D0078215

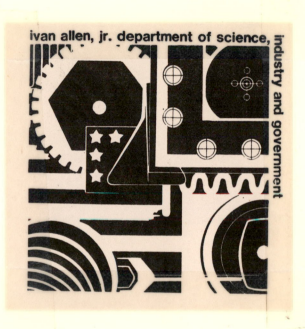
ivan allen, jr. department of science, industry and government

Women and the American Left

a guide to sources

G. K. Hall

W♀MEN'S STUDIES

Publications

Barbara Haber
Editor

Women and the American Left

a guide to sources

MARI JO BUHLE

G.K. HALL & CO.

70 LINCOLN STREET, BOSTON, MASS.

Library of Congress Cataloging in Publication Data

Buhle, Mari Jo, 1943-
  Women and the American left.

  Bibliography
  Includes index.
  1. Feminism—United States—Bibliography. 2. Right
and left (Political science)—Bibliography. 3. Radical-
ism—United States—Bibliography. I. Title.
Z7964.U49B84 1983   016.3054'2'0973   83-6158
[HQ1420]
ISBN 0-8161-8195-0

This publication is printed on permanent/durable acid-free paper
MANUFACTURED IN THE UNITED STATES OF AMERICA

Contents

The Author vi

Introduction vii

Acknowledgments. xi

General Works. 1

1871–1900
  Histories and General Works. 7
  Autobiographies and Biographies. 13
  Books and Pamphlets on the Woman Question. 24
  Periodicals. 37
  Fiction and Poetry 38

1901–1919
  Histories and General Works. 55
  Autobiographies and Biographies. 65
  Books and Pamphlets on the Woman Question. 93
  Periodicals. 108
  Fiction and Poetry .111

1920–1964
  Histories and General Works. 123
  Autobiographies and Biographies. 126
  Books and Pamphlets on the Woman Question. 154
  Periodicals. 169
  Fiction and Poetry .170

1965–1981
  Histories and General Works. 195
  Autobiographies and Biographies. 198
  Books and Pamphlets on the Woman Question. 206
  Periodicals. 226
  Fiction and Poetry .228

Selected References. 247

Index. 253

The Author

Mari Jo Buhle, assistant professor of American civilization and history at Brown University, is a specialist in the field of American women's history. She is coeditor of The Concise History of Woman Suffrage (1978) and author of Women and American Socialism, 1870-1920. She has contributed chapters to several books on the history of women and has published in Signs and in Feminist Studies. Professor Buhle has held fellowships from the Wellesley Center for Research on Women in Higher Education and the Professions and from the Bunting Institute of Radcliffe College.

Introduction

The political and cultural upheavals of the 1960s--the civil rights and antiwar campaigns, the New Left, and the women's liberation movement--restored questions of women's rights and status to a central place within the American radical tradition, and at the same time, inspired a literary and scholarly revival in various fields. Writers speculated on the nature of the relationship between the struggle for women's emancipation and the reconstruction of American society, past and present, along collectivist or cooperative lines. Within a decade, scholars trained in the academy, journalists for underground as well as commercial presses, and political activists themselves produced a sizable body of literature on the subject. Publishing houses in the early 1970s responded to a growing audience and reprinted important texts, such as the little-remembered novels of feminist visionaries and the autobiographies of long-forgotten radical women. Former luminaries such as Charlotte Perkins Gilman, Emma Goldman, and Victoria Woodhull received attention after several decades of obscurity, as subjects of doctoral dissertations, scholarly monographs, popular vignettes, and even children's books. At the local level, state historical magazines fairly blossomed with cameo studies of their favorite radical daughters.

In the early 1980s it is too early to evaluate the net result of this activity. Much work remains in progress; many outstanding scholars are still near the beginning of their careers. Yet it is possible to document a tradition of publication spanning over a century of American history and to present it as an aid to further work along this line.

This volume reviews sources on women and the American Left beginning in 1871, the year of the Paris Commune. This year, a symbolic turning point, ushered in the era of modern or "scientific" socialism and placed issues of women's rights squarely on the revolutionary agenda. Although American radicals had pursued a variety of causes prior to the Civil War, they moved only gradually toward a political philosophy informed by the notion of class struggle as the principal means of social reconstruction. The events surrounding the Paris Commune served to sharpen their perspectives on class relations in their own country and to underscore the role of the working class as revolutionary agency. It was within this historic context that a small group of radical women first formulated what they termed the "Woman Question": how could women make claims on behalf of the liberation of their sex and simultaneously, and with equal commitment, advance the struggles of the working class? In other words, what was the categorical relationship of class and gender in theories, strategies, and practices of social change?

This volume takes their question as its central theme and reviews primary and secondary sources tracing its evolution from 1871 to 1981. Materials are organized within four major periods of the American Left: 1871-1900; 1901-1919; 1920-1964; and 1965-1981. The last three periods designate major shifts in the organizational history of the Left: 1901 marks the formation of the Socialist Party of America; 1920 the emergence of the Communist movement; 1965 the ascendancy of the New Left. Within each period, sources are grouped under specific headings: general works and histories; autobiographies and biographies arranged by subject; books and pamphlets that specifically address the Woman Question as defined above; periodicals with a discernible Socialist feminist content; and works of fiction-- novels, plays, and poetry. Omitted are books and essays written by radical women on topics outside the Woman Question; their inclusion would have doubled, perhaps tripled, the length of this volume and weakened its thematic framework. For similar reasons, literary criticism in nonbook form is excluded as too voluminous to incorporate within a guide to primarily historical sources. Materials on civil rights, peace, temperance, and other movements radical in their own right have been included only when issues concerning the specific relationship of class and gender predominated.

Although I have tried to review sources as comprehensively as possible, some areas presented formidable obstacles. The nineteenth-century materials seemed as elusive as the radical movement itself, and consequently constitute a sample rather than definitive survey. So, too, the publications of the last decade, when the proliferation of pamphlets and books served the movement foremost and only slowly came to the attention of scholars and librarians; one might hope that improved retrieval systems will advance the identification of such recondite sources. For readers interested in studying the important role of women in radical movements not included in this volume, such as the antebellum communitarian settlements, the mainstream women's rights campaigns, or struggles for racial equality, a list of reference works on related topics appears in the final section.

Several libraries house excellent collections of the books, pamphlets, and periodicals reviewed in this volume. The Library of Congress, the New York Public Library, and the Boston Public Library hold many old works of fiction that have not yet been reprinted. The State Historical Society of Wisconsin and Tamiment Library of New York University have collected scores of primary sources covering the

entire period. Most of the materials concerning the Women Question
in the twentieth century are available on microfilm at Tamiment
Library. Dozens of pamphlets from the late nineteenth and early
twentieth centuries have been microfilmed by Research Publications,
Inc., and are so designated in the text. This series as well as the
bulk of post-1965 sources are located in the Arthur and Elizabeth
Schlesinger Library on the History of Women at Radcliffe College.
For location of individual entries, I refer readers to the <u>National</u>
<u>Union Catalog</u>.

Acknowledgments

I wish to thank the many librarians who aided my research.
Barbara Haber, of the Arthur and Elizabeth Schlesinger Library on the
History of Women in America, suggested this project in 1977 when I
was engaged in writing a related book. Her patience and guidance
have sustained me over the years between conception and completion of
this volume. Karen Morgan, also of the Schlesinger Library, helped
me locate sources and check citations. Dorothy Swanson at the Tamiment Library of New York University guided me through its rich collections. My gratitude extends to the librarians at the New York
Public Library, the Boston Public Library, Widener Library of Harvard
University, the State Historical Society of Wisconsin and Memorial
Library of the University of Wisconsin, the Library of Congress,
Smith College Library, Chicago Historical Society, and the Rockefeller
and John Hay libraries of Brown University.

My students at Brown University, both graduate and undergraduate,
have contributed significantly to this research. I wish to thank all
the adventuresome young scholars who struggled through experimental
seminars on women and the American radical tradition during the fall
terms of 1980 and 1981. Funded by Brown University, several students
worked directly on this project. Mary Trigg and Pamela Gordon re-
searched some particularly obscure sources, while Jane Levine worked
diligently on utopian socialists. Michael Staub performed laborious
and usually tedious chores filling in missing citations and retrieving
elusive books from the library. Lesley Dretar volunteered some as-
sistance and shared with me her appreciation of radical women writers,
particularly Josephine Herbst. Deborah DeBare merits an extra round
of thanks, as she worked for an entire summer without financial com-
pensation. She tracked down scores of socialist feminist publications
from the recent period, located major reviews, and drafted a few an-
notations herself. Now returned to campus after completing a year's
work in the Equal Rights Amendment campaign, she will, I hope, be able
to use her fine research in further study.

Other scholars have aided in different ways. Annette T.
Rubinstein, Nancy Joyce Peters, and Paul Lauter reviewed my selection
of radical women novelists and offered helpful advice. Ethelbert

Acknowledgments

Miller brought to my attention the works of some black poets. Ann D. Gordon read and summarized several books that slipped by me during a summer's research stint in Madison, Wisconsin. Susan Ware supplied information about her aunt, Dorothy McConnell. Don Davis reviewed my selection of pamphlets published by Pathfinder Press. Linda Gordon read the entire manuscript and spotted gaps in coverage and in logic.

I wish to thank most wholeheartedly the person who saw this work to completion. Paul Buhle shared with me his wide-ranging knowledge of American radical history, took an avid interest in this project when mine sometimes flagged, tracked down sources for me during his own research trips, and helped me understand more fully the purpose of our joint work.

General Works

No scholar has yet attempted to write a comprehensive history of women in American radical movements, although several have studied particular topics such as sex, labor, and architecture, or the colorful personalities of the most remembered activists. More often aimed at general readers rather than specialists, the majority of books in this category reflect the renewed interest in women's liberation of the late 1960s and seek to establish a feminist and radical tradition within American history.

1   COTT, NANCY F., and ELIZABETH PLECK, eds. A Heritage of Her Own: Toward a New Social History of American Women. New York: Simon & Schuster, 1979, 608 pp.
      This volume is perhaps the finest collection of the new scholarship in women's history. It gathers twenty-four essays on various topics and covers the sweep of American history. Several concern aspects of women's radical activism, such as Linda Gordon's "Birth Control and Social Revolution," a chapter from Woman's Body, Woman's Right, and Blanche Wiesen Cook's "Female Support Networks and Political Activism: Lillian Wald, Crystal Eastman, Emma Goldman," which had been published previously in Chrysalis. The editors also include Barbara Easton's "Feminism and the Contemporary Family," which appeared first in Socialist Review.

2   DITZION, SIDNEY. Marriage, Morals and Sex in America: A History of Ideas. New York: Bookman Associates, 1953, 440 pp. Reprint. New York: W.W. Norton, 1978, 460 pp.
      Published in 1953, over a decade before the new wave of women's history and family history began, Ditzion's book stands as a marker. In one sense it is old-fashioned. As the subtitle indicates, it is a history of ideas. His analysis, therefore, ultimately falls short by today's standards in that the social or behavioral sides of sexuality play no significant role. Nevertheless, Ditzion deserves credit as a pioneer, for he managed to break new ground merely by treating the history of sexual morality as a legitimate, scholarly enterprise. Rather than casting his

actors as cranks or eccentrics—or worse, as malevolent agents
determined to destroy the family—Ditzion opened the way for
serious, enlightened discussion.

The text covers a long period. Ditzion begins his narrative by discussing the late eighteenth-century treatises on
marriage and sexual morality produced by British writers and
assesses their influence in the United States. The bulk of the
book concentrates on the nineteenth century. Ditzion provides a
virtual catalog of the major and minor works on marriage and sexuality. He summarizes and interprets the liberal tradition established by Wollstonecraft and Godwin, the communitarian and utopian
alternatives, the free-thought and anarchist strains, as well as
the debates raging within the women's rights movement. The chapters on the postfreudian era, when discussions of sexual behavior
became more open, are surprisingly thin compared to early portions
of the book.

Ditzion is comfortable with the large role radicals played
in the various movements for sexual reform. He offers judicious
assessments of figures usually subjected to harsh or comical
treatment. Frances Wright, Victoria Woodhull, Ezra Heywood, and
Emma Goldman do not suffer at his hands. The chapter entitled
"The Socialist View of the Family" surveys the contribution of
utopian thinkers in the late nineteenth century, the German-
American free-thinkers, Marx, Engels, and Bebel, Daniel DeLeon,
Kate Richards O'Hare, and a score of writers close to the Socialist and Communist parties. Ditzion demonstrates that radicals
held a variety of opinions on the question of sex relations, but
were joined by a common desire to elevate woman's status by what-
ever reform they advocated. Ditzion also credits Socialists and
anarchists with elevating the level of discussion of such subjects
to a more serious plane than was common among other intellectuals.

Because he chose to write a full-length history, he examined no one figure or movement in depth. The book serves best as
an introductory survey of ideas on sexual morality. Although the
text is dotted with references, there are no footnotes, and the
bibliography is skimpy.

3 FONER, PHILIP S. Women and the American Labor Movement from
   Colonial Times to the Eve of World War I. New York: The Free
   Press, 1979, 621 pp.
   Foner's massive survey includes significant information on
the role of Socialist women in the labor movement. A section on
the Illinois Woman's Alliance and its sister organization, the
New York Working Women's Society, brings to life the women who
participated in the important labor and political movements of
the late 1880s. A chapter on the Socialist party focuses on its
position on woman suffrage and concludes with a brief biography
of Mother Jones. Coherent chapters on organization in the garment
trade and the textile industry, 1909-1916, contain valuable information on women activists and concise narratives of the major
strikes of the era.

4 _____. Women and the American Labor Movement from World War I
   to the Present. New York: The Free Press, 1980, 682 pp.
      Foner's second volume emphasizes the role Communist women
have played in labor organizations since World War I. He takes a
hard line against Socialists, particularly in discussing the
internecine warfare in the garment unions during the 1920s, and
underscores the contribution of Communists, especially to the
formation of the CIO. A later section reviews the Communist
party's position on the proposed Equal Rights Amendment. The
second volume of Foner's history, like the first, is an invaluable
guide to the labor activities of women in the Left.

5 GORDON, LINDA. Woman's Body, Woman's Right: A Social History
   of Birth Control in America. New York: Grossman Publishers,
   1976, 479 pp. Reprint. New York: Penguin Books, 1977, 479
   pp.
      A massive study of birth control in the nineteenth and
twentieth centuries, Gordon's text contains a lengthly chapter
that details the radical origins of the first major political movement to address this issue. In her analysis, Gordon minimizes
the contribution of Margaret Sanger and focuses instead on the
Socialist party, the IWW, Emma Goldman, and local birth-control
groups organized by rank-and-file activists. She claims that by
1916 birth control was both a radical and a large movement in the
United States. Its later decline, Gordon explains, resulted less
from the political vacillation of Sanger than from the waning
Socialist and women's movements and the unwillingness of radicals
and feminists to defend the birth-control movement against attacks
by conservatives. In Gordon's provocative reading, the birth-
control campaigns constituted a major event in the history of the
Left.

6 GRIFFIN, FREDERICK C., ed. Woman as Revolutionary. New York:
   New American Library, 1973, 256 pp.
      This collection of short documents records the sentiments
of a broadly defined group of revolutionary women of several con-
tinents, beginning with Christine de Pisan and including American
radicals Helen Keller, Emma Goldman, Isadora Duncan, Margaret
Sanger, and Joan Baez. Anne Fremantle writes a brief introduction
to this eclectic assortment of primary sources.

7 HAYDEN, DOLORES. The Grand Domestic Revolution: A History of
   Feminist Designs for American Homes, Neighborhoods, and Cities.
   Cambridge: MIT Press, 1981, 367 pp.
      This book details the efforts of various visionary reformers
to use architectural and technological innovations in the household to advance women's status in American society. It explores
the feminist and socialist traditions dating to the 1820s.
Hayden's subjects for the most part are men and women influenced
by either Charles Fourier or Edward Bellamy. They took as their
task a communal solution to the drudgery of the household; or

they advanced schemes to collectivize industry, including domestic industry, on a grand, national scale. Hayden is sensitive to the nuances of the various programs and produces a veritable catalog of major plans and minor schemes for a "grand domestic revolution."

The section "Communitarian Socialism and Domestic Feminism" considers in detail the outlooks of Charles Fourier and Catharine Beecher. In later chapters, Hayden traces the contributions of practical innovators, beginning with the first cooperative housing experiment in 1868 in Cambridge, Massachusetts, conducted by Mesulina Fay Peirce. Marie Stevens Howland, an advocate of free love and socialism, advanced the principle of women's economical independence in her work to proselytize the familistère idea in the 1870s; in the 1880s Mary Livermore and various associates in the women's clubs and Woman's Christian Temperance Union brought these ideas into the mainstream women's movement by advocating both cooperative housekeeping and a system of professionalized home maintenance. By the 1890s the impact of new technology and the permanence of the American urban landscape led to a host of futuristic novels about domestic reform, Edward Bellamy's Looking Backward being the prime example. Hayden follows this development into actual programs, such as the public kitchens advocated by Ellen Swallow Richards and the model settlement established by Jane Addams. Charlotte Perkins Gilman receives special consideration for her landmark contribution. Hayden concludes with an examination of the work of Ethel Puffer Howes, a domestic reformer who continued to campaign in the 1920s.

Hayden writes that the "great theoretical contribution of communitarian socialism was the view that women's work was essential to economic and social life and must be valued accordingly in any system which attempted to combat industrial capitalism."

8 _____. Seven American Utopians: The Architecture of Communitarian Socialism, 1790-1975. Cambridge: MIT Press, 1976, 401 pp.

Hayden is not primarily concerned with the role of women in utopian settlements. Her main purpose is "to explore the relationship between social organization and the building process in particular community groups." She examines in detail seven such groups--Shakers, Mormons, Fourierists, Perfectionists, Inspirationists, Union Colonists, and Llano Colonists--and seven sites. As sex roles are major factors in all systems of social organization, Hayden pays close attention to the design of the various colonies as a reflection of their founders' conception of women's place. She thus studies the architectural arrangements of both social life and material production, and delineates the planners' intentions in regard to women's role. The chapter "The Architecture of Complex Marriage" has special insights.

The most thorough treatment of women's role as a function of design appears in Chapter 10, "Feminism and Eclecticism," which focuses on the Llano del Rio colony organized by Socialist Job

Harriman after his mayoral defeat in Los Angeles in 1910. The
Llano colony opened in 1914 in California, moved to Louisiana in
1917, and survived for twenty-four years. Its principal planner
was Alice Constance Austin, a self-trained architect and feminist.
Believing that women's oppression was reinforced by the design of
traditional dwellings, Austin planned Llano to reduce the physical
burdens of housework so that women might fill their obligations
of wife and mother in relative leisure and beauty. She designed
model family homes to meet the needs of an egalitarian society.

A study of architectural design, Hayden's book is richly
illustrated.

9 NEIDLE, CECYLE S. American Immigrant Women. Boston: G.K.
   Hall & Co., 1975, 312 pp. Reprint. New York: Hippocrene
   Books, Inc., 1976, 312 pp.

   Neidle's history surveys the contribution of immigrant
women to American social and political development. Beginning in
the colonial period, the author catalogs the noble deeds of wives
and daughters of the British settlers. In later chapters she
focuses on groups from continental Europe, and concludes with a
brief treatment of successful professional women in the midtwentieth century. The strongest chapters, which cover the peak
period of European immigration, record the activities of mainly
Irish and Jewish women in the trade-union movement.

   Lacking a conceptual framework, Neidle's book presents a
series of short biographies of immigrant women who achieved
prominence in the United States, including a few representative
radical activists. An early chapter entitled "Social Change"
summarizes the crusades of the "dynamic Scotswoman" Frances
Wright, and Ernestine Rose and Mathilde Giesler-Anneke. Chapters
on the labor movement contain vignettes about "Mother" Mary Jones,
Rose Schneiderman, Pauline Newman, Bessie Abramowitz Hillman, and
Dorothy Jacobs Bellanca; these sections are especially interesting
because they are based on personal interviews conducted by the
author. An entire chapter on Rose Pastor Stokes and Emma Goldman
is very revealing. Neidle aptly describes Stokes as one who
"twisted and turned from one set of ideas to another and from one
ambition to the next until too ill to care" and Goldman as one
who "never deviated from her views." A handy reference, American
Immigrant Women aims at a popular readership.

10 NIES, JUDITH. Seven Women: Portraits from the American Radical Tradition. New York: Viking Press, 1977, 235 pp. Reprint. New York: Penguin Books, 1978, 235 pp.

   Judith Nies aims to disprove the myth that women, by their
nature, eschew radical activism. On the contrary, the author
claims, women claim a rich tradition as major actors in movements
for social justice. To bolster her argument, Nies chose seven
women representative of various endeavors and designed a series
of biographical sketches to trace a distinctive narrative of
women's radicalism.

She begins with a study of women involved in the antebellum antislavery and women's rights movements: Sarah Moore
Grimké, Harriet Tubman, and Elizabeth Cady Stanton. She then
turns to activists more commonly associated with the cause of
labor and modern socialism: "Mother" Mary Harris Jones,
Charlotte Perkins Gilman, Anna Louise Strong, and Dorothy Day.
Each chapter provides essential vital statistics on its subject,
her youthful influences, major involvements, and finally, her
overall significance to the history of American radicalism.
Compensatory history with all its strengths and weaknesses, Seven
Women successfully documents women's important contributions to
the "radical political movements that fashioned the substance of
America's growth and maturity." Nies not only recreates a tradition of women's radicalism but offers her readers unblemished
heroines.

11 SOCHEN, JUNE, ed. The New Feminism in 20th-Century America.
    Lexington, Mass.: D.C. Heath & Co., 1971, 208 pp.
        This anthology of primary sources is an entry in the Prob-
lems in American Civilization series. Many of Sochen's selections
represent the Left edge of the women's movement at the turn of
the century. The first section of the book focuses on the woman
suffrage movement at the turn of the century. The second section
documents feminist ideas and activities in the 1910s, the
editor's field of expertise, and includes essays by socialists
Floyd Dell, Charlotte Perkins Gilman, Margaret Sanger, Crystal
and Max Eastman, and Henrietta Rodman. The women's movement of
the 1960s is represented in the third section; essays by Naomi
Weisstein, Jo Freeman, Margaret Benston, and Roxanne Dunbar are
included.

12 WERTHEIMER, BARBARA MAYER. We Were There: The Story of
    Working Women in America. New York: Pantheon Books, 1977,
    427 pp.
        Wertheimer's broad survey, designed for trade-union educa-
tion courses, includes sections on Socialist women who were
active in the labor movement. Chapters on the Women's Trade
Union League and the garment unions contain brief biographical
sketches of Rose Schneiderman, Leonora O'Reilly, Clara Lemlich,
and Dorothy Jacobs Bellanca, and information on Pauline Newman
drawn from personal interviews.

1871-1900

HISTORIES AND GENERAL WORKS

Although German-Americans dominated the organized Socialist movement until the twentieth century, native-born radicals forged a distinctive tradition of their own. The contributing elements, however,
represented several sometimes antagonistic strains: anarchism and
free love; temperance and women's rights; agrarian revolt and urban
reform. Throughout the 1870s activists hewed separate paths, but in
the next decade, amid upheavals in city and country alike, many envisioned a grand alliance of radicals and reformers of various kinds.

Women found congenial places in two major sectors. In the anarchist or free-love movements, they gained a modicum of freedom in
sexual relations and developed principled criticisms of the institution of marriage as governed by church or state. Although their
numbers remained small, anarchist women and free-lovers achieved
notoriety for their controversial opinions and practices. Many more
women took political roles within the comparatively benign mainstream
women's movement. Beginning in the 1870s, temperance agitation
served as the major vehicle for activism, and over the next decades,
the Woman's Christian Temperance Union, under the skilled leadership
of Frances Willard, would prepare thousands of women for broader
public roles. Although temperance activists and free-lovers rarely
joined hands, together they catalyzed the radical sentiments of
native-born women across the country.

The sources in this section highlight several aspects of this
parallel development, although in piecemeal fashion. Only recently
have historians explored the connections between the women's movement,
especially its temperance component, and the radical movements of the
late 1880s and early 1890s. The role of women in agrarian radical
movements from the Farmers' Alliance of the 1870s to the Populist
upsurge of the 1890s, in the urban intellectual circles that blossomed
into Christian Socialist and Bellamy Nationalist clubs in the late
1880s, and in the separate anarchist enclaves--this is a history just
now coming to the fore.

13 BLOCKER, JACK S., Jr. "The Politics of Reform: Populists, Prohibition, and Woman Suffrage, 1891-1892." Historian 34 (August 1972):614-32.

In the late 1880s labor and agrarian radicals gathered under the Populist banner. Thousands of women under Frances Willard's leadership also joined the movement and expected to participate fully in the political reconstruction ahead. To ensure women's role in this new venture, Willard called a meeting in Chicago of leading reformers and radicals and presented a set of demands to be considered by delegates to the historic St. Louis Industrial Conference of 1892, which gave birth to the People's party.

Blocker discusses the events at this major conference. He records Willard's instrumental activities to secure a broad platform for the new party and the subsequent schism between farmers and laborers over the burning issues of prohibition and woman suffrage. Fearing a potential loss of German and Irish votes, Blocker explains, trade unionists strongly opposed both measures and defeated Willard's proposal.

Blocker interprets Willard's failure as a sign that "the Populists had taken a step away from their middle-class ideology in the direction of a class party uniting the interests and demands of farmers and laborers." This conclusion indicates Blocker's disregard for the importance of women's issues to contemporary activists, especially those associated with the vibrant women's movement of the period. His account, therefore, differs from the feminist interpretation offered by Mary Earhart Dillon in Frances Willard: From Prayers to Politics.

14 BORDIN, RUTH. Woman and Temperance: The Quest for Power and Liberty, 1873-1900. Philadelphia: Temple University Press, 1981, 221 pp.

Because so many native-born radical women grew to political maturity within the Woman's Christian Temperance Union, the nineteenth-century history of this organization is a key to their world view. In Bordin's finely detailed study, the transformation of the WCTU from a single-issue to a multifaceted organization of national proportion proceeds smoothly and logically under Willard's leadership. Although Bordin focuses on the institution itself rather than on its charismatic president, she describes the many programs that Willard introduced during the 1880s. The chapter "Woman's Mighty Realm of Philanthropy" shows how Willard's do-everything policy embodied feminists goals that came to be accepted by the somewhat reluctant general membership and pushed women into scores of activities unrelated to temperance agitation. Bordin shows, too, how Willard planned to arrange a broad political coalition in the late 1880s, as she moved from home protection to gospel socialism. The first full study of the first mass organization of American women, Woman and Temperance provides the necessary background for understanding the aspirations of thousands of women who participated in the Populist movement in the

1890s or the Bellamy Nationalists clubs, and who, more often than
not, continued their agitation under the banner of the Socialist
Party of America after the turn of the century.

15 EPSTEIN, BARBARA LESLIE. The Politics of Domesticity: Women,
    Evangelism, and Temperance in Nineteenth-Century America.
    Middletown, Conn.: Wesleyan University Press, 1981, 188 pp.
         It is Epstein's thesis that as the industrial revolution
    removed production from the home and created in its wake a sepa-
    rate culture of domesticity, a fateful shift occurred in the
    balance of power between men and women. To regain the status
    they had lost, women struggled in arenas where they could exert
    influence, mostly in the great religious events of the midnine-
    teenth century. The Woman's Christian Temperance Union repre-
    sented, in Epstein's analysis, a culmination of these activities
    and stood as a direct political challenge to male hegemony.
    Epstein examines the program of the WCTU and discovers its major
    intention to restore the equality within the family lost since
    preindustrial times.
         Epstein covers briefly Frances Willard's crucial role in
    wedding the WCTU to the principle of sex equality. She examines
    Willard's ties with the labor movement and her espousal of social-
    ism. Although Epstein judges the WCTU as insufficiently feminist,
    she does raise important questions about the relationship of
    woman's domestic culture and the politics carried under the tem-
    perance banner. Because so many native-born radical women at the
    turn of the century emerged from the temperance movement,
    Epstein's interpretation sheds light, albeit indirectly, on their
    activities.

16 HAYDEN, DOLORES. "Two Utopian Feminists and their Campaigns
    for Kitchenless Houses." Signs 4 (Winter 1978):274-90.
         Hayden examines the careers of Marie Stevens Howland and
    Constance Austin, who promoted architectural innovations to unite
    feminist domestic reform and utopian socialism in the cities of
    Topolobampo, Mexico, and Llano del Rio, California. She describes
    their experiments with housing designed to reduce drudgery and to
    free women to greater participation in society. Hayden portrays
    Howland and Austin as architectural visionaries, forecasters of
    the suburban renovations that would take place in the twentieth
    century.

17 JEFFREY, JULIE ROY. "Women in the Southern Farmers' Alliance:
    A Reconstruction of the Role and Status of Women in the Late
    Nineteenth-Century South." Feminist Studies 3 (Fall 1975):72-
    91.
         This essay analyzes the position of women in the Farmers'
    Alliance in North Carolina and shows how their role deviated from
    the norms of Southern womanhood. Jeffrey found a great deal of
    support for women's participation in the organizational life of
    the Alliance. "Within the framework of the Alliance," she writes,

"southern women had the opportunity to discuss pressing economic, political, and social questions, to try out ways of behaving in mixed groups and to gain confidence in newly acquired skills."

The Alliance thus endorsed the economic equality of women and envisioned them as co-workers for a better society. Jeffrey also considers the limitations of the Alliance's attitude, especially the leadership's reluctance to grapple with the major controversial issue, woman suffrage. A balanced treatment, this essay is an invaluable monographic study of women in the agrarian movement of the 1880s and 1890s.

18   LEACH, WILLIAM. "Looking Foward Together: Feminists and
     Edward Bellamy." Democracy 2 (January 1981):120-34.
     Leach is concerned with a strategic problem in feminist theory: reliance on the state to achieve sex equality. He studies the attraction of nineteenth-century feminists to the Nationalist program of Edward Bellamy to illustrate some of the more problematical aspects of this tendency.

After outlining some of the principal tenets of Nationalism, especially its emphasis on material gratification and consumption over the value of productive labor, Leach follows several important feminists into Bellamy's camp. Zerelda Wallace, Frances Willard, Elizabeth Cady Stanton, Harriot Stanton Blatch, and Charlotte Perkins Gilman stand prominently among those women influenced by his ideas.

Leach asks: "Why did so many feminist leaders, some of whom one would hardly expect to find in such company, choose to join the Nationalist movement?" He answers that Nationalism's recognition of sex equality as well as its serious consideration of women's domestic situation proved the major drawing cards. Unfortunately, he concludes, feminists failed to perceive that Bellamy's faith in the technocratic, centralized state would ultimately destroy the basis for individual autonomy and thus negate its potential to liberate women.

19   _____. True Love and Perfect Union: The Feminist Reform of
     Sex and Society. New York: Basic Books, 1980, 449 pp.
     Leach presents a sensitive and complex analysis of nineteenth-century feminist ideology and discusses its applications to both the private world of sexual relations and the public realm of social reform. Chapters cover topics ranging from health reform, to romantic love, the sexual division of labor, and social science. The author develops a forceful critique of feminists' political world view, especially their fatal attraction to possessive individualism and consequential failure to create a genuinely democratic and cooperative political strategy.

Although Leach does not focus on radical women, he sets the scene for their political journey from mainstream to Left movements. He examines the beliefs and activities of several women who eventually affiliated with various radical causes in the 1880s and 1890s. His account of Lucinda Chandler is acute; he handles well Chandler's simultaneous advocacy of spiritualism, social purity, and socialism.

20   MANN, ARTHUR. Yankee Reformers in the Urban Age: Social Reform in Boston, 1880-1900. Cambridge: Belknap Press of Harvard University, 1954, 314 pp. Reprint. New York: Harper & Row, 1966, 314 pp.
         Mann's invaluable local study includes a chapter on women reformers, most of whom became Christian Socialists or Bellamy Nationalists in the late 1880s. Mann mentions the reform activities of Lucy Stone, Julia Ward Howe, and Mary Livermore, and treats in detail the career of Vida D. Scudder. Mann's analysis, developed decades before the emergence of the new scholarship in women's history, is now outdated. He concludes, for example, that the emancipation of women was "almost complete by 1900."

21   MARSH, MARGARET S. "The Anarchist-Feminist Response to the 'Woman Question' in Late Nineteenth-Century America." American Quarterly 30 (Fall 1978):533-47.
         Marsh begins her essay by comparing anarchist feminists with participants in the mainstream women's movement. She contends that most American feminists emphasized by 1870 differences between the sexes and asked for women's rights on a basis of feminine moral superiority. Anarchists, in contrast, espoused an "equality based on a shared humanity" and thus chose the more radical course. Marsh claims that anarchist feminism developed logically from anarchism's advocacy of the absolute liberty of the individual. From this premise, anarchist feminists criticized women's subordination in the family, aimed to reorder the household, advocated "free unions" in place of conventional marriage, and insisted on women's financial independence.
         Marsh discusses briefly the social movement and characterizes two types of anarachist women: the anarchist communists who were often Jews from Russia or from eastern Europe; and individualist anarchists who were native-born Americans of various backgrounds. Differences in origins or philosophical orientation, however, had little bearing on women's commitment. Marsh presents Voltairine de Cleyre as a prominent example, and suggests that de Cleyre's anarchism was essentially, although not exclusively, an outgrowth of her feminist beliefs. She concludes that twentieth-century feminists may find appealing the anarchist feminist emphasis on the similarities between the sexes.

22   ____ . Anarchist Women 1870-1920. Philadelphia: Temple University Press, 1981, 214 pp.
         March sets anarchist women apart from other nineteenth-century feminists by emphasizing their rejection of contemporary norms of femininity and, particularly, domesticity. She examines their philosophical underpinnings in the cornerstone of anarchist philosophy, the sanctity of personal liberty. This premise led anarchist women to believe in the absolute equality of the sexes and the necessity to abolish female dependency upon men as in-

stituted in legal marriage and within the family. Thus Marsh devotes a long chapter to anarchist sexual theory and the program-
matic alternative, free love. She also studies the propaganda
messages and techniques of leading figures in both the individualist and Communist tendencies. Emma Goldman and Voltairine de
Cleyre play large parts in her study.

Marsh recognizes that anarchist women represented a small
number in the history of American feminism. Their significance
rests, however, neither on the size of their following nor on
their influence within the broader society. Rather, anarchist
feminists responded to the major historical shifts in women's
role by testing the limits of custom and convention; they also
addressed the question of institutional change as the prerequisite
for women's emancipation. Because anarchist women issued such a
direct challenge to the prevailing sentiments about marriage and
family, they engendered hostile opposition from mainstream society.
Nevertheless, their contribution is lasting, Marsh concludes, because anarchist feminists issued a lasting radical declaration
against the gender distinctions that prevent women from partici-
pating freely and fully in society.

Adding to her intellectual and political analysis, Marsh
offers an interesting sociobiographical sketch of individual
women. She also includes an appendix in which she compares ten
anarchist women with a comparable sample of Socialist, mainstream
suffragist, and labor activist women, on places of birth, ethnic
backgrounds of parents, educational attainments, social class,
occupations, and attitudes toward marriage and violence. Limited
to English-language sources, Anarchist Women 1870-1920 is the
first major study of the feminist tradition within American
anarchism.

23 SEARS, HAL D. The Sex Radicals: Free Love in High Victorian
    America. Lawrence: Regents Press of Kansas, 1977, 342 pp.
        Throughout New England and in small towns in the Midwest,
settlements of anarchists and free-lovers formed to explore a
variety of economic and sexual arrangements. Sears surveys their
activities from the Civil War to the turn of the century, and
brings to life their unconventional ideas about sex, their dedication to women's emancipation, and their connections with various
radical movements. To identify the basic tenet of free love,
Sears quotes the American anarchist Josiah Warren, who insisted
that the individual is "at liberty to dispose of his or her person, and time, and property in any manner in which his or her
feelings or judgment may dictate, WITHOUT INVOLVING PERSONS OR
INTERESTS OF OTHERS." A rejection of the prerogatives of either
church or state over the private affairs of the individual was at
the heart of this doctrine.

Sears presents fascinating case studies of leading free-
lovers, such as Moses Harman, E.B. Foote, and Ezra Heywood. He
also records rare information about their female associates.
Brief sketches of Elmina Slinker, Lois Waisbrooker, Dora Forster,
and Lillie White increase the value of Sears's contribution.

AUTOBIOGRAPHIES AND BIOGRAPHIES

The lives of the women represented in this section spanned the American radical movements of the late nineteenth century, and more often than might be expected, their paths crossed. They left a fragmentary record of their activities, as if to underscore the difficulty of interpreting this curious era even by the surviving veterans themselves. For decades afterward, scholars, too, seemed frankly puzzled by the mixture of free love and social purity, spiritualism and scientific socialism espoused by these radicals. At times they sought to vindicate an individual crusader like Frances Willard, at others to sensationalize a character such as Victoria Woodhull. Only in recent years has a newer scholarship, still in its formative stages, begun the necessary reassessment.

Yet the dramatis personae are so individually fascinating that an anecdotal history already exists. The Christian Socialist sentiments of temperance leader Frances Willard offer one example, the multi-various careers of Florence Kelley and Lucy Parsons another. The mysticism and checkered histories of Victoria Woodhull and Martha Moore Avery serve as pieces in some as yet unfinished history.

Avery, Martha Moore (1851-1929)

24 CARRIGAN, D. OWEN. "Martha Moore Avery: Crusader for Social
    Justice." Catholic Historical Review 54 (April 1968):17-38.
        Martha Moore Avery, a native of Steuben, Maine, moved to
    Boston in 1886 and became a prominent Socialist lecturer and
    writer. In 1886 she became a charter member of the Boston
    Nationalist Club and for the next several years wrote frequently
    for Nationalist publications. In 1890 she joined the Socialist
    Labor party and served it actively until 1900, when dissension
    split its ranks. Avery made the Massachusetts Socialist party
    her political home until its 1902 state convention defeated her
    motion to repudiate any Socialist who condoned free love or
    attacked religion. Having converted to Catholicism by 1903, she
    produced, together with an associate, David Goldstein, a pamphlet
    entitled Socialism: The Nation of Fatherless Children (1903).
        Carrigan traces Avery's political activities after she re-
    nounced socialism for Catholic social action. After her 1903 con-
    version, she spent the next several years serving the anti-
    Socialist crusade of the Catholic Church. She lectured widely on
    various subjects, but made her central theme the threat of social-
    ism to the family and to woman's role. In 1920 Avery and her
    coauthor, Goldstein, published their second major denunciation of
    socialism, Bolshevism: Its Cure. Through a series of involve-
    ments, such as the Militia of Christ for Social Service, the
    Common Cause Society, the Catholic Truth Guild, and the Phila-
    matheia Club (a women's auxiliary to Boston College), Avery be-
    came one of the most prominent lay activists in the New England

Catholic Church. Carrigan aptly ends his essay by quoting the inscription on her gravestone: "Martha Moore Avery, Convert from Marx to Christ."

25 _____. "A Forgotten Yankee Marxist." New England Quarterly 42 (March 1969):23-43.
          In this essay Carrigan focuses on Avery's role in the Socialist Labor party. He surveys her many entries in the socialist press, summarizes her political philosophy, and judges her faithful to the "marxian line." He also describes her endorsement of popular reform measures, such as woman suffrage, and her allegiance to Daniel DeLeon's controversial Socialist Trades and Labor Alliance. Carrigan documents Avery's major educational venture, the Karl Marx Club, which she organized in Boston to teach the more theoretical precepts of socialism. Despite her later renunciation of socialism, Carrigan believes Avery was sincere in her early convictions and fully deserving of a detailed scholarly examination.

Donnelly, Katharine (1833-1894)

26 KREUTER, GRETCHEN. "Kate Donnelly versus the Cult of True Womanhood." In Women in Minnesota; Selected Biographical Essays, edited by Barbara Stuhler and Gretchen Kreuter, pp. 20-33. St. Paul: Minnesota Historical Society Press, 1977.
          Katharine Donnelly was the wife of Ignatius Donnelly, the author of Caesar's Column (1890) and a leading Populist politician from Minnesota. Kreuter describes Kate Donnelly as a strong and jovial woman who, although not active herself, supported her husband's political ambitions and offered tactical advice. She played an important role in encouraging her husband to take a strong stand in favor of women's emancipation.

Kelley, Florence (1859-1932)

27 BLUMBERG, DOROTHY ROSE. Florence Kelley: The Making of a Social Pioneer. New York: Augustus M. Kelley, 1966, 194 pp.
          Florence Kelley, best remembered for her work for the National Consumers' League, was a dedicated albeit independent-minded Socialist for most of her life. In 1883, while studying in Zurich, Kelley met a group of students fired by Socialist idealism and enthusiastically joined their cause. In 1884 she married her new comrade, Lazare Wischnewetzky, a Russian medical student, and in 1886 returned with him to the United States. Settled in New York City, the young couple joined the intensely sectarian, German-dominated Socialist Labor party, and Kelley set herself to translating into English Friedrich Engels's The Condition of the Working Class in England in 1844, which was published in New York in 1887. Expelled from the SLP that same year, Kelley sought an alternative outlet and in 1891 moved to Chicago where she divorced Wischnewetzky and found a congenial milieu at

Hull House. Although Kelley joined the Socialist Party of America in 1912, she never again became active in a Left party organization, and worked instead for legislative reform of working
conditions.

Blumberg treats in detail Kelley's Socialist years and
follows her activities until the turn of the century. A more
scholarly work than Josephine Goldmark's, her biography is based
on primary research in foreign-language materials, including
letters at the Institute of Marxism-Leninism, Moscow, and the extensive correspondence between Engels and Kelley. Blumberg aptly
describes the late nineteenth-century Socialist Labor party and
Kelley's uncomfortable relationship with its dogmatic leaders.
She concludes that at the heart of Kelley's political striving
was a desire to achieve an "American" brand of socialism as a
means best to use theory for social change.

28 GOLDMARK, JOSEPHINE. Impatient Crusader: Florence Kelley's
    Life Story. Urbana: University of Illinois Press, 1953,
    217 pp.
    Josephine Goldmark (1877-1950), an investigator of labor
conditions and legislative reformer, was a close friend of
Florence Kelley and co-worker in the National Consumers' League.
Her uncritical biography touches lightly on Kelley's Socialist
sympathies and focuses primarily on her efforts to improve the
working conditions of women and children. The descriptions of her
early years are drawn almost entirely from Kelley's personal
reminiscences published serially in the Survey in 1926 and 1927.

29 HARMON, SANDRA D. "Florence Kelley in Illinois." Journal of
    the Illinois State Historical Society 74 (Autumn 1981):163-78.
    Harmon records Kelley's work as chief factory inspector
for the state of Illinois, 1893-1897. It was during this period,
the author contends, that Kelley sharpened her professional and
political skills and gained a national reputation as legislative
reformer. Moreover, as chief factory inspector, Kelley acted
forcefully to improve the working conditions of women and children,
a campaign she would later develop under the auspices of the
National Consumers' League.

Kellie, Luna Sanford (1857-1940)

30 BAKKEN, DOUGLAS A., ed. "Luna E. Kellie and the Farmers'
    Alliance." Nebraska History 50 (Summer 1969):184-205.
    The leading Populist woman in Nebraska, Luna E. Sanford
Kellie performed editorial and secretarial services for the
Farmers' Alliance in the 1890s and wrote several Populist songs.
She also raised eleven children and, like so many Populist women,
participated in the local temperance movement.
    Bakken introduces a manuscript written by Luna Kellie in
1926 in which she recounts her stewardship in the Nebraska Alli-
ance. The original copy is held by the Nebraska State Historical
Society.

Kelly, Florence Finch (1858-1939)

31 KELLY, FLORENCE FINCH. <u>Flowering Stream: The Story of Fifty-Six Years in American Newspaper Life</u>. New York: E.P. Dutton & Co., 1939, 571 pp.

From a Midwestern rural background, Kelly worked her way through college to become a leading journalist in the twentieth century. She held positions at various times on the <u>Boston Globe</u>, <u>San Francisco Examiner</u>, and <u>Los Angeles Times</u>, and served for three decades on the staff of the book review magazine of <u>The New York Times</u>.

In the 1880s, while working at the <u>Boston Globe</u>, Kelly met Benjamin Tucker, and under his sway she became an anarchist. In this discursive autobiography focused on her newspaper career, Kelly minimizes her youthful bent toward anarchism but states that "the chief attraction of Tucker's anarchist philosophy was that it recognized so strongly the rights of the individual and envisioned a world that was not a man-made world, for men, but a world made up of equal individuals, regardless of sex."

Although the passage concerning Kelly's involvement in the Boston anarchist circle is brief, it conveys vividly the centrality of feminist issues. Kelly describes her rapid disenchantment with anarchism but claims a lifelong commitment to feminism. She records her dependence on women's networks, such as her Kansas association with Populist Annie Diggs and her professional relationship with Boston's Lilian Whiting.

Lease, Mary Elizabeth (1850-1933)

32 BLUMBERG, DOROTHY ROSE. "Mary Elizabeth Lease, Populist Orator: A Profile." <u>Kansas History</u> 1 (Spring 1978):3-15.

Blumberg's essay is to date the best biography of Mary E. Lease, foremost orator among the ranks of Populist women. Born in Pennsylvania, Lease spent the years of her marriage and political activism in Kansas. There she took up the causes of Irish nationalism and agrarian revolt. In 1885 she supported the Union Labor party, which ran on a popular antimonopoly platform. In the next several years she became a prominent member of both the Knights of Labor and Farmers' Alliance.

Between 1890 and 1894 Lease reached her stride as a fiery speaker and militant leader. She developed a spell-binding lecture style and entranced audiences across the Midwest, far West, and South. "Our Queen Mary," as she was known among her ranks, became a legendary figure in her own lifetime. She wrote only one book, <u>The Problem of Civilization</u> (1895), a rambling text advocating reform on an international level.

Blumberg traces Lease's remarkable career and assesses her contribution to radical history. Although Lease adhered to a strict economic analysis of society and stressed the evils of class division, she supported the women's movement and joined many of its campaigns. Blumberg credits this activity and

documents the origins of Lease's public role in a speaking engagement, her first, before a local Woman's Christian Temperance
Union in Texas. From temperance, woman suffrage, and women's
club work, Lease moved into broader political networks. Although
her radical sympathies waned after the turn of the century, she
maintained a commitment to women's rights. She supported Margaret
Sanger's campaigns and served for a time as president of the
National Society for Birth Control. Blumberg's essay successfully relates the various aspects of Lease's political activities.

33 CLANTON, O. GENE. "Intolerant Populist? The Disaffection of
    Mary Elizabeth Lease." Kansas Historical Quarterly 34
    (Summer 1968):189-200.
        Clanton traces the evolution of Lease's career and assesses
its shortcomings. He describes Lease as a woman who had "an ex-
aggerated sense of her own importance," a fanatical hatred of
Democrats, and a shallow understanding of the political situation.

34 JAMES, EDWARD T. "More Corn, Less Hell? A Knights of Labor
    Glimpse of Mary Elizabeth Lease." Labor History 16 (Summer
    1975):408-9.
        James attempts to penetrate the legend attached to Mary E.
Lease, the much-quoted admonition to Kansas farmers to "raise
less corn and more hell." He suggests a member of the Knights of
Labor first coined this expression, but hostile newspaper writers
attributed it to Lease in an effort to cast aspersion on her
character and on the Populist movement.

35 LEVINSON, HARRY. "Mary Elizabeth Lease: Prairie Radical."
    Kansas Magazine (1948):18-24.
        This spare journalistic essay traces Lease's career as
Populist leader through her turn toward the Republican party and
McKinley and into her later life as a counselor to the poor in
New York City. Although the author draws no profound conclusions,
he captures aspects of Lease's contradictory character.

Modjeska, Helena (1840-1909)

36 MODJESKA, HELENA. Memories and Impressions of Helena Modjeska;
    An Autobiography. New York: Macmillan & Co., 1910, 571 pp.
        Born in Cracow, Poland, Modjeska was both a famous actress
in her homeland and activist in the cause of Polish nationalism.
In 1876 she joined a group of Polish immigrants who formed a
cooperative farm in the Santa Ana valley of California.
        Modjeska devotes a small portion of her memoirs to her
brief encounter with communal living. By January 1877 the farm
began to fail and Modjeska, to provide the needed funds, resumed
her acting career. She learned English and conducted a successful tour of Eastern United States, but by the summer of 1878 the
colony had disbanded.

Morgan, Elizabeth Chambers (1850-?)

37 RITTER, ELLEN M. "Elizabeth Morgan: Pioneer Female Labor
    Agitator." Central States Speech Journal 22 (Winter 1971):
    242-51.
        Born in England, Elizabeth Morgan was a major figure in
the Chicago labor movement in the 1880s and 1890s. During this
period she brought together trade unionists, Socialists, and
women reformers in a campaign to improve the working conditions
of women and children. In June 1888 she helped form the Ladies'
Federal Labor Union no. 2703, one of the most important women's
affiliates in the American Federation of Labor. Under Morgan's
guidance, the Ladies' Federal Labor Union sought the cooperation
of the city's Trade and Labor Assembly and local women's organizations to campaign actively to enact legislative reforms to
ameliorate the poor conditions in the sweated trades. The
Illinois Woman's Alliance, formed in November 1888, became a
landmark institution. It secured changes in the Illinois Compulsory Education Act, the appointment of women factory inspec-
tors, the construction of new schools, a municipal child labor
law, and public bathhouses in the working-class neighborhoods in
Chicago. Its major campaign, inspired by Morgan's hard labors,
resulted in the Illinois Factory and Workingshop Inspection Act
of 1893.
        Focusing on Morgan's investigation of the sweatshop con-
ditions of Chicago's garment industry, Ritter examines in particular the rhetoric Morgan employed in her speeches and in her published reports. She also measures Morgan's contributions to the
legislative campaigns of the 1890s.

38 SCHARNAU, RALPH. "Elizabeth Morgan, Crusader for Labor Re-
    form." Labor History 14 (Summer 1973):340-51.
        Scharnau provides a factual summary of Morgan's activities
to improve the conditions of labor for Chicago's women and children. As wife of the English-language leader of the local Socialist Labor party, Morgan believed in the efficacy of legislative
campaigns. Scharnau writes: "She saw trade unions as a necessary
and valuable outgrowth of the worker's desire for protection
against the profit system. But her attitude toward labor organizations was always conditioned by her belief that political
action offered the only really effective way of combatting the
evils of capitalism."

Parsons, Lucy (1853-1942)

39 ASHBAUGH, CAROLYN. Lucy Parsons: American Revolutionary.
    Chicago: Charles H. Kerr, 1976, 288 pp.
        Lucy Parsons became involved in Socialist organizations in
1874, when she and her husband Albert made their home in Chicago.
In the late 1870s, when the Chicago movement was at its peak,
Lucy began to contribute essays and poems to the Socialist, a

newspaper edited by Albert, and together with Alzina Parsons
Stevens and Lizzie Swank (Holmes) she helped organize the local
Working Women's Union. Throughout the 1880s, Parsons, a "fashion-
able" dressmaker by profession, sought to improve the conditions
of Chicago's working women, especially those employed in the
city's expanding garment trades. At this time, she was also
drawn to "revolutionary socialism." In the mid-1880s, Lucy and
Albert resigned from the politically oriented Socialist Labor
party and joined the International Working People's Association.
Lucy wrote her most notorious essays, such as her plea "To
Tramps," for its newspaper <u>Alarm</u>, edited by her close friend
Lizzie Swank and by her husband, Albert Parsons. She and her
husband emerged militant advocates of "propaganda by the deed,"
or individual acts of terrorism.

The fatal bombing and shootings at Haymarket Square on
May 3, 1886 became the focal point of Lucy Parson's activities
for the remainder of her life. With seven others, Albert Parsons
was implicated in an alleged conspiracy, was indicted and tried
for the bombing, was found guilty, and was executed on November
11, 1887. On behalf of the eight men held as prisoners, Lucy had
conducted an extensive lecture tour and suffered repeated arrests,
and throughout the 1890s she continued to use this incident as
the basis of her political work. After the turn of the century
Lucy joined the Industrial Workers of the World and the Socialist
Party of Amerca; after the Russian Revolution, she became close
to the Communist party. In November 1937 she spoke in Chicago on
the fiftieth anniversary of the execution of the Haymarket martyrs.

Carolyn Ashbaugh reconstructs Lucy Parsons's life from
only fragments of information. She also supplies a broad context.
Ashbaugh documents the turmoil and violence rife in Chicago during
the 1870s and 1880s, and details the activities of various labor
and political organizations. Her description of the Haymarket
incident and trial, uniquely and imaginatively told through Lucy's
eyes, is especially dramatic. The author tends, however, to make
Lucy Parsons a one-dimensionally heroic figure despite obvious
flaws in her character and philosophy. For example, Ashbaugh
underscores Parsons's background as Afro-American, an identity
Parsons herself repeatedly denied. Ashbaugh also apologizes for
Parsons's conservative attitudes toward sexual relations and marriage, and dismisses Emma Goldman's criticisms of Parsons;
Goldman, Ashbaugh contends, was merely exhibiting her middle-
class feminist bias, whereas Parsons shaped her ideas around her
origins in and loyalty to the working class.

<u>Valesh, Eva McDonald (1866-1956)</u>

40 GILMAN, RHODA D. "Eva McDonald Valesh, Minnesota Populist."
    In <u>Women of Minnesota; Selected Biographical Essays</u>, edited by
    Barbara Stuhler and Gretchen Kreuter, pp. 55-76. St. Paul:
    Minnesota Historical Society Press, 1977.
        Eva McDonald Valesh was the most prominent woman in the

Minnesota Populist movement; she ranked nationally next to Annie
L. Diggs and Mary E. Lease. Her political dedication dates to
1888, when she conducted an investigation of factory conditions
among local working women and reported her findings in a column
in the St. Paul Globe. Valesh soon joined the Knights of Labor
and within a few years became a key figure in the Farmers' Alliance. She was instrumental in supporting women's rights and in
encouraging women to play a larger role within the agrarian movement.

Gilman provides ample details on the peak era of Valesh's
political activity. She also traces her drift toward conservatism
in 1896, when Populism and a short-lived marriage collapsed simultaneously. Valesh then moved East, where she worked for a time
for the American Federationist, official journal of the American
Federation of Labor. Later, she and her second husband published
the American Club Woman. After the end of her second marriage in
the 1920s, Valesh supported herself as a proofreader until her
retirement from the staff of the New York Times in 1951.

Whitney, Anne (1821-1915)

41   PAYNE, ELIZABETH ROGERS. "Anne Whitney, Art and Social
     Justice." Massachusetts Review 12 (Spring 1971):245-60.
     Anne Whitney, one of the few nineteenth-century American
women to achieve success as a sculptor, made social justice the
theme of her life's work. Her sculpture memorialized heroes of
freedom, especially the emancipation of women and blacks, or
portrayed the victims of oppression.
     Payne's essay surveys Whitney's major works; it also
acknowledges her role in the Bellamy Nationalist movement,
particularly as financial angel to the flagging Boston section.

Willard, Frances E. (1839-1898)

42   WILLARD, FRANCES E. Glimpses of Fifty Years: The Autobiog-
     raphy of an American Woman. Chicago: Woman's Temperance Pub-
     lication Association, 1889, 698 pp. Reprint. New York:
     Source Book Press, 1970, 698 pp.
     Frances Willard, president of the National Woman's Chris-
tian Temperance Union during its most militant period, is remembered primarily for her work among women. Social purity,
woman suffrage, and world peace were among her most arden concerns. In the late 1880s Willard began to relate these various
activities to a unified vision of social change: Christian
socialism.
     In her last address to a national WCTU convention in 1897,
Willard said that if she had her life to live over she would de-
vote it to Christian socialism. She did manage to contribute
significantly to its popularity among many women in her ranks.
She established formal ties between the WCTU and the Knights of
Labor, became a principal supporter of the Bellamy Nationalist

movement, and tried, although unsuccessfully, to forge a national political alliance of the major radical and reform organizations of the late 1880s. Equally important, she preached socialism to women's audiences throughout the 1890s, preparing large numbers, especially in the Midwest, to take active parts in the Socialist Party of America when it formed after the turn of the century.

First published in 1889, Willard's autobiography is an invaluable record of her activities until the late 1880s. She describes many events in elaborate detail and includes pertinent documents such as texts of speeches, favorite poems, and passages from her diaries. A large section, as might be expected, is a history of the National Woman's Christian Temperance Union, but choice anecdotes and sketches of her friends add a personal touch. Although it is discursive and unwieldy, the autobiography offers essential insights into Willard's public persona and social vision, both well characterized by the inscription on the title page: "Nothing makes life dreary but lack of motive."

43 DILLON, MARY EARHART. Frances Willard: From Prayers to Politics. Chicago: University of Chicago Press, 1944, 417 pp. Reprint. Washington, D.C.: Zenger Publishers, 1975, 417 pp.

Until the publication of Dillon's book in 1944, Frances Willard was remembered primarily for her temperance work. Her friends and associates, all co-workers in the Woman's Christian Temperance Union, had produced early studies of the organization's most dynamic president, and they had eulogized Willard as "Saint Frances" and minimized the complexity of her political world view. Dillon demolishes many myths, and portrays Willard as a shrewd politician and tactical genius.

Dillon combed the archival records at the national headquarters of the WCTU in Evanston, Illinois, and recreated the story of Willard's rise within the organization. She shows how Willard planned to push the WCTU beyond its temperance advocacy to a multifaceted campaign of social and economic reform. Under her presidency, the WCTU adopted a do-everything policy, which by the 1880s involved hundreds of thousands of women in nearly forty fields of work and agitation. By offering women such a diverse program, Willard hoped to bring them under her leadership and to train them for a larger role in American society. Dillon carefully underscores Willard's achievements along this line, especially her hard-won victory of bringing the WCTU into the suffrage camp. Unlike the earlier biographers who erased Willard's Socialist leanings from the historical record, Dillon details her aspirations as well as her attempts to build alliances with radical organizations in the late 1880s and early 1890s.

Woodhull, Victoria Claflin (1838-1927)

44 MARTIN, VICTORIA (CLAFLIN) WOODHULL. A Fragmentary Record of Public Work Done in America, 1871-1877. London: G. Norman & Son, 1877, 44 pp.

Victoria Claflin Woodhull reigns as the most unconventional and notorious woman in American radical history. She has many credits to her name: the first "lady" broker on Wall Street; president of the American Spiritualist Association; candidate for the presidency of the United States; first American publisher of Karl Marx's The Communist Manifesto; and the most renowned advocate of free love of her generation. A wide-ranging reformer, Woodhull also joined the International Workingmen's Association, the first modern Socialist organization in the United States; she also was the precipitating agent in a fatal rift between rival American and German-dominated sections in 1872. In 1877, suffering from ill health and a decline in popularity, Woodhull departed for England, where she soon resumed her public activities. In 1883 she married John Biddulph Martin, an ardent admirer and London banker.

Compiled shortly after her departure from the United States, this anthology includes selected notices published in newspapers announcing Woodhull's public lectures, 1871-1876. She carefully selected only praiseful reviews of her performances during extensive lecture tours.

45 MARTIN, Mrs. JOHN BIDDULPH (VICTORIA WOODHULL). Brief Sketches of the Life of Victoria Woodhull. London: n.p., 1893, 29 pp. Microfilm. History of Women, Reel 577, no. 4502.

Late in her life, Woodhull collected miscellaneous tributes to her assorted contributions. The five sketches in this volume, written at various points in her career, emphasize her mystical and inspirational qualities, especially her talent for spellbinding oratory. The concluding essay, "The Apostle of Womanhood," signed by Roslyn D'Onston, names Woodhull the "prophetess" of "the new cult of womanhood," which is to supersede spiritualism and even socialism as the coming faith.

46 ARLING, EMANIE SACHS. "The Terrible Siren": Victoria Woodhull. New York: Harper, 1928, 423 pp. Reprint. New York: Arno Press, 1978, 423 pp.

In the studies of American cranks, Victoria Woodhull is a favorite character. Few popular writers have been able to resist her appeal; most portray Woodhull as a comic figure from America's colorful past.

Arling's biography, published originally in 1928, is the first and best full-length source available to scholars, but it, too, capitalizes on the more bizarre features of Woodhull's life. Arling passes lightly over Woodhull's involvement in the First International and focuses instead on her more notorious deed, precipitating the Beecher-Tilton free-love scandal of the early 1870s. Arling also assigns the bulk of Woodhull's eccentricities to her impoverished childhood and unusual parents, and thereby institutionalizes the flamboyant rags-to-riches flight that dominates later interpretations.

Despite a fascination with the more extraordinary aspects

of Woodhull's public activities, the author manages to create the
first detailed narrative of her life based on path-breaking research into family geneology and local newspaper reportage.
Aimed at popular audiences, Arling's biography nevertheless claims
more scholarly merit than later productions. A combination of
anecdotes and unique perceptions, it reads easily and engagingly.
The Arno reprint preserves the numerous illustrations published
in the first edition.

47 EK, RICHARD A. "Victoria Woodhull and the Pharisees." Jour-
    nalism Quarterly 49 (Autumn 1972):453-59.
        Ek focuses on Woodhull's public addresses during the
Beecher-Tilton free-love scandal of 1873, and assesses her role
in promoting the right of free speech.

48 JOHNSTON, JOHANNA. Mrs. Satan: The Incredible Saga of
    Victoria C. Woodhull. New York: G.P. Putnam's Sons, 1967,
    319 pp.
        Johnston presents Woodhull as a principled fighter against
the rigid and oppressive code of victorian morality. She focuses
primarily on Woodhull's advocacy of free love and touches only
lightly upon her Socialist activities. A popular rather than
scholarly work, this biography builds on Arling's earlier contribution but delves more deeply into the Beecher-Tilton scandal
and trial. Like Arling, Johnston attributes Woodhull's determined personality to her impoverished childhood, so much so that
a contemporary reviewer found a parallel between Woodhull's rise
to notoriety and the saga of Marilyn Monroe, who also experienced
a "sordid" youth.

49 MARBERRY, M. MARION. Vicky: A Biography of Victoria C.
    Woodhull. New York: Funk & Wagnalls, 1967, 344 pp.
        Less substantial than Johnston's biography, Marberry's
study takes a similar, popular approach. Victoria Woodhull
appears a colorful character and, most of all, an extraordinarily
beautiful woman. These two attributes alone seem sufficient to
explain her unique role in American history.
        Marberry acknowledges his inability to interpret the sig-
nificance of Woodhull's political career, including her dramatic
role in the infamous Beecher-Tilton scandal, which he covers in
familiar detail. He concludes: "What the ultimate judgment of
posterity on Victoria C. Woodhull will be, no one knows. Yet
surely few people today will deny that she was sui generis." As
one reviewer noted, Marberry's biography is really a "slapstick
burlesque," a catalogue of Woodhull's antics.

50 TILTON, THEODORE. Victoria C. Woodhull. A Biographical
    Sketch. New York: Golden Age Tract No. 3, 1871, 33 pp.
    Microfilm. History of Women. Reel 414, no. 3010.
        Theodore Tilton wrote this brief biography of his close
associate when she was thirty-two years old. He tells a melo-

dramatic tale of her unhappy childhood and first marriage and portrays Woodhull as distanced spiritually and intellectually from the surrounding depravity of her youth. He credits her spectacular rise to public acclaim to her nobility of character and spiritualistic leanings.

Tilton's sketch is one of the first contributions to set the stage for the myth of Victoria Woodhull.

BOOKS AND PAMPHLETS ON
THE WOMAN QUESTION

In the late nineteenth century, various radicals began to construct a framework for discussing aspects of the Woman Question in relation to a changing economic and political order. Members of the first generation to witness the dramatic alterations accompanying the industrial revolution, they perceived that sex roles, rather than fixed by nature, were determined by social and cultural forces. They therefore set themselves to examining contemporary conditions, to studying historical development, and to imagining a system that would allow woman to rise to her full potential. At the heart of most analyses was a critique of woman's dependency on man, especially within the economic arrangements of marriage.

The essays and tracts in this section illustrate the elementary and fragmentary quality of these early speculations. Only August Bebel in Germany and Charlotte Perkins Gilman made lasting contributions that are readable today. Yet the various writers hit upon a common theme, that woman's self-determination would be guaranteed only by a truly republican government and cooperative economic order. The outlines of what would become the modern Socialist feminist analysis of sex relations are apparent here.

Few writers, however, broke entirely with midcentury notions about the essential differences between the sexes, but rather predicted that freedom from artificial and unjust restraints would allow woman to find her preferred sphere and restore sex relations to a natural harmony.

51 ANDREWS, STEPHEN PEARL. Love, Marriage and Divorce and the Sovereignty of the Individual. Edited by Charles Shively. Weston, Mass.: M. & S. Press, 1975, 13, 121, 55 pp. Microfilm. History of Women. Reel 422, no. 3083.1.
    Stephen Pearl Andrews (1812-1886), Victoria Woodhull's mentor, expounded the philosophical basis of free love. In this volume, he updates an exchange on sexual relations between Henry James, Sr., Horace Greeley, and himself. Published originally in the New York Tribune in 1853, and reprinted by Benjamin Tucker's press in 1889, this expanded version contains Andrews's essay "Love, Marriage, and the Condition of Women."

Editor Charles Shively interprets Andrews's contribution:
"Andrews provided an anarchist/socialist critique of existing
marriage and sought to delineate another system of male/female
relations based upon love and equality."

52 AVERY, MARTHA MOORE. Woman: Her Quality, Her Environment,
     Her Possibility. Boston: Socialist Press, [1901], 29 pp.
         Like many native-born Socialists, Avery was deeply touched
     by mysticism. In this short treatise she makes a case for equal
     rights but adds an extra one for women--the right to fulfill
     their role as mothers of the race. Women have two unique and
     compelling reasons to become Socialists, Avery contends: the
     desire to protect their right to wifehood and motherhood; and the
     need for political citizenship. The Socialist revolution, more-
     over, requires their participation because only together can men
     and women endure. Avery posits a duality of masculine and femi-
     nine qualities as the building blocks of the new civilization.
     She designates woman the "receptive force," man the "projective
     force," and their union the source of a "more beautiful and
     divine future for the race."
         Although published after the turn of the century, this
     address won the favor of Socialist crowds throughout the 1890s.

53 BEBEL, AUGUST. Woman Under Socialism. New York: Schocken
     Books, 1971, 379 pp.
         Published originally in Germany in 1883, Bebel's text
     stands as a classic argument for women's emancipation. Bebel
     opened: "Woman and workingmen have, since old, had this in com-
     mon--oppression." He then elaborated the historical drama of
     simultaneous subjugation of women and the division of society
     into opposing classes. He traced this history through three
     major epochs until the nineteenth century, when industrial capi-
     talism had increased the immiseration of the proletariat and at
     the same time intensified the oppression of women.
         The bulk of the text focuses on women's situation in con-
     temporary nineteenth-century society, especially their new place
     in the labor force. Unlike many of his comrades, Bebel did not
     seek to restore women to the home, but instead encouraged their
     broader participation in economic and political life. He thus
     appealed to woman "not to remain behind in this struggle in which
     her redemption and emancipation are at stake," but to join the
     working class in its struggles for a better future.
         Although Bebel established a firm precedent within the
     European Socialist movement in his advocation of women's rights,
     he set the goal of their emancipation squarely within the Social-
     ist revolution and nowhere else.
         Woman Under Socialism became, after Karl Marx's Capital,
     the most important book in the Socialist movement until after the
     turn of the century. This edition, translated into English by
     Daniel DeLeon, was first published in the United States in 1904.
     In 1971 Lewis Coser provided an introduction stressing the rele-
     vance of Bebel's work to a new generation of activists.

54 BELLAMY, EDWARD. Talks on Nationalism. Chicago: The Peerage
    Press, 1938, 191 pp. Reprint. Freeport, N.Y.: Books for
    Libraries Press, 1969, 191 pp.
        This volume reprints a series of short essays that appeared
    originally in the Nationalist publication the New Nation in the
    1890s. Compiled in 1938, the collection was designed to revive
    Bellamy's program as a solution to the Great Depression.
        Written in the form of a conversation between "Mr. Smith"
    and a representative individual, Bellamy's essays address a vari-
    ety of topics. Three selections addressed to women take up
    women's rights, dress reform, and the problems of household labor.

55 BLACKWELL, ELIZABETH. Christian Socialism; Thoughts Suggested
    by the Easter Season. Hastings, England: sold by D. Williams,
    [1882], 15 pp. Microfilm. History of Women. Reel 935, no.
    7926.
        Elizabeth Blackwell (1821-1910), physician and women's
    rights advocate, is known primarily for her work to advance women
    in the medical profession and her concern for women's health.
    In the 1880s, while practicing in London, Blackwell followed her
    friend Charles Kingsley and became a Christian Socialist.
        In this pamphlet, Blackwell reviews various social prob-
    lems, such as agrarian unrest, sickness, and poverty, as well as
    the inequitable relations between the sexes. She endorses the
    Christian teaching of brotherhood, especially as applied to a
    system of greater distribution of wealth and social insurance.

56 BRISTOL, AUGUSTA COOPER. Present Phase of Women's Advancement
    and Other Addresses. Boston: Christopher Publishing House,
    1916, 136 pp. Microfilm. History of Women. Reel 882, no.
    7253.
        Augusta Cooper Bristol (1835-1910) was a public speaker on
    women's rights and a variety of radical causes, especially the
    problems between labor and capital. In the early 1880s she spent
    three months at the familistère in Guise, France, and returned to
    the United States dedicated to the principles of cooperation in
    industry. She served for a time as a national lecturer for the
    Patrons of Husbandry and as a national superintendent of the
    Labor and Capital Department of the National Women's Christian
    Temperance Union.
        This volume, introduced by her daughter, collects her best
    essays and addresses, most dating to the 1880s and early 1890s.
    They reflect Bristol's socio-economic approach to the Woman
    Question and her understanding that women's self-support or fi-
    nancial independence was the paramount issue of her generation.
    Bristol advocated a system of cooperation and a major role for
    women in creating a truly republican form of government, one
    based on the reciprocity and interdependence of the sexes and ex-
    tolling the end of special privilege and inequalities of class.

57 CAMPBELL, RACHEL. The Prodigal Daughter; or, The Price of

Virtue. Valley Falls, Kan.: Lucifer, 1888, 31 pp.
Rachel Campbell (1834-1892) read this essay before the New
England Free Love League in Boston in 1881. She describes the
natural superiority of women and demands institutional recognition of their role in evolution. She explains that menstruation
purifies the female body by regularly sloughing away "the grosser
particles" and supplying women with "a higher grade of matter out
of which to build the next generation of babies." To complement
this biological process, society must assist genetic selection by
providing women the best in culture and education. Moreover, at
age eighteen, Collins insists, every women should receive a
stipend that would allow her to fulfill her evolutionary role
with dignity and independently from men.

58 CHICAGO TRADE AND LABOR ASSEMBLY. The New Slavery: Investigation into the Sweating System. Chicago: Detwiler Printers,
1891, 24 pp.
In 1891, Socialist Elizabeth Morgan and two other members
of the Trade and Labor Assembly formed a committee to begin a
systematic campaign to alert the public to the injustices regularly levied against the city's working women and children. In
her report, Morgan detailed the abysmal conditions in twenty-six
clothing establishments and argued for the abolition of the
sweating system by drawing a parallel between the horrors of
chattel slavery and the suffering endured in the "new slavery" of
the garment industry. Raising Britain's factory law as a successful precedent, Morgan demanded similar legislation in the United
States, as well as enforcement of the city's existing child and
sanitary laws.
Both the Trade and Labor Assembly and the Illinois Woman's
Alliance responded to Morgan's report and helped inaugurate a
campaign to abolish the sweating system. Morgan herself drew
such acclaim for her endeavors that she was invited to appear
before a House of Representatives Committee on Manufactures and
to present her findings on Chicago's situation. The Illinois
Bureau of Labor Statistics also acknowledged her contribution and
began a similar investigation. In 1893 the Illinois Factory Inspection Act stood as the culmination of Morgan's efforts.

59 COLLINS, MAY. A Plea for the New Woman. New York: Truth
Seeker Library, 1896?, 32 pp. Microfilm. History of Women.
Reel 523, no. 4004.
This rambling address, delivered before the Ohio Liberal
Society in February 1896, examines women's condition within the
framework of social evolution. Collins contends that given the
progressive tendencies of social development, women's position
as inferior is illogical. "Place women in their normal sphere,"
she predicts, "and like the laws of mechanical force, they will
follow the line of least resistance." Sex equality and harmony
will reign together.

60 COOK, TENNESSEE C. CLAFLIN. <u>Constitutional Equality: A Right of Woman</u>. New York: Woodhull, Claflin, & Co., 1871, 148 pp. Reprint. Westport, Conn.: Hyperion Press, 1976, 148 pp. Microfilm. <u>History of Women</u>. Reel 375, no. 2607.

Overshadowed by her more famous sister, Victoria C. Woodhull, Tennie C. Claflin (1845-1923) was a radical activist in her own right. She accompanied her sister through many political ventures in the early 1870s, including a stint in the First International, and published essays on women's equality.

Subtitled "A consideration of the various relations which she sustains as a necessary part of the body of society and humanity," this tract is Claflin's best-known work on women. It comprises a series of essays on various aspects of the Woman Question. Claflin considers in detail the legal ramifications of women's rights as guaranteed by the Constitution, but insists that the issue is not merely one of justice but the welfare of humanity. She writes: "The whole tendency, then, of the Woman Question is toward the perfection of the relation between the sexes."

61 _____. <u>Essays on Social Topics</u>. Westminster, England: The Roxburghe Press, 1898, 284 pp. Microfilm. <u>History of Women</u>. Reel 375, no. 2608.

Claflin moved to England in the late 1870s; in 1885 she married Francis Cook, proprietor of a substantial London dry goods firm, and assumed the title "Lady Cook."

This collection of essays documents Claflin's lifelong dedication to woman's rights and social justice. Mostly written during her years abroad, they concern women's sexual status and maternal duties. Included are several short tracts on "virtue" and "seduction" reprinted from <u>Woodhull & Claflin's Weekly</u> from 1871 and 1872.

62 CRANE, JOHN MAYO. <u>The Evolution of the Family</u>. Chicago: Moses Harman Publishing Co., 1900, 48 pp. Microfilm. <u>History of Women</u>. Reel 527, no. 4032.1)

An entry in the Light-Bearer Library series, Crane's essay comprises several rambling arguments against the institution of marriage. The author takes an evolutionary, ethnologic approach popular among Socialists and anarchists, and underscores the relative nature of morality. He claims that man, by nature polygamous, has created a variety of forms of sexual association that need not be regulated. His major purpose is to demonstrate "the futility of attempting to regulate morality by either ecclesiastical or governmental authority."

63 DIAZ, ABBY MORTON. <u>Only a Flock of Women</u>. Boston: D. Lothrop, 1893, 224 pp. Microfilm. <u>History of Women</u>. Reel 531, no. 4081.

Abby Morton Diaz (1821-1904), a successful writer of children's literature and New England local-color stories for young

people, devoted herself to improving the condition and status of
women. She joined the Women's Educational and Industrial Union
of Boston at its founding in 1877 and served as president from
1881 to 1892 and vice president from 1892 to 1902. She believed
in the efficacy of cross-class alliances among women and hoped to
uplift all to a position of financial and spiritual independence
from men. In 1888, she joined the First Nationalist Club of
Boston and became an ardent advocate of Christian socialism.

Only a Flock of Women is Diaz's Nationalist tract based on
her frequent lectures on the subject. She calls for government
ownership of utilities and transportation as a means to lessen
the competition, which brings the country "under the unscrupulous
rule of self-interest." She discusses a plethora of social injustices and considers carefully women's position as workers in
the labor market and in the household. Diaz's book is one of the
few full-length interpretations of Nationalism from women's perspective.

64 ENGELS, FRIEDRICH. The Origins of the Family, Private Property
    and the State in the Light of the Researches of Lewis H.
    Morgan. New York: International Publishers, 1942, 176 pp.
        First published in Germany in 1884, The Origins of the
Family became the leading theoretical statement on the origins of
women's oppression in class society. Engels drew freely from the
empirical work of Lewis Henry Morgan, an American ethnologist who
studied the Iroquois Indians in New York state, and described the
evolution of the family from its origins in savagery, through
barbarism, and into civilization. He related various forms of
social organization to the prevailing mode of production at each
stage, and pinpointed "the world historical defeat of the female
sex" at the overthrow of the mother-right that marked the onset
of private property and class society. Thus women's oppression
and class oppression shared a common historical setting, which
could be eradicated only by the overthrow of capitalism and the
inauguration of socialism.

        The Charles H. Kerr press published the first American
edition in 1902, but by the turn of the century most Socialists
were familiar with the contours of Engels's analysis. August
Bebel's Woman Under Socialism, which incorporated Engels's outline
of historical development, proved a popular vehicle for dissemina-
tion. Socialist women in study clubs across the United States
routinely examined the three major epochal stages of historical
development and located women within the distinct form of family
organization. Later generations of Communist women similarly em-
braced Engels's treatise as a singly important contribution to
the marxist canon.

65 FALES, IMOGENE C. The New Civilization. New York: n.p.,
    188?, 14 pp.
        In 1882 Imogene C. Fales helped organize the Sociologic
Society of America, an association advocating industrial coopera-

tion. She later joined the Bellamy Nationalist movement and, at the turn of the century, the Social Democracy of America. She was instrumental in spreading the ideas of socialism among activists in the late nineteenth-century women's movement.

Fales presented this address to the 1884 congress of the Association for the Advancement of Women. She tackled the problem of competition versus combination in the political economy of the nation and predicted that unless a solution to the discordant situation is found "there will be, sooner or later, a war of races, a war of classes." She called for a higher form of civilization based on the principle of cooperative action.

66 _____. The Fall and the Restoration: A Story in Social Science. Louisville, Ga.: P. Davidson, 1900, 58 pp.
    This essay surveys women's status in civilization by interpreting various mystic symbols and myths about the fall from paradise. "The present imperfect order of things," Fales concludes, "dates from the time when the masculine and feminine principles were sundered in the divorce between reason and intuition." She predicts a new, harmonious social order when the original and divine balance between sexes is restored.

67 _____. The Religion of the Future. Boston: Esoterica Publishing Co., 1889, 29 pp.
    Originally presented to the annual congress of the Association for the Advancement of Women in 1885, this tract argues for the "second coming" of Christ in the form of a new religion based on "the divine idea of human brotherhood." Fales places civilization at a major turning point, "on the threshold of a change from a social order representative of the egoistic instincts of man's nature, to one expressing altruistic sentiments." The advancing civilization, Fales predicts, will put an end to industrial competition and realize cooperation in all spheres of society; in this grand evolutionary process the life force is Jesus Christ, the assembling movement for cooperation the human agency of His will.

68 GAY, BETTIE. "The Influence of Women in the Alliance." In The Farmers' Alliance History and Agricultural Digest, edited by Nelson A. Dunning, pp. 308-12. Washington, D.C.: Alliance Publishing Co., 1891.
    Bettie Gay, a leading figure in the Texas Farmers' Alliance and advocate of temperance and woman suffrage, affirms the dedication of Populists to women's emancipation. She writes that "the Alliance has come to redeem woman from her enslaved condition, and place her in her proper sphere." She stresses the importance of woman's role in the family and shows how the Alliance honors that position in the structure of its organization. Like other Populists, Gay glorifies womanhood for its civilizing qualities.

69 GILMAN, CHARLOTTE PERKINS. Women and Economics: A Study of
    Economic Relation Between Men and Women as a Factor in Social
    Evolution. Edited and with an introduction by Carl N. Degler.
    Boston: Small, Maynard & Co., 1898, 356 pp. Reprint. New
    York: Harper Torchbooks, 1966, 356 pp. Microfilm. History
    of Women. Reel 549, no. 4236.
         Gilman's classic treatise, originally published in 1898,
    has inspired Socialists and feminists across the generations.
    Limited by a darwinist conception of social evolution and by an
    unbounded faith in progress, Women and Economics continues never-
    theless to attract a political audience because it offers a de-
    tailed examination of the impact of the industrial revolution on
    women's status, especially as determined by their changed rela-
    tionship with productive labor. Gilman described the epochal
    shift in production from home to marketplace, but focused pri-
    marily on the concurrent degradation of women's domestic work and
    their exploitation in wage-labor. Strongly influenced by Edward
    Bellamy, she outlined a system of collectivized housework similar
    to the one sketched earlier in Looking Backward: modern, effi-
    cient laundries, food and cleaning services, and nurseries would
    eliminate most chores routinely performed by women in their homes
    and thereby free them for the more exciting and fulfilling em-
    ployments enjoyed by men. As women became less trapped by
    archaic forms of domestic work, Gilman believed, they would ad-
    vance smoothly into wage-labor, become in the process economically
    and politically independent, and emerge as noble representatives
    of the female species. The end product of this evolution would
    be, in Gilman's imagination, not merely a new social order of
    sexual harmony, but an improved race, one ensured by women's
    unique capacity for maternity.
         Recent scholars have questioned Gilman's commitment to
    socialism; they have underlined the fact that Gilman's vision of
    a transformed political economy retains the essentials of com-
    petitive capitalism. Similarly, today's readers are often dis-
    turbed by her emphasis on women's capacity for motherhood. Others
    might find peculiar Gilman's reliance on analogies from the animal
    kingdom. Yet as a historical source, Women and Economics provides
    innumerable insights into the philosophical modes and personal
    aspirations of Socialist women at the turn of the century.
    Degler's introduction helps to establish its enormous popularity
    among Gilman's comrades in radical movements of various shades.

70 GRONLUND, LAURENCE. The Cooperative Commonwealth: An Exposi-
    tion of Socialism. Edited by Stow Perkins. Boston: Lee &
    Shepard, 1890, 304 pp. Reprint. Cambridge: Belknap Press of
    Harvard University, 1965, 251 pp.
         The Cooperative Commonwealth, published originally in 1884,
    was the first popular American exegesis of socialism written in
    English. A simplified version of the Germanic outline, except
    for a notable absence of the class-struggle thesis, Gronlund's
    text includes a revealing section on women.
         Gronlund (1846-1899) considered women's liberation a major

component of socialism and traced the roots of their oppression
to an economic system that demanded their dependency upon men in
marriage. He did not, however, favor an equal status for men and
women. Gronlund believed that men and women were fundamentally
different and therefore should not compete in the world of work.
Referring to "certain notorious physiological facts" that allegedly demanded a unique role for women, Gronlund assumed that
under socialism women would find their true place under a natural
division of labor. Similarly, he did not advocate woman suffrage.
Rather, Gronlund promised that socialism would enable every man
and woman to form a happy family, with man the chief breadwinner
and woman the homemaker.

Although never a best seller, The Cooperative Commonwealth
influenced many of Gronlund's contemporaries and reached a large
number of readers in serialized form in Socialist and labor newspapers. It provides an important insight into the prevailing
attitude toward women and their rights within the Socialist Labor
party of the late nineteenth century.

71 HARMAN, LILLIAN. Marriage and Morality. Chicago: Moses
    Harmon Publishing Co., 1900, 48 pp.
        Daughter of Moses Harman and wife of Edwin C. Walker,
Lillian Harman shared their controversial free-love beliefs. She
worked as a compositor on her father's journal, Lucifer, the
Light-Bearer, and at age sixteen, on September 19, 1886, joined
Walker in an "automistic marriage" that rejected both state and
church intervention. The day following the ceremony, Harman and
Walker were arrested and spent their second night in a Valley
Falls, Kansas, jail. In October they were brought to trial on
charges of living together outside wedlock, convicted, and
sentenced to prison.
        Lillian Harman held firm to her principles through a
highly publicized trial before a higher court in January 1887,
and during the next several decades of political agitation. She
wrote and lectured regularly on free love and women's rights.
This pamphlet constitutes the text of a speech delivered before
the Ohio Liberal Society in 1899, wherein she argued for a higher
morality than civil or religious.

72 HARMAN, MOSES. Love in Freedom. Chicago: Moses Harman Pub-
    lishing Co., 1900, 45 pp.
        Moses Harman (1830-1910), outspoken advocate of free love
and editor of Lucifer, the Light-Bearer, criticized the role of
church and state in governing marriage. A free-thinker and anarchist, he believed that love was an especially personal matter
that should recognize no greater authority than the individual.
In this pamphlet, he calls marriage "love's greatest enemy."

73 HEYWOOD, EZRA. Cupid's Yokes: or, The Binding Forces of Con-
    jugal Love. Princeton, Mass.: Cooperative Publishing Co.,
    1876, 23 pp. Microfilm. History of Women. Reel 387, no.

2744.

Ezra H. Heywood (1829-1893) of Princeton, Massachusetts, led New England anarchists and free-lovers during the decades after the Civil War. In 1873 he and his wife, Angela Tilton Heywood, founded the New England Free Love League and marked this historic event by introducing a new calendar beginning with "Y.L." the Year of Love.

Cupid's Yokes, subtitled "An Essay to Consider Some Moral and Physiological Phases of Love and Marriage, Wherein It is Asserted the Natural Right and Necessity of Self-Government," attacked the "Comstock" Postal Act of 1873, which banned "obscene" matter from the mails. Heywood insisted that only the individual could judge morality. This dictum applied equally to men and to women.

Cupid's Yokes also describes the beauty of love and sex. "Love stimulates enterprise, quickens industry, fosters self-respect, reverences the lowly and worships the Most High," Heywood contended. Indeed, love, he notes, is the "regnant force in social life."

Heywood was arrested and tried under the Comstock Act for sending this pamphlet through the mails. His friends, however, called a huge rally in his behalf, and Heywood was granted a presidential pardon in 1878, after he had served a six-month term. The United States attorney general then declared that Cupid's Yokes was not obscene.

74 JAMES, C.L. The Law of Marriage: An Exposition of Its Use-lessness and Injustice. St. Louis: Time Printing House, 1871, 22 pp. Microfilm. History of Women. Reel 962, no. 9953.
        A British immigrant, Charles Leigh James (1846-1911) was described by Voltairine de Cleyre as "the most learned of American Anarchists." James resided outside the political mainstream in Eau Claire, Wisconsin, but wrote frequently for Lucifer, the Light-Bearer, Free Society, Mother Earth, and other anarchist and free-thought publications.
        In this tract he argues that the laws of marriage enforce the subjection of women and consequently are morally wrong. Sexual intercourse without love or passion, James contends, is an evil sanctioned by the institution of marriage.

75 _____. Future Relation of the Sexes. St. Louis: n.p., 1872, 27 pp. Microfilm. History of Women. Reel 962, no. 9954.
        Like many nineteenth-century anarchists, James emphasized the differences between the sexes. In this tract he focuses on "female philoprogenitiveness," examines marriage practices among Shakers, Mormons, and Oneidans, and concludes that only absolute freedom from regulation will ensure women their rights and human-ity its destiny.

76 LEASE, MARY E. "Women in the Farmers' Alliance." Philadel-phia: J.B. Lippincott Co., 1891. Reprint. In Transactions

of the National Council of Women of the United States, 1891,
edited by Rachel Foster Avery, pp. 157-160; 214-216.
Farmingdale, N.Y.: Dabor Social Science Publications, 1978.
    Addressing the major national assembly of women, Lease be-
gins by acknowledging the contributions of the Kansas Farmers'
Alliance to the temperance and woman suffrage campaigns. She
focuses, however, on the pervasive condition of class strife and
economic hardship in America, and documents women's role in the
"great uprising of the common people." Although more rhetorical
than substantive, Lease's speech and appearance at the meeting
indicate the association of Populist women and the mainstream
women's movement.

77 POTTER-LOOMIS, HULDA L. Social Freedom, The Most Important
    Factor in Human Evolution. Chicago: Moses Harman Publishing
    Co., n.d. [189?], 21 pp. Microfilm. History of Women. Reel
    956, no. 9628.
    A lecture delivered to the Social Science League of Chi-
cago, this tract for free love advocates complete freedom in sexual matters for both men and women. Potter-Loomis bases her
argument on the proposition, "Love is the savior of the world,
and the world will not be saved until it ceases to crucify love."

78 RHINE, ALICE HYNEMAN. "Woman's Work in Industry." New York:
    Henry Holt & Co., 1891. Reprint. In Woman's Work in America,
    edited by Annie Nathan Meyer, pp. 276-322. New York: Arno
    Press, 1972. Microfilm. History of Women. Reel 579,
    no. 4525.
    Alice Hyneman Rhine was one of the very few native-born
women who joined the Socialist Labor Party in the late 1870s.
She combined a commitment to socialism and woman's rights.
    In this essay, first published in 1891, Rhine reviews the
programs of various institutions designed to protect and assist
wage-earning women, the role of labor organizations like the
Knights of Labor, the Grange, and trade unions, and the results
of contemporary reports on the conditions of labor. She concludes
by strongly endorsing the program advocated by Edward Bellamy.

79 SAYLES, LITA BARNEY. "Co-operation, the Law of the New Civili-
    zation." In Report of the International Council of Women,
    March 25 to April 1, 1888, assembled by the National Woman
    Suffrage Association, pp. 152-53. Washington, D.C.: National
    Woman Suffrage Association, 1888.
    Sayles's report constitutes a brief history of the Socio-
logic Society of America and the work of its first president,
Imogene C. Fales. It surveys the educational programs conducted
by the Society as well as its alliances with advocates of industrial cooperation in England and France.

80 SEVERANCE, JULIET H. Marriage. Chicago: Moses Harman Pub-
    lishing Co., 1901, 34 pp. Microfilm. History of Women. Reel
    956, no. 9641.

A prominent physician and reformer, Juliet H. Severance began taking a radical stand on marriage in the 1860s. An officer of several spiritualist societies and of the Liberal League, a Master Workman in the Knights of Labor, Severance was described by a contemporary as "a radical of the radicals."

In this address, delivered at the International Conference of Free Thinkers in Chicago, October 4, 1893, Severance attacked marriage as an institution that enslaves women. She contends that the time is ripe "for an advance along the line of sex life."

81 TODD, MARION MARSH. Prof. Goldwin Smith and His Satellites in Congress. Battle Creek, Mich.: Wm. C. Gage & Son, Printers, 1890, 167 pp.

Marion Marsh Todd (1841-1913) participated in several radical movements in the 1880s and 1890s. She ran for office on the California Greenback ticket, joined the Knights of Labor, and helped organize the Midwestern Union Labor Party. She was also well known for her populist tracts, Protective Tariff Delusions (1886) and Railways of Europe and America (1893).

This tract is a reply to an antiwoman-suffrage essay by Professor Smith, which was published in the Forum. Todd answers in a rambling, discursive fashion, but ultimately insists that women's enfranchisement is an inevitable factor in the progress of civilization, and Professor Smith's efforts to retard its achievement are not only "fruitless" but "unworthy."

82 VAN ETTEN, IDA. The Condition of Women Workers Under the Present Industrial System. New York: Concord Co-operative Printers, 1891, 16 pp. Microfilm. History of Women. Reel 943, no. 8560.

For brief periods in the late nineteenth century, the Socialist Labor party attracted native-born activists such as Ida Van Etten. A member of the New York Working Women's Society, a precursor to the Consumers' League, she presented this address to the national convention of the American Federation of Labor in December 1890. She described the low status of women in the labor force, with special reference to conditions in New York City. She lamented the fate of workers in the sweatshops and endorsed a program of protective legislation and hours limitation. Above all, she called for the organization of working women into trade unions.

83 WAISBROOKER, LOIS. A Sex Revolution. 2d ed. Topeka, Kan.: Independent Publishing Co., 1894, 61 pp. Microfilm. History of Women. Reel 615, no. 4896.1.

Lois Nichols Waisbrooker (1826-1909) was by the 1870s a leading advocate of free love, spiritualism, and woman's rights. During the next two decades she published her own journal, Foundation Principles, which was dedicated to "Humanitarian Spiritualism."

This pamphlet concerns various free-love, free thought,

and antiwar sentiments. It takes the form of a dream fantasy.
Margaret Mulgrove, a widow who has also lost her only child,
falls into a reverie while reading Strike of a Sex, a British
novella loosely constructed on the theme of Lysistrata, in which
women stage a strike against men's wars and for the right to
their own bodies. Two discussants, Selferedo and Lovella, represent the dual forces in civilization. Because women embodied the
"love-element of the God-forces in nature," the author argues,
society should let "the subservient sex become the dominant one
for a time." The women organize themselves and confront their
menfolk, and the men eventually agree to a five-year experiment
wherein women hold positions of leadership. It is assumed that
under women's reign, peace and love will flourish.

84 WOODHULL, VICTORIA C. The Victoria Woodhull Reader. Edited
    by Madeleine Stern. Weston, Mass.: M. & S. Press, 1974, un-
    paginated.
        Scholarly accounts of Victoria C. Woodhull are rare.
Copies of her many publications are equally scarce and available
only in a few libraries. Stern has provided an extremely useful
collection of Woodhull's major essays and speeches; moreover, she
has included a short yet informed introduction that contains
essential biographical information and underlines Woodhull's significance in the history of American feminism.
        Stern organized Woodhull's tracts within three categories
and wrote short introductions to each section. The first,
"Sociology," contains Woodhull's statements on sexual relations,
including exposés of the Beecher-Tilton scandal, and on eugenics.
The second section, "Political Theory," collects Woodhull's most
important contributions on woman suffrage and on women in political office, written during the period of her peak feminist activism in the early 1870s. The final section, "Economics," includes
her early address "A Lecture on the Great Social Problem of Labor
and Capital . . . May 8, 1891," and several tracts on revolution
and on finance. All entries, reprinted from the Miriam Y. Holden
Library of Books By and About Women and the New York Public
Library, are facsimile reproductions of original publications.
Important tracts not reprinted here are listed in a short bibliography of primary and secondary references on Woodhull.

85 WOODHULL, VICTORIA C., and TENNESSEE CLAFLIN. Woodhull &
    Claflin's Weekly: The Lives and Writings of Notorious Victoria
    Woodhull and Her Sister Tennessee Claflin. Edited by Arlene
    Kisner. Washington, N.J.: Times Change Press, 63 pp.
        Kisner's anthology contains selections from Woodhull &
Claflin's Weekly pertaining to woman's rights and free love. It
also includes an excerpt from Theodore Tilton's biographical
sketch of Woodhull. Concise headnotes place the various selections within their historical context.

PERIODICALS

Although women's literature flourished in a wide variety of
politically mainstream periodicals, like the suffragist Woman's Journal, few left-of-center women's publications appeared during this era.
The sparse number, the short runs, and the eclectic interests suggest
how limited remained the resources of radical women in the late nineteenth century.

86   Farmer's Wife. Topeka, Kan., 1891-1894.
     The Farmer's Wife, edited by Emma D. Pack, was the official
organ of the National Woman's Alliance Incorporated, which was
formed in September 1891 by leading Populist women. The newspaper addressed itself primarily to issues central to farm women,
such as isolation and household drudgery. It also reported activities of the woman's movement, the People's party, and local organizations like the Woman's Progressive Political League of
Kansas, which was an auxiliary to the People's party. The front
page featured a masthead proclaiming "Equal rights to All, Special
Privileges to None" and poems by Populist women. The reports on
women's issues and Frances Willard's role at the St. Louis Industrial Conference of 1892 are detailed and informative. The
Farmer's Wife is a principal source for the study of women and
Populism.

87   Lucifer, the Light-Bearer. Valley Falls and Topeka, Kan.;
     Chicago, 1883-1904.
     Edited by Moses Harman, Lucifer, the Light-Bearer achieved
a national reputation in the 1880s as an anarchist and free-
thought journal. Harman described its chief function as preaching
"the gospel of discontent." He believed in the value of education,
naming it an absolute prerequisite to self-determination. Hence,
"the Light-Bearer" illuminated the dark spots of American culture,
especially sex relations and matters of personal morality.
     Unlike most anarchist publications, Lucifer addressed a
female audience. Harman viewed woman, "the slave of a slave," as
the principal factor in social revolution, and called upon her to
play a leading part in the struggle. Harassed by postal authori-
ties for violating the Comstock Postal Act that prohibited the
mailing of "obscene" literature, Harman endorsed free love and
woman's right to control her own body. In 1907 Harman changed
the name and format of his publication to the more scholarly
American Journal of Eugenics, which died with its editor in 1910.

88   Woodhull & Claflin's Weekly. New York, 1870-1876.
     Woodhull & Claflin's Weekly, emblazoned by the motto
"Progress! Free Thought! Untrammeled Lives!", addressed a number of contemporary radical causes including divorce reform,
women's rights, and socialism. Among its more controversial de-
votions were free love and spiritualism. Founded originally to

advance Woodhull's campaign for presidency, the newspaper became
the organ of the synthetic philosopher, Stephen Pearl Andrews, who
filled its pages with his program for universal government, the
Pantarchy. Columns on women's political rights and sexual freedom
appeared prominently alongside a regular page of poetry and boxed
advertisements for patent medicines and various nostrums. Throughout 1872-1873 the newspaper served as Woodhull's voice on the
notorious Beecher-Tilton scandal, which she exposed in November
1872.
        Woodhull & Claflin's Weekly also contained news of the
first organized Socialist movement in the United States, the
International Workingmen's Association. The sisters joined New
York sections of the First International, and struggled to win
recognition for the Woman Question. Their newspaper remains the
most informative primary source on the American sections of the
First International and has distinction of being the first publisher in the United States of a full English-language version of
Marx and Engels's The Communist Manifesto.

FICTION AND POETRY

In the decades following the Civil War, writers of fiction addressed a series of moral and economic questions posed by the con-
solidating order of industrial capitalism. Edward Bellamy is the
most widely known. His best-selling Looking Backward inspired a
generation to search for collectivist solutions to the problems of
the day. Dozens of lesser-known novelists, including many women,
also hoped to educate a reading public through entertaining yet
thoughtful stories about contemporary American society.

The authors represented in this section advocate a variety of
political programs, from the anarchism of free-lover Florence Finch
Kelly to the state socialism of Bellamy himself. The majority take a
middle ground and discuss the benefits of industrial cooperation, a
system of profit-sharing, and joint management based on precepts of
Christian brotherhood.

Although a developing social realism dominated the literary form
in this era, utopian romances gained in popularity in the wake of
Bellamy's success. The women utopian writers informed their vision
of cooperation with a study of transformed sex roles. Like essayists
on the Woman Question, these writers shared the era's belief in basic
differences between men and women, especially the masculine inclina-
tion toward aggressive and selfish behavior and the feminine propensity for altruism, peace, and love. Female protagonists often
serve as the moral imperative, the beacon of the cooperative commonwealth so desired.

89 BARBER, HARRIET BOOMER [Faith Templeton]. Drafted In; A

Sequel to "The Breadwinners," A Social Study. New York:
Bliss Publishing Co., 1888, 348 pp.

A sequel to John Hay's famous work, this novel continues
the story and some of the same characters, although less successfully. Arthur Farnham, Hay's protagonist, renounces his former
antilabor stand and becomes a staunch advocate of cooperation.
The author paints scenes of poverty, labor conflict, and "fierce
assemblages of thwarted manhood," and her prediction that a "Day
of Reckoning" will come seems to foreshadow class warfare rather
than peaceful reconciliation.

90 BARTLETT, ALICE ELINOR [Birch Arnold]. A New Aristocracy.
New York: Bartlett Publishing Co., 1891, 316 pp.

This story hopes to inspire "a new aristocracy, wherein
moral worth and purpose count first, with brain and healthy
digestion a good second, and where wealth doesn't stand any show
at all." It narrates the lives of three orphan children, Meg,
Elsie, and Gilbert Murcheson, who in struggling to earn a livelihood enlighten their community to the principles of cooperation.
After describing their many adventures in town and city, the
author closes by outlining the philosophy of the Society of Universal Brotherhood.

As Benjamin O. Flower commented (Arena, January 1896),
Bartlett concerns herself primarily with the moral development of
the individual. She considers neither the economic causes of
poverty nor the political forces at work. Bartlett (1848-1930)
envisions a cooperative society but asks only that individuals
put into practice the Golden Rule.

91 BELLAMY, CHARLES J. An Experiment in Marriage; a Romance.
Albany, N.Y.: Albany Book Co., 1889, 286 pp. Reprint.
Delmar, N.Y.: Scholars' Facsimiles & Reprints, 1977, 286 pp.

Brother of Edward Bellamy, the author constructed a novel,
originally published in 1889, about a utopian settlement similar
in Socialist principles to the outline of Looking Backward.
Charles Bellamy (1852-1910), however, did not focus on the bare
economic and political arrangements but on the personalities of
his emancipated protagonists.

The narrator, Harry Vinton, sends his friends to Grape
Valley, a medium-sized socialistic settlement where true love
flourishes. He explains why life is so blissful in Grape Valley
compared to the rest of the country. He says, "The woman question
has not been solved, and until it is solved, society will have to
stay in a bad way. Until the relations of the sexes are properly
adjusted, we can have no real reform, nor progress." And, as
long as marriage is "a lottery, love is a delusion." Thus the
women of Grape Valley are economically independent as the first
principle, and consequently only passion, physical and spiritual,
draw men and women together. With a free-divorce system, men and
women change partners as they move through various stages of
their personal development and thereby achieve a yet higher

plateau of love, mutual enjoyment, and respect.
    Bellamy is relatively candid on the sources of physical
attraction that draw men and women together, and for this reason
his novel is unique in its visionary content.

92 BELLAMY, EDWARD. Looking Backward. Boston: Ticknor & Co.,
    1888, 470 pp. Reprint. Edited by R. Jackson Wilson. New
    York: Modern Library, 1981, 320 pp.
    Originally published in 1888, Looking Backward was the
most popular book at the turn of the century and a favorite among
women readers. Frances Willard called Looking Backward "an
evangel" and urged her temperance followers to study it carefully; Lucy Stone, Mary Livermore, Helen Campbell, Zerelda
Wallace, among others, praised its author and joined the Nationalist movement that formed shortly after its publication. Decades
later, Looking Backward still served as a clarion call to socialism, and brought thousands of men and women to active service.
    Looking Backward was the first popular novel in the
English language to describe the economic basis of women's emancipation and to grant women an equal role in the political and
cultural affairs of the utopian state. The novel offered a blueprint of a society founded on cooperation rather than competition
and showed how this goal might be reached by peaceful, electoral
means. The mechanism guaranteeing equality between the sexes was
an industrial army that pooled the labor of all citizens between
the ages of twenty-one and forty-six. Alongside men, women
served except during brief periods of maternity, and thereby
gained their economic independence, hence their freedom. "That
any person should be dependent for the means of support upon
another would be shocking to the moral sense," the narrator explained, "as well as indefensible on any rational social theory."
Financially self-sufficient, women gained control over their personal relationships with men and entered marriage for love's sake
alone. They also enjoyed full political rights.
    Although a few contemporary reviewers accused Bellamy
(1850-1898) of stealing such ideas from August Bebel's Woman
Under Socialism, it is more likely that he drew inspiration from
the women's movement itself. A newspaper journalist, Bellamy
covered many meetings of women and was thoroughly familiar with
their methods and goals. In Looking Backward, he incorporated
their vision into a socialistic framework and thereby spoke
directly to a receptive audience of activist women. Especially
compared to Laurence Gronlund, whose Cooperative Commonwealth
appeared just a few years earlier, Edward Bellamy understood his
audience.

93 _____. Equality. New York: D. Appleton & Co., 1897, 412 pp.
    Reprint. New York: AMS Press, 1970, 412 pp.
    The sequel to Looking Backward continues the romance of
Julian West and Edith Leete as well as the exegesis of Bellamy's
vision of socialism. Like Looking Backward, Equality contains a

chapter on women entitled "What the Revolution Did for Women."
After absorbing almost a decade of criticism from fellow Socialists and feminists, Bellamy was able to produce a clearer analysis
of gender and class relations. He wrote: "It was the economic
key, the control of the means of subsistence. Men, as a sex,
held that power over women, and the rich as a class held it over
the working masses. The secret of the sexual bondage and of the
industrial bondage was the same--namely, the unequal distribution
of the wealth power, and the change which was necessary to put an
end to both forms of bondage must obviously be economic equaliza-
tion, which in the sexual as in the industrial relation would at
once insure the substitution of co-operation for coercion."
Bellamy also criticizes the mainstream women's rights movement
for failing to achieve this insight, for criticizing, in his
opinion, the consequences rather than the underlying causes of
women's oppression.
    Published in 1897 shortly before Bellamy's death, Equality
never achieved the mass popularity of Looking Backward. Historians, however, consider it Bellamy's best statement on socialism
and his sharpest criticism of the capitalist system.

94 CAMPBELL, HELEN. Mrs. Herndon's Income. Boston: Roberts
    Brothers, 1886, 534 pp.
    This novel is a metaphorical statement on women's position
under capitalism. The plot concerns two female protagonists who
represent the twains of women's existence as well as the common
fate all women share under men's rule. Margaret Herndon, recently
widowed by an unloving husband, has inherited a small sum of
money and now must explore the alternatives for useful applica-
tion. Her opposite number, Meg, is a working-class woman trying
to escape from a marriage marked by violence and destitution.
Together Margaret and Meg effect a position of strength. They
also find a solution to their quandaries by finding new mates:
Margaret marries a middle-class Christian Socialist who draws her
away from philanthropy; Meg marries a proletarian German immigrant
revolutionary.
    Helen Stuart Campbell (1839-1918) wrote this novel at a
turning point in her career as she moved from humanitarian reform
endeavors toward the Socialist movement. A successful writer of
children's stories and philanthropic tracts, Campbell conducted
several important investigations of the conditions of women
workers. Her Prisoners of Poverty, also published in 1886, established her as an authority in the field. In 1889 Campbell gave
formal expression to her new political faith and joined the
Bellamy Nationalist movement.

95 CONVERSE, FLORENCE. The Burden of Christopher. Boston:
    Houghton Mifflin Co., 1900, 315 pp.
    Converse (1871-?), a Christian Socialist, modeled her
story on the religious parable of St. Christopher: her protagonist tries, metaphorically, to carry the working class to its

emancipation. The story opens as Christopher Kenyon inherits a
New England shoe factory. Appalled by the heartless employment
practices of his fellow capitalists, Kenyon decides to run his
factory on a semicooperative basis, sharing profits with his 1200
workers and allowing them a voice in management. His plan fails
because the reorganized operation cannot compete successfully
with the ruthless capitalists who keep their costs lower by
staving off labor unions and thereby keeping wages at starvation
level. Kenyon realizes that he should have turned over the
factory to the workers at once rather than hoping to move gradually toward full cooperation. His failure to carry their dreams
drives him to his death.

In advocating cooperation, Converse also endorses equality
of wages for women and government ownership of the railroads.
She enlivens her story by adding the spice of romance.

96　DONNELLY, IGNATIUS. The Golden Bottle; or, The Story of
Ephraim Benezet of Kansas. New York: D.D. Merrill Co., 1892,
313 pp. Reprint. Upper Saddle River, N.J.: Gregg Press,
1968, 313 pp.
Donnelly's novel is an important source documenting the
ideological affinity between Midwestern Populists and the contemporary women's movement. The heroine, a Kansas farm girl
forced to the city to find work, emerges as a revolutionary
leader. Sophie first works hand in hand with her bethrothed,
Ephraim Benezet, the novel's protagonist, and organizes the women
of the nation into a grand alliance. The Woman's League of America conducts reforms similar to those currently popular among
women activists, such as the formation of a cross-class alliance
to foster the independence and dignity of wage-earning women.
The League also replicates the prevailing faith in womanhood to
elevate the race. At the novel's conclusion, Sophie, now married
to Benezet, rides a white horse across the steppes of Tsarist
Russia, thus carrying the revolutionary message to the politically
darkest corners of the earth.

A leading Populist in the Midwest, Donnelly (1831-1901)
first published The Golden Bottle in 1892.

97　DOUGLAS, AMANDA M. Hope Mills; or, Between Friend and Sweet-
heart. Boston: Lee & Shepard, 1880, 372 pp.
Amanda Minnie Douglass (1831-1916), born in New York, was
not a political activist. She was a popular author, best known
for her children's stories. Many of her adult novels concern
women's struggle for financial independence and dignity; her
typical heroine flaunts the prescribed role of idleness and comes
to manage a successful business career. Inventive herself,
Douglas favored the entrepreneurial woman.

Hope Mills, however, is not a story of women's fate, although two supporting characters, the "sweethearts," serve to
illustrate Douglas's commitment to womanly resourcefulness. It
concerns two male protagonists, Jack Darcy and Fred Lawrence,

friends from childhood; it is also a study in the morality of
class society. Fred is the son of the "great man" of Yerbury,
the owner of the local woolen mill. Jack, fatherless from a
tender age, is an employee at the mill and the main provider for
his mother and aged grandmother. Fred, a Harvard graduate, is a
gentleman scholar but knows no practical trade. Jack, trained in
the school of life, has little polish but is richly endowed in
both common sense and sensitivity. Whereas their opposite qualities provided a strong childhood bond--Jack protecting Fred in
tough situations, Fred offering Jack refinement in return--class
antagonism dominates their adult relationship: Fred has un-
abashedly snubbed Jack, his social inferior. The main plot
follows Fred and Jack en route to a renewed friendship, as Fred
comes to terms with the errors of his upper-class, hence foolish,
ways.

The vehicle for their reunion makes Hope Mills an interesting document. Fred's father has proved an unwise capitalist,
like the many rash speculators who brought on the panic of 1873.
At his death, the amount of devastation is finally revealed. His
family is left penniless, the mills are closed, and the major
workforce of Yerbury stands idle, near ruination. Whereas Fred
is reduced to drifting and misery, Jack responds creatively. He
locates a financial angel and for a relatively small sum buys the
old mortgage on the mills from the Lawrence estate. He then turns
Hope Mills into a workers' cooperative on a five-year trial basis.
At first he hires the workers back at only three-quarters salary;
having endured lengthy unemployment, they gladly accept. For the
first few years the experiment struggles along, for the economy
has not yet recovered from the depression. Finally and despite
the disgruntlement of some impatient and selfish workers, the
mills achieve a modicum of success. Cooperation--"Honesty,
industry, and fidelity"--emerges victorious.

It is, of course, Jack who embodies these noble virtues
because he is a worker. As manager of the reoganized mills, he
offers his destitute friend, Fred, a job in the design department.
Although his family is shocked by such demeaning prospects, Fred
gladly accepts the position. The experience of work cleanses him,
and by the story's end he stands transformed. The friendship is
renewed on the higher ground of equality, and the protagonists
may now claim their sweethearts.

Hope Mills is not a radical novel. Douglas disavows communism, trade unions, and strikes, but she does offer credence to
cooperation and the participation of workers in the productive
process. She also takes up related social issues. The sound-
thinking citizens of Yerbury address the temperance question, not
by preaching but by opening up a coffee shop convenient to the
mills; practical-minded women establish a cooking school to teach
the wives domestic economy and nutrition. A pious and sincere
writer, Douglas lambasts ministers and politicians. In their
stead, she advocates respect for labor and self-help as the road
to a classless society. Of marginal literary merit, Hope Mills

nevertheless offered serious criticism of capitalist industry and morality.

98 FITCH, THOMAS, and ANNA M. FITCH. Better Days; or, A Million-aire of To-Morrow. San Francisco: Better Days Publishing Co., 1891, 373 pp.

Dedicated "To the 8,000 Millionaries of America," this didactic novel implores capitalists to help workers help them-selves. Professor John Thornton is the teacher who analyzes the Chicago World's Fair as a perfect example of class division in American society. Although he bemoans the concentration of cap-ital and the corruption of government that have all but negated the Civil War victory, the protagonist hopes that cooperation on a large scale will set things aright.

99 FORD, MARY HANFORD. Which Wins? A Story of Social Conditions. Boston: Lee & Shepard, 1891, 312 pp.

Mary Hanford Ford (1856-?) was a prominent Chicago Social-ist in the 1890s. She wrote for Nationalist publications and respectfully dedicated this novel to the Farmer's Alliance.

Which Wins? follows a well-to-do New Yorker, John Thurston, as he comes to terms with a growing "socialistic philosophy in his soul." Thurston surveys the massive poverty and starvation in a land where prosperity for a few abounds. He decides he can never achieve an inner peace until he divests himself of his worldly possessions and takes his stand on "an equality with the poorest son of Mother Earth." Thurston hopes to begin anew on a Nebraska farm, where a sactuary from the urban blight might allow a new order to bloom. Soon, however, he discovers the ruthless railroad monopolists and grain barons who for personal profit wreak havoc with the rural economy. He eventually realizes that only the People's party has the potential for salvation, for leveling class differences, elevating the cultural order, re-creating marriage into a true partnership between husband and wife, and inaugurating a brotherhood of man.

As reviewers noted, Ford's message was essentially moral. She wrote: "If you can plainly tell one half of the world how the other half lives, how it suffers, how it strangles and dies daily under the exactions of injustice, humanity will rise as one man, and strike down its oppressors, and never rest until it stands free under heaven."

100 GILMAN, CHARLOTTE PERKINS. In This Our World. Boston: Small, Maynard & Co., 1898, 217 pp.

Published originally in 1893, the fifth edition of this book of verse established Gilman as a leading poet of contemporary social issues. The largest section, entitled "The World," ad-resses an assortment of metaphysical themes, humanitarian causes, and the beauty of nature. Poems grouped under the heading "Woman" found an appreciative audience. Edward Bellamy, in a letter to Gilman, thanked her for writing the poems "expressive

of faith in and aspiration toward the larger life which seems to
be opening to women." Contemporary newspapers and magazines re-
printed many selections, especially the satirical verse, "The
Holy Stove," which asked if "The Holy Stove is the altar fine, /
The wife the priestess at the shrine-- / Now who can be the god?"
This volume comprises about seventy-five poems.

101 HOWLAND, MARIE STEVENS. The Familistère. Boston: Christopher
     Publishing House, 1918, 547 pp. Reprint. Introduction by
     Robert S. Fogarty. Philadelphia: Porcupine Press, 1975,
     547 pp.
        Marie Howland (1836-1921), one of the most remarkable
     figures in nineteenth-century American radicalism, lived, for
     those times, a free life and conducted a range of activities that
     spanned the First International, the Grange, and utopian coloniza-
     tion. Impoverished during her childhood, Marie Stevens worked in
     a Lowell, Massachusetts, cotton factory and later moved to New
     York where she married a noted radical lawyer. There she taught
     school, lived in a cooperative boarding house where a circle of
     literary intellectuals gathered, and met her second husband,
     Edward Howland. With him, she spent the Civil War years in
     France, where she observed firsthand a system of communal living
     pioneered by the utopian Socialist, Charles Fourier. When she
     returned to the United States she took up the task of creating
     familistères in the United States and in Mexico, most devotedly
     in the utopian colony at Topolobampo, Mexico. In her later years,
     she moved to a single-tax colony in Fairhope, Alabama.
        The Familistère, first published as Papa's Own Girl in
     1874, is based upon New England family life and the utopian ven-
     ture that most impressed Howland, in Guise, France. Fathered by
     Jean Baptiste Bodin, a self-made philanthropist, the original
     familistère housed at its peak in the 1880s some 1700 persons,
     with child care and cooperative workshops that especially im-
     pressed visitors. Howland applies this visionary idea to village
     life in New England. The novel's main plot describes the system
     of communal living and the organization of work in this trans-
     formed mill town.
        The Familistère also blends this utopian promise with the
     message of women's emancipation. Papa's Own Girl, the original
     title of the novel, is the protagonist, Clara Forest, who draws
     immeasurable strength from her father, a kind and understanding
     physician. This freethinker encourages his daughter's aspirations,
     despite opposition from his old-fashioned wife and the rascality
     of his only son. Clara therefore grows to a precocious self-
     awareness, "saves" a girl "ruined" by her brother, and establishes
     with her a nursery "sworn never to employ a man where a woman
     could be found to do the work required." Clara becomes separated
     from her conventional husband, and eventually is drawn to Count
     Frauenstein, a highly educated millionaire infatuated by visions
     of utopia. With him she plans a Social Palace--a familistère--
     dedicated to cooperative living, social justice, and women's

rights. Clara's instinctual hostility to all prejudice—class, sexual, or racial—is thus vindicated. She achieves complete happiness with the birth of her child. She is the finest promise of American democratic aspirations, "Papa's own girl."

102   JONES, ALICE ILGENFRITZ, and ELLA MERCHANT. Unveiling a
       Parallel: A Romance. Boston: Arena Publishing Co., 1893,
       269 pp.
           This utopian novel takes as its central theme the equality
       of the sexes as envisioned by many late-nineteenth-century women.
       The story relates an earthling's visit to two Martian cities,
       Thursia and Caskia, where women have achieved not only equality
       of rights but have ushered in a single standard of morality that
       transforms their society into a cooperative and peaceful order.
       In contrast, a parallel existence on Earth is described in which
       women play important political and economic roles but have failed
       to gain control over morality. In Earth's cities, women follow
       masculine norms; they drink, smoke, and even frequent baudy
       establishments filled with comely young men.

103   KELLY, FLORENCE FINCH. Frances: A Story for Men and Women.
       New York: Sanfred & Co., 1889, 221 pp.
           Set in Boston in the 1880s, this unusual story exposes the
       weaknesses in the existing system of sexual relations. It con-
       cerns four main characters: Eva and Harris Collquit, an unhappily
       married couple; Frances, a former prostitute and Harris's mis-
       tress; and Jack Malquam, a speculator and Eva's lover.
           Kelly first describes the unhappiness caused by sexual
       incompatibility in marriage. The Collquit marriage dissolves
       when Eva discovers her husband's infidelity. Eva, however, is
       "cold," a condition that drove Harris to seek pleasure in Frances,
       a working-class woman endowed with a full complement of sensuality.
       Harris eagerly leaves his wife just as their baby dies. The
       tragic consequences of a forced relationship are thus underscored.
           In following Frances's life, Kelly attacks the hypocrisy
       of organized religion. Frances is the illegitimate child of a
       famous minister, and when she discovers that she is pregnant with
       Harris's child and Harris has disappeared, she turns to her father
       for assistance. Although this highly respected minister secretly
       acknowledges his sin against womanhood, he cannot risk atoning
       for it. He refuses to help, and Frances drifts aimlessly.
           Meanwhile, Eva and Jack have become lovers, and in studying
       their relationship Kelly reaffirms the tragedy of female frigidity.
       Jack is just about to desert Eva when he learns that he has lost
       his fortune in a stock-market crash. Devastated, Jack puts a gun
       to his head and kills himself, and Eva, upon discovering his body,
       believes he has died because of their sexual difficulties. She,
       too, kills herself.
           Kelly does not fully articulate her major points and ends
       the story on an equally ambivalent note. Eventually Harris finds
       Frances, who has just witnessed the death of their baby. Sudden-
       ly, however, a happy ending appears. Frances and Harris reunite,

although they neither pledge fidelity nor marry. Free love thus triumphs over conventional marriage.

104 ____. On the Inside. New York: Sanfred & Co., 1890, 238 pp.
Published shortly after Frances, Kelly's novel continues to relate the shortcomings of marriage and conventional sexual relations in general and, in a less explicit sense, the evils of capitalism. It is set in New York City in the 1880s, and narrates the unusual experiences of Isabelle Fairmont, a young typist who has left her safe home in Prairieville to secure a good-paying job in the East.

Isabelle soon finds work, but just as quickly confronts evil in the person of her employer, Brokken. A married man, Brokken is totally degenerate. He keeps a mistress, Helen Le Strange, who happens to be a friend of Isabelle. Adultery is only one of Brokken's sins, however. In a fit of passion, he attempts to rape Isabelle. He fails to harm her, but is soon arrested on charges of having murdered his business partner.

To her good fortune, Isabelle has also met a true friend, Reberfell. An anarchist, he explains the causes of poverty and other social injustices. Most important, in Isabelle's hour of need, he offers both political guidance and personal support. At the story's end, with Brokken safely behind bars, Isabelle and Reberfell have become "not only lovers and friends, but comrades and intellectual companions." Once again, free love triumphs.

105 KNAPP, ADELINE. One Thousand Dollars a Day: Studies in Social Economics. Boston: Arena Publishing Co., 1894, 132 pp.
This small book is a collection of short parables about labor and capital. Knapp (1860-1909), a close friend of Charlotte Perkins Gilman, discusses the distribution of wealth and methods of production, and calls for fraternity rather than competition as an alternative system of social economy.

106 LANE, MARY E. BRADLEY. Mizora: A Prophecy. New York: G.W. Dillingham, 1890, 312 pp. Reprint. Boston: Gregg Press, 1975, 147 pp.
A feminist utopia, Mizora is an island community under the North Pole inhabited solely by women. In recounting its development, the Preceptress of the island relates a history closely resembling that of the United States until the era of Reconstruction. At that point, the parallel ends, for the women of Mizora managed to create a new society free from the civil disorder and social strife that characterized the Gilded Age. After gaining access to education, Mizoran women formed their own republic. Although they intended to exclude men from the political process for only a century, the male species, too accustomed to competition and greed, could not survive in an environment of cooperation and became extinct. As men disappeared so did corruption in government, poverty, disease, and war. Under womanly virtue,

peace and enlightenment reigned supreme. As the author affirmed: "The future of the world, if it be grand and noble, will be the result of UNIVERSAL EDUCATION, FREE AS THE GOD-GIVEN WATER WE DRINK."

The story is told by Vera Zarovitch, a shipwrecked political exile from czarist Russia. Vera describes Mizora's charms, its architectural beauty and natural splendor, the loving relations among its inhabitants, the total absence of social distinctions, and the perfect mental and physical health that prevails. The Mizorans, Vera discovers, enjoy the benefits of extremely modern technology: they travel in airships, eat synthetic foods, and most important, reproduce parthogentically. An enlightened population, the Mizorans are bound by no religion but celebrate Great Mother Nature and womanhood.

An important feminist utopian novel, Mizora aptly illustrates the separatist tendencies of the era's women's movement. It first appeared in serial form in the newspaper Cincinnati Commercial in 1880-1881 and later reached a larger audience as a paperback book issued in 1890. This new edition contains a short introduction by Stuart A. Teitler and Kristine Anderson. Nothing is known about its author.

107 LONG, LILY A. Apprentices to Destiny. New York: Merrill & Baker, 1893, 348 pp.

This book "toys with socialism to a certain extent—almost enough to make it a novel of tendency—but," the contemporary reviewer noted, "the dangerous fascination of that subject for generous and over-emotional minds has not . . . distorted the writer's sympathies from a just appreciation of the social problem." The novel concerns various approaches to what the author calls the Day of Deliverance. Lily Long uses an array of character types to represent various inclinations, but chooses two for emphasis. Joyce Mabie, the female protagonist, is a novice activist who writes a column for a local Socialist newspaper. Karl Bardt, the stereotyped German-American Socialist, is her employer; he edits Justice, and also guides Joyce in her political awakening. These two characters, one in the early stages of growth, the other fixed in his ways, serve as yardsticks for the various reformist measures suggested throughout the novel.

As the same reviewer noted, there are some "wordy pages" and imperfectly drawn characters; the plot comes into focus only slowly. Eventually, the major event concerns a militant labor protest, the burning of the local mill works. Joyce Mabie is the inadvertent instigator of this outburst; it is her essay in Justice that incites the workers to destroy their place of employment. Mabie and Bardt must share the responsibility for this tragedy and reassess their strategies. They learn that a clear solution to the social problem is not at hand. But, as Bardt says to Mabie as the story moves toward its end, "The hope of the world rests with its women and its workers." In addition to this enduring insight, the conclusion ties up the romantic subtheme:

Joyce and a newly made capitalist, who is confused by his humanitarian sympathies toward his workers, find true happiness in
marriage.

108 McCORMICK, FANNIE. A Kansas Farm; or, The Promised Land. New
     York: J.B. Alden, 1892, 163 pp.
          Fannie McCormick of Kansas, a "foreman" in the Knights of
     Labor, was president of the National Woman's Alliance, an organi-
     zation of Populist women formed during the movement's peak in the
     early 1890s. In this unusual novel she discusses populism from
     woman's perspective.
          The story is narrated by a young woman whose new husband
     has uprooted her from her childhood home in rural Pennsylvania
     and transplanted her in frontier Kansas in the 1870s. She de-
     scribes the life of a typical farm woman, presenting vivid de-
     criptions of her isolation and the complete silence of farm
     existence. She also portrays the odd nature of her domestic
     drudgery, which includes the burdensome care and feeding of paid
     help. As the story progresses, politics overshadow the plot.
     Chapters describe in grim detail the impact of blight and drought,
     especially the grasshopper invasion of 1874; the usury-level
     mortgage rates that favor the money lender over the farmer; and
     the growing discontent among the farmers. At the conclusion, the
     farmers and their wives organize a Farmers' Alliance. Although
     the narrator underscores the economic import of populism, she
     nevertheless presents the ultimate vision of harmony along femi-
     nine lines: a future of well-furnished homes replete with kitchen
     appliances, and the elevation of women's role in the family and
     in the state.
          The volume includes a selection of McCormick's poetry, a
     similar testament to women's role in the radical agrarian move-
     ments.

109 MASON, CAROLINE A. A Woman of Yesterday. New York: Double-
     day & Page, 1900, 367 pp.
          Anna Benigna, she is called by those who recognize her ab-
     solute virtue. She is also a woman easily thwarted. As a child
     she managed to break through the oppressive chains of calvinism,
     and determined to become a foreign missionary. She secures the
     appropriate religious training and finds the proper mate, Keith
     Burgess, who also plans to devote himself to missionary work.
     Burgess, however, is cursed with a weak constitution. During a
     bout of illness, he persuades Anna to marry him immediately. Al-
     though hesitant, Anna relents. In a short time she learns that
     her husband will never fully recover from his affliction and must
     therefore forsake all plans for foreign service.
          The bulk of the story follows Anna's humdrum routine as a
     small-town minister's wife. Her husband is emotionally distant
     and leaves his young wife to his self-righteous, narrow-minded
     mother who shares their home. After years of lying fallow, Anna
     meets John Gregory, a distinguished British utopian Socialist.

Gregory persuades Anna to take part in his communal experiment,
Fraternia. The plot takes several more turns, but in the end,
Anna, a young widow, regains her opportunity to become a foreign
missionary. She has no regrets about the delay, for had she gone
into service as a youth she would have carried a hard and narrow
message. Gregory has opened to her "the great truth of the unity
of the race."

Riddled with ambiguities, A Woman of Yesterday is interesting for its interpretations of calvinism and depictions of woman's
powerlessness. The Christian Socialist message is comparatively
vague. Little is known about Caroline A. Mason (1853-1939).

110 PITTOCK, Mrs. M.A. (WEEKS). The God of Civilization; A Ro-
     mance. Chicago: Eureka Publishing Co., 1890, 135 pp.
     A utopian romance, Pittock's fanciful story describes an
idyllic society in which money and competition are unknown. The
setting is the tropical island of Kaahlanai in the South Seas,
where a group of Americans are shipwrecked. The men and women of
the party discover a native population living peacefully and
blissfully, so contentedly that they eagerly adopt the island
customs and assimilate.

The marriage relationship plays an important part in
Pittock's presentation. The author describes the island's peculiar mating custom, a form of yearly probation that allows women
to take the initiative. At an annual feast, all eligible men
line themselves in a row, and each available woman performs a
dance that ends as she places a scarf about her chosen mate. The
man must either submit or die at her hands. At the next feast,
however, he may if he desires rejoin the marriage line and again
take his chances.

The wisdom of this freedom of choice in marriage is underscored by a comparison between the fates of two cousins, Mabel
Miller and Lucy Maynard. Mabel, age twenty, has eagerly sought
adventure and delights in exploring the new civilization on
Kaahlanai. She falls in love and "marries" the native Akleha,
described as a "black Apollo." Lucy, meanwhile, back home in San
Francisco, has pursued a sensible society match. When the two
women are later reunited, they discover how different their experiences have been. While Mabel has found an adoring husband
and happiness, Lucy has known only despair with a husband who
ignores her, and she suffers the loneliness and humiliation of a
marriage rooted in economics rather than romance. At the story's
close, Mabel and Akleha flee the artificialities of civilization.
They return to Kaahlanai, taking Lucy and her child with them.

For its time, this novel presents a bold critique on
social relations in marriage. Its handling of interracial marriage is equally daring.

111 PORTER, LINN BOYD [Albert Ross]. Speaking of Ellen. New York:
     G.W. Dillingham, 1890, 345 pp.
     One of the best Nationalist novels, Speaking of Ellen is a

lively account of New England mill strife with a nearly believable
female protagonist. It features vivid descriptions of factory
towns and a study of sexual intimacy daring for its day. Linn
Boyd Porter (1851-1916), a prolific pulp author, announced candidly in his introduction that Bellamy's Looking Backward had
provided the solution to social problems his previous reform
interests had evaded. Porter's novel serves as an exchange of
ideas as well as a propagandistic vehicle for romance.

Ellen, the "Marchioness of Riverfall," is the illegitimate
daughter of a mill girl and a United States senator. Deserted by
her father, Ellen proudly disclaims any surname just as she disavows the propriety of the millowners' claim upon her labor. A
member of a wronged class, she is also a self-taught intellectual,
in touch with all the important ideas of the time. When she
meets Philip Westland, a lawyer for a mill corporation, Ellen
overwhelms him with her persuasive style. They quickly fall in
love, but only with difficulty do they reconcile their differences.
Philip must be shown through events as well as arguments.

When the Great Central Corporation resolves to reduce the
already pitiful wages of its workers, a strike becomes inevitable.
The expulsion of the strikers from company-owned houses turns
anger to desperation, and an immigrant anarchist, preaching "fire
and blood," convinces some strikers to set a factory ablaze.
Only Ellen's moral suasion and strategic acuity forestall widespread retribution. The brutality of the millowners, the street
clashes of police and strikers, and the heated rhetoric of the
confrontation might have been taken from journalistic reports of
the strike wave of 1885-1886.

Porter also puts the Woman Question at the center of
events. At one point a wealthy blind woman, who sees better than
her fortunate sisters the plight of her sex, becomes an important
symbol, as does an impoverished French-Canadian girl who becomes
a manufacturer's lover. Neither is much overdrawn. Even the
sexual liaison is described as a natural relation, strained by
class differences but not in itself immoral. The message,
muddied through overextended and clumsy dialogue, eventually becomes clear: the cause of labor and of woman are one; only by
advancing beyond private property can society make true love
possible for all.

The novel's ending collapses into romantic improbabilities.
Ellen's father bestows his fortune upon her through the guardian-
ship of his friend and her beau. Still, she experiences a very
realistic crisis at becoming Westland's wife, a sense of madness
at being torn between love and class loyalty. One can almost believe that Ellen and Philip find their happiness by reducing
hours, introducing a profit-sharing system, and living in a
modest cottage among the workers as they wait the day of the cooperative commonwealth.

112   SHERWOOD, MARGARET POLLOCK. An Experiment in Altruism. New
      York: Macmillan & Co., 1895, 215 pp.

A thirty-nine year old woman narrates a thin story about her attempts to understand more fully the nature of social injustice. She mainly criticizes mainstream charity workers, especially their patronizing and callous attitude toward the poor. Social settlements, however, pique her interest because they bring together on equal terms individuals of various social classes and backgrounds. Social settlements, she contends, also provide a forum for discussing programs such as anarchism and socialism. Toward the conclusion of her narration, the author leans toward a vaguely socialistic solution to the problem of poverty, admits the difficulty of the struggle, but asks for a closing of ranks among radicals and reformers and for a continuing faith in God and in humanity.

Sherwood (1864-1955) published <u>An Experiment in Altruism</u> under her pen name, Elizabeth Hastings. She was at the time a professor of English literature at Wellesley College, a position she maintained from 1889 to 1930.

113 ____. <u>Henry Worthington, Idealist</u>. New York: Macmillan & Co., 1899, 294 pp.

This novel served well as a tract for the Consumers' League. It studies "the big cheap department stores where they advertise great bargains that aren't there at all, and maltreat their clerks, and underpay their women. . . ." The story centers on a university endowment underwritten by the heartless owner of a department store chain, and on a youthful idealist's opposition to his institution's acceptance of such ill-begotten funds. It also follows the budding romance between Henry Worthington and the merchant's daughter, who fully understands her father's role in the exploitation of his cash-girls and saleswomen.

114 STONE, Mrs. C.H. <u>One of "Berrian's" Novels</u>. New York: Welch, Fracker Co., 1890, 210 pp.

"Sorrowfully dedicated to all who believe 'competition' to be the only incentive to progress," <u>One of "Berrian's" Novels</u> attempts to answer some of the criticisms leveled against Edward Bellamy's utopian vision. Mrs. Stone protests the notion that monotony of character and condition would result under Nationalism. She believes that human nature is strong and capable of evolving toward a great complexity under harmonious conditions. The novel thus concerns the psyche as it has evolved after the Revolution in the year 1997.

A frustrated romance is the vehicle for delivering the political message. The protagonist, Fleur-de-Lys Standish, must learn to respond in unison to her spiritual and physical passions.

115 WAISBROOKER, LOIS. <u>The Wherefore Investigating Company</u>. Topeka, Kan.: Independent Publishing Co., 1894, 313 pp.

Inspired by the agrarian and Henry George movements of the late 1880s and early 1890s, this loosely plotted novel set in the Midwest adds an anarchist touch to what the author calls the

question of land emancipation. Waisbrooker calls for the abolition of private property in land and especially for a restraint
upon the government's hand in selling millions of acres to cor-
porations. To carry out this plan, the male hero instigates a
mass educational campaign, which the author describes as modeled
on the garrisonian agitation that changed public opinion and
brought an end to slavery.

116 WOODS, KATHARINE PEARSON. Metzerott, Shoemaker. New York:
     Thomas Y. Crowell, 1889, 373 pp.
          Charity worker, teacher, and writer, Katharine Pearson
     Woods (1853-1923) was one of the most politically notable authors
     of the gilded-age novel. She was an ardent Christian Socialist
     whose idealism had been deepened by reading Edward Bellamy's
     Looking Backward.
          Metzerott, Shoemaker, her first novel, has a unique ethnic
     and regional character. Between 1876 and 1886 Woods taught
     school in Wheeling, West Virginia, a Southern center of indus-
     trialization and a militant German-American radical community.
     Influenced by her friend Richard T. Ely, progressive political
     economist of Johns Hopkins University, Woods sought to provide a
     faithful description of the social scene and to construct a nar-
     rative pitting violence against cooperation and bringing together
     immigrant and "old American" values.
          Woods's talent proved no match for this undertaking. Her
     tragic protagonist, Karl Metzerott, is unable to marry his
     Socialist convictions to Christian morals. As leader of a local
     commune, he loses his reason when the local mill reduces wages
     and starves workers' families. At his behest, workers attack the
     millowner, and in the riot Metzerott witnesses the death of his
     own son. Chastened, Metzerott becomes a truly pious Christian,
     now mindful of the necessarily peaceful methods that true social
     change demands. To this poor characterization, Woods adds a
     sentimental style of plot development.
          Published only three years after the brutal repression of
     German-American anarchists and the destruction of the Knights of
     Labor by an employers' counteroffensive, this novel had a wide
     readership but little influence. Yet, as one contemporary re-
     viewer noted, Woods's "story is only one of many straws that show
     how the wind of popular aspiration blows toward social changes of
     a radical sort" (Overland Monthly, March 1890).

117 _____. A Web of Gold. New York: Thomas Y. Crowell, 1890,
     307 pp.
          Set in an arcadian mill village, Hillhope, the story
     weaves romance and politics into a characteristic late nineteenth-
     century fantasy. The two protagonists are Victor Maurice, a
     foreign-born idealist and member of a secret anarchist society,
     and Agatha Godfrey, the winsome, pious daughter of the paternalist
     millowner. Maurice has come to Hillhope to carry out the plans
     of his political sect, which aims to disrupt the harmonious labor

relations prevailing under Godfrey's charitable rule. Meanwhile, Nathaniel Hazard, another local capitalist, has his own evil plans to destroy Philip Godfrey. Hazard eventually lures Maurice into a scheme to undercut his rival and to create a giant trust that would set prices throughout the region's flour mills. The plot is one of espionage, the capitalist hoping to profit, the anarchist aiming to incite a revolution. In the end Maurice's love for Agatha and her strength of character and Christian faith lead to the alternative vision: socialism.

As a reviewer at the time noted, A Web of Gold is a "clever story with a moral." Katharine Pearson Woods uses her stylized characters to voice various political philosophies. Hazard speaks for monopoly capitalism, Godfrey for capitalist beneficence. Victor Maurice, Woods adds in an introduction, is less credible, for he represents an organized anarchist society more likely to be found in Russia than in the United States; nevertheless, his viewpoint must be delivered. Each character, and the philosophy he holds, fails so that the true, American solution may arise at the story's close.

118 _____. Mine and Thine: A Story of Conflicting Interests.
   Philadelphia: Journal of the Knights of Labor, 1894, 86 pp.
      Woods, who joined the Knights of Labor in 1888, wrote this novelette as a tract against labor violence and a plea for social harmony. Set in a New England town, the plot involves the ruthless behavior of a railroad president and a bitter strike. Although many characters appear in this brief tale, the chief female protagonist is Eileen Leroy, wife of the local labor leader. Eileen's family has been grievously injured by the railroad magnate, and her hatred has made her the easy prey of a group of Italian anarchists. At the story's gripping climax, Eileen has taken part in their violent deed against an oncoming train, which she believes is carrying only freight but turns out to be a passenger train with her nephew, whom she has raised since childhood, and his new bride. Although Eileen succumbs to madness as a result of her act, the railroad president learns a profound lesson. He calls a conference with the strike leaders and offers to settle, announcing that he now understands "that one cannot injure one's brother man without also injuring one's self!"

1901-1919

The first two decades of the twentieth century marked a high
point for radical women in that it was an era that encouraged a joint
dedication to socialism and women's rights. In 1901 the Socialist
Party of America formed, bringing together aging veterans from the
nineteenth-century campaigns and young activists fired with optimism
about the political future. In major urban areas and in growing
industrial towns, in the rural centers of the Midwest, to the western
frontiers of Washington and Alaska, the Socialist party provided an
organizational home for thousands. For those women who had heeded
Frances Willard's admonitions, or who had responded enthusiastically
to Edward Bellamy's vision, the new Socialist movement rekindled
political passion. They were joined by professional women from the
colleges and settlements, from the Women's Trade Union League and
woman suffrage movement, and by "new immigrant" women such as Russian
Jews, Finns, Slavs, and Italians. Indeed, the movement comprised a
population marked by differences in age, ethnicity, religion, regional
identity, and even class. And within this wide-ranging movement
women found unprecedented support for their participation and for
their programs. By 1910 a genuine Socialist women's movement had
taken shape.

The sources noted in this section speak both to the cultural
variation within the Socialist women's movement and to the large
degree of sisterhood found there. All save one were published since
1970, after the New Left of the 1960s had fostered the rebirth of
Socialist feminist politics. Many of the scholars therefore address
contemporary as well as historical issues: how do radical women relate to the politically mainstream women's movement? How do they relate to the male-dominated Left? How do radical women bring working-
class women into their movement and meet their special needs? How do
radical women combat discrimination within the Left and build support
networks among themselves? To uncover the history of a feminist radical tradition, one with lasting significance, is a goal that unites
their various endeavors.

119 BUHLE, MARI JO. "Socialist Women and the 'Girl Strikers,'
     Chicago, 1910." Signs 1 (Summer 1976):1039-51.
         In 1910 women led a strike of over 41,000 workers in the
     Chicago garment industry. In response, local Socialists rallied
     the community to support their efforts. This essay describes the
     role of Socialist women in strike activities and reprints selec-
     tions from the Chicago Daily Socialist that document their ex-
     pectations.

120 _____. "From Sisterhood to Self: Woman's Road to Advancement
     in the 20th Century." In Men, Women, and Issues. Vol. 2, rev.
     ed., edited by Howard H. Quint and Milton Cantor, pp. 170-84.
     Homewood, Ill.: Dorsey Press, 1980.
         This essay examines three Socialist women--Kate Richards
     O'Hare, Rose Schneiderman, and Margaret Sanger--as archetypal
     "new women" of the turn of the century. The author compares
     their varying degrees of reliance on networks of women. Thus
     O'Hare's social purity agitation, Schneiderman's activity within
     the Women's Tade Union League, and Sanger's birth-control cam-
     paigns are interpreted as symbols of the progressive dissolution
     of the female collectivity that sustained women's reform activi-
     ties in the nineteenth century.

121 _____. Women and American Socialism, 1870-1920. Urbana:
     University of Illinois Press, 1981, 344 pp.
         The major work in the field, this history is at once polit-
     ical and cultural. Buhle traces the story through three genera-
     tions and several ethnic groups to understand the complex tradi-
     tion of Socialist feminist struggles in the early decades of the
     twentieth century. She uncovers little-known collective endeavors,
     reveals their multivarious influence upon the larger Socialist
     movement, and roots their political forms in the lives of activ-
     ists themselves.
         Buhle begins by examining nineteenth-century heritage.
     She compares the political evolution of the principal constitu-
     ents, German-American and native-born women, and their distinctive
     contributions. German-American women were for the most part
     active in auxilliary organizations to the male-dominated Social-
     ist movement. They developed a network of cultural activities
     for their friends and families, played instrumental roles in
     training children for party membership and lives of dedication,
     and laid the groundwork for agitation in the immigrant blue-
     collar neighborhoods. Above all, they expressed loyalty to the
     class struggle and understood their work exclusively within that
     context. Native-born women, descended from the antebellum
     women's right tradition, maintained their own organizations and
     political world view. In the 1880s they carried their gender-
     conscious sensibility into broader struggles, hoping to build an
     alliance among temperance, suffrage, agrarian, and working-class
     movements. From their stellar leader, Frances Willard, native-
     born radical women took to heart the lesson of female autonomy

and leadership in the reconstruction of American society. In different ways, both native and foreign-born women contributed to the "golden day" of American socialism just ahead.

The formation of the Socialist Party of America in 1901 heralded a more active role for women, as activists of all kinds forced their attention upon the leadership. Internecine struggles between groups and generations--women loyal first to the working class and second to their sex, aging veterans of suffrage and temperance agitations, young professionals and settlement workers-- prompted disagreements over tactics and strategy. The decentral- ized character of the Socialist movement, however, permitted a wide range of local options, and within the first decade of the twentieth century a genuine Socialist women's movement thrived.

By 1908 Socialist women established within the party their own representative form, the Woman's National Committee, which afforded individuals opportunities for leadership at both local and national levels. Socialist women thus assisted working women in great battles for unions in the garment and textile industries. They played pivotal roles in directing several local campaigns for woman suffrage in the decade beginning in 1910. With the inspiration of Margaret Sanger, Socialists and anarchists pio- neered the agitation for birth control and enlightened attitudes on issues of sexuality.

Buhle studies this history in great detail and concludes her narrative in the political upheaval during World War I and the Russian Revolution. As the leading actors of the movement at its peak passed from the scene amid factional disputes and govern- ment repression, the Left moved into its next period. Rebuilding the movement along different ethnic lines, the next generation of activists forged their own traditions, many recalling the auxil- iary forms of former times. The heroic era of the Socialist women's movement had come to an end.

Within this framework, Buhle presents brief biographies of leading activists such as Augusta Lilienthal and her daughter Meta, Theresa Malkiel, Kate Richards O'Hare, Josephine Conger- Kaneko, and May Wood Simons, among others. She also describes the networks that served the political movement and the rituals that gave it vitality.

122 COOK, BLANCHE WIESEN. "Female Support Networks and Political
      Activism: Lillian Wald, Crystal Eastman, Emma Goldman."
      Chrysalis, no. 3 (1977), pp. 44-61.
      Cook's paper, first presented at the Berkshire Conference
on the History of Women in June 1976, is an eloquent testimony to
the importance of personal relationships in the study of history.
It examines the female networks that allowed politically active
women to conduct their work. Each section begins with a brief
statement outlining the political beliefs of the woman under discussion and then turns to a detailed description of the nature of
her close friendships and emotional attachments. The relationship between politics and personal lifestyle forms the heart of
Cook's analysis.

123 DANCIS, BRUCE. "Socialism and Women in the United States,
1900-1917." Socialist Revolution 6 (January-March 1976):81-
144.
        Dancis offers a two-tiered analysis of the women's sector
of the Socialist Party of America. He first discusses the Socialist position on several political issues: marriage and free love,
the home, sexual relations, woman suffrage, the nature of womanhood, and the interrelation of socialism and feminism. He devotes
the bulk of his essay to an examination of Socialists' participation in the major contemporary campaigns for women's equality.
He highlights specific strategic problems, such as the question
of separate women's organizations within the larger Socialist
movement, the role of the Woman's National Committee, and the
place of factional politics within the women's sector itself. He
concludes that although Socialist women developed a richer political theory than did their counterparts in the mainstream women's
movement, they suffered a similar tactical disorientation after
passage of the Nineteenth Amendment. Like suffragists, Socialist
women failed to plan an alternative to the single-issue campaign
and thus witnessed the fatal decline of their movement after
World War I.

124 DYE, NANCY SCHROM. As Equals & As Sisters: Feminism, Unionism, and the Women's Trade Union League of New York. Columbia:
University of Missouri Press, 1980, 200 pp.
        The Women's Trade Union League, formed in 1903, attracted
many radical women to its ranks, especially during its first
decade of activity. A cross-class alliance of trade unionists
and middle-class "allies," the League also tested an individual's
loyalty to the women's movement or labor movement.
        Nancy Schrom Dye's book covers the history of New York
League until the 1920s, when it began to play a marginal role in
the city's labor movement. Dye studies in detail the continual
struggles between feminists and unionists and between working-
class and upper-class members. She also highlights the League's
unequaled leadership in the organization of working women in the
early twentieth century, and especially in the education of these
women to positions of organizers, writers and speakers, and
negotiators. She concludes: "Without doubt, the Women's Trade
Union League went further than any other American women's organization to ameliorate working women's situation and to come to
terms with the problems women of different classes and ethnic
backgrounds have in relating to one another."
        Dye also provides acute cameos of Socialist unionists like
Leonora O'Reilly, Rose Schneiderman, Pauline Newman, and Helen
Marot, and discusses the factional role of Socialists within the
League, especially their criticism of the alliance with wealthy
and often antiradical suffragists.

125 GORDON, LINDA. "Are the Interests of Men and Women Identical?"
Signs 1 (Summer 1976):1101-18.

Gordon collects and introduces three short essays from the
Socialist press, 1908-1912, which underscore the theoretical difficulty of rooting a Socialist feminist perspective in the experiences of the American working class. The selections address
several issues of historical and contemporary interest, namely
the role of housework in the capitalist economy and the relationship of women's organizations to the male mainstream Left.

126 HUMPHREY, ROBERT E. The Children of Fantasy: The First
     Rebels of Greenwich Village. New York: John Wiley & Sons,
     1978, 267 pp.
     Humphrey examines the romantic outlook of six prominent
male bohemians of the decade beginning in 1910 and judges it
politically vapid. Unlike previous historians who have admired
the stylistic rebellion of the Villagers, Humphrey uncovers
motivations both self-centered and childish. Men such as Floyd
Dell and Max Eastman truly wanted to be free of repressive conventions, the author concludes, but they lacked the fortitude for
serious work of social reconstruction, and created instead their
own personal playground in lower Manhattan.
     The most disappointing aspect of this book is its failure
to deal adequately with the many women who found a similar escape
in Greenwich Village. Humphrey admits that scores gravitated
toward this select community of artists and intellectuals because
they, too, hoped for an opportunity to explore less restricted
lifestyles. But Humphrey considers women's experiences only
through the eyes of their male lovers. Thus he describes Hutchins
Hapgood's frustrating marriage to Neith Boyce; Dell's passion for
Edna St. Vincent Millay; Eastman's unsatisfying relationship with
Ida Rauh; John Reed's tempestuous affair with Mabel Dodge Luhan;
and George Cram Cook's literary partnership with Susan Glaspell.
Humphrey also examines these men's attempt to construct a theory
of sexual emancipation that successfully justified their promis-
cuous ways. In the few passages that discuss women's role, he
makes a similar assessment, calling their view of women's liberation narrow and self-centered. He concludes: "Feminism was
supposed to liberate Villagers from old-fashioned attitudes and
establish open, trusting relationships between men and women.
But there was no consensus on feminist goals and few rebels of
either sex were capable of equality."

127 KARVONEN, HILJA J. "Three Proponents of Women's Rights in the
     Finnish-American Labor Movement from 1910-1930: Selma Jokela
     McCone, Maiju Nurmi and Helmi Mattson." In For the Common
     Good: Finnish Immigrants and the Radical Response to Indus-
     trial America. Superior, Wis.: Työmies Society, [1977], pp.
     195-216.
     Although women participated avidly in the foreign-language
sectors of the Socialist movement, there are few published accounts
of their activities. Karvonen's essay provides essential information on the experiences of Finnish-American women. Among the

several ethnic groups that constituted the immigrant sector,
Finns were represented by a disproportionate number of women.
Women not only served in the rich cultural network of Finnish-
American radicalism, but sustained their own forms of agitation
around the questions of temperance and woman suffrage.

In this essay Karvonen traces the development of the
Toveritar, a Socialist newspaper founded in 1909, edited by women
and devoted primarily to women's issues. Its early editors,
especially Selma Jokela McCone, struggled to keep the newspaper
alive and to make it responsive to its female readership. Under
McCone's management, the Toveritar achieved a circulation of
nearly 5,000 in 1915 and became a genuine women's newspaper,
replete with household tips, advice columns, a children's department, and the usual run of literary and political articles. The
Toveritar's subsequent editors, Maiju Nurmi and Helmi Mattson,
brought the newspaper through wartime censorship of radical
periodicals into the 1920s. Karvonen provides important biographical information on these leading women in the Finnish Socialist
Federation of the United States.

128 LAGEMANN, ELLEN CONDLIFFE. A Generation of Women: Education
     in the Lives of Progressive Reformers. Cambridge: Harvard
     University Press, 1979, 207 pp.
         Lagemann's book is a series of educational biographies
     that emphasize not the formal, institutional setting of learning,
     but education as a lifelong "process of interaction that changes
     the self." She interprets the roles of parents, relatives, col-
     leagues, and especially mentors in shaping the lives of several
     outstanding activists. Although less concerned with their ideo-
     logical proclivities than with their educational development,
     Lagemann includes Socialists Leonora O'Reilly and Rose Schneiderman.
     Based on standard secondary and primary sources, Lagemann's
     sketches of their lives break no new research ground but concisely
     summarize the major influences on the two women during their
     formative years.

129 MILLER, SALLY M., ed. Flawed Liberation: Socialism and
     Feminism. Contributions in Women's Studies no. 19. Westport,
     Conn.: Greenwood Press, 1981, 211 pp.
         The seven original essays in this anthology examine the
     position of women in the American Socialist movement at the turn
     of the century and address the philosophic and strategic tension
     between socialism and feminism that beset the pioneering activ-
     ists. Editor Sally Miller describes the context of the Woman
     Question in an essay detailing the role of women in the bureau-
     cracy of the Socialist Party of America and traces the rise and
     fall of the Woman's National Committee. William C. Pratt updates
     an earlier study of women in the Socialist party of Reading,
     Pennsylvania, 1927-1936; he concludes that few Socialists, male
     or female, questioned sexual inequalities in the movement or in
     their private lives. John D. Buenker describes the uneasy

alliance between Socialists and suffragists during the great campaigns in New York and Wisconsin.

Several essays focus on major and minor figures in the
Socialist movement. L. Glen Seretan traces Daniel DeLeon's stand
on the Woman Question to conventional ideas on gender roles and
to the unique dynamics of the preeminent Socialist's childhood.
Gretchen and Kent Kreuter grapple with the complex personality of
May Wood Simons, a leading writer on women's issues and influential member of the Woman's National Committee; they provide rare
insights into Simons's post-Socialist feminism of the 1920s.
Mari Jo Buhle adds a biographical note on Lena Morrow Lewis, one
of the most prominent women in the leadership of the Socialist
party before World War I; she studies Lewis's ambivalent attitude
toward the Woman Question. The essays on Simons and Lewis provide an interesting study of contrasting dilemmas faced by Socialist women. Neil K. Basen unearths the histories of several rank-
and-file radical women of the Southwest, the "Jennie Higginses"
who served to undermine the prevailing image of demure Southern
ladies.

The book contains twelve rare illustrations of Socialist
women and a useful bibliographic essay. An appendix reprints
May Wood Simons's major essay, "Woman and the Social Problem."

130 SHOWALTER, ELAINE, ed. These Modern Women: Autobiographical
     Essays from the Twenties. Old Westbury, N.Y.: Feminist
     Press, 1978, 147 pp.
     In 1926, the Nation invited a group of prominent women to
explore the sources of their feminist idealism and to assess its
resilience during the decade following the suffrage victory.
"Our object," the editors stated, "is to discover the origin of
the modern point of view toward men, marriage, children, and jobs.
Do spirited ancestors explain their rebellion? Or is it due to
thwarted ambition or distaste for domestic drudgery?" Seventeen
women replied, and with the assurance of anonymity disclosed
intimate details of their childhoods and marriages. Three psy-
chologists analyzed the completed series and evaluated the personalities of these women and their responses to life's challenges.

Although the group of contributors represented a broad
political spectrum, several were Socialists or close to various
radical movements that began around 1910: Mary Alden Hopkins,
Ruth Pickering, Genevieve Taggard, Crystal Eastman, Victoria
McAlmon, and Wanda Gag. Elaine Showalter, whose introductory
essay outlines the quality of feminism in the twenties, identifies
each contributor and provides relevant biographical data. This
collection offers a rare insight into the personal aspirations of
a pivotal generation of radical women, a generation which attempted
to apply its political ideals to the task of forging a new,
liberated lifestyle.

131 SICKELS, ELEANOR M. Twelve Daughters of Democracy; True
     Stories of American Women, 1865-1930. New York: Viking

Press, 1942, 256 pp.
        Sickels writes popular biographies of eleven women who in-
fluenced the "growth of democracy" in the United States, including
Mother Jones and Kate Richards O'Hare.

132 SNYDER, ROBERT E. "Women, Wobblies, and Workers' Rights: The
        1912 Textile Strike in Little Falls, New York." New York
        History 60 (January 1979):29-57.
        The Little Falls textile strike, led by Socialists and
Wobblies, was one in a series of strikes by recent immigrants
from southern and eastern Europe. Lasting for three months, from
October 9, 1912, until January 4, 1913, the Little Falls strike
involved over 1,300 unskilled workers, of which an estimated
seventy percent were women. Although the strikers gained significant wage increases and forced a major investigation of labor
conditions in their city, their IWW local soon collapsed, as many
of its most active leaders faced imprisonment for their strike
activities.
        One of the most interesting sections of Snyder's essay
concerns the role of Socialist women in providing relief services
for the strikers and their families and in rallying the community
to support their efforts. Foremost was M. Helen Schloss, a former
settlement house nurse from New York City. Schloss had been recently hired by the local women's club, the Fortnightly, as its
chief agent in a war against consumption, which raged in the
city's working-class neighborhoods. As soon as the strike broke
out, Schloss, a Socialist, resigned her position to become a
principal organizer within her community. Helen Keller, who was
also a member of the Socialist party and IWW enthusiast, added
her words of encouragement. Snyder's essay documents the activities of these women; it provides a basic narrative of the 1912
strike and relates the event primarily to the statewide movement
for protective legislation for women workers.

133 SOCHEN, JUNE. The New Woman: Feminism in Greenwich Village,
        1910-1920. New York: Quadrangle, 1972, 175 pp.
        Sochen studies five turn-of-the-century feminists who ab-
jured the prescribed domestic role for exciting careers and political involvements. Living in Greenwich Village during its bohemian prime, these women joined the cultural avant-garde, contributed to its premier magazine, the Masses, and sometimes took
parts in an experimental theatrical group, the Provincetown
Players. They also supported the woman suffrage and birth-control
movements, the Women's Trade Union League, the Industrial Workers
of the World, and the Socialist party; and they helped form two
small but significant women's societies, Heterodoxy and the
Feminist Alliance.
        Crystal Eastman, Henrietta Rodman, Ida Rauh, Neith Boyce,
and Susan Glaspell emerge as the star players in this study.
Sochen opens her narrative with a short biography of each woman
and stresses their common backgound in the educated and secure

middle class. Shocked by the sordid conditions of New York City's poor, repelled by the callousness of the majority, and sickened by the patriotism of World War I, these women asked a question still valid today: "How do you create effective cultural reform within the traditional American legislative framework?"

Sochen traces the development of their political ideology. She notes that Rodman and Eastman adapted many ideas of Charlotte Perkins Gilman to their own purposes and became Socialists; they hoped to restructure industrial society to realize its potential to liberate women from domestic drudgery. They also aimed to eradicate sex-role stereotyping by reaching children during their formative years. Glaspell and Boyce, on the other hand, were more romantic and interpreted the feminist quest as a search for love and happiness. With their companion Village writer, Floyd Dell, they fashioned short stories, novels, and plays that challenged traditional sexual morality and femininity. Together, these feminists shaped a novel ideology, although only the romantic view remained intact in the decade after the war.

Sochen offers a mixed assessment of their contribution. She describes their role in various campaigns and organizations and devotes a chapter to their courageous peace activities during World War I, particularly in the Woman's Peace party. Although Sochen admires their vivacity and bravado, she nevertheless concludes that their bohemian lifestyle and bold political stance alienated the mainstream of American women. Moreover, in their enthusiasm they tried too many things at once and left no permanent organization in their wake. Only in their pacifism did they hit upon a fundamentally radical critique of their society. Thus Sochen concludes: "While feminists failed partly because of their inability to marshall support for their beliefs, it was more decisive that the substance of their program was too radically removed from reality." In the end, their failures outnumbered their successes.

134 TAX, MEREDITH. The Rising of the Woman: Feminist Solidarity and Class Conflict, 1880-1917. New York: Monthly Review Press, 1980, 332 pp.
Tax aims to fill the gap in our theoretical as well as historical understanding of the relationship of the class struggle to the movement for women's liberation. She shapes her analysis around a distinct concept, the united front of women, which she defines as more than a temporary coalition organized for a specific campaign, but rather an alliance of Socialists, feminists, and trade unionists who work routinely together for a common goal. Tax examines several cross-class alliances of women between the late 1880s and World War I, and judges the political success of each institution within its historical context. She considers such factors as the strength of the labor movement and the Left, the Left's position with regard to the women's movement, the attitude of the women's movement toward the Left and the labor movement, and the overall political and economic quality of the

period under discussion. Rather than positing an unvarying opinion on the efficacy of cross-class alliances, in the past as well as in the future, Tax advocates a feminist strategy capable of adapting to the exigencies of the situation.

The strongest section of this book centers on the Illinois Woman's Alliance formed in Chicago in 1888. Tax opens by describing the nature of industrial capitalism at the turn of the century: the low status of women in the labor force, the hardships endured by blacks and by immigrants, the state of the labor movement, and the attitude of Socialists toward the plight of working women. The scene thus set, Tax traces the history of the premier "united front of women" of the nineteenth century in precursive organizations in the early 1880s to the Haymarket Square riot. Tax also studies its immediate origins in the Ladies' Federal Labor Union, which heralded the beginning of a women's labor movement in Chicago. Tax examines in detail the work of the Illinois Woman's Alliance along four lines: its campaigns against the sweating system; its child-labor agitation; its drive to improve the conditions in public institutions that housed women and children; and its efforts to secure bath houses in working-class neighborhoods. Although the middle-class members ultimately failed to sustain loyalty to the labor movement at a moment of crisis, Tax judges the Illinois Woman's Alliance a model enterprise during its accomplished, if brief, tenure.

In this survey no other alliance achieves the stature of the Illinois Woman's Alliance. Tax evokes less sympathy for the middle-class women who pioneered the Women's Trade Union League. She weaves her story around the case study of Leonora O'Reilly who exemplifies "all the contradictions of the united front of women in her own person": attracted to the amenities of middle-class society and its opportunities for personal advancement, O'Reilly suffers a repeated conflict sparked by her greater receptivity to the stirrings of her own class. In contrast to the Women's Trade Union League, the Industrial Workers of the World stand as a model of working-class solidarity, but only reluctant supporter of women's rights. Despite its weakness on feminist issues, the IWW nevertheless ranks higher than the Women's Trade Union League on Tax's scale because it brought the class struggle into the community and the demand for birth control into the labor movement. The case of the problematical alliance between the Socialists and suffragists reveals yet another paradigm. An effective alliance never jelled, in Tax's opinion, because both groups were marred by serious political flaws. The Socialist party, Tax claims, did not understand the value of united front agitation, and the mainstream women's movement, single-mindedly devoted to suffrage, represented a conservative force in an era of reform and social unrest. The Illinois Woman's Alliance, Tax concludes, represented a crossroad in the history of united fronts.

The remaining section of The Rising of the Women considers in detail the New York shirtwaist strike of 1909-1910 and the

Lawrence textile strike of 1912, and judges the work of the
various coalitions that offered support to the strikers. Tax
closes her study by offering "practical conclusions" drawn from
history and stresses that "never has the need for unity and for
a newly energetic approach to organizing been more clear."

135   WOROBY, MARIA. "Ukrainian Radicals and Women." Cultural
      Correspondence 6, 7 (Spring 1978):50-56.
           Woroby summarizes and interprets the activities of
      Ukrainian-American Socialist women as "the intellectual and po-
      litical outgrowth of community formation and institutionalization
      among the various Ukrainian settlements in the U.S." This pro-
      cess began with their immigration in the early years of the
      century, and accelerated after 1910. Although relatively small,
      the Ukrainian community sustained a vigorous Socialist section.
      Organized in "Agitational Committees," particularly strong in
      Hamtramck, Michigan, and New York City, its women conducted study
      groups and the Ukrainian Workers' Schools for children. They
      also played a major, if less formal, role in the preservation of
      Ukrainian language and culture, especially by linking their
      feelings of ethnic oppression to the struggles against imperial
      Germany, czarist Russia, and the ruling economic and political
      forces in the United States.

AUTOBIOGRAPHIES AND BIOGRAPHIES

     Despite involvement of thousands of women in the radical move-
ments of the early decades of the twentieth century, fewer than
twenty recorded their experiences for the public. Mother Jones, Emma
Goldman, Elizabeth Gurley Flynn, and Charlotte Perkins Gilman, among
a few others, achieved such renown that the autobiography became a
form suitable to political expression in later life. Their memoirs
often serve as testaments to the comrades and the cause that sustained them for decades. Only a small portion reflect on the inner,
psychic life; Goldman, Mabel Dodge Luhan, and Vida Scudder thus stand
out as unusually reflective, almost indulgent, compared to the many
who chose to write factual narratives of their lives and times. The
majority of radical women, however, remained silent about themselves,
playing the highly honored role of "Jennie Higgins," the hard-working
yet unassuming activist so necessary to the success of the movement.
Women like Mary Marcy, Bertha Howe, and Corinne Brown left few records
of their lives save the tributes of their comrades. Recently,
scholars have recaptured a few personalities and described their contributions. The stories of Voltairine de Cleyre, Kate Richards
O'Hare, Theresa Malkiel, and other radical women prominent in their
own lifetimes are only now coming to the fore.

Anderson, Margaret Carolyn (1886-1973)

136 ANDERSON, MARGARET. <u>My Thirty Years' War</u>. London: Alfred A. Knopf, 1930, 274 pp. Westport, Conn.: Greenwood Press, 1971, 274 pp.

Anderson founded the <u>Little Review</u> in 1914 as a monthly magazine "fresh and constructive, intelligent from the artist's point of view." In its pages she introduced works by avant-garde writers Joyce, Elliot, Lowell, Pound, and Yeats, as well as her friend Emma Goldman.

Anderson describes her life until 1929, when she stopped publishing the <u>Little Review</u>. Although she lived mostly in France since the early 1920s, she writes here in detail about her all-too-American childhood and youthful adventures. In this first of a three-volume autobiography, her mother emerges as a powerful stimulus to Anderson's lifelong rebellion against middle-class mores. The autobiography is primarily valuable, however, for the author's insights into the personalities of leading artists and writers of her generation. Floyd Dell, Amy Lowell, Theodore Dreiser, James Joyce, and Max Eastman, among others, receive unique treatment. Anderson also devotes considerable space to her association with Emma Goldman, the source of her anarchist sympathies, and especially to her relationship with Jane Keep, her companion and copublisher of the <u>Little Review</u>.

First published in 1930, <u>My Thirty Years' War</u> received a warm review from Sherwood Anderson, who aptly captured its flavor: "This is not a book. It is a flash-back of yourself. It is charming, Margaret, as you are charming. . . ." (<u>New Republic</u>, June 11, 1930).

Brown, Corinne Stubbs (1850-1914)

137 <u>Memorial--Corinne Stubbs Brown</u>. [Chicago, n.p., 1914?], 17 pp.

Corinne Stubbs Brown became a Socialist shortly after the Haymarket affair, and helped organize the Ladies' Federal Labor Union no. 2703. Active in the local women's club movement, she was instrumental in gathering the variety of representatives who formed the Illinois Woman's Alliance. After the turn of the century, Brown joined the Socialist Party of America and continued to work primarily among women.

This pamphlet attests to the prominence Brown achieved in Chicago and contains tributes from the city's leading Progressive, labor, and Socialist activists. It also includes a letter from Eugene V. Debs and the program of the memorial meeting held in Brown's honor.

de Cleyre, Voltairine (1866-1912)

138 AVRICH, PAUL. <u>An American Anarchist: The Life of Voltairine de Cleyre</u>. Princeton, N.J.: Princeton University Press, 1978, 266 pp.

Voltairine de Cleyre ranked with Emma Goldman and Louise Michel as the leading anarchist women of the century. Born in

the Midwest to a poor family, educated against her will in a con-
vent, de Cleyre entered the radical movement in the 1880s as a
free-thought lecturer. Like so many of her generation, she found
her radical sympathies swelling after the Haymarket affair, and
she soon declared herself an anarchist.

Avrich skillfully describes de Cleyre's role as an activist
and propagandist. He portrays her as a less flamboyant lecturer
than her contemporary, Emma Goldman, but more thoughtful.
Voltairine de Cleyre relished the spoken and written word. As a
child she dabbled in poetry and verse and continued to do so
throughout her life. She earned her living as a teacher of English to the Russian-born Jews in the Philadelphia neighborhood
where she made her home. She also contributed regularly to free-
thought and anarchist journals, after the turn of the century
especially to Mother Earth, published by Emma Goldman and
Alexander Berkman. Because of her contributions and unswerving
dedication to the cause, de Cleyre became one of the most re-
spected representatives of American anarchism.

Although Avrich does not focus on the significance of
de Cleyre's role as a rare woman within the anarchist movement,
he does record her vivid awareness of sex oppression. Dedicated
to individual liberty, de Cleyre viewed marriage as slavery and
held firm to this position in both her private as well as public
life. Avirch narrates a series of unhappy affairs with men whom
de Cleyre loved but nevertheless resisted in their desire to
domesticate her. Avrich also notes de Cleyre's work among women,
particularly her founding of the Ladies' Liberal League, an organization that promoted anarchist and feminist propaganda.

This biography draws on the memories of de Cleyre's
friends and relatives and serves to correct earlier misleading
accounts of her life. It provides a rich character study of this
unusual figure. Most of all, it rings with tragedy. An unhappy
childhood, ceaseless battles against poverty, betrayals in love,
and recurring ill health threatened but failed to sap de Cleyre's
energy.

139 GOLDMAN, EMMA. Voltairine de Cleyre. Berkeley Heights, N.J.:
Oriole Press, 1932, 41 pp.
Goldman and de Cleyre vied for title of leading anarchist
woman. They played similar roles as movement propagandists,
writing tracts and addressing mass audiences. Whereas Goldman
starred as a spell-binding lecturer, de Cleyre excelled as a
sensitive, careful writer. Neither woman enjoyed a retiring disposition, and each viewed the other as potential rival. Their
relationship was never easy, sometimes loving and supportive, but
often hostile and distant.

In this limited edition, published long after de Cleyre's
death, Goldman celebrates the memory of her contemporary. She
lavishes praise upon de Cleyre's strength of character, her
ability to carry on despite a weak body and tormented spirit.
Goldman emphasizes de Cleyre's artistic contribution, her fine

literary sketches, and strong prose style.

140 PERLIN, TERRY M. "Anarchism and Idealism: Voltarine [sic] de
     Cleyre (1866-1912)." Labor History 14 (Fall 1973):506-
     20.
         Perlin presents Voltairine de Cleyre as "an apostle of
     toleration among anarchist factions." Because she was so philo-
     sopically eclectic, he argues, de Cleyre was able to bridge the
     individualist and Communist tendencies in the anarchist movement.
     Perlin also insists that de Cleyre was unique because she drew
     principally upon a native radical tradition, thus standing apart
     from the immigrant majority. Inevitably, the author compares his
     favorite to Emma Goldman.

141 SHULMAN, ALIX. "Viewing Voltairine de Cleyre." Women: A
     Journal of Liberation 2 (Fall 1970):5-7.
         Shulman presents a capsule biography of de Cleyre to sec-
     tions of the women's liberation movement that were reviving
     anarchist ideals in the 1970s.

Flynn, Elizabeth Gurley (1890-1964)

142 FLYNN, ELIZABETH GURLEY. The Rebel Girl: An Autobiography,
     My First Life (1906-1926). Originally, I Speak My Own Piece:
     The Autobiography of The Rebel Girl, New York: Masses & Main-
     stream, 1955, 326 pp. New York: International Publishers,
     1973, 351 pp.
         Born in Concord, New Hampshire, descendent of Irish rebels,
     Elizabeth Gurley Flynn grew up in the South Bronx. As a teenager
     she read Edward Bellamy's Looking Backward, Kropotkin's Appeal to
     the Young, and Upton Sinclair's The Jungle. She took in her
     father's Socialist convictions, but felt the more adventurous
     spirit of the newly born Industrial Workers of the World. At
     sixteen she began street-speaking and almost immediately became a
     public hit as the "girl orator." She soon dropped out of high
     school, conducted a Western lecture tour, and established the
     pattern of her life's work as agitator rather than journalist or
     theoretician, public speaker above all.
         At seventeen she married an IWW organizer in his thirties,
     but soon realized she had made an unhappy match. One child died
     at birth, another born in 1910 she deposited with relatives while
     she returned to the road. The uncertainty of her love life, its
     distinctly secondary status to her political commitment, forms a
     modest undercurrent in Rebel Girl. Flynn rarely reflects upon it,
     but according to many accounts she suffered extensively from dis-
     appointments and loneliness.
         By 1909 she emerged as champion of the IWW's free-speech
     fights across the West, and was arrested time and again for her
     activities. In 1912-1913 her talents carried her to the industrial
     cities of the East where the IWW staged its boldest drive among
     the unskilled, unorganized, mostly immigrant workers. Her spec-

tacular success in Lawrence, Massachusetts, showed her ability
not only for speaking but for publicizing (with the help of
Margaret Sanger) the plight of the strikers and their children,
who were ferried away to comrades in other cities. During this
strike, Flynn also became close to Carlo Tresca, Italian-American
anarchist leader who became her companion for more than a decade.
     Flynn's career, like that of the IWW, proved meteoric.
When the Eastern organizing drive failed, Flynn began to pull
back, eventually breaking with the leadership over handling of
strikes and defense campaigns. She found herself increasingly
involved in the defense of labor and political prisoners, helping
to form a Workers' Defense Union in 1918. A founder of the American Civil Liberties Union in 1920, Flynn slipped into a quieter
niche.
     Her activities on behalf of Sacco and Vanzetti, the last
major incident in this volume, proved her only significant involvement for a decade. Illness diagnosed as heart trouble side-
lined her until the CIO and the Communists' Popular Front brought
her back to the harness in 1936. Her fame and energy catapulted
her into the leadership of the Communist party. She in turn gave
it an unstinting service, privately critical of its sectarianism
but publicly a major spokesperson among liberal organizations
and women's groups. After World War II, the disintegration of
the party and the deteriorating political climate deprived her of
all but the vestiges of renown. She remained doggedly in the
struggle, through three years in prison under the Smith Act,
through the calamitous party split of 1957, to her own personal
ascendance as the first woman to chair the Communist party in
1961. Three years later, on an official visit to the Soviet
Union, she died and received a lavish state funeral.
     Flynn had been handicapped in pursuing her commitment to
women's emancipation, although she herself had made that issue
secondary to the class struggle. Similarly, her fervent support
of Irish nationalism became in later years mere sentiment. Although she resisted being transformed into "Mother" (like Mother
Bloor or Mother Jones), she became a symbol decades before her
death. There was something democratic in her personal bearing,
indigenous in her radical style, that triumphed over ideology and
affiliation. That quality comes through in the pages of her
autobiography.

143   _____. Memories of the Industrial Workers of the World (IWW).
     New York: American Institute for Marxist Studies, 1977, 40 pp.
     On November 8, 1962, Elizabeth Gurley Flynn spoke to the
students and faculty of Northern Illinois University. This
pamphlet is a transcript of a tape recording of her remarks on
this occasion, including questions from the audience and her
brief replies.
     Flynn recalled incidents in the history of the IWW and
described its leading personalities, like William D. Haywood and
Joe Hill. She compared the native-born itinerant workers of its

Western sections with the foreign-born of the East. She also re-
counted her role in the famous Lawrence, Massachusetts, textile
strike of 1912 and in the free-speech campaigns of World War I.
    At age seventy-two Flynn offers an interesting insight
into her past, especially the source of her initial attraction to
the IWW. Her parents were both members of the Socialist party,
and compared to the stodgy character of her elders' affiliation,
the IWW seemed youthful and vibrant. Heavily influenced by
Kropotkin's Appeal to the Young, she chose to become an agitator
of the IWW.

144 BAXANDALL, ROSALYN FRAAD. "Elizabeth Gurley Flynn: The Early
    Years." Radical America 9 (January-February 1975):97-115.
        Baxandall provides a brief overview of Gurley Flynn's pre-
Communist involvements, with special attention to the IWW strike
in Lawrence, Massachusetts, and her labor defense work in the
decade beginning in 1910. A few intimate details of Gurley
Flynn's love affairs with Jack Jones, her husband, and Carlo
Tresca enliven the essay. Scholars might note that Baxandall
bases her analysis on research conducted in the American Institute
for Marxist Studies, which holds many of Elizabeth Gurley Flynn's
personal papers.

145 HOHL, MARDEN WALKER. "The Rebel Girl--Elizabeth Gurley Flynn."
    Women: A Journal of Liberation 1 (Spring 1970):25-27.
        Writing in the heady days of the women's liberation move-
ment, Hohl offers a brief chronology of Gurley Flynn's activities
to 1917, but attempts primarily to justify her foremost commitment to socialism over women's rights.

Ganz, Marie

146 GANZ, MARIE. Rebels: Into Anarchy--and Out Again, in collab-
    oration with Nat J. Ferber. New York: Dodd, Mead & Co., 1920,
    282 pp. Reprint. Millwood, N.Y.: Krause Reprint Co., 1976,
    282 pp.
        Rebels is the memoir of a Jewish woman who had a brief en-
counter with anarchism. Marie Ganz grew up amid poverty in New
York City at the turn of the century. Her father deceased, she
worked in a sweatshop to support her mother and brothers, and
came into contact with assorted radical activists. Ganz first
joined unemployment demonstrations, and eventually drifted toward
a circle of prominent anarchists associated with Emma Goldman's
magazine, Mother Earth. Influenced by the passionate propagandist
of the deed, Alexander Berkman, Ganz soon found herself in jail
for her own misdeeds. At this point a major event occurred that
shattered her new faith: soon after her release from prison, she
learned that several of her close friends had been killed by a
premature explosion of their home-made bomb. Emotionally devas-
tated, Ganz renounced anarchism, and found a substitute in a
fierce patriotism stimulated by World War I.

Rebels is the author's attempt to refute her earlier radical beliefs. Ganz additionally offers a fascinating portrait of
Jewish immigrant life and working conditions. Her depiction of
New York anarchist circles, however, is primarily interesting because it is told from the point of view of an outsider. Because
Ganz came into the movement without a radical tradition rooted in
family or community experiences, she tells a story of a woman
with few resources to understand or appreciate even her own inclinations.

Gilman, Charlotte Perkins (1860-1935)

147 GILMAN, CHARLOTTE PERKINS. The Living of Charlotte Perkins
Gilman: An Autobiography. Foreword by Zona Gale. New York:
D. Appleton-Century Co., 1935, 341 pp. Reprint. New York:
Harper Colophon Books, 1963, 341 pp.
Charlotte Perkins Stetson Gilman was a prolific and popular
writer on the Woman Question and an independent Socialist throughout most of her life. Born in Hartford, Connecticut, Gilman
spent her youth in Providence, Rhode Island, where she lived in
genteel poverty with her mother and brother. She married Charles
Walter Stetson, a local artist, in 1884; the following year she
gave birth to her only child, a daughter named Katherine. Marriage did not suit her disposition, and in an attempt to recover
from a nervous breakdown, she separated from Walter.
Gilman moved to California in 1888, and within a few years
became a locally prominent political speaker. Attracted to
Bellamy Nationalism, she lectured frequently before local audiences and outlined the ideas that would later serve as the basis
for her leading publications, notably Women and Economics. She
also moved into feminist circles and related many of her collectivist notions to the situation of contemporary women. A firm
advocate of woman suffrage, Gilman presented her strongest case
for financial autonomy and the right of women to engage in productive labor. She still stands as a major figure in the realm
of feminist theory.
Although Gilman never joined the Socialist party, she was
after the turn of the century a leading Socialist. In 1896 she
had served as a delegate to the International Socialist and Labor
Congress in London and came under the influence of George Bernard
Shaw and Sidney and Beatrice Webb. She published in the American
Fabian in the 1890s, and continued to espouse a faith in collec-
tivism through political action in her own journal, the Forerunner, after 1909. Opposed to marxian notions of "class
struggle," Gilman preferred the label "humanist."
Published posthumously in 1935, Gilman's autobiography
provides a detailed picture of her public life and insight into
her lifelong depression. Gilman devotes almost half of her narrative to her troubled childhood and fills the remainder with
descriptions of her friends, travels, and public events. She records her life as a constant struggle against the draining effects

of emotional depression, as a triumph of her remarkable will to
serve humanity. She touches only lightly upon her political beliefs, primarily to dissociate herself from marxism. She laments
in later life that socialism, which had always had a weak following in the United States because of its mistaken similarity to
anarchism, "has been fairly obliterated in the public mind by the
Jewish-Russian nightmare, Bolshevism." Like many nineteenth-
century converts to radicalism, Gilman could not survive the
dramatic political shifts accompanying the Russian Revolution;
nor could she handle the equally poignant changes in sexual
morality of the pre-World War I decade. In trying so hard to
create a persona for herself, Gilman unfortunately began in her
autobiography the legend of herself as quintessential victorian.

148 BERKIN, CAROL RUTH. "Private Woman, Public Woman: The Con-
     tradictions of Charlotte Perkins Gilman." In Women in America:
     A History, edited by Carol Ruth Berkin and Mary Beth Norton,
     pp. 150-76. Boston: Houghton Mifflin Co., 1979.
     Designed for undergraduate readers, this essay examines
Gilman's attempt to secure for women a full measure of humanity,
especially her efforts to realize that goal in her own life.
Berkin traces the contours of Gilman's biography within the
framework of her philosophical and sociological writings.

149 DEGLER, CARL N. "Charlotte Perkins Gilman--the Economics of
     Victorian Morality." Ms. 1 (June 1973):22-28.
     Degler offers a brief synopsis of Gilman's life and dis-
cusses the importance of her contribution to the feminist canon.

150 HILL, MARY A. Charlotte Perkins Gilman: The Making of a
     Radical Feminist, 1860-1896. Philadelphia: Temple University
     Press, 1980, 362 pp.
     The first in a projected two-volume study, Hill's biography
covers the first half of Charlotte Perkins Gilman's life, the
period before the publication of Women and Economics and national
acclaim. Its greatest and most welcomed achievement is a reeval-
uation of Gilman's childhood and young adulthood. Hill's interpretation serves as a necessary corrective to Gilman's own record
of her life, and the portrait that emerges is one of a more complex personality than Gilman described in her autobiography.
     Hill adapts Gilman's reflective mode with great success
and continues her analysis of the major tension in her middle
years: the desire "to communicate her insights more effectively
and to find a greater measure of peace and happiness within herself." Hill reexamines Gilman's relationships with her mother
and first husband; her decisions to divorce Walter Stetson and to
send her daughter to live with him and his new wife; and her
close friendships with Martha Luther, Grace Ellery Channing,
Adeline Knapp, and Helen Campbell. Hill also critically assesses
Gilman's role within the Nationalist movement.

Glaspell, Susan (1882-1948)

151 WATERMAN, ARTHUR. Susan Glaspell. New York: Twayne Pub-
     lishers, 1966, 144 pp.
          Raised in Des Moines, Iowa, Susan Glaspell became a leading
     feminist playwright in Greenwich Village during the decade be-
     ginning in 1910. She and her husband, George Cram Cook, were
     prime movers in the Provincetown Players and friends with the
     leading figures of the cultural Left. More concerned with women's
     dilemma than social revolution, Glaspell dabbled lightly in
     Socialist themes but helped create a fictional genre focused on
     the "new woman."
          Waterman traces Glaspell's literary career from her days
     as a Midwestern local-colorist to her prime as an avant-garde
     playwright. He provides plot summaries of her major works and
     informed critical analyses. He concludes that Glaspell, despite
     her attraction to the bohemian life, remained at heart a Mid-
     western idealist and regional writer.

Goldman, Emma (1869-1940)

152 GOLDMAN, EMMA. Living My Life. 2 vols. New York: Alfred A.
     Knopf, 1931, 993 pp. Reprint. New York: De Capo Press, 1970,
     993 pp.
          Emma Goldman, the best-known anarchist in the United States
     or elsewhere, reveals her life in sometimes garish colors: her
     massive autobiography is a vehicle for sensationalism and self-
     justification. Nevertheless, by way of anecdote Goldman draws a
     detailed picture of her surroundings, her life, friends, and
     activities. Biographies have been written of this remarkable
     woman, but none offer so much to the scholar.
          Born in Kovno, now Lithuania, to a failing shopkeeper,
     Goldman moved with her family to Koenigsberg, Prussia, where she
     gained a preliminary education despite her resistance to disci-
     pline. She rapidly became a political radical and personal dis-
     sident, and immigrated to the United States to gain freedom from
     her family. For a brief spell she lived and worked in Rochester,
     New York, but a mistaken marriage and emotional reaction to the
     murder of the Haymarket martyrs sent her on a new course. She
     moved to New York City where she became acquainted with the
     leading anarchist personalities. Johann Most, famed agitator and
     editor of the Freiheit, gave her ideological inspiration and for
     a short time became her lover. She and Alexander Berkman estab-
     lished a friendship that endured for the rest of their lives.
          Under Most's tutelage, Goldman became a lecturer. Her
     stirring phrases, good humor, and deep moral commitment attracted
     large audiences, and within a few years she had gained a stellar
     reputation. Socialists, liberals, and self-styled freethinkers
     sought her message, while a bourgeois citizenry was titillated by
     her free-love advocacy. Had she not been so single-minded in her
     twin aims--building the anarchist movement and achieving a free

life for herself--she might have become one of America's favorite
rebels. Even with her fanatical attachments, she almost succeeded
in this at various times in her life.

In the 1890s, while Goldman was still young, much of her
energy went into personal relationships. Not only Berkman and
Most, but a half-dozen other men drew her to them, emotionally
and physically, and figure prominently in her autobiography. Although she may have been inclined, especially in this period, to
judge men by their sexual magnetism, she displayed an unusually
generous spirit in judging character; later, that spirit would
extend further and further, even to the Bolsheviki of the early
days of the Russian Revolution.

The decline of Most, the imprisonment of Berkman following
his attempted assassination of steel magnate Henry Clay Frick,
and the general demise of the anarchist movement thrust Goldman
forward as a personality. She loomed larger than the pitifully
small anarchist publications and circles of comrades she continued
to serve in her own way. President McKinley's assassination by a
deranged young man vaguely associated with anarchism provoked a
public wave of irrational fear and anger toward Goldman and her
associates, and at the same time evoked liberal sympathy among
those who cherished free speech. Goldman meanwhile began to excel
in lecturing on cultural topics ranging from Ibsen to Nietzsche,
and promoted free literature and a little-theatre movement.

A liaison with anarchist Ben L. Reitman and an engagement
with the IWW's free-speech crusade involved Goldman in another
round of excitement and actual danger in the early decades of the
twentieth century. Her support of the nascent birth-control movement carried that danger even further. Her avowed opposition to
war and especially to conscription made her once more a public
enemy in the eyes of American law-enforcement officials. Hardened
to repeated arrests, Goldman yet again became a symbol of free
speech. Imprisoned for more than two years, she was deported to
the Soviet Union in late 1919.

Goldman's well-known disillusionment with communism swiftly
followed and became her chief subject for discussion in later
life. Marrying the Welsh James Colton in 1925, she continued to
lecture and to write her autobiography. A decade later, near the
end of her life, she threw herself into support for anarchists in
the Spanish Civil War. In Canada raising money for the cause in
1939, she suffered a fatal stroke. To the end Emma Goldman had
continued her crusades.

153 _____. Living My Life. Edited by Richard and Anna Maria
      Drinnon. New York: New American Library, 1977, 754 pp.

      Richard and Anna Maria Drinnon have skillfully reduced
Goldman's lengthy autobiography by preserving the significant
sections that deal with her years of activism in the United
States. They cut the last six chapters of the original version
published in 1931 and have replaced them by an afterword sum-
marizing the last two decades of Goldman's life, the years since

1919, which she spent in exile. A new index and bibliographical essay, which underscores Goldman's appeal to the New Left of the 1960s, add to the value of this edition.

154 _____ . My Disillusionment in Russia. Introduction by Rebecca West; biographical sketch of Emma Goldman by Frank Harris. New York: Thomas Y. Crowell, 1970, 263 pp.

In December 1919 in the midst of the Red scare, Goldman was deported to the Soviet Union. She sailed to her destination with great expectations: "All my life Russia's heroic struggle for freedom was a beacon to me." For the next two years she worked for the new Soviet government by collecting artifacts for the Museum of the Revolution at Petrograd. She traveled extensively, from Moscow to Kiev to Archangel, and simultaneously gathered data for her memoirs of disillusionment.

As a contemporary reviewer pointed out, Goldman's "disillusionment" with a centralized Socialist government is somewhat baffling. For decades she had promoted a cooperative anarchist commonwealth and bitterly attacked marxian Socialists. What is truly surprising is even her temporary infatuation with the Bolsheviks as the "symbol of the revolution." Goldman thus relates her disappointment and constructs yet another format to expound anarchist philosophy.

This edition includes the full text of Goldman's essay. Originally it appeared in two volumes, My Disillusionment in Russia, published in 1923, and My Further Disillusionment in Russia. Due to a failure of the post office to deliver the second installment of her manuscript, or mismanagement by Doubleday & Page, her publishers, the last twelve chapters were missing in the first volume, including the afterword, which Goldman deemed the most important chapter, an analysis of her opinions from an explicitly anarchist point of view.

155 GOLDMAN, EMMA, and ALEXANDER BERKMAN. Nowhere at Home: Letters from Exile of Emma Goldman and Alexander Berkman. Edited by Richard and Anna Maria Drinnon. New York: Schocken Books, 1975, 282 pp.

Goldman scholars Richard and Anna Maria Drinnon have edited a rich collection of correspondence, 1918–1938. Many letters reflect Goldman and Berkman's strong attachment to one another and the unique nature of their lifelong relationship. Others serve as commentary on political issues, especially Goldman's opinion of the Russian Revolution and life in the Soviet Union.

156 DRINNON, RICHARD. Rebel in Paradise: A Biography of Emma Goldman. Chicago: University of Chicago Press, 1961, 349 pp. Reprint. New York: Harper Colophon Books, 1976, 349 pp.

Drinnon's book is the first full biography of Goldman. As such, it adds a scholarly dimension to the tale created by Goldman herself in her two-volume biography without altering its major contours. Unfortunately, Drinnon and Goldman share an unrestrained admiration for their subject. Moreover, as reviewers at the time noted, Drinnon tends to use the biography as a platform for his own anarchist views. Thus his portrayal of Goldman is one-dimensionally heroic, and the line between description and interpretation is too thinly drawn.

Despite these limitations, this biography provides a sound and succinct narrative of Goldman's life based on exhaustive research into formerly untapped primary sources. Drinnon not only records her many exploits, but discusses in detail her anarchist philosophy, which he describes as a mixture of cooperationist ideas borrowed from Peter Kropotkin and a propensity toward individualism derived from Henrik Ibsen. Goldman comes across as a remarkable woman, which she undoubtedly was, campaigning for the full gamut of revolutionary causes of her day. Drinnon underscores, for example, her early birth-control activities, hoping to reclaim for his heroine the title of pioneer, which he feels has been unfairly assigned to Margaret Sanger. The idea that Goldman, too, felt overshadowed by other women remains unexplored.

157 MADISON, CHARLES A. Critics and Crusaders: A Century of American Protest. New York: Henry Holt & Co., 1947, 572 pp. Reprint. 2nd ed. New York: Frederick Ungar Publishing Co., 1959, 662 pp.
In this book narrating episodes in the struggle for freedom in America, Madison offers one of the first historical and sympathetic accounts of Emma Goldman. The narrative of her life, based primarily on Goldman's autobiography, is straightforward. Madison describes her as the "most active and audacious rebel of her times," as the only American woman "to suffer such persistent persecution." Published originally in 1947, Madison's short chapter provides a useful summary.

158 REICHERT, WILLIAM O. Partisans of Freedom: A Study in American Anarchism. Bowling Green, Ohio: Bowling Green University Popular Press, 1976, pp. 385-406.
As one of twenty-seven chapters insightfully cataloguing anarchism in the United States, the essay subtitled "High Priestess of American Anarchism," establishes Goldman within a major and multifaceted tradition. Reichert provides a brief biography and discusses in detail Goldman's role as orator and editor of Mother Earth, which he describes as "the major vehicle for disseminating the ideas of militant anarchist communism in America." Reichert dissociates Goldman from those anarchists who, like her lifelong friend Alexander Berkman, advocated violence, and emphasizes instead her pacifist leanings. He also imaginatively traces her antiauthoritarian idealism to both Henry David Thoreau and Max Stirner. Reichert describes Goldman as a broad-minded libertarian, as more interested in art than politics, and dedicated to women's emancipation from all forms of tyranny. These central aspects of her social and political thought, particularly its

focus on individualism, were the source, Reichert concludes, of
Goldman's condemnation of the Soviet bureaucratic and centralized
state.

159 SHULMAN, ALIX KATES. "Emma Goldman--Feminist and Anarchist."
     Women: A Journal of Liberation 1 (Spring 1970):21-24.
          Shulman's short essay relates standard biographical infor-
     mation about Goldman and offers a brief assessment of her anar-
     chist beliefs. It focuses on Goldman's perspectives on sexual
     morality and women's oppression. Shulman concludes that Goldman,
     in establishing her political distance from the women's rights
     and suffrage movements, cast herself into the role of philosophi-
     cal forerunner of women's liberation.

160 _____. To the Barricades: The Anarchist Life of Emma
     Goldman. Lexington, Mass.: D.C. Heath & Co., 1970, 255 pp.
          A sympathetic treatment, Shulman's biography for young
     people contains an important chapter on the Woman Question that
     places Goldman's contribution within the context of the women's
     liberation movement of the late 1960s.

161 SOCHEN, JUNE. Consecrate Every Day: The Public Lives of
     Jewish American Women, 1880-1890. Albany: State University
     of New York Press, 1981, 167 pp.
          Sochen's book documents the contributions of Jewish women
     to American life. A chapter on radical Jewish women activists
     features Emma Goldman. Sochen claims that Goldman, who rejected
     all formal religions, nevertheless found her true inspiration in
     Judaism. Goldman frequently addressed Jewish audiences and spoke
     in Yiddish; she also published translations of the stories and
     poems of Yiddish writers. Sochen concludes: "Emma Goldman's
     faith in anarchism did not make her forget her Jewish identity or
     the particular burden Jews faced in a hostile world."

162 WEXLER, ALICE. "Emma Goldman on Mary Wollstonecraft."
     Feminist Studies 7 (Spring 1981):113-33.
          This essay reprints in full the text of Goldman's lecture
     "Mary Wollstonecraft, the Pioneer of Modern Womanhood." As
     Wexler explains, the lecture is valuable to scholars because it
     provides insight into the nature of Goldman's anarchist feminist
     beliefs through her portraiture of the eighteenth-century author
     of A Vindication of the Rights of Women.
          Wexler examines parallels in the lives of the two, and
     posits that Goldman herself discovered these similarities when
     she read G.R. Stirling Taylor's Mary Wollstonecraft: A Study in
     Economics and Romance, which appeared in 1911 shortly before
     Goldman's own essay. Misreading Taylor's account, Goldman cast
     Wollstonecraft into a tragic role, one marked by both public
     scorn and inner conflicts. Thus Goldman presented Wollstonecraft
     as a brave and determined fighter for freedom as well as an
     individual bound by "fate" and "destiny" to unhappiness. Wexler

concludes that Goldman focused on the tragic quality in
Wollstonecraft's life because she felt her own life was following
a similarly depressing course toward isolation and loneliness.

Hillman, Bessie Abramowitz (1895-1970)

163 JULIANELLI, JANE. "Bessie Hillman: Up From the Sweatshop."
     Ms. 1 (May 1973):16-20.
          Bessie Abramowitz Hillman played a leading role in the
     Chicago garment strike of 1910. Together with her future husband,
     Sidney Hillman, she became a founder of the Amalgamated Clothing
     Workers of America and later, a prominent union organizer.
          Julianelli's essay offers a brief biography, which like
     the Hillmans of the New Deal era, downplays their Socialist back-
     ground.

Howe, Bertha W. (1866-1966)

164 HOWE, BERTHA W. An American Century: The Recollections of
     Bertha W. Howe, 1866-1966. Edited by Oakley C. Johnson. New
     York: Humanities Press, 1966, 142 pp.
          Bertha Washington Howe, a court stenographer by trade, was
     a lifelong rank-and-filer in the Socialist and Communist move-
     ments, and acquaintance of many leading radical personalities.
     She joined the Socialist party in 1906, wrote occasional essays
     and reviews for the New York Call, and served on the editorial
     board of the New Review. She later moved into the Communist
     party and became a close friend of Grace Hutchins.
          This volume contains a brief biography by Oakley C.
     Johnson, a transcript of the tape recording made by Howe at her
     retirement home in Orlando, Florida, November 8-17, 1964, a few
     photographs, and a collection of several of her short essays
     written between 1906 and 1910. The book constitutes a testimony
     to a certain indigenous strain of radicalism, a blending of
     several political traditions from women's rights, anarchism, and
     spiritualism to modern communism in the life of an ordinary
     person.

Jones, Mary Harris (1830-1930)

165 JONES, "MOTHER" MARY. The Autobiography of Mother Jones.
     Edited by Mary Field Parton; foreword by Clarence Darrow;
     introduced by Fred Thompson. Chicago: Charles H. Kerr, 1925;
     2d ed., 1972, 242 pp.
          Born in Cork, Ireland, Mary Harris (Mother) Jones was the
     foremost woman in the American labor movement. After losing her
     four children and husband in a typhoid epidemic in 1867, Jones
     established herself as a dressmaker in Chicago, only to witness
     the destruction of her business in the great fire of 1871. In
     the aftermath she began attending meetings of the Knights of
     Labor, and by the early 1880s she was taking part in coal strikes.

In 1891 she took a position as an organizer for the United Mine
Workers of America and stayed with the union for most of her life.
    Mother Jones was more militant than radical. She joined
the Socialist Party of America in 1901 and supported its candi-
dates in many elections; but her energies were centered in the
labor movement. She had little time for politics, and was fond
of saying, "You don't need a vote to raise hell."
    The Autobiography of Mother Jones, first published in 1925,
is a chronicle of her strike activity. Jones offers few insights
into her personal life but rather presents a picture of the famed
agitator as she liked to be recognized: never a lady. Thus she
heroically narrates her many adventures; especially poignant are
her renditions of the 1903 march of the mill children and the
great strikes in Colorado in 1903 and 1913-1914.
    Opposed to the woman suffrage movement, Jones enjoyed
working among women. She relates with pride her treasured tactic,
the dishpan-and-mob brigade that drove the scabs away. She quotes
a newspaper reporter: "'Mother Jones was raising hell up in the
mountains with a bunch of wild women!'" There is no doubt that
Mother Jones believed her concluding words: "The future is in
labor's strong, rough hands."

166 FETHERLING, DALE. Mother Jones, the Miners' Angel: A Por-
     trait. Carbondale: Southern Illinois University Press, 1974,
     263 pp.
         In this competent biography, Fetherling assesses the sig-
     nificance of Mother Jones's contribution to the labor and Social-
     ist movements. He acknowledges that no coherent or consistent
     philosophy guided her work; she was, rather, a "benevolent
     fanatic." Nevertheless, Mother Jones was "a folk heroine whose
     inspiration reached down to those people who were unimportant in
     name or wealth or title but all-important in numbers."
         Much like Jones's autobiography, Fetherling's narrative
     skips over her youth and focuses instead on her post-1900 activ-
     ities in the coal fields of America. He includes a chapter on
     her notable attitude toward women, her fierce antipathy toward
     the suffrage movement, and her affinity with what the author
     terms the "matriarchal pattern" found in coal-mining communities.
     Mother Jones was, in other words, a traditionalist on the Woman
     Question.

167 LONG, PRISCILLA. Mother Jones, Woman Organizer. Cambridge,
     Mass.: Red Sun Press, 1976, 40 pp.
         Long focuses on the charismatic, maternal quality of Mother
     Jones to explain her organizing success among miners and their
     wives. She examines Jones's conservative view of women's role
     and her reluctance to leave "her boys" for the six million women
     in paid employment at the turn of the century. Even the Women's
     Trade Union League could not soften her hostility toward middle-
     class women or change her fundamental belief that women belonged
     at home not in industry.

168 McFARLAND, C.K. "Crusade for Child Laborers: 'Mother' Jones
and the March of the Mill Children." Pennsylvania History 38
(July 1971):283-96.
In 1903 Mother Jones left the coal fields to take part in
the textile strike in the Kensington section of Philadelphia. To
her dismay, she discovered among the strikers over 10,000 children, many under ten years of age. McFarland narrates her historic march of 150 adults and 50 factory children from Philadelphia to New York City, a grand parade to call attention to the
evils of child labor.

169 STEEL, EDWARD. "Mother Jones in the Fairmont Field, 1901."
Journal of American History 57 (September 1970):290-307.
In this monographic account of the defeat suffered by the
United Mine Workers of America in the northern West Virginia coal
strikes at the turn of the century, Steel focuses on the role of
Mother Jones. Although the militant orator and organizer suc-
ceeded in the southern mining area, she found herself "badly out-
generalled" by the management of the Fairmont Field, due in part,
Steel concludes, to her adherence to a simple socialistic economic
philosophy.

Keller, Helen (1880-1968)

170 KELLER, HELEN. Midstream: My Later Life. Garden City, N.Y.:
Doubleday, Doran & Co., 1929, 362 pp. Reprint. Westport,
Conn.: Greenwood Press, 1968, 362 pp.
Helen Keller is remembered primarily for her valiant
struggles against limitations imposed by blindness and deafness
and for a lifelong determination to assist the handicapped. Her
sometimes controversial political involvements, in contrast, have
faded from public memory. Keller was in fact a champion of
humanitarian causes, including socialism and women's rights. In
1909 she joined the Socialist Party of America and over the next
several years conducted lecture tours on behalf of working
people.
Although this volume covers the major period of Keller's
radical activity, it contains few references to once noteworthy
acts. Keller mentions her Socialist faith only in passing, in an
anecdote about a conversation with capitalist Andrew Carnegie.
She provides instead descriptions of her daily life and meetings
with prominent figures, such as Samuel Clemens and Alexander
Graham Bell. There are, however, a few interesting insights into
her relationship with John Macy, her teacher's husband who fur-
thered her political education. First published in 1929, this
volume of Keller's autobiography captures best the spirit of her
youthful activism.

171 HARRITY, RICHARD, and RALPH G. MARTIN. The Three Lives of
Helen Keller. Garden City, N.Y.: Doubleday & Co., 1962, 189
pp.

Harrity and Martin divide their study into logical sections: Keller's early childhood; her education by teacher Anne
Sullivan; and her adult life of dedication to others. Valuable
as a photo essay on Keller, this biography offers no new insights
into her remarkable life.

172   LASH, JOSEPH P. Helen and Teacher: The Story of Helen
      Keller and Anne Sullivan Macy. New York: Delacorte Press,
      1980, 811 pp.
         Although his description of the Socialist movement is
      weak, Lash treats seriously Keller's conversion and role as
      spokesperson in the decade beginning 1910. He writes: "Socialism
      gave direction and excitement to Helen's life and provided a
      theme for her writing. . . . Her participation in the socialist
      movement gave her a sense of comradeship with millions throughout
      the world." He calls her a "Socialist Joan of Arc" in describing
      her public role, but details as well the impact of her dedication
      on her private life. He describes Keller's brief and tragic love
      affair with her fellow Socialist and secretary, Peter Fagar, and
      her relationship with John Macy, a prominent Socialist and erratic
      husband of her teacher.

Lilienthal, Meta Stern (1876-1947)

173   LILIENTHAL, META. Dear Remembered World: Childhood Memories
      of an Old New Yorker. New York: Richard R. Smith, 1947, 248
      pp.
         Meta Stern Lilienthal was one of the most important jour-
      nalists among women in the Socialist party. She produced several
      pamphlets, scores of leaflets and short essays, and edited a
      women's page in the New Yorker Volkszeitung and a "Votes for
      Women" column in the New York Call. Her autobiography, however,
      does not focus on her political accomplishments; it relates,
      often in charming detail, her childhood memories of New York City.
      Nevertheless, Lilienthal provides scattered insights into the
      German immigrant radical milieu of the late nineteenth century,
      for her parents were ardent Socialists and prominent activists in
      the Socialist Labor party.
         Meta's parents emigrated from Germany in 1861. Her
      father, Frederick Lilienthal, was a physician and noted Jewish
      freethinker; her mother, Augusta, was a lecturer and advocate of
      woman's rights. Both parents were active in the Socialist move-
      ment of the 1870s, but Augusta was by far the more renown.
      Standing in strong opposition to the marxist leadership, she in-
      sisted that Socialists support campaigns for woman suffrage and
      accept the permanence of women's wage-labor. A rare political
      figure of her day, Augusta Lilienthal bequeathed this women's
      rights legacy to her talented daughter, who played a similar role
      among Socialists after the turn of the century. Meta Lilienthal
      writes fondly of her parents, although she fails to underscore
      her mother's contributions or personal influence.

She describes instead her childhood friends around Tompkins
Square, the parks, beaches, and other city landmarks, trips to
the country and abroad, and the family's circle of friends.
Short sketches of her parents' associates include such colorful
personalities as Helene Von Doenninges, the woman for whom the
leading German Socialist Ferdinand Lassalle gave his life in an
ill-fated duel. Lilienthal also describes the visits of Russian
nihilists and German Socialists, including August Bebel and
Wilhelm Liebknecht who solemnly addressed her as "Comrade Meta."
Lilienthal remembers becoming enthusiastically involved in the
Henry George campaign of 1886, resolving at an early age to work
for socialism. Her parents' ideal—"economic security, physical
well-being and personal happiness for the great mass of mankind"—
seemed to her, writing during the last years of her life, as "the
goals most worthy of human achievement."

Luhan, Mabel Dodge (1879-1962)

174 LUHAN, MABEL DODGE. Movers and Shakers. New York: Harcourt
     Brace, 1936, 542 pp. Reprint. New York: Kraus Reprint Co.,
     1971, 542 pp.
          The daughter of a wealthy banker of Buffalo, New York,
     Mabel Dodge Luhan became a leading patron of avant-garde artists
     and a host of radical intellectuals. By 1912 she had been
     widowed, remarried, and separated from her second husband, Edward
     Dodge, and was settled comfortably on lower Fifth Avenue where
     she had established a famous salon. Best known as an engaging
     conversationalist, Luhan supported some radical activities. In
     1913 she sponsored the famous Armory Show, which featured the
     most modern European painters, and helped organize a pagent
     staged in Madison Square Garden to draw attention to the plight
     of the Paterson, New Jersey, textile strikers.
          Luhan wrote several volumes of her fascinating and highly
     introspective memoirs, four published under the title Intimate
     Memoirs. Movers and Shakers, first published in 1936, describes
     her life in the decade beginning in 1910. She opens appropriately,
     with a description of her famous Manhattan apartment where she
     entertained the radical prominenti of her day. Luhan recalls her
     many friends and acquaintances and offers unique perceptions of
     women like Emma Goldman, Margaret Sanger, and Isadora Duncan.
     She also discusses in detail her romantic involvements with
     Hutchins Hapgood and John Reed.
          Luhan's autobiography is essential reading for scholars of
     Greenwich Village radicalism. Amid its rambling discursions are
     reprinted portions of Luhan's personal correspondence and selec-
     tions of poetry.

175 HAHN, EMILY. Mabel: A Biography of Mabel Dodge Luhan.
          Boston: Houghton Mifflin & Co., 1977, 228 pp.
          A popular novelist and writer, Hahn offers a comparatively
     brief sketch of Luhan's life and assessment of her character.

Although she presents little information not found in her subject's multivolume autobiography, she situates Luhan socially in
an era that bid middle-class women to idleness and neuresthenia.
Hahn does not downplay the complexity of Luhan's personality, or
ignore her vanity and egotism, but she delivers a sympathetic and
sometimes perceptive account of her adventuresome life.

176 LASCH, CHRISTOPHER. The New Radicalism in America (1889-
     1963): The Intellectual as Social Type. New York: Alfred A.
     Knopf, 1965, 349 pp. Reprint. New York: Vintage Books,
     1967, 349 pp.
          Mabel Dodge Luhan, who enjoyed a reputation as a demanding
     lover and high-strung personality, features prominently in a
     chapter subtitled "Sex as Politics." Despite Luhan's preference
     for experience over intellect, Lasch presents her as a special
     case study in the cultural alienation of the middle-class intel-
     lectual at the turn of the century. Because Luhan exhibited many
     symptoms that marked the personalities of her peers, she too
     represented a generation that was painfully dissatisfied with the
     existing route toward personal happiness and fulfillment.
          Lasch traces Luhan's erratic adult behavior to her child-
     hood in a typical upper-middle-class family beset by declining
     patriarchal authority and bereft of human emotion. As Luhan
     matured she searched for alternative forms of social relations,
     turning repeatedly and desperately for help to sympathetic men.
     By following a tortuous path toward spiritual regeneration, Luhan
     became, in Lasch's opinion, a modern, albeit neurotic, prophet of
     sexual liberation.

Macy, Anne Sullivan (1866-1936)

177 BRADDY, NELLA. Anne Sullivan Macy: The Story Behind Helen
     Keller. Garden City, N.Y.: Doubleday, Doran & Co., 1933,
     165 pp.
          Anne Sullivan, an orphan of Irish immigrants, grew up in a
     state almshouse near Boston. Nearly blind from a fever contracted
     in childhood, she enrolled in the Perkins Institution for the
     Blind in Boston when she was fourteen. An operation partially
     restored her sight, and after her graduation, at age twenty,
     Sullivan became the tutor and governess of Helen Keller, who was
     then seven years old. They stayed together until Macy's death.
          Sullivan came to share her pupil's Socialist convictions.
     In 1905 she married John Albert Macy, a Harvard instructor who
     had helped Keller write her early autobiography. Macy first con-
     verted Keller to socialism, but the Lawrence textile strike of
     1912, especially Keller's public role in behalf of the strikers,
     moved his wife.
          Braddy's biography contains only brief passages on Anne
     Sullivan Macy's Socialist activities but instead downplays her
     involvement in radical politics. The author concludes: "She has
     had flurries of the evangelical spirit, but they have never

lasted. She still has an incredible, heartbreaking faith in people, but she has left to others the task of making them over."

Malkiel, Theresa Serber (1874-1949)

178 MILLER, SALLY M. "From Sweatshop Worker to Labor Leader: Theresa Malkiel, a Case Study." American Jewish History 68 (December 1978):189-205.
Theresa Serber Malkiel (1874-1949) was an organizer in the Jewish labor movement in the 1890s and a prominent activist and propagandist in the New York Socialist party after the turn of the century. Born in Bar, Russia, Malkiel emigrated to the United States in 1891 and immediately entered the infant cloak-makers' industry. As a young garment worker, she led her union into the Knights of Labor and served as delegate to the Socialist-dominated Central Labor Federation. She joined the Socialist Labor party in 1893 and later broke, along with other dissidents, to form the Socialist Party of America. In 1900 she married fellow-Socialist Leon A. Malkiel, left the shops, and settled into a domestic routine. Within a few years she had organized other housewives of her hometown, Yonkers, and formed the first branch of the Socialist Women's Society of Greater New York. Malkiel later served on the Woman's National Committee of the Socialist party and also the New York branch of the Women's Trade Union League. A prolific writer, Malkiel produced many leaflets, pamphlets, and newspaper articles, many of which were published in the New York Call and in the New Yorker Volkszeitung. She was opposed to cooperating with the mainstream woman suffrage movement and chaired the instrumental New York Socialist Suffrage Campaign Committee in 1915 and 1917.
Miller's essay offers essential biographical information on this little-known activist. Miller describes Malkiel's concern for women as a facet of Jewish immigrant activity and judges her feminism "narrow, if not contradictory, less expansive than her commitment to socialism."

Marcy, Mary Tobias (1877-1922)

179 CARNEY, JACK. Mary Marcy. Chicago: Charles H. Kerr, 1923, 12 pp.
Mary Marcy was a leading writer and intellectual in the Chicago Socialist movement. Orphaned at a young age, she held several secretarial positions, for a time working on the clerical staff of the University of Chicago and simultaneously attending classes. When she joined the Socialist party in 1903, Marcy devoted herself to writing on social questions and economics. Out of the Dump (1909), an exposé of charity work, Shop Talks on Economics (1911), and Stories of Cave People (1917) for young folk were her major contributions. On the editorial board of the International Socialist Review, she wrote mainly for this publication.

Although Marcy was an advocate of free love, she never
participated in the women's sector of the Socialist movement, nor
did she share its political leanings. Rather, she considered herself an orthodox marxist and an expert on economics. In 1918 she
joined the Industrial Workers of the World.

This pamphlet was written as a tribute to Marcy and was
published shortly after her death. "To the rebels throughout the
movement," its author concluded, "she was sister, brother, sweet-
heart and lover."

O'Hare, Kate Richards (1877-1948)

180 O'HARE, KATE RICHARDS. The Kate O'Hare Booklets. St. Louis:
     Frank O'Hare, 1919, 104 pp.
     Kate Richards O'Hare was the most popular female propa-
gandist in the Socialist party before 1920. Born on a Kansas
farm, she grew up in Kansas where she joined the bustling reform
movements at the century's end. As a young woman she became an
ardent advocate of Populism, temperance, and woman suffrage, and
worked for a time at a local Florence Crittenton mission, a refuge
for "fallen women" and home for unwed mothers. In 1901 she
joined the Socialist party; the following year she married Frank
O'Hare. Until World War I, Kate O'Hare devoted herself to
spreading the Socialist gospel.
     In 1917 she chaired the Committee on War and Militarism,
convened at the Socialist party's Emergency Convention in St.
Louis. Over the next months, she conducted a nationwide lecture
campaign to protest the United States' involvement in war. She
had delivered one of her prepared lectures seventy-five times
before she was arrested at Bowman, North Dakota. A few days
later, a federal grand judge indicted O'Hare for interfering with
the enlistment and recruiting service of the U.S. Army. She
stood trial in December 1917 and was found guilty of violating
the wartime Espionage Act. She was sentenced to five years in
prison at hard labor. On April 14, 1919, Kate O'Hare entered the
Missouri State Penitentiary. Due to massive Socialist agitation,
her sentence was commuted in May 1920; she was later granted a
full pardon by President Coolidge.
     The Kate O'Hare Booklets were published by the Socialist
party to bring attention to the case. They include "Socialism
and the World War," the lecture that brought her arrest in North
Dakota; "Americanism and Bolshevism," the address delivered on
her final tour before imprisonment; and W.E. Zeuch's "The Truth
About the O'Hare Case," which details the events leading to her
arrest.

181 _____. Kate O'Hare's Prison Letters. Girard, Kan.: Appeal
     to Reason, [1919], 95 pp.
     Frank O'Hare, Kate's first husband, collected and intro-
duced a collection of her letters written during her stay in
prison. He writes that the letters were not intended for

publication but are rather "personal expressions" to him and
their four children. The letters contain family gossip as well
as detailed descriptions of prison conditions, especially O'Hare's
daily routine and her growing interest in the subject of prison
reform. Upon the advice of his comrades, Frank O'Hare chose to
publish these intimate letters to bring forward his wife's
"loyalty to a great ideal" and the flagrant injustice of her imprisonment.

182   _____. In Prison. New York: Alfred A. Knopf, 1923, 211 pp.
          O'Hare records how the political prisoners of World War I,
mainly a group of trained journalists and educators, used their
internment to study the penal system and conditions in the
prisons. O'Hare describes her own fourteen months in a federal
penitentiary, including such details as food, clothing, and the
role of religion among the inmates. She indicts the entire
prison system for conditions in general and for its refusal to
differentiate between crimes against the individual and those
against the state, especially what she deems the waste of tax-
payers' money spent for the prosecution and confinement of "spies."
With publication of this book, O'Hare began a long campaign to
reform the prison system.

183   BASEN, NEIL K. "Kate Richards O'Hare: The 'First Lady' of
          American Socialism, 1901-1917." Labor History 21 (Spring
          1980):165-99.
          Basen attempts to delineate O'Hare's political philosophy
and role within the Socialist Party of America. Too often, he
contends, historians have simplified her contribution, portraying
her alternately as a right-wing Socialist and a flaming revolutionary. Basen insists that O'Hare does not fit neatly into
fixed categories. She was a complex figure: "Militant in tone
and temperament, moderate in theory and tactics, and 'American as
apple pie,' she was a pragmatic, conciliatory, constructive, and
centrist Socialist who courageously devoted twenty years of her
life to building a viable, democratic mass movement."
          On the Woman Question, Basen views O'Hare as a "transi-
tional figure" and emphasizes her devotion to traditional ideals
of womanhood as well as her attraction to twentieth-century
feminist goals. O'Hare clung to romantic notions of marriage and
family, but after 1910, with the rise of the birth-control movement, she began to advocate family limitation and woman's control
of her body. Like most Midwestern Socialist women, O'Hare took
a firm stand on woman suffrage and against war.

184   BROMMEL, BERNARD J. "Kate Richards O'Hare: A Midwestern
          Pacifist's Fight for Free Speech." North Dakota Quarterly 44
          (Winter 1976):5-19.
          This essay provides a detailed account of the 1917 arrest
and trial of Kate O'Hare for her antiwar activities. Brommel
provides basic biographical data on her early years in the

Socialist movement, but focuses on the chain of events that led
to her conviction on charges of violating the Espionage Act.

185   LOVIN, HUGH. "The Banishment of Kate Richards O'Hare." Idaho
      Yesterdays 22 (Spring 1978):20-25.
            This essay details the abduction of Kate Richards O'Hare by
      a band of American Legionnaires who determined to prevent her
      from speaking in postwar Twin Falls, Idaho.

186   MALLACH, STANLEY. "Red Kate O'Hare Comes to Madison: The
      Politics of Free Speech." Wisconsin Magazine of History 53
      (Spring 1970):204-22.
            After her release from prison in 1920, O'Hare continued
      her protest activities. In 1922 she and her husband led the
      Children's Crusade, a march on Washington of children whose
      parents were still in prison for their antiwar activities. She
      also moved into civic work to reform conditions in American
      prisons.
            Invited by students in the local Social Science Club,
      O'Hare delivered a lecture on "Crime and Criminals" to a Madison,
      Wisconsin, audience in 1922. In this essay, Mallach describes
      the controversy caused by her appearance.

Ovington, Mary White (1865-1951)

187   OVINGTON, MARY WHITE. The Walls Came Tumbling Down. Intro-
      duction by Charles Flint Kellogg. New York: Harcourt, Brace
      & World, 1947, 307 pp. Reprint. New York: Schocken Books,
      1970, 307 pp.
            Mary White Ovington was a founder and for many years an
      officer of the National Association for the Advancement of Colored
      People. She advocated many reforms in behalf of blacks, labor,
      and women. In 1905 she joined the Socialist party in New York
      City and remained a Socialist throughout her life.
            In her autobiography, first published in 1947 when
      Ovington was eighty-two years old, she recalls her lifelong
      struggle to improve conditions for Afro-Americans. After study-
      ing for two years at Radcliffe College, Ovington worked from 1895
      to 1903 at Greenpoint Settlement in Brooklyn. There she acquainted
      herself with working-class life and moved into circles of con-
      cerned reformers and radicals. In 1903, at a meeting of the
      Social Reform Club, she heard a lecture by Booker T. Washington
      that made her acutely aware that racism existed as forcefully in
      the North as in the South. The next year she joined the Greenwich
      House Settlement and began an extensive research project on
      blacks in Manhattan, which was published as Half a Man: The
      Status of the Negro in New York (1911). Ovington also joined
      several uplift organizations, like the National League for the
      Protection of Colored Women and the Committee for Improving the
      Industrial Condition of Negroes in New York. It was the dynamic
      W.E.B. DuBois who gave a clear direction to her work, and in 1908

Ovington joined him in creating the NAACP. She describes in
vivid detail the events leading up to this historic event, her
experiences among blacks in both North and South, and the leaders
of the NAACP in its formative years.

Pemberton, Caroline Hollingsworth

188 FONER, PHILIP S. "Caroline Hollingsworth Pemberton: Phila-
     delphia Socialist Champion of Black Equality." Pennsylvania
     History 43 (July 1976):227-52.
        Descended from an old Quaker family, Pemberton was an
     active member of the Socialist party 1900-1903, and wrote books
     and essays on the Negro Question. Foner provides summaries of
     her various publications.

Sanger, Margaret (1879-1966)

189 SANGER, MARGARET. An Autobiography. New York: W.W. Norton,
     1938, 504 pp. Reprint. New York: Dover Publications, 1971,
     504 pp.
        Remembered primarily for birth-control activities, Margaret
     Sanger began her public career as a flamboyant radical. In 1910
     she joined one of the most vibrant branches of the New York
     Socialist party. Her friends were avant-garde artists, bohemian
     intellectuals, and leading figures in the labor and Socialist
     movements. Prompted by the forceful personalities around her,
     Sanger experienced a political awakening. By 1912 she emerged as
     a prominent agitator, known for her lectures and essays that
     appeared in the New York Call, and eager to rally her comrades in
     the first organized campaign for birth control.
        Sanger published her autobiography in 1938, decades after
     her disillusionment with radical politics. As a result, her tone
     throughout is somewhat condescending toward her youthful comrades,
     her words occasionally bitter about the old-guard Socialist
     leadership that failed to support her activities. Sanger's prin-
     cipal narrative thread traces her gradual withdrawl from radical
     circles and increasing reliance upon middle-class backers and the
     medical profession. In heroic proportions, Sanger presents her-
     self as uniquely determined to wage this risky struggle against
     social and legal proscriptions.
        Despite a marked distance from her early radical ventures,
     Sanger manages to preserve many memories of the exciting times of
     the 1910s. She offers perceptive cameos of radical luminaries
     such as Elizabeth Gurley Flynn, William D. Haywood, and Mabel
     Dodge Luhan. She succeeds, perhaps inadvertently, in documenting
     the instrumental role Socialists and anarchists played in foster-
     ing the birth-control movement.

190 DASH, JOAN. A Life of One's Own: Three Gifted Women and the
     Men They Married. New York: Harper & Row, 1973, 388 pp.
        Inspired by recent discussion of careers and marriage, the

author decided to examine the conflicting demands in the lives of
three highly ambitious and notable married women: Margaret
Sanger, Edna St. Vincent Millay, and Maria Goeppert Mayer. Dash
built upon the common knowledge of Sanger's life but concentrated
on the fine details of her relationships with her first and
second husbands. She concluded that neither marriage nor sex was
a major factor in comparison to Sanger's "will to power." She
argued similarly that despite Millay's longing for security and
companionship, she was first and foremost a poet.

191 DOUGLASS, EMILY TAFT. Margaret Sanger: Pioneer of the Future.
     New York: Holt, Rinehart & Winston, 1970, 274 pp.
          This popular biography enshrines Sanger as a modern-day
     saint. Focused on her postwar activities, it describes her
     valiant efforts to spread the birth-control movement to foreign
     countries. Douglass has little interest in Sanger's origins in
     the radical movements in the early decades of the twentieth cen-
     tury, and understands even less about the political complexities
     of her later international crusades. Rather, she presents Sanger
     as a pioneer of women's liberation, and a key figure in the
     achievement of the 1960s--the birth control pill.

192 KENNEDY, DAVID M. Birth Control in America: The Career of
     Margaret Sanger. New Haven, Conn.: Yale University Press,
     1970, 320 pp.
          Kennedy's prize-winning history is the first major icono-
     clastic treatment of Margaret Sanger. Although he grants Sanger's
     contribution to the historic birth-control movement, Kennedy does
     not portray her as a one-dimensionally heroic figure. Rather, he
     traces her early, somewhat erratic career as a function of a com-
     bative disposition and desire to be in the limelight.
          Kennedy examines various influences on Sanger's political
     development. Drawing from her autobiography, he recounts her
     Catholic childhood in Corning, New York, and her relationships
     with a radically inclined father and a mother driven to an early
     grave by successive childbirths. Beyond the personal factors
     Kennedy also delves into the nineteenth-century legacy on sexual
     relations and situates Sanger within a widespread awakening in
     the first decades of the twentieth century. The free-love prac-
     tices of Sanger's anarchist friends, the texts of Freud and other
     popular theorists, and a close friendship with the British sex
     radical Havelock Ellis all proved instrumental in shaping Sanger's
     early perspectives on sexual emancipation.
          But Sanger was too easily caught in the political whirl-
     pool in the years before World War I, Kennedy maintains, and
     changed with the currents. She drifted from the relatively staid
     circles of the Socialist party when they proved too constraining,
     toward the Industrial Workers of the World, and ultimately to the
     ultra-Left position embodied in her flamboyant journal, Woman
     Rebel. After her arrest on charges of conspiracy and obscenity.
     Sanger fled to Europe. When she returned to the United States,

World War I had fragmented her milieu, and she, too, underwent a gradual ideological retrenchment, turning away from radicals and toward middle-class volunteers and the medical profession. Ruled too often by emotions, Sanger could not weather the difficult trials of this period. She was, in Kennedy's opinion, a politically unstable campaigner.

193 SABAROFF, NINA. "Margaret Sanger and Voluntary Motherhood." Women: A Journal of Liberation 1 (Spring 1970):28-32.
    Sabaroff aims to set straight the record and to redeem Sanger from the charges of revisionist historians. Emphasizing the nobility of Sanger's intentions, she offers a brief summary of the birth-control pioneer's early development and landmark campaigns between 1910 and 1920. Unlike Kennedy who faults Sanger for an increasing conservatism in later life, Sabaroff maintains that her "primary struggle was to relieve the burden of working women who were married and who already had children." The revolutionary implications of this stand, however, unrealized, should not, in the author's opinion, be forgotten.

Schneiderman, Rose (1882-1972)

194 SCHNEIDERMAN, ROSE. All for One, with Lucy Goldthwaite. New York: Paul S. Ericksson, Inc., 1967, 264 pp.
    Rose Schneiderman, an immigrant from Russian Poland, was a labor activist throughout her adult life. In the mid-1890s, shortly after her father's death, she found her first job in a New York department store. Oppressed by the long working hours and poor pay, and over her mother's objections, she took a better job in a cap factory. Here she began a notable career in trade unionism and gained her first contact with radical activists. In 1903, with two co-workers Schneiderman organized the first women's local of the Jewish Socialist United Cloth Hat and Cap Makers' Union. She emerged a local leader, a delegate to the New York Central Labor Union, and a militant agitator during a capmakers' strike in 1905.
    After 1907 the Women's Trade Union League became her organizational home. At first she harbored reservations about the middle-class and wealthy women who served as League "allies," but she eventually adapted to the new environment. She served for a time as vice president of the New York league and in 1910 became a full-time organizer. From 1909-1914 she assisted the crucial union drive of the International Ladies' Garment Workers' Union. The famous shirtwaist makers' strike of 1909-1910 saw Schneiderman in her prime. In 1918, after working in the dramatic campaign for woman suffrage during that decade, she became president of the New York Women's Trade Union League, a position she filled until 1949.
    Schneiderman wrote her autobiography late in life, after a close association with Eleanor Roosevelt and appointment on the labor advisory board of the National Recovery Administration of

the New Deal had shaped her memories. Never an active Socialist even during her youth, Schneiderman had little room for politics outside the Democratic party since the 1930s. The single thread in her autobiography is her commitment to the labor movement and its special work among women.

Scudder, Vida Dutton (1861-1954)

195   SCUDDER, VIDA DUTTON. On Journey. New York: E.P. Dutton & Co., 1937, 445 pp.

Vida Dutton Scudder is best known for her important contribution to the settlement movement and her role as a leading Christian Socialist at the turn of the century. Born to Congregationalist missionaries in India, reared in Europe, educated at Smith College and Oxford University, Scudder emerged as an accomplished scholar of Christian social thought. She held a teaching position at Wellesley College from 1887 until 1928, when she retired. The author of sixteen books, Scudder also devoted her life to social activism. She helped initiate the College Settlement Association, and for twenty years was the guiding force at Denison House in Boston's South End.

In her autobiography Scudder explains how she achieved this synthesis of intellectual achievement and social reform. A series of lectures by John Ruskin at Oxford College in 1884 had opened her eyes to social injustice, but life at Denison House, especially daily contact with working people and organized labor, proved, in her mind, an "excellent preparation for later reading of Marx." Christianity, however, was "the ultimate source" of her Socialist convictions.

Scudder's autobiography provides rich insights into the Socialist movements at the turn of the century. She describes "the good years" of Boston Christian Socialism in the 1890s and her later role in the Lawrence textile strike of 1912. After World War I she continued her efforts but focused primarily on establishing a dialogue for socialism within the Episcopal Church.

Most reviewers praised Scudder's autobiography when it appeared. Candid and thoughtful, written in a simple form, it reflects her appreciation of intimate details and the inner life.

196   CORCORAN, THERESA, S.C. "Vida Scudder and the Lawrence Textile Strike." Essex Institute Historical Collections 115 (July 1979):183-95.

Corcoran discusses the reaction to Vida Scudder's marginal involvement in the Lawrence textile strike of 1912. She interprets the public censure of Scudder's innocuous actions--she did little more than address an audience of strikers and offer words of encouragement--as a telling sign of a growing conservatism within the Boston reform community.

197   FREDERICK, PETER J. Knights of the Golden Rule: The Intellectual as Christian Social Reformers in the 1890s. Lexington:

University of Kentucky Press, 1976, 323 pp.
        In expanding his essay in the New England Quarterly,
Frederick constructs a chapter on Vida Dutton Scudder that places
her within her social and political milieu. He compares her with
fellow Bostonians B.O. Flower and W.D.P. Bliss, and concludes
that she alone understood the chief limitation of the intellectual, the ineffectiveness of, in her words, "the appeal to purely
moral incentives." Because Scudder tried to confront this weakness by becoming an activist, Frederick concludes that she was
more subject to self-doubts and disappointments than were her
armchair colleagues.

198 _____. "Vida Dutton Scudder: The Professor as Social Activ-
        ist." New England Quarterly 43 (September 1970):407-33.
        Frederick explores Scudder's career as a college teacher
and as a reformer, especially the tensions between the two voca-
tions. Influenced by Ruskin and Tolstoy, she traveled a smooth
path to Christian socialism only to face a crucial personal
dilemma: how to balance a commitment to social activism with a
desire for the contemplative, ascetic life of the scholar.
Frederick follows Scudder's attempt to resolve this problem
through three types of activity: teaching, settlement-house work,
and socialism. He concludes that although Scudder judged her own
life one of "defeat," "the fulfillment of her quest for right conduct and for beauty was her achievement."

199 MAGLIN, NAN BAUER. "Vida to Florence: 'Comrades and Com-
        panions.'" Frontiers; A Journal of Women Studies 4 (Fall
        1979):13-20.
        Published in a special issue on lesbian history, this
essay focuses on the close friendship of Vida D. Scudder and
Florence Converse. Maglin examines their novels, personal relationships, and forms of political and religious involvement as
examples of a "feminine-sororial community" and "a system of
female values and priorities."

Thompson, Bertha

200 REITMAN, BEN L. Sister of the Road: The Autobiography of
        Box-Car Bertha as Told to Dr. Ben L. Reitman. New York:
        Sheridan House, 1937, 314 pp. Reprint. New York: Harper &
        Row, 1973, 314 pp.
        This fascinating, anecdotal memoir allegedly relates the
life of a woman familiar with both bohemian anarchist circles and
the ways of the lumpen-proletariat. Although Ben Reitman, Chicago
anarchist, birth-control agitator, and erstwhile lover of Emma
Goldman, projected some of his sentiment into the tale of this
remarkable figure, the story rings true. If there was a real-
life counterpart to Hutchins Hapgood's Anarchist Woman, it is
Box-Car Bertha.
        Bertha's character had the imprint of her origins, the

grassroots free-thought and eccentricity of the small town in
Middle America. Her grandfather, Moses Thompson, aided John
Brown, later published the Woman's Emancipator from Valley Forge,
Kansas, and went to jail twice for defying "moral" statutes. Her
father, IWW notable Walker C. Smith, passed through Valley Forge,
met and bedded Bertha's mother, then proudly shared an unwed
parenthood that outraged the neighborhood. Bertha's mother gave
her the nickname, "Box-car," a prediction of the rambling life
ahead.

Bertha grew up in a Little Rock, Arkansas, cooperative
colony, where she learned about the theories of free love and the
practice of birth control. For fifteen subsequent years she hit
the road, traveling by train or hitchhiking on the roads, living
as shoplifter or prostitute, and occasionally touching the intellectual circles of anarchists and Wobblies. She thus gratified
her interest in "abnormal" people until, at the end of her road,
she joined a New York social-service agency and worked as a re-
searcher.

Vorse, Mary Heaton (1874-1966)

201 VORSE, MARY HEATON. A Footnote to Folly: Reminiscences of
     Mary Heaton Vorse. New York: Farrar & Rinehart, 1935, 407 pp.
     Reprint. New York: Arno Press, 1980, 407 pp.
          A leading labor journalist, Vorse enjoyed a career spanning
     five decades. She covered the great strikes in Lawrence, Massa-
     chusetts; Passaic, New Jersey; Gastonia, North Carolina; and
     Flint, Michigan, and maintained throughout her life a deep sym-
     pathy for the rights of labor. She never joined the Socialist or
     Communist parties, and after World War II became increasingly
     mainstream in her support of the union movement. But from 1910
     through the 1930s, Vorse not only reported but participated in
     scores of major labor events.
          Her autobiography is a testament to her faith in socialism,
     shaped in the mid-1930s by the Soviet model of a planned economy.
     It opens appropriately with a recounting of Vorse's first big
     assignment, the story of the Lawrence textile strike of 1912.
     Vorse weaves in a few personal details, sketches some leading
     personalities like Elizabeth Gurley Flynn, Vida Scudder, and
     Floyd Dell, and describes life with Greenwich Village radicals.
     A large section covers labor and peace activities during World
     War I and Vorse's tours of Europe and the Soviet Union at its
     close. The autobiography, first published in 1935, is a journal
     of many years of hard work.

BOOKS AND PAMPHLETS ON
THE WOMAN QUESTION

The Socialist and anarchist writers listed in this section served
their movements as propagandists and agitators. They made no

significant contributions to Socialist feminist theory, but instead
built upon the pioneering works by August Bebel, Edward Bellamy, and
Charlotte Perkins Gilman. Most brought a materialist analysis to
bear on their subject, be it women's economic role in home or marketplace or sex relations in contemporary society. The anarchists--
Adeline Champney, Voltairine de Cleyre, Dora Forster, Emma Goldman,
and Moses Harman--criticized marriage as an institution and advocated
free love; while the Socialists, more in keeping with their social
purity and temperance heritage, took an opposing view, lamenting
women's degradation by male lust in prostitution or imperfect marriages under capitalism. Their respective arguments, however different in substance, shared a form both didactic and simplistic.
They aimed to reach working-class men and women and to bring them
into the radical fold. The work of serious education in the finer
points of analysis would take place after these essays and lectures
piqued their interest.

202 CHAMPNEY, ADELINE. Woman Question. Pamphlets in American
     History: Women WO 18. New York: Concord Co-operative
     Printers, 1903, 30 pp.
         A contributor to Mother Earth and Liberty, Champney de-
     livered this address to the Boston Social Science Club. Marriage
     and motherhood were her principal subjects, and she framed an
     argument for sexual freedom by describing materially the evolution
     of these institutions parallel to the rise of private property.

203 CLARK, W[ALTER] E[RNEST]. Woman, Man and Poverty: Some
     Startling History. Kansas City, Mo.: The Author, 1902, 30 pp.
         This essay constitutes a radical defense of woman's con-
     tribution to civilization, inspired by Matilda Joslyn Gage's
     popular tract, "Woman, Church and the State." After conducting
     an intensive study of history, Clark concluded that "Mother was
     the first diety," that her overthrow by savage man to create a
     patriarchal god destroyed the early egalitarian and beneficent
     order. In the future, the author asserts, "Man's nature to keep
     must be brought into cooperation with woman's nature to give,
     before Justice can be established among men."

204 CONGER-KANEKO, JOSEPHINE. Woman's Slavery--Her Road to
     Freedom. Chicago: Progressive Woman Publishing Co., [1911?],
     31 pp.
         Conger-Kaneko examines women's servitude across the cen-
     turies and considers the impact of the industrial revolution,
     particularly the mechanization of household labor, on women's
     role. She explains how modern women have gained a presence in
     civil society and why they now want a voice in the affairs of
     state. This pamphlet is addressed to mainstream suffragists and
     aims to document the case that women's ultimate freedom will come
     only with socialism.

205 CONGER-KANEKO, JOSEPHINE, ed. Woman's Voice: An Anthology.
     Boston: The Stratford Company, 1918, 294 pp. Microfilm.
     History of Women. Reel 901, no. 7482.
         A compilation of very short statements, stories, poems,
     and aphorisms, Woman's Voice presents a variety of perspectives
     on the Woman Question in the first decades of the twentieth cen-
     tury. Among the representative authors are Socialists May Beals,
     Mary Garbutt, Miriam Allen de Ford, Gertrude Breslau Fuller,
     Margaret Haile, Caroline Lowe, Anna Maley, Theresa Malkiel, Kate
     Richards O'Hare, Mary O'Reilly, Lida Parce, Leonora Pease, Meta
     Stern, Marian Craig Wentworth, and Josephine Conger-Kaneko. The
     selections are reprinted from a wide range of publications but
     are not dated.

206 CREEL, HERR GLESSNER. Prostitution for Profit. St. Louis:
     National Rip-Saw Publishing Co., 1911, 40 pp.
         Around 1910 Socialists became involved in the major cam-
     paigns to eradicate prostitution in the nation's cities. They
     were especially active in Chicago, where the white-slave traffic
     inspired a major investigation of vice and political corruption.
         Drawing upon his firsthand observations as a journalist
     for metropolitan dailies, Creel tells the "real facts" about
     Chicago's "red light" district, a story about the involvement of
     the rich that he could not publish in mainstream newspapers.

207 De CLEYRE, VOLTAIRINE. Selected Works of Voltairine de Cleyre;
     Pioneer of Women's Liberation. Edited by Alexander Berkman.
     New York: Mother Earth Publishing Assoc., 1914, 480 pp.
     Reprint. New York: Revisionist Press, 1972, 471 pp. Micro-
     film. History of Women. Reel 808, no. 6469.
         This large volume collects de Cleyre's major poems, essays,
     short stories, and sketches. The bulk deal with anarchism or
     free thought, although several selections address the Woman
     Question. The poem to "Mary Wollstonecraft" celebrates her un-
     dying spirit: "In the heart of the world at rest/She liveth
     still." An essay on "Sex Slavery" proclaims: "The earth is a
     prison, the marriage-bed is a cell, women are prisoners. . . ."
     In another entry de Cleyre recounts her intellectual journey
     toward anarchism, especially the impact of the Haymarket affair.
         The brief introduction by Hippolyte Havel provides a bio-
     graphical sketch and overview of de Cleyre's essays. He writes:
     "Voltairine de Cleyre belongs to this gallant array of rebels who
     swore allegiance to the cause of universal liberty, thus forfeit-
     ing the respect of all 'honorable citizens,' and bringing upon
     their heads the persecution of the ruling class. In the real
     history for human emancipation, her name will be found among the
     foremost of her time." Published shortly after her death, this
     collection, along with Havel's praiseful commentary, is a testa-
     ment to de Cleyre's standing within the anarchist community.

208 DeLEON, DANIEL. Woman's Suffrage. New York: New York Labor

News Co., 1909, 48 pp. Microfilm. History of Women. Reel
808, no. 6472.
The chief ideologue of the small, dogmatic Socialist Labor
party at the turn of the century, Daniel DeLeon (1852-1914) outlined his position on the Woman Question. He stated: "Woman's
disenfranchisement is an incident in the division of society in
classes, the consequent Class Struggle, and the rise of Class
Rule." Women's full civil enfranchisement, he reasoned, could be
obtained only by the overthrow of capitalism. DeLeon thereby
undermined arguments for an independent movement for women's
emancipation.
This pamphlet constitutes the text of a speech delivered
under the auspices of the Socialist Women's Society of Greater
New York, May 9, 1909.

209 DELL, FLOYD. Women as World Builders: Studies in Modern
Feminism. Chicago: Forbes & Co., 1913, 104 pp. Reprint.
Westport, Conn.: Hyperion Press, 1976, 104 pp. Microfilm.
History of Women. Reel 808, no. 6473.
During his youth, Floyd Dell (1887-1969) was an ardent
feminist and publicist of the "new woman." An editor of the
Masses and chronicler of Greenwich Village life, he considered
the Woman Question to be at the heart of Socialist endeavors.
This collection of short essays, first published in 1913,
assesses the contribution of ten women who embodied "the soul of
feminism." Dell introduces his method by explaining that he is
primarily concerned with woman's role as producer rather than as
lover or mate. His sketches of Charlotte Perkins Gilman, Olive
Schreiner, Beatrice Webb, Jane Addams, Margaret Dreier Robins,
and Emmeline Pankhurst carry out his intention. His most forceful essays, however, betray his deeper fascination with women who
address more sensual matters. Thus Isadora Duncan, Emma Goldman,
Ellen Key, and Dora Marsden emerge as true prophets of feminism.
As Dell admitted years later in his autobiography, Homecoming (1933), each page of his first book belied its stated
purpose: "I was, and remained, incurably romantic about women.
I thought them perfectly wonderful, and would never cease to
think so." If Women as World Builders fails as a deep analysis
of feminism, it succeeds in providing, albeit unintentionally, an
insight into Dell's intellectually fatal attraction to sexually
liberated women.

210 EASTMAN, CRYSTAL. Crystal Eastman on Women and Revolution.
Edited and introduction by Blanche Wiesen Cook. New York:
Oxford University Press, 1978, 388 pp.
"Life is a big battle for the complete feminist." Cook
opens her book with this true statement by Crystal Eastman (1881-
1928). Writing in 1918, Eastman believed that women would emerge
victorious in their battles for emancipation--and Eastman played
no small part in that struggle. A Socialist as well as feminist,
she participated in as many progressive campaigns as possible in

the decade before World War I and remained true to her colors in
the difficult period of reaction and isolation that followed.

Cook has gathered nearly seventy of Eastman's strongest
essays into a definitive collection and provides an introduction
informed equally by scholarship and empathy. Cook concentrates
on Eastman's attempt to forge a coherent philosophy from her dual
commitments to socialism and feminism. This focus allows the
editor to restore her subject to history, a necessary first step
because during the decades that followed Eastman's peak activity,
the Red scare, the Great Depression, and the Cold War all miti-
gated against an appreciation of her militant and radical ideas.
Cook recaptures the spirit of unconventionality in Eastman's life
and treats with sensitivity and perception her complex vision,
political involvements, and personal relationships. She closes
with a eulogy: "Crystal Eastman left the legacy of her life,
her determination and her work. Her vision, lost for so long,
enables us to build with more clarity."

The documents themselves reaffirm Cook's promise. More
than most feminists of her generation, Eastman wrote with an
almost universal appeal, certainly with an uncanny ability to
transcend the intellectual gap between her generation and the
next. Her essays on feminism and lifestyle, on women's place,
and the issue of equal rights versus protective legislation stand
as statements with more than mere historical significance.
Eastman was perhaps the first truly modern feminist whose Socialist vision comfortably encompassed both the workplace and the
bedroom. As Joan Kelly wrote when this collection first appeared,
"The most astonishing thing about Crystal Eastman is how contemporary her socialist and feminist consciousness is."

211 FORSTER, DORA. <u>Sex Radicalism as Seen by an Emancipated Woman
of the New Time</u>. Chicago: Moses Harman, 1905, 48 pp. Microfilm. <u>History of Women</u>. Reel 652, no. 5200.
Forster identifies the three major evils of the present
sex system as celibacy, marriage, and prostitution. To transform
sexual relations, she advocates investigations into patterns of
behavior, a widespread campaign to enlighten the populace, and a
program ensuring sex equality. Physicians and scientists,
Forster contends, are too afraid to risk censure, and timidly
stand in the wings of this controversial and awesome crusade.
She therefore envisions a grand alliance of spiritualists, anarchists, and Socialists leading the way to free love.

212 GOLDMAN, EMMA. <u>Anarchism and Other Essays</u>. New York: Mother
Earth Publishing Assoc., 1911, 277 pp. Reprint. New York:
Dover Publications, 1969, 271 pp. Microfilm. <u>History of
Women</u>. Reel 893, no. 7395.
This collection contains Goldman's own selection of essays
representing, she writes, "the mental and soul struggle of twenty-
one years,--the conclusions derived after many changes and re-
visions." Included are statements on anarchism and political

violence as well as Goldman's often-reprinted essays on women's
condition. Hippolyte Havel contributed a synopsis of Goldman's
life and appraisal of her contribution.
    This edition offers a new preface by Richard Drinnon.

213 _____. Red Emma Speaks: Selected Writings and Speeches.
    Compiled and edited by Alix Kates Shulman. New York: Random
    House, 1972, 413 pp.
        Amid the revival of interest in Emma Goldman in the early
    1970s, Shulman compiled a representative selection of her works.
    She includes Goldman's earliest testament, "What I Believe,"
    first published in 1908, and concludes with a complementary piece,
    "Was My Life Worth Living?" that appeared in 1934; together they
    attest to the steadfastness of Goldman's principles.
        Shulman groups Goldman's essays under four headings: po-
    litcal and economic organizations of society; social institutions,
    which includes perspectives on women; violence, both individual
    and institutional; and the Russian Revolution and the Spanish
    Civil War. Headnotes to each section place the essays within the
    appropriate historical context and assess their importance.

214 _____. Social Significance of the Modern Drama. Boston:
    Richard G. Badger, 1914, 315 pp.
        Goldman studies a group of European writers who "mirror in
    their work as much of the spiritual and social revolt as is ex-
    pressed by the most fiery speech of the propagandist." The plays
    of Ibsen, Wedekind, Brieux, Shaw, and Tolstoy, among others, thus
    mirror Goldman's own desire to overthrow stifling social conven-
    tions, victorian morality and its accompanying sexual repression,
    the subordination of the individual, especially woman, and "the
    hidden viciousness of purity and Christianity."
        Like so many others in her milieu, Goldman did not con-
    sider any American authors worthy of inclusion.

215 _____. The Traffic in Women and Other Essays on Feminism.
    Introduction by Alix Kates Shulman. Washington, N.J.: Times
    Change Press, 1970, 63 pp.
        This pamphlet brings together three essays by Emma Goldman
    from 1917. "Traffic in Women" criticizes reformers' attitudes
    toward prostitution and calls for sexual enlightenment and an end
    to the cash nexus in marriage. In "Marriage and Love" Goldman
    continues her argument by describing marriage as primarily an
    economic arrangement that sexually oppresses women and destroys
    the potential for true comradeship between men and women. "Woman
    Suffrage" is a strong critique of political reform as a means to
    liberate women.
        Shulman's introductory essay first appeared in Women: A
    Journal of Liberation (Spring 1970).

216 GREER, J.H. The Social Evil and the Remedy. Chicago:
    Charles H. Kerr, n.d., 64 pp.

Greer, a physician, relates the existence of prostitution
to women's oppression under a system rooted in private property.
A large portion of his pamphlet traces the grand historical narrative popularized earlier by Frederick Engels and August Bebel.
Greer thereby demonstrates that woman was the first slave and
necessarily succumbed to degradation. Prostituion, he contends,
results from this condition: it is "the logical outcome of centuries of abuse, oppression and robbery. . . ." He concludes by
discussing some of the contemporary reform programs, the opening
of "homes" for fallen women, and the proposed changes in the
legal structure. He rejects these efforts: "Nothing but a complete change in the social and economic institutions and systems
of our civilization will effect a cure" for the social evil.

217 HARMAN, MOSES. Institutional Marriage. Chicago: The Author,
     1901, 45 pp. Microfilm. History of Women. Reel 659, no.
     5252.
     The Light-Bearer Library published this text of Harman's
address before the Chicago Society of Anthropology on March 31,
1901. Framed as an imaginary discussion among Martians about
sexual relations on Earth, the essay contains Harman's main argument on behalf of free love. It begins with the premise: "Man
is the creator of institutions and creatures can have no rights
as against their creator." Marriage is Harman's prime example,
with woman's subjugation within the institution the proof of the
injustice of artificial restraints.

218 HOWE, ROBERT HARRISON. A Woman's Place. Chicago: Charles H.
     Kerr, [1900?], 24 pp.
     Evidently published in the mid-1910s, after several
Western states had approved woman suffrage referenda, this tract
argues in classic materialist fashion that the old social systems
have become outmoded for woman's purposes, but that a kernal of
the ancient collectivity remains intact for a future Socialist
order. "The spirit of the matriarchal gens that has so long laid
dormant is awakening and will lead every woman to recognize a
sister in every other woman," Howe writes, "and that she has a
mother's duty to perform for every child in the world." Like
many other Socialist tracts, A Woman's Place emphasizes the need
for home life and the expansion of the domestic sentiment, but
insists that, "A woman's place IS in her home, but her home is
now the world."

219 JOHNS, DOROTHY. Victims of the System; How Crime Grows in
     Jail and City Hall. Chicago: Charles H. Kerr, n.d. [1908?],
     31 pp.
     During the summer of 1908 Los Angeles Socialists waged a
campaign for the right to speak freely on the city's streets. To
gain public sympathy, they refused bail when arrested and often
served the usual sentence of twenty-one days in jail. After a
few months and considerable press coverage, Socialists succeeded,

and the city council changed the ordinances to open the streets for public speaking.

Dorothy Johns was one of those protestors arrested and imprisoned. While in jail she recorded her impressions of conditions and managed to forward several reports to local newspapers. As a result of such efforts, the Socialist-led free-speech campaign grew into a widespread assault on the city's penal system. This pamphlet contains Johns's descriptions of the sordid life of prison inmates, especially the vile conditions in the women's cells; it is a forceful statement on behalf of free speech and prison reform from the Socialist perspective.

220 JOHNSON, OLIVE M. Woman and the Socialist Movement. New York: New York Labor News, 1908, 48 pp. Microfilm. History of Women. Reel 739, no. 5917.

In the first decades of the twentieth century, the Socialist Labor party emerged gradually from its Germanic origins but nevertheless maintained a rigid position on the Woman Question. Olive Malberg Johnson (1872-1954) was the party's chief female propagandist, and she routinely criticized any theoretical deviations from a narrow class analysis. In this pamphlet, Johnson rails against the mainstream women's movement and middle-class women in general. She states emphatically that Socialists care only about working-class women. Moreover, she argues that Socialists uphold traditional roles for women, wifehood, and motherhood as alternatives to women's participation in wage-labor. Industrial labor, she explains, "unsexes" women and "nothing is more repugnant than the unsexed, boldfaced, rude, masculine girl, unless it be the weazened, physically deteriorated, effeminate man." Under socialism, Johnson affirms, women will enjoy their "natural" status as men's helpmeet. Woman and the Socialist Movement is a representative document from this era in the history of the Socialist Labor party.

221 KELLER, HELEN. Helen Keller, Her Socialist Years: Writings and Speeches. Edited and with an introduction by Philip S. Foner. New York: International Publishers, 1967, 128 pp.

Between 1910 and the early 1920s, Keller wrote frequently for the Socialist press and spoke in behalf of striking workers. In 1909 she joined the Massachusetts Socialist party and became an active member in 1912, at the time of the Lawrence textile strike. She wrote in the New York Call of that year: "I am no worshipper of cloth of any color, but I love the red flag and what it symbolizes to me and other Socialists. I have a red flag hanging in my study."

Keller published some of her early essays on socialism and woman's rights in Out of the Dark, which appeared in 1913. Foner reprints several selections from the original anthology and adds many essays covering the next decade of Keller's political career. The range of topics is broad: antimilitarism and world peace, birth control, woman suffrage, mass strikes, and the Russian

Revolution. Although Keller worked chiefly for the American
Federation for the Blind after 1921, she retained her faith in
socialism throughout her life.

222 KERR, MAY WALDEN. <u>Socialism and the Home</u>. Chicago: Charles
     H. Kerr, 1901, 32 pp.
         Published in Kerr's Pocket Library series, this small
     pamphlet addresses female readers. Kerr discusses things "about
     which we women think the most of; the things which come to us and
     help to make or mar the happiness of our daily lives," most es-
     pecially the home. An advocate of cooperative living, May Walden
     Kerr blames capitalism for women's woes, their isolation in the
     home, endless rounds of household drudgery, and need to marry for
     a livelihood rather than love. Socialism, she contends, will ex-
     tend cooperation throughout industry and into the home.
         May Walden was a prominent Socialist organizer among women
     in Chicago. Born in 1965, she became a Socialist in 1900 with
     her husband, Charles H. Kerr, the leading Socialist publisher of
     the era. Walden wrote frequently for the <u>Chicago Daily Socialist</u>
     and ran for local office on the Socialist party ticket. She also
     conducted several major speaking tours through the Midwestern
     states. Kerr and Walden separated early in their marriage; they
     had one daughter, Katherine Kerr.

223 _____. <u>Woman and Socialism</u>. Chicago: Charles H. Kerr, n.d.
     [1907], 24 pp.
         In this educational pamphlet, the author discusses three
     main points: the differences between utopian and scientific
     socialism; the "scientific" account of the changes in social in-
     stitutions as a function of economic development from prehistoric
     times to the era of modern capitalism; and the emergence of the
     Socialist perspective on these events. Only a small portion of
     this essay concerns women's status. Walden describes the efforts
     of class-conscious workers to "agitate, organize, and educate
     their fellow men and women for the coming change from Capitalism
     to Socialism," and asks women to consider seriously their part in
     this process. She mentions briefly some relevant issues, such as
     suffrage, women's working conditions, and maternity. Once free,
     women will develop their maternal instincts, Walden concludes,
     and lift the race to its highest level of development.

224 LILIENTHAL, META STERN. <u>From Fireside to Factory</u>. New York:
     Rand School of Social Science, 1916, 66 pp. Microfilm. <u>His-
     tory of Women</u>. Reel 905, no. 7532.
         Lilienthal analyzes the impact of industrialization on
     women's work. She begins her historical narrative with a descrip-
     tion of the mechanization of the textile industry. She writes
     that once the power loom replaced the old-fashioned hand loom,
     "when one time-honored woman's work after another was transferred
     from the home to the factory, it was only natural and inevitable
     that woman should follow her work, that she, too, should accomplish

the transition from her age-long work-shop, the family homestead,
to the world's new work-shop, equipped with machinery and steam-
power, the factory." Lilienthal verifies this development by presenting a statistical survey of women's wage-labor and notes that
between 1890 and 1910 the number of female breadwinners increased
significantly. Economic necessity forced them to find new fields
of employment and, she concludes, consequently weakened the barriers between man's work and woman's work.

The social implications of this development, according to
the author, are manifold. Men and women share a greater portion
of public life. "This entirely new relation of the sexes,"
Lilienthal writes, "a relationship of comradeship and co-operation,
is one of the greatest gains to humanity brought about by the industrial revolution." Furthermore, because woman is no longer
isolated within the narrow confines of her home, she has awakened
to a new social consciousness: she recognizes the economic basis
of her desire for independence, and will join the labor movement
in a common struggle for a "better, juster, happier, more humane
civilization." In rooting the labor movement and the women's
movement in the industrial revolution, Lilienthal hopes to demonstrate their political interdependence.

225 _____. Women of the Future. New York: Rand School of Social
Science, 1916, 31 pp. Microfilm. History of Women. Reel 905,
no. 7533.

When Karl Marx outlined scientific socialism, women, because they had not yet taken their modern roles, were a slight
consideration. Now that women had become important factors in
public life and in economic affairs, Socialists must consider the
movement in its relation to women. So Meta Stern Lilienthal begins her pamphlet.

She defines socialism as "the social ownership of all
things that are socially used" and indicates women's role and
status in the cooperative commonwealth. At the core of her statement is the prediction that men and women will share in the world's
work and will enjoy a full education. Socialism will bring universal peace, and it will establish women on a plane of full
equality with men. Lilienthal predicts that socialism will destroy the home only insofar as it is a workshop, and the family
insofar as it is founded on the economic dependence of women.
She explains how the socialization of housework, much along the
lines suggested by Charlotte Perkins Gilman, will afford women
the opportunity to participate in a variety of occupations and
will reorganize marriage on the principles of mutual love of husband and wife instead of on its present economic basis. Through
an expansion of the public school system, socialism will be the
"paradise of childhood"; at the same time, it will preserve the
sacredness of individual motherhood. Lilienthal concludes that
socialism, in fact, holds out its greatest promise to women. She
asks her reader to pass her "little book" along, to help "spread
the gospel of Socialism, the hope of humanity!"

226 LOWE, CAROLINE. The New Social Structure. Oakland, Calif.:
     n.p., n.d., 24 pp.
          Caroline A. Lowe (1874-1933) joined the Socialist party in
     1903 and soon thereafter became a popular regional organizer in
     Kansas and Oklahoma. Between 1910 and 1912 she served as national
     correspondent of the party's Woman's National Committee. Later
     she returned to field work and the free-speech battles conducted
     by the Industrial Workers of the World.
          The New Social Structure is the text of a lecture she de-
     livered in Oakland, California. She called for the abolition of
     private property in the nation's basic resources, and maintained
     that only through collective ownership and democratic management
     could each citizen enjoy the fruits of his labor. Lowe briefly
     considered women's status; she named capitalism the cause of
     prostitution and predicted the restoration of the home and women's
     position therein with the coming of socialism.

227 MALEY, ANNA A. Our National Kitchen. Minneapolis: People's
     Press, [1916], 62 pp.
          Anna A. Maley Ringsdorf (1873-1918) served as national
     organizer of women for the Socialist party in 1909-1910. After
     resigning this position, she moved to Everett, Washington where
     she edited the Commonwealth, a Socialist weekly newspaper. In
     1912 she became the first qualified woman in any state to stand
     as candidate for governor; she polled over 37,000 votes for this
     office.
          Our National Kitchen is the text of a lecture wherein
     Maley developed an analogy between the national economy and house-
     hold management. "Industry is, after all," she posited, "no more
     and no less than our national housekeeping. It is the process of
     feeding, clothing, housing, and educating our people." Despite
     the similarity between her argument and woman suffrage propaganda,
     Maley mentioned women's political rights only in passing.

228 MALKIEL, THERESA. Woman and Freedom. New York: Socialist
     Literature Co., 1915, 14 pp. Microfilm. History of Women.
     Reel 935, no. 7986.
          Malkiel brings to bear the classic Socialist materialist
     analysis on woman's condition and traces her evolution from primi-
     tive times to the era of the industrial revolution. "In a word,"
     Malkiel writes, "woman woke from her long sleep, the tide turned;
     the force which developed the age of industrialism sounded the
     knell of woman's subjection, the age of enlightenment opened its
     doors to her." The pamphlet concludes with a brief examination
     of modern conditions and calls upon women to join the struggle to
     overthrow capitalism.

229 _____ . Woman of Yesterday and Today. New York: Co-operative
     Press, 1915, 16 pp. Microfilm. History of Women. Reel 935,
     no. 7987.
          Similar in analysis to Woman and Freedom, this pamphlet

traces women's social development from ancient society to the
industrial revolution. Malkiel calls the nineteenth century "a
great iconoclast" because it destroyed the prevailing conception
of women's sphere as the home, and sent them into the larger
society where they took their places alongside men.

230 MARCY, MARY. Breaking Up the Home. Chicago: Charles H. Kerr,
     n.d., 12 pp. Microfilm. History of Women. Reel 956, no.
     9675.
          The pamphlet outlines the commonplace Socialist interpreta-
     tion of the impact of the industrial revolution on women's work.
     Marcy describes work in the old-fashioned home of "Grandmother
     Hopkins, a beautiful old lady of eighty-eight" to emphasize its
     intense yet satisfying quality. The advent of factory production,
     she continues, witnessed the transformation of the home into a
     shell of its former self. Modern women can no longer afford the
     luxury of a domestic life, Marcy contends, but are forced into
     wage-labor where they "grind out profits for some capitalist."
     But just as the capitalist system has broken up the old-fashioned
     home, socialism promises a new future.

231 MARCY, MARY, and ROSCOE BURDETTE TOBIAS. Women as Sex Vendors;
     or, Why Women Are Conservative. Chicago: Charles H. Kerr,
     1918, 59 pp.
          To answer the many authors claiming expertise on human
     sexuality, Marcy and her brother, Roscoe Burdette Tobias, wrote
     this booklet. It contains a historical materialist analysis of
     sex relations focused on woman's subordinate status, the source
     of her alleged reticence in matters of sex and morality.

232 MARTIN, PRESTONIA MANN. Is Mankind Advancing?. New York:
     Baker & Taylor Co., 1910, 302 pp.
          Prestonia Mann Martin (1861-1945) became a lifelong disci-
     ple of Edward Bellamy. In the 1890s she served as editor of the
     American Fabian; in the 1930s she revived Bellamy's schemes in
     Prohibiting Poverty (1932), a proposal for a national work-army
     to do away with unemployment.
          In this book Martin examines the concept of progress as
     applied to human beings rather than to material objects, and con-
     cludes that since the downfall of the Greek civilization two
     thousand years ago, few substantive gains have been made. The
     author advocates a plan of state socialism to maintain responsi-
     bility for the welfare of the common people, to redistribute the
     national wealth, and to restore women to their role as "priest-
     esses of the private, inner life," the family.

233 O'HARE, KATE RICHARDS. The Sorrows of Cupid. St. Louis:
     National Rip-Saw Publishing Co., 1912, 253 pp. Microfilm.
     History of Women. Reel 843, no. 6855.1.
          O'Hare's major publication, The Sorrows of Cupid reflects
     her Midwestern background and formative political experiences in

the 1890s. Originally published in 1904 as <u>What Happened to Dan?</u>,
the enlarged and revised edition reads as an old-fashioned social
purity tract, albeit from a Socialist perspective. O'Hare begins
by asking a fundamental question: how does modern civilization
affect love between men and women? "Love, home and babies are
the three graces that make the trials, struggles and suffering of
life worthwhile," she writes. But modern civilization had prevented the realization of basic happiness, as indicated by the
rising divorce rate, the decrease in family size, the later age
at which people marry, and the growing number not marrying at
all. O'Hare investigates the causes for this "rift in the lute"
and finds the source in capitalism--in the competitive struggle
for a livelihood and greed for profit, in the exploitation of
young working women and men, and in the domestic drudgery of the
housewife. Such conditions make it impossible for men and women
to form stable, happy marriages, O'Hare concludes, and "race
suicide" and prostitution result.

    This book circulated widely among Socialists, especially
in the Midwest. It is a testament to the lingering popularity of
nineteenth-century sentiments, a reverence for womanhood and the
family among modern-day Socialists. It also suggests the continuity of the leading reform crusades of the era, from the temperance movement of the 1880s through populism, and into the
Socialist movement after the turn of the century. O'Hare's own
political development, which she traces in part in this book, was
typical of that of many radical women of her generation.

234   PARCE, LIDA. <u>Lesson Outlines in the Economic Interpretation</u>
     <u>of History</u>. Girard, Kan.: Humanist Publishing Co., 1908,
     62 pp.
    Believing the principal value of history is to train the
judgment rather than to celebrate conspicuous characters, sustain
governments, or applaud nations, Parce offers a series of brief
lessons in the materialist conception of history. For individuals, she places at the forefront the history of people; for the
"Will of God" she names the motive force as the process of evolution. Parce then traces social development from its primitive
beginnings in savagery, through barbarism, and into modern times.
Like Engels before her, she relates the particular form of production at each historical stage to the organization of the family
and women's condition. She thereby hopes her readers will understand that "the normal habit of the human race is the communal
habit."

    Born in 1867, Parce began her political work in Arizona,
where she served for a time as president of the state's Equal
Suffrage Association. She gained her first appreciation for
formal study in the local women's club, which prompted her interest
in sociology and economics. Parce moved to Chicago where she
joined the Socialist party and pursued her studies at the University of Chicago.

235 RAPPAPORT, PHILIP. Looking Forward; A Treatise on the Status
     of Women and the Origin and Growth of the Family and the State.
     Chicago: Charles H. Kerr, 1906, 234 pp. Microfilm. History
     of Women. Reel 759, no. 6085.
          Rappaport's volume served Socialists as a readable and
     simple materialist history of the family and women's status
     patterned on the analysis outlined earlier by Frederick Engels
     and Lewis Henry Morgan. He includes chapters on divorce, prosti-
     tution, and the modern political and economic systems.

236 RICKER, ALLEN W. Free Love and Socialism: the Truth as to
     What Socialists Believe about Marriage. St. Louis: National
     Rip-Saw Publishing Co., n.d., 31 pp.
          Ricker's pamphlet is similar in perspective to O'Hare's
     The Sorrows of Cupid. It, too, focuses on capitalism's role in
     destroying the home, and presents "race suicide" and prostitution
     as the two prime examples. Ricker also argues for women's con-
     trol over sexual matters on the grounds of their moral superiority,
     their "instinctive" preference for monogamy, and their material
     natures.

237 SIMONS, MAY WOOD. Woman and the Social Problem. Chicago:
     Charles H. Kerr, [1907], 31 pp. Microfilm. History of Women.
     Reel 766, no. 6142.1.
          Simons intends to describe the "vital influence of social-
     ism upon woman's condition" and accordingly, woman's influence on
     the Socialist movement. She develops her essay historically,
     beginning with a summary of women's economic status from savagery
     through the industrial revolution. Simons gathers evidence from
     classic texts, like Lewis Henry Morgan's Ancient Society, and
     concludes that capitalism, by bringing women into wage-labor,
     makes the condition of men and women more similar. Yet she re-
     cords the detrimental effects of this process, particularly capi-
     talism's misuse of women workers. She describes working women as
     low-paid, unorganizable factors in the labor market, and compet-
     itors who worsen the situation of working men. She catalogs the
     evil effects of capitalism on personal life, such as various in-
     juries to health and home. "It is to socialism alone," Simons
     writes, "that home life must look for its rescue and purifica-
     tion." Similarly, it is to socialism alone that women must look
     for economic equality and political freedom.
          Simons's background in the Socialist Labor party shows it-
     self in this essay. Unlike women who came into the Socialist
     party from the women's movement, Simons has little faith in those
     of her sex as progressive agents in society. She believes,
     rather, that conditions have made women "physically weak, men-
     tally narrow, politically powerless," such that they constitute
     "a conservative reactionary body." As she warns against the lure
     of the mainstream women's movement, she describes the rise of the
     proletarian movement according to the prediction of Karl Marx.
     Woman's primary responsibility, Simons ends, is to join the ranks
     of class-conscious working men.

This pamphlet is reprinted in the appendix to <u>Flawed Liber-ation: Feminism and Socialism</u>, edited by Sally M. Miller.

238 SPARGO, JOHN. <u>Socialism and Motherhood</u>. New York: B.W. Huebsch, 1914, 128 pp.

Spargo, one of the Socialist movement's chief intellectuals, did not endear himself to its women's sector with the publication of this volume, which takes as its premise: "There is nothing in the philosophy or programme of Socialism which is incompatible with the maintenance of the private family based upon monogamic marriage." Defending socialism against charges of free love, Spargo refutes Bebel and glorifies woman's maternal nature. He claims that a woman does not strive for rights as man experiences his in politics or labor, but desires instead, "freedom to remain with her child to nourish and guard its body and soul during all the dependent years."

239 TICHENOR, HENRY MULFORD. <u>Woman Under Capitalism</u>. St. Louis: National Rip-Saw Publishing Co., 1912, 32 pp.

Born in 1858, Tichenor evinced a sentimental outlook on the Woman Question throughout his life. He was a pioneering Missouri poet who became a popular agitational writer for the <u>National Rip-Saw</u> (St. Louis), publisher of his own free-thought magazine, the <u>Melting Pot</u> (St. Louis), and a philosopher of reli-gion in later life. He took a hard stand against "bourgeois hypocrisy," as in this pamphlet, and raised prostitution and woman's sexual subjugation as his chief examples.

240 WALLING, WILLIAM ENGLISH. <u>The Larger Aspects of Socialism</u>. New York: Macmillan & Co., 1913, 406 pp.

Walling's book represents his attempt to move beyond the materialist framework of Second International theory and present in its place a more pragmatic, cultural conception of socialism. Thus he views socialism as a revolution in politics and economics as well as in history, science, literature, and art.

His concluding chapter, "Man, Woman, and Socialism," is an especially important indication of the popularity of feminism among party intellectuals in the 1910s. Walling begins by ac-knowledging the historic contribution of Bebel to the Woman Ques-tion, but underscores the outdated notions about sexuality, partic-ularly female sexuality, in <u>Woman Under Socialism</u>. He turns to what he considers the most significant modern works by Charlotte Perkins Gilman and Olive Schreiner. He praises most of all the ideas of the Scandinavian writer, Ellen Key, who represents the feminist thinker most liberated from the fetish of evolutionism. Walling's exegesis of Key's philosophy provides an essential in-sight into shifting intellectual currents within the Socialist movement during the decade of World War I.

241 WENTWORTH, FRANKLIN HARCOURT. <u>The Woman's Portion</u>. New York: Socialistic Co-Operative Publishing Association, [1910], 24 pp.

Microfilm. <u>History of Women</u>. Reel 779, no. 6229.
     This pamphlet is the text of an address delivered in
Carnegie Hall, New York City, February 27, 1910, at the annual
Woman's Day celebration sponsored by Socialist women. Wentworth
discusses the effect of women's oppression upon womanhood and
society in general. He frames his argument in a traditional
manner: the enslavement beginning with the onset of private
property locked women behind a barrier, her special sphere--"a
region vast in pettiness and futility"; economic development,
however, created the preconditions for women's entry into social
life. Wentworth predicts that the ascent of the free woman will
benefit the race, for her superior instinct will uplift the
civilization. He calls upon his fellow Socialists to assist
women in their advancement, and to welcome the "world of love and
liberty" that will accompany their emancipation.

PERIODICALS

     The first decades of the twentieth century might be called the
golden era of radical women's magazines, not excelled--if at all--
until the women's liberation movement of the 1970s. For the first
time the Socialist and women's movements could sustain financially a
handful of magazines that reached a sizable audience. Radical women
writers became in a small way the vogue, and a few found paying
positions as editors and publishers. The Socialist <u>New York Call</u> and
several other radical newspapers introduced women's pages or columns,
adding to this short-lived but impressive journalistic flurry.

242 <u>Forerunner</u>. New York, 1909-1916.
     The <u>Forerunner</u> is the unique expression of a remarkable
individual, for it was edited, published, and written solely by
Charlotte Perkins Gilman. She produced the first thirty-two-page
issue, priced at ten cents per copy, in November 1909 and continued single-handedly to crank out monthly issues until December
1916. Renouncing the class struggle doctrines of marxism, she
termed her magazine a venture in Socialist journalism; similarly
she preferred to stress its advocacy of humanism rather than
feminism. Over the years of publication, Gilman ran serially
seven novels and seven major essays, which constitute the bulk of
her published work. She hoped to attract 3,000 subscribers to
cover operating costs, but never came near that goal. Nevertheless, with Gilman shouldering much of the financial burden, the
<u>Forerunner</u> reached a select audience of leading women reformers,
suffragists, and Socialists. The Rand School of Social Science
in New York City and the Socialist Literature Company distributed
the magazine to an intellectual constituency and helped make the
idiosyncratic production a staple among radical periodicals.

243 <u>Masses</u>. New York, 1911-1917.

A monthly journal edited during its most creative period
by Max Eastman, the Masses boldly proclaimed itself "A Revolutionary And Not A Reform Magazine." It was the liveliest, most
innovative Left production to combine political journalism and
the arts. Its covers by Robert Minor, cartoons by Art Young and
John Sloan, and poetry and short stories by avant-garde writers
conveyed a flexible editorial policy and a sense of humor that
betrayed the cultural sobriety of most Second International
Socialists.

Eastman and his partner, Floyd Dell, made the Masses a
premier feminist journal. They wrote on prostitution, woman
suffrage, working women, birth control, and the more intimate
aspects of social relations between the sexes. Contributions by
leading women activists--Elizabeth Gurley Flynn, Dorothy Day,
Mabel Dodge Luhan, Helen Marot, Elsie Clews Parsons, and Mary
Heaton Vorse, for example--strengthened their commitment. For
historians, the Masses is an invaluable measure of the shift in
feminist consciousness during the decade before World War I, a
rare insight into the revolt against formalism and the upsurge of
militant tactics that marked the era.

244 Mother Earth. New York, 1906-1918.
Founded in 1906 by Emma Goldman and edited from 1908 by
her close friend Alexander Berkman, Mother Earth appeared monthly
to August 1917. It appealed to small circles of anarchists and
other radicals, reaching a peak audience of perhaps 10,000. It
was primarily a political magazine focused on anarchist doctrines
and the defense of free speech and civil rights of activists.
Mother Earth also touched upon the arts. Never as lively as the
Masses, Goldman's journal published her leading essays on women
and on sexual liberation; especially in its last years it followed
the birth-control campaigns, offering both endorsements by leading
radical women, including Margaret Sanger, and detailed reportage
of Goldman's nationwide tours. Barred from the mails in 1917,
Mother Earth was succeeded in October 1917 by the short-lived
Mother Earth Bulletin, which lost its mailing privileges the
following May.

245 Socialist Woman/Progressive Woman/Coming Nation. Girard,
      Kan.; Chicago, 1907-1913.
The Socialist Woman, founded in 1907 by Josephine Conger-
Kaneko, became the official organ of the Woman's National Committee of the Socialist Party of America. Although Conger-Kaneko
soon changed its name to Progressive Woman to reach a larger
audience, the magazine never achieved a mass circulation; it grew
from an initial mailing list of 120 subscribers to a peak of
3,000, most undoubtedly close to the women's sector of the
Socialist party. Several issues on special themes suitable for
mass distribution at rallies and fund-raising or political events
enjoyed print runs near 20,000 copies. Between 1908 and 1912,
the Progressive Woman sustained a thriving Socialist women's

movement and published news of its accomplishments, biographical
sketches of leading lights, short essays and stories by organizers
and theoreticians, lesson outlines on "scientific socialism,"
poetry, and large samples of letters from grateful readers across
the country. During this successful period, Conger-Kaneko struggled to make the fifty-cent subscription price cover her bills,
and blessed the volunteer labor of local Girard women and the
comfortable facilities of the Appeal to Reason's press. During
the spring of 1911, facing major technical problems, Conger-
Kaneko moved the operation to Chicago, the seat of the National
Office of the Socialist party and its women's department. The
financial responsibilities proved more difficult to maintain outside Girard, and the venture eventually folded into a general
interest, short-lived magazine, the Coming Nation. In its last
issue, the embittered editor related the history of the demise of
her life's work.
     The Progressive Woman was the product of Josephine Conger-
Kaneko's imagination. It tapped the sensibility of its predomi-
nantly small-town readership centered in the Midwest, and carried
older traditions of womanhood into the twentieth-century Socialist
movement. The Progressive Woman advocated women's economic independence and political rights, temperance, social purity, and
domestic harmony, and never abandoned its appealing sentimental
vision of women's emancipation.

246 Toveritar--Työläisnainen--Naisten Viiri. Astoria, Ore.;
     Superior, Wis., 1911-present.
     Finnish-American women in the Western and Central states
constituted the readership of the sister paper of Toveri (Comrade), Toveritar (Comradess). The first issue appeared on July
11, 1911, and its goal was to bring enlightenment to working
women so they might join the broader struggle for socialism.
Under the successful management of Selma Jokela McCone, Maiji
Nurmi, and Helmi Mattson, who served as editors from 1911 through
the 1920s, Toveritar was the voice of women organized in the
Finnish Socialist Federation of the United States. Toveritar
bore the imprint of its Scandinavian ancestry: its editors
boldly advocated woman suffrage and temperance as well as brought
special attention to the well-being and education of children;
its literary quality was consistently high. The paper contained
some of the best of Finnish-American political essays, short
stories, and poems. During the period following the Russian
Revolution, Toveritar achieved a circulation of over 10,000. In
the 1930s, Toveritar was moved to Superior, Wisconsin, its name
changed to Työläisnainen (Workingwoman) and later to Naisten
Viiri (Women's Banner). For the next twenty years, Emma Mattila
served as editor. Naisten Viiri celebrated its sixty-fifth anniversary in July 1976. A special English supplement appeared on
July 9, 1976. Naisten Viiri is the only Finnish women's paper
published in the United States; it is also the nation's oldest
Socialist women's journal.

247 Woman Rebel. Alex Baskin, editor. New York: Archives of
     Social History, 1976, 56 pp.
          This edition is a facsimile reproduction of the original
     newspaper edited and produced by Margaret Sanger. Baskin includes
     an introduction, which offers a short history of the Woman Rebel
     as well as a chronicle of Sanger's activities at the time.
          The Woman Rebel appeared monthly during the months of
     March through August 1914. It was an eight-page, triple-column
     newspaper printed on common stock. Its intended audience was
     working-class women, and it was, in Sanger's own opinion, "red
     and flaming." Its first issue was declared unmailable under a
     section of the criminal code. Sanger continued to test the limit
     of the law in subsequent numbers. In July she published an essay
     found especially objectionable by the courts of New York, Herbert
     A. Thorpe's "A Defense of Assassination." In August, Sanger was
     indicted for violating the Comstock Postal Act of 1873 and arraigned
     before the U.S. District Court for southern New York. Soon there-
     after she fled, first to Canada, and then to Europe, to begin a
     lengthy period of exile.
          Ostensibly devoted to birth control, the Woman Rebel was
     an anarchist journal. It spoke in the name of free love, anti-
     clericalism, and labor militancy, and often lashed out at those
     feminists who failed to take an unconventional stand. In one
     issue Sanger reprinted the preamble of the Industrial Workers of
     the World; in others she republished short essays by Ellen Key,
     Olive Schreiner, Helen Keller, Emma Goldman, and other anarchist
     writers. The journalism was laced with short epigrams calling
     for personal bravado, with poems of a similar sort, and with
     short sketches of revolutionary heroines. Its motto, "No Gods,
     No Masters," set the tone throughout. Although Sanger determined
     its editorial content, she wrote relatively few articles. Her
     occasional editorials, however, were strident, and serve to illus-
     trate her political mentality during this period of her life.

                              FICTION AND POETRY

     Socialists developed no distinctive literary tradition, but con-
tinued the realist and didactic forms established in the late nineteenth century. Many writers seemed to revive the sentimental flavor
associated with a much earlier era. Josephine Conger-Kaneko, for
example, steeped in the social-purity vision of sexual harmony, was
decidely old-fashioned in both form and content. Even Rose Pastor
Stokes, who argued cautiously for sexual freedom, reduced the complexities of her story to a simple moral of good triumphant over evil.
Only Reginald Wright Kauffman achieved recognition in his day, his
novel on the social evil a contemporary best-seller.

     It must be added that these writers produced scores of short
stories and poems but published them primarily in radical newspapers
and magazines, which enjoyed large circulations. Books, even cheap

                                 111

productions, were undoubtedly beyond the financial means of their intended working-class audience, whereas newspapers were the centerpiece
of literature designed for entire families.

248 BAKER, ESTELLE. The Rose Door. Chicago: Charles H. Kerr,
     1911, 202 pp.
         A novel about prostitution, The Rose Door relates the
     stories of three young women and their entrapments. Rebecca is a
     recent immigrant, waiting for her bethrothed to join her in the
     new country, but she is meanwhile duped by a man who poses as her
     friend. Anna, who had been seduced by the family boarder, later
     orphaned, and reared as a poorly treated servant, runs away with
     a Berkeley student only to be deserted by him. Grace, a student
     at the University of Minnesota, represents yet another case. The
     three women eventually find themselves working at "The Rose Door,"
     a San Francisco brothel. The main message is delivered by a
     patron, a Socialist who explains that prostitution is merely a
     business enterprise like any other. The author, however, has
     added her own interpretation on the dedication page:
                   "Count me once for all enslaved;
                   Twice for women, twice enslaved."

249 BEALS, MAY. The Rebel at Large. Chicago: Charles H. Kerr,
     1906, 184 pp.
         May Beals Hoffpauir (1879-1956) worked as an organizer for
     the Socialist Party of America among the field workers of Louisiana
     and coal miners of Tennessee. She edited the Red Flag, a cul-
     tural magazine published in Abbeville, Louisiana, in 1907-1908.
         The Rebel at Large is a collection of her short stories
     and vignettes reprinted in a form suitable for propaganda work.

250 BULLARD, ARTHUR [Albert Edwards]. Comrade Yetta. New York:
     Macmillan & Co., 1913, 448 pp. Reprint. Upper Saddle River,
     N.J.: Gregg Press, 1968, 448 pp.
         Arthur Bullard (1879-1929) published Comrade Yetta in 1913.
     It is the story of the political and emotional maturation of
     Yetta Rayefsky, a Jewish immigrant. Poverty forces the orphaned
     Yetta into the garment industry of New York's Lower East Side.
     Lured into the dance halls, she survives a close call with a pimp.
     Fortunately, she becomes the ward of Mabel Train, an idealistic
     middle-class official of the Women's Trade Union League who recog-
     nizes Yetta as a diamond in the rough. With just a little
     prompting from her new mentor, Yetta emerges a heroine during a
     strike in her trade, patterned no doubt on the soul-stirring
     shirtwaist makers' strike of 1909-1910. Now an organizer for the
     League, Yetta opens a new chapter in her life.
         As she gains an increasingly sophisticated perspective on
     the struggle for bread, Yetta also grows from romantic infatua-
     tion with a middle-class scholar to true love with a dedicated
     Socialist, Isadore Braun. At the end of the novel, Yetta has

reached a poetic synthesis in her life. She and Isadore are
working together on the Clarion, a newspaper modeled on the
Socialist New York Call, which Bullard edited for a period. They
are "comrades" in the full meaning of the word, mates as well as
class-conscious revolutionaries.

Comrade Yetta is a story with both insight and good character development. Bullard deals sensitively with the tensions between working-class activists like Yetta and the well-meaning
benefactors of the Women's Trade Union League. He portrays effectively the oppressive pace of labor in the early garment factories,
the misery of life in the tenements. He also provides a rare
glimpse into the daily life of the Socialist movement, its spirit
of camaraderie, and the complex personalities of its loyal supporters. One of the more interesting if didactic sections of the
book concerns Yetta's sexual enlightenment. Bullard was a pioneer
in the field of sex education; he not only wrote convincingly
about the evils of prostitution but made a strong case for sexual
liberation for women. As a reviewer at the time noted, Arthur
Bullard writes with "freshness and power."

251 CONGER-KANEKO, JOSEPHINE. Little Sister of the Poor. Girard,
     Kan.: Progressive Woman Publishing Co., 1909, 103 pp.
        When Josephine Conger-Kaneko was on the staff of the
Appeal to Reason (Girard, Kansas), she took an assignment in
Chicago investigating slum life and the white-slave traffic. She
later confirmed her impressions by visiting New York and other
Eastern cities.
        This novelette, which was serialized in part in the Coming
Nation in 1913, is based on Conger-Kaneko's explorations into in-
vestigative reporting. To present her data and analysis in an
appealing form, she chose the medium of fiction. The subject is
women's sexual exploitation in both country and city. There are
two plots, one about a young Polish woman, Vera Oblinsky, who
lives in Chicago's West Side, and another about Mary Elizabeth
Ray, a resident of a small town in Indiana. Both women experience
lives of poverty and confront their oppressor, the male seducer.

252 CONVERSE, FLORENCE. The Children of Light. Boston: Houghton
     Mifflin Co., 1912, 308 pp.
        Told in autobiographical form, this story traces the matu-
ration of an idealistic child. Clara was born in New Hope, a
failing Southern communitarian settlement that had been pioneered
by her deceased parents. At a critical moment in her upbringing,
a fortuitous inheritance takes her to New England, where relatives
inspired by St. Francis serve as interesting role models. A
plethora of erudite discussions on the nature of social change
fill Clara's adolescence. After college she turns to settlement
work and eventually faces a major test of her as yet abstract
political notions. Amid a tense electoral campaign between a reform candidate and a Socialist and a general strike led by working
women, Clara emerges philosophically unscathed. She has become a

dedicated Socialist as well as prospective bride of the hero of
the hour.
    The plot is incidental. The author focused instead on
character development to draw archtypal representatives of various
strands of progressive thought, and through their voices she
argues the relative merits of contending political theories.
Converse thus created a tract for socialists that underscored the
necessity of individual dedication.

253 GILMAN, CHARLOTTE PERKINS. The Charlotte Perkins Gilman
     Reader. Edited and introduced by Ann J. Lane. New York:
     Pantheon Books, 1980, 208 pp.
        Lane collected several of Gilman's best short stories and
selected portions of her major novels to fill this volume representing "the fictional world of Charlotte Perkins Gilman." As
Lane points out, although Gilman considered herself a Socialist
and imagined cooperative societies in her utopian fiction, she
presented "strangely conservative" strategies in her realistic
stories. She routinely addressed the plight of women circumscribed by the domestic sphere, and underlined the necessity of
opening up the world of work to encompass and make use of women's
creative energies. Gilman nevertheless envisioned a solution to
household problems that relegated chores to servants or capitalist
industries rather than cooperative or socialistic enterprises.
Thus these collected stories, most published originally in the
Forerunner, understate Gilman's broader vision of social change
outlined in Women and Economics and in her philosophical tracts
and essays.

254 _____. Herland. New York: Pantheon Books, 1979, 146 pp.
        Gilman's utopian novel, first published serially in the
Forerunner in 1915, studies cultural attitudes about sex roles.
The scene is an island community of women, described by a man who
has journeyed with two friends to witness this amazing phenomenon.
As the men come to terms with the female society, they reveal
their own cultural conditioning about the relationship between
the sexes and woman's place in particular. They must learn to
relate to women who are strong, self-sufficient, and orderly, and
the road to understanding is a hard one, although softened by
Gilman's witty commentary.
        The story serves as a vehicle for Gilman to explore the
cultural and biological determinants of gender. She also describes a harmonious society governed by the New Motherhood, where
the feminine propensity for cooperation has triumphed over the
competitive marketplace relations of man's world.
        This new edition contains a brief introduction by Ann J.
Lane, a noted Gilman scholar.

255 GLASPELL, SUSAN. The Visioning. New York: Frederick A.
     Stokes Co., 1911, 464 pp.
        Writing in the tradition of radical women novelists,

Glaspell fulfills symbolically the desire for social harmony in
the mutual growth of two female characters from opposite classes.
The well-to-do Katherine Wayneworth Jones, daughter of an old
army family, experiences a political awakening to the reality of
class society as she comes to understand the tragic circumstances
surrounding Ann Forest. As the story opens, Kate saves desolate
Ann from suicide. At first confused by Ann's attempt to end her
life, Kate follows her to Chicago where she discovers a world unknown to her, a city "too loathsome for civilized man and woman
of today to set foot in." As she views firsthand urban poverty
and squalor, she finally grasps the meaning of degradation and
why Ann might want to end her life. Kate also finds solutions in
good causes, including women's rights and socialism. She eventually affirms her new faith by marrying Alan Mann, a Socialist
and ex-military man who brings to her "a vision" of a world without armies, a world at peace. Ann, too, grows and emerges a
strong woman; she marries Kate's brother, who under her influence
rejects his military preoccupations and becomes a forest ranger.
     The Visioning, supposedly written under the influence of
Glaspell's friends Floyd Dell and George Cram Cook, marks her departure from local-color fiction. Nevertheless, despite its
Socialist idealism, a romantic theme prevails as a signature of
her early writing.

256   _____. Plays. Boston: Small, Maynard & Co., 1920, 315 pp.
     This volume collects Glaspell's most innovative plays
written from 1910 on, including Trifles, her most popular production, and Suppressed Desires, a satirical skit about Greenwich
Village's infatuation with Freud and psychoanalysis, which she
wrote with her husband, George Cram Cook.

257 HAPGOOD, HUTCHINS. An Anarchist Woman. New York: Duffield &
     Co., 1909, 309 pp.
     Hapgood (1869-1944) prefaced his novel by representing it
as "an effort to throw light on what may be called the temperament
of revolt." Two major characters serve his purpose. Hapgood
first introduces his heroine, Marie, who at twenty-three "had
lived enough for a woman twice her age." Born in 1884 to poor
immigrants, Marie had grown up in the slums of Chicago's West
Side. She became hardened to life's miseries not only by her impoverished environment but by her parents' frequent beatings and,
later, a series of boring, degrading jobs. Neither factory work
nor domestic service satisfied her longings; searching for a
spark of love or excitement, Marie drifted casually into prostitution. At this point Marie crosses the path of a fervent young
anarchist, Terry. Terry sees in Marie the material for a living
experiment in social propaganda: a girl from the working class,
unrestrained by social convention, Marie needs only to be enlightened to the philosophy of life she has already lived. They
conduct an anarchist salon, and Marie imbibes the heady spirit.
She lives and loves freely and tries to respond to Terry's demand

for a spiritual relationship. Terry, too cerebral and impatient,
becomes increasingly individualistic and makes friendship impossible. After several attempts at reconciliation, Marie departs
for California where she "feels the ecstacy of the aesthetic
fanatic." The experiment has proved a success, for Marie has derived from their relationship "an assured sense of her own
essential dignity and worth." Terry, on the other hand, has
succumbed to bitterness and isolation.

> The story is a metaphor. As Hapgood reveals:
> Marie's relative good sense, her vitality
> and love of life, finally rebelled against
> an idealism so exquisite that it became
> cruelty and almost madness. The world can-
> not, in the end, endure the idealist, though
> it has great need of him. The world can en-
> dure a certain amount of irritation, a cer-
> tain amount of fundamental revolt, but when
> that revolt reaches the point of absolute
> rejection, the world rebels, the worm turns.
> Marie represents the world and the worm.
> (p. 297)

258 HIRSCH, CHARLOTTE TELLER. The Cage. New York: D. Appleton &
Co., 1907, 340 pp. Reprint. New York: AMS Press, 1977, 340
pp.

Charlotte Teller Hirsch (1876-19?) interwove two themes:
woman's awakening and the class struggle. Inspired by the Haymarket tragedy, she set her story in Chicago at the close of the
nineteenth century. Her female protagonist, Frederica Hartwell,
lives with her father, a minister, in the slums of the city's
South Side. Frederica meets and falls in love with Eugene Harden,
an Austrian-born labor agitator who challenges the philanthropic
sentiments of Reverend Hartwell and pushes his beloved in the
direction of class-conscious socialism.

The feminist theme revolves around "the cage" that the law
places around love by prescribing marriage as the only legitimate
form of expression, as well as Frederica's intellectual maturation. Although Eugene brings political enlightenment to his wife,
he maintains a very Old-World opinion of woman's role. It is
Frederica who becomes the instructor in the realm of gender relations, for in rejecting the rigid standards of victorian morality
she emerges as the most reflective character in the novel, out-
shining not only her father and his Christian platitudes, but
even Eugene and his formalistic abstractions.

A free-thought, quasi-free-love tract, The Cage nevertheless sets anarchism against socialism as its main political message. The preferred strategy for the emancipation of labor is
explained through the character of Eugene Harden who at first is
suspected as being a perpetrator of the propaganda of the deed,
but emerges after a series of violent and tragic mishaps as the
advocate of socialism.

116

259 HUNT, GERTRUDE BRESLAU. <u>An Easy Wheel, and Other Stories of</u>
     <u>Real Life</u>. Norwood Park, Ill.: The Author, n.d., 48 pp.
        A leading writer for the Socialist party, Gertrude Breslau
Hunt frequently addressed questions of women's role and status.
In this volume of journalistic fiction about working class and
rural life, she portrays the miseries, lost opportunities, and
poverty of common folk. Several stories feature women characters.

260 KAUFFMAN, REGINALD WRIGHT. <u>House of Bondage</u>. New York:
     Grosset & Dunlap, 1910, 480 pp. Reprint. Upper Saddle River,
     N.J.: Gregg Press, 1968, 479 pp.
        This novel is the premier Socialist tract on white slavery.
The plot traces the unhappy life of a working-class girl from
Pennsylvania, Mary Denbigh, who is ensnared by a procurer for a
New York brothel. To escape a violent home life, Mary accepts an
offer of marriage from a handsome, flashy suitor, takes a train
with him to the big city, and becomes a prisoner in a house of
prostitution run by Rose Légère. Drugged and raped, deprived of
her street clothes, Mary is forced to become "Violet," a fallen
woman.
        A sympathetic customer helps Mary escape, and some friendly
settlement workers hope to set her on a new path. She tries
several jobs but soon turns to the streets.
        Reginald Wright Kauffman (1877-1959) examines the plight
of distressed womanhood within a <u>system</u> of poor wages and economic
discrimination, corrupt politicians and businessmen, and ineffec-
tive reformers and shows how all well-meaning schemes to uplift
the fallen woman are bound to fail. Because the system of industrial capitalism is the source of social evil, only a revolution
will eradicate this heinous exploitation of women. The solution,
explained by a German Socialist who has befriended Mary, is
clear: "Do avay vith poverty. Reorganize de whole of de industrial system; gif effery man und voman a chance to vork; gif
effery man und voman effery penny dey earns." Only the overthrow
of capitalism will restore human dignity.
        Originally published in 1910, <u>House of Bondage</u> enjoyed a
large audience and favorable reviews. It still stands as a major
contribution to a genre of literature about the fallen woman.

261 MALKIEL, THERESA SERBER. <u>Diary of a Shirtwaist Striker</u>. New
     York: Co-operative Press, 1910, 96 pp.
        Subtitled "A Story of the Shirtwaist Makers' Strike in New
York," Malkiel's major publication is not a diary but a work of
fiction. She creates a native-born character who records her
development from a casual observer of working-class life, to
strike militant, and finally, to dedicated Socialist. The context is the so-called uprising of thirty thousand, the famous
strike of garment workers in New York's Lower East Side, 1909-
1910.
        First published serially in the <u>New York Call</u>, the <u>Diary</u>
is also a vehicle for Malkiel as political strategist. Actively

involved in strike support work, she could accurately describe
the poor conditions in the shop, the complacency of male trade
unionists, but also some of the crucial disagreements among women
themselves. Malkiel, who worked for the New York Women's Trade
Union League, grew increasingly bitter as the strike progressed
and as some middle-class "allies" moved to limit the public participation of Socialists. To counter their actions, Malkiel led a
vigorous campaign within the Socialist party to proscribe cooperation with mainstream women activists. Although Diary of a Shirtwaist Striker focuses on the growing solidarity and class-con-
sciousness among the strikers, it also issues a strong attack on
the "class enemies" within the ranks of the woman's movement.

262 MARCY, MARY. A Free Union: A One-Act Drama of "Free Love."
     Chicago: Charles H. Kerr, 1921, 64 pp.
          Dedicated to the author's sister, Inez Stephens, the play-
let features "free woman" Sonia Barowski, a self-indulgent lover
who wishes freedom but foresakes responsibility. For the past
year she has been living with a common-law husband, a decent,
caring man, while forming liaisons on the side. One especially
intrepid bohemian boyfriend even asks to borrow money and clothes
from her husband as Sonia recites a seemingly endless monologue
about the prerogatives she enjoys as a free woman. Finally, her
husband flees for the prospect of a conventional marriage and
satisfying relationship with a compassionate woman. Thus Sonia
pays the price for misunderstanding the principles of free love.

263 O'HARE, FRANK P. and KATE RICHARDS. World Peace; a Spectacle
     Drama in Three Acts. St. Louis: National Rip-Saw Publishing
     Co., 1915, 61 pp.
          This play takes the form of a dialogue among the working
people and the rulers of nations on the question of war. The
rulers reveal their weak, selfish, and spurious reasons for
waging war, the workers their opposition. The women, however,
organize to resolve the impending conflict. They propose the
establishment of a world federation for peace and human brotherhood. As the play closes, a woman from each nation takes a strip
of red from her country's flag and carries it forward, where the
strips are fastened into a great crimson banner.

264 RIDGE, LOLA. The Ghetto, and Other Poems. New York: B.W.
     Huebsch, 1918, 101 pp.
          Born in Dublin, Ireland, Lola Ridge (1873-1941) came to
the United States via New Zealand and Australia, where she spent
her childhood. In 1908 she settled in Greenwich Village and became an important figure in the "little magazine" movement of
Left cultural circles. She contributed frequently to Mother
Earth.
          This volume contains her early poems, written in the
imagist tradition. "The Ghetto," first published in the New Republic in 1918, established Ridge as a noteworthy poet. The poem

is a tribute to the vitality of life among the Jewish working
class of New York's Lower East Side.

265 SCUDDER, VIDA D. A Listener in Babel; Being a Series of Imag-
     inary Conversations Held at the Close of the Last Century and
     Reported by Vida D. Scudder. Boston: Houghton Mifflin Co.,
     1903, 322 pp.
          A semiautobiographical novel, A Listener in Babel traces
     the intellectual growth of a wealthy, sensitive woman who gives
     up a promising art career and marriage to do practical work in
     Langley House, a Boston social settlement. There Hilda Lathrop
     becomes "a listener in Babel" and hears the discourses of a
     variety of types: fellow residents, a young lawyer, a labor
     organizer, a Russian anarchist, a charity worker, a religious
     leader, a businessman, a philanthropist, a group of working women,
     and an Anglican priest. Each presents a unique solution to the
     contemporary problems of poverty and social unrest. At the
     novel's close, Scudder, writing in the persona of Hilda Lathrop,
     presents her own choice, a synthesis of ideals drawn from Ruskin
     and Tolstoy, the application of art to the modern production
     process in the creation of a new esthetic and economic justice.

266 SINCLAIR, MARY CRAIG. Sonnets by M.C.S. Pasadena, Calif.:
     Upton Sinclair, [192?], 39 pp.
          Between 1914 and 1919 Sinclair published sonnets in various
     newspapers and magazines. Several years later, her husband, the
     muckraking novelist Upton Sinclair, collected the best in this
     small volume. The poet focused thematically on three areas: the
     sexual double standard that restricts women's freedom; the trag-
     edies of World War I; and the possibilities of a social order
     based on cooperation and love.

267 STOKES, ROSE PASTOR. The Woman Who Wouldn't. New York: G.P.
     Putnam's Sons, 1916, 183 pp. Microfilm. History of Women.
     Reel 924, no. 7766.
          This play in four acts is set in a working-class home in a
     small mining village in Pennsylvania. The story focuses on Mary
     Lacey, a hard-working daughter who supports the family while her
     father is on strike. Her sacrifice is great, for Mary and her
     fiancé cannot marry because her family depends on the meagre
     wages she earns making artificial flowers. Mary finds that she
     is pregnant and discovers that Joe, who is tired of waiting, has
     taken up with another woman. Mr. Lacey, however, insists that
     Joe marry his daughter, but Mary refuses and is driven from her
     home. Years later, the heroine returns and finds her father
     living alone and her former fiancé a widower. Meanwhile, she has
     become a famous labor leader known as Mother Mary, and is re-
     turning to take part in a strike. She is accompanied by her
     young daughter, Joey. Mary and her father eventually reconcile
     but on her terms, for she has remained firm in her stand that her
     personal freedom and integrity will not yield to patriarchal

customs. Mary stars as the truly moral person, and her devotion
to her child and to the working class underscores the nobility of
her character.

The published version of The Woman Who Wouldn't was reviewed widely in 1916. Most critics noted its lack of originality
but conceded that it was a strong, realistic play with a powerful
message about the double standard of morality. The prestige of
its author undoubtedly inspired such favorable assessments. Rose
Pastor Stokes (1879-1933) had recently charmed the public with
her Cinderella role in the media. A Russian immigrant and former
cigar worker, she had married the wealthy settlement worker James
G. Phelps Stokes. In 1906 the newsworthy couple joined the
Socialist party, and over the next decade Rose Pastor Stokes
achieved fame as a dedicated labor and Socialist agitator. She
wrote The Woman Who Wouldn't while recuperating from illness
exacerbated by her exhausting labors in a series of strikes in
1913.

268   TAGGARD, GENEVIEVE, ed. May Days; an anthology of verse from
      Masses-Liberator. New York: Boni & Liveright, 1925, 306 pp.
      This anthology is the most representative collection of
poetry from the flowering of the cultural Left before World War I.
It includes many prominent writers like Edna St. Vincent Millay,
Max Eastman, Floyd Dell, and Louise Bogan, as well as personages
less remembered for their poetry such as Rose Pastor Stokes,
Babette Deutsch, Miriam Allen de Ford, and Marya Zaturensky.
Taggard writes a brief but very perceptive introduction to "the
most significant group that managed to dominate, for a time, an
entire generation."

269   WALLING, ANNA STRUNSKY. Violette of Père Lachaise. New York:
      Frederick A. Stokes Co., 1915, 198 pp.
      Ostensibly a novel, Violette is a tract for socialism
heavily influenced by the precepts of nihilism and the writings
of Nietzsche. The plot centers on the maturation of the orphan,
Violette, who lives with her loving, aged grandfather on the
street facing the cemetary, Père Lachaise. The cemetary holds a
special fascination for this sensitive, precocious child.
Violette spends many days and evenings within its walls and there
acquires an all-consuming love for life. As she approaches young
womanhood, Violette learns of the many dimensions of love; and it
is love that teaches Violette the meaning of death. Whereas her
first awakening in the cemetary was personal, the second, at the
failure of first love, is social. Violette emerges from her
youthful disappointment a full person. She dedicates herself to
the revolutionary struggle, not as an act of self-abnegation or
martyrdom but as "the full flowering of her whole personality."
In a short essay on Nietzsche published in the New Review
(August 1915), Walling (1878-1964) explicated the relationship
between the philosopher's central idea and socialism. "It is
this will to power which Socialism recognizes and upon which it

places a wholly different interpretation," she wrote. "It is the
will to power as a living principle of life that is steadily
directing itself at the abolition of all oppressive power, at the
destruction of castes and the resurrection and the elevation of
Superman which dwells in every man." Violette of Père Lachaise,
a lyrical novel in the modern mode, is based on this premise.

1920-1964

In 1919, following the Russian Revolution, the American Left
entered a new era marked by the formation of the Communist International. The 1920s, however, was a period of slow reorganization.
The Socialist party lost the bulk of its membership and never regained
its political strength. Driven underground by the Red scare of 1919,
Communists gathered members cautiously and slowly. During the 1930s,
amid the Great Depression, the Communist Party USA, emerged as a significant political and cultural force in American society, uniting
diverse populations of cadre and fellow-travelers. The initial success of the Soviet Union, the threat of fascism abroad, and a burgeoning labor movement drew many men and women into the growing circles
of the Old Left.

With the decline of organized feminism after the passage of the
woman suffrage amendment in 1919, the Woman Question receded from
public view. Consequently, women in the Old Left lacked the support
that the women's movement had given to their radical counterparts between 1871 and 1919. Indeed, feminism became associated with middle-
class aspirations and "bourgeois individualism," termed an inappro-
priate ideology for proletarian revolutionaries. Despite this dramatic change in policy, many women, especially from first- and second-
generation immigrant and working-class backgrounds, found an organizational home in the Communist party and created their own sustaining
networks in neighborhood and cultural clubs.

The sources in this section underscore the dearth of secondary
literature on the history of women in the Old Left. A full, scholarly
examination has not yet been published.

270 COWL, MARGARET. "Women's Struggle for Equality." Political
     Affairs 53 (May 1974):40-44.
          Margaret Cowl was a member of the Communist party's first
     National Women's Commission in 1922. Published posthumously, her
     essay records the party's contributions to various struggles for

sex equality. Cowl discusses the Communists' opposition to the
Equal Rights Amendment and participation in the Women's Charter
group launched in 1936. She emphasizes the party's influence
among middle- as well as working-class women, especially its mass
work among housewives during the Depression. Writing in response
to the rise of the women's liberation movement, Cowl quotes Lenin
and faithfully calls upon the CPUSA to strengthen its commitment
to women's rights.

271   GORNICK, VIVIAN. The Romance of American Communism. New York:
      Basic Books, 1977, 265 pp.
          Disappointed by the sterile histories of American commu-
      nism, unconvinced by the bitter diatribes characteristic of ex-
      Communist reminiscences, Gornick decided to tap the wellspring of
      dedication that held so many activists for decades. She traveled
      across the country and interviewed dozens of former Communists
      about their experiences in the party, mostly in the 1940s and
      1950s. Although she met a wide variety of responses, she un-
      covered a universal thread in their lives: "What I remember most
      deeply about the Communists is their passion. It was passion
      that converted them, passion that led them, passion that lifted
      them up and twisted them down. Each and every one of them ex-
      perienced a kind of inner radiance: some intensity of illumina-
      tion that tore at the soul."
          Gornick includes a large selection of interviews with
      women. Many told how their marriages were shaped, for better or
      worse, by joint party membership with their husbands. Gornick
      lends, sometimes quite subtly, a feminist interpretation to their
      stories. As one reviewer noted, the reader might do well to
      realize that Gornick's descriptions represent foremost her per-
      ceptions, not facts. Unfortunately, she uses pseudonyms through-
      out.
          The greatest insight is contained in the author's personal
      statement on her own political past. Born in 1935 to a New York
      Jewish family, Gornick grew up with politics the daily substance
      of dinner-time conversation. At age fifteen she had been a member
      of the Labor Youth League, but broke in 1956 following the
      Khrushchev report. Twenty years later, she longed to understand
      the milieu of her childhood and undertook the research for this
      book. She hoped to understand, moreover, the "passion" of her
      own life--feminism. She concludes by drawing a parallel between
      the drift toward rigidity and dogmatism that ruined many Commu-
      nists as their movement passed its prime, and what she perceives
      as a similar tendency in the women's movement.

272   KLEHR, HARVEY. Communist Cadre: The Social Background of the
      American Communist Party Elite. Stanford, Calif.: Hoover
      Institute Press, 1978, 141 pp.
          Klehr's study provides a biographical profile of the Com-
      munist party leadership, the members of the Central Committee
      from 1921 to 1961. A chapter on female leadership concludes that

although women's role was not as central as the Communist party
contends, their representation on the Central Committee "probably
reflected fairly accurately the percentage of women in the entire
party." Klehr does admit that women advanced from the ranks more
slowly than men did, and held leadership positions only for brief
periods. As in most political parties, men secured themselves in
the most prestigious and influential offices.

273 PRATT, WILLIAM C. "Women and American Socialism: The Reading
     Experience." Pennsylvania Magazine of History and Biography
     99 (January 1975):72-91.
          Pratt traces the rise in Socialist women's activity fol-
     lowing the Socialist victory in the Reading municipal elections
     of 1927. The Women's Socialist League raised money and organized
     recreational events for the party membership, while a sister or-
     ganization, the Berks County Women's Political Committee, sought
     to bring women into political campaigns and to encourage working-
     class women to use their voting rights. Although women represented
     a sizable portion of party membership during the period 1927-1936,
     they played primarily an auxiliary role. Several exceptions were
     Lilith Martin Wilson, Hazelette Hoopes, Annie Pike Zechman, Bertha
     Tyson Weidner, and Gertrude Hiller--all successful candidates for
     public office. Pratt follows their accomplishments until 1936,
     when the local Socialist party fell into a fatal factional squab-
     ble. He concludes that the Reading Socialist experience was
     probably typical of other local movements. "Social Democracy in
     the United States and elsewhere," Pratt writes, "has not had an
     exceptional record on women."

274 SHAFFER, ROBERT. "Women and the Communist Party, USA, 1930-
     1940." Socialist Review 45 (May-June 1979):73-118.
          In this essay Shaffer assesses the role of the Communist
     party in organizing women and in addressing their issues during
     the crucial decade of the 1930s, when the CPUSA enjoyed its
     greatest level of influence in American society. While not deny-
     ing its limitations, Shaffer portrays the Communist party as an
     important arena for the struggle for women's emancipation, es-
     pecially because it drew in relatively large numbers of working-
     class women. Its major shortcomings were due, the author contends,
     to the absence of an organized feminist movement at large that
     would have forced Communists to take up women's cause more vocif-
     erously.
          Shaffer divides his study into two periods and relates
     each to women's status within the Communist party. He charac-
     terizes the "Third Period" (1929-1935) as sectarian in regard to
     women's issues. The party was then relatively small in member-
     ship, and its unified leadership and rigid political program
     placed a low priority on the woman question; instead, Communists
     aimed to organize primarily among industrial workers, the unem-
     ployed, and blacks. Where women fit those categorical descrip-
     tions, they could claim a role, not as women, however, but as

"workers." This attitude was best illustrated in the party's
major book on women, Grace Hutchins's Women Who Work, published
in 1934. Lacking an explicit strategy to appeal to women, the
party attracted only about 3,000 during this period; women represented sixteen percent of its membership. Shaffer measures the
change in policy during the "Popular Front" (1935-1939) by the
rapid rise in women's membership to upwards of forty percent
during wartime. During this period, the Communist party conducted
"mass work" among women, softened its line on "bourgeois feminism,"
and created alliances with mainstream women's groups. It also
took more seriously women's position within the home, as exempli-
fied by Mary Inman's controversial In Woman's Defense, published
in 1939, which emphasized the economic and psychological contributions of working-class housewives. The party's magazines Working
Woman and Woman Today also showed more openness on feminist
issues, while the party leadership enlarged its program to incorporate special demands designed to improve women's status. It
was during this era that International Woman's Day reemerged as
an important proletarian holiday.

Shaffer's essay is well-researched, adequately footnoted,
and conceptually well-organized. His conclusions are equally
judicious. Although he judges the "Popular Front" successful in
recruiting women and in addressing issues of women's emancipation,
he also notes that the glorification of the working-class housewife and the adoption of a conservative view toward sexuality and
the family weakened the overall effectiveness of the Communist
party's political program. In his final statement Shaffer emphasizes this ambiguous legacy by referring to the conflicting
memories of women who concluded that their work in the Communist
party was meaningless and of those who believed they could not
have lived without the movement. Obviously, no unilateral assessment is possible, and Shaffer provides interesting insights into
the paradoxical history of women and the Left.

AUTOBIOGRAPHIES AND BIOGRAPHIES

The books and essays below attest to the diversity within the Old
Left. Women of various backgrounds and ideological leanings left
their marks on the period. Leading dancers, poets, novelists, and
dramatists contributed artistically to the cause, while scores of
rank-and-file activists served the labor movement, anti-Fascist and
civil-rights organizations, and community and fraternal associations.
Some, like Agnes Smedley and Anna Louise Strong, achieved international prominence, bridging the domestic and foreign Communist movements.

Autobiographies and memoirs fill most of this section. Written
at various points in the history of the Old Left, they reflect the
ever-changing political currents of the midtwentieth century. Those
writers before 1940 tend to emphasize the continuous history of

American radicalism; they trace their roots if not to the American
Revolution than to the great abolitionist crusade of the nineteenth
century and to the Socialist and Communist movements of their own
experience. Ella Reeve Bloor, Mother Bloor of American communism,
sets the standard in this genre. With the advent of the Cold War in
the late 1940s, several leading activists succumbed to the pressure
and recorded their life stories in an effort to recant publicly their
former political faith. Elizabeth Bentley and Bella Dodd, in different ways, give witness to the times. Only in the 1960s, with the
revival of the Left in the civil-rights and student movements and
antiwar campaigns, did veterans feel free to write without shame or
fear about their Communist activities. Ella Winter, Peggy Dennis,
Jessica Mitford, and Vera Buch Weisbord thus round out perspectives
on the period, writing more personally than their predecessors and
more self-consciously about their role as women in the Old Left.

Andres, Chaya Rochel (1899-   )

275 ANDRES, CHAYA ROCHEL. Years Have Sped By: My Life Story.
Edited by Jeannette Cohen. Dallas: The Author, 1981, 194 pp.
A rare if elliptical autobiography, Years Have Sped By reflects the dedication of the immigrant generation for whom the
preservation and enrichment of Yiddish has become a mission. The
author, a wife and mother in Dallas, Texas, since the early 1920s
took direct part in political activities only through her husband's affiliation with the Arbeter Ring (Workman's Circle), a
Socialist fraternal order. She was drawn to the Communist literary circuit, the most lively sector of Yiddish culture between
1920 and 1970. She contributed poetry to left-wing journals in
Canada and the United States, corresponded with leading radical
Yiddish poets, and generally conducted her intellectual life by
mail. More recently, she took part in Redet mit mir Yiddish
(Speak Yiddish with Me) circles in Dallas, an effort by oldtimers to hold onto the language virtually destroyed by the
Holocaust.
Andres is one of perhaps a hundred Yiddish women writers
in the United States, radical because of their moral commitment
and their milieu, publishing their books at their own expense or
through fund-raising committees, and extremely active in Yiddish
cultural life of clubs, choruses, and reading circles. Few have
risen to prominence, yet they have played an important part in
shaping the radical Jewish heritage and women's place within it.

Bentley, Elizabeth (1908-1963)

276 BENTLEY, ELIZABETH. Out of Bondage: The Story of Elizabeth
Bentley. New York: Devin-Adair Co., 1951, 311 pp.
In the decade following World War II, many radical activists fell victim to the pressures of the Cold War and recanted
their youthful political beliefs. The autobiography-as-confession

emerged as a popular literary form.

Elizabeth Bentley was at the forefront of this movement. She had joined the Communist party in 1935 when she was a graduate student at Columbia University, and became a spy for the Federal Bureau of Investigation ten years later. At the close of the war she made yet another career for herself in selling her confessions to the press. In 1949 her testimony aided in the conviction of eleven Communist party leaders, including the Rosenbergs, on conspiracy charges.

First serialized in McCall's Magazine, her story aims to "let the decent people of the world know what a monstrous thing Communism is." Contemporary reviewers, however, judged her tales "unbelievable" and her presentation "childish."

Berger, Meta Schlichting (1873-1944)

277 BERGER, META. I Saw Russia; Socialism in the Making. New York: American Friends of the Soviet Union, [1935], 23 pp.

Meta Schlichting Berger, widow of the architect of "constructive socialism," Victor Berger, was an important activist in her own right. For many years she served as an elected Socialist member of the Milwaukee school board. Although she did not support the party's women's committees, she worked assiduously for woman suffrage. She was a prominent member of the National American Woman Suffrage Association and later, of the Congressional Union.

Representing the Wisconsin Federation of Teachers, Berger toured the Soviet Union in 1935. In this pamphlet she records her impressions, noting especially employment conditions and the status of women and children.

Blatch, Harriot Stanton (1856-1940)

278 BLATCH, HARRIOT STANTON, and ALMA LUTZ. Challenging Years; The Memoirs of Harriot Stanton Blatch. New York: G.P. Putnam's Sons, 1940, 347 pp. Reprint. Westport, Conn.: Hyperion Press, 1976, 347 pp.

Daughter of Elizabeth Cady Stanton and prominent suffragist in her own right, Blatch first aligned herself with the Socialist movement in England. In the 1880s and 1890s Blatch served on the executive committee of the Fabian Society and worked closely with Sidney and Beatrice Webb and George Bernard Shaw. In 1902 she returned to the United States and its woman suffrage movement. For the next decade, she helped revitalize the campaign by infusing it with the militant tactics she had learned abroad. After the passage of the Nineteenth Amendment, Blatch renewed her ties with the Socialist movement and became an active member of the party. Proud to gain such a prominent recruit, the party issued Blatch's statement, "Why I Joined the Socialist Party," as a four-page leaflet. In the 1920s, Blatch ran for several offices on the party ticket. Like Alice Stone Blackwell (1857-1950), the

Socialist daughter of Lucy Stone, Blatch continued her radical
activities into the 1920s. Like Blackwell, she campaigned against
the Red scare and for amnesty for political prisoners, supported
the Non-Partisan League, and endorsed the 1924 Robert M.
LaFollette presidential campaign.

Described by a reviewer as a "solid, earnest, but good-
humored history of the women's-rights movement," Blatch's memoirs
emphasize her woman suffrage activities in England and the United
States. They touch only lightly on her sojourn with the American
Socialist movement.

Bloor, Ella Reeve (1862-1951)

279 BLOOR, ELLA REEVE. We Are Many; An Autobiography. New York:
International Publishers, 1940, 319 pp.

Ella Reeve Bloor, better known to her admirers as Mother
Bloor, relates her half-century odyssey with the American Left.
Born on Staten Island, New York, Bloor enjoyed a middle-class
Protestant childhood. She later attended a young ladies' seminary
and gradually found her way into activist circles. An association with Quakers, she recalled, stimulated her interest in the
Woman Question. She became an ardent suffragist and, as did so
many Socialist women of similar background, gained her primary
education as an organizer within the Woman's Christian Temperance
Union. Bloor credits Frances Willard for having introduced the
neophyte activist to the Knights of Labor. Well rooted in the
contemporary women's movement, Bloor carried her commitments into
the heart of the Socialist movement. She became a labor agitator
for the Socialist Labor party during the 1890s and switched allegiance to the Socialist Party of America shortly after its formation in 1901. Bloor writes vividly of her adventures during the
first two decades of the twentieth century. She served as a
relentless organizer throughout the period, working for the
miners and for the garment unions, loyally following her beloved
Eugene V. Debs, and still finding time to campaign for woman
suffrage. Her chapters on the impact of World War on the Socialist movement, and on the political repression that followed,
offer significant insights into her personal history.

The remainder of the autobiography, about half, is devoted
to Bloor's years with the Communist movement, which she joined
shortly after the Russian Revolution. Bloor was no less active
for the cause than during her prime. At age sixty-three, in 1925,
she hitch-hiked across the country on a party mission, delivering
bundles of its new organ, the Daily Worker. She recalls the
1920s in detail, relating at length her organizing experiences
in the new industrial unions, in textiles and mining, which
helped lead to the formation of the CIO. Labor events and the
Sacco-Vanzetti case fill out this section of the book.

Writing before the era of the self-centered, confession-
style memoir, Bloor devotes considerable space to her friends and
associates. Although she traces her own evolution as a radical

activist, she allots comparatively little space to her personal
life, such as her marriages or children. Instead, her devotion
to the cause stands foremost in the narrative. She concludes:
"It has been a privilege and joy to carry the torch of socialism,
and that torch must be kept bright in the days that are to come."
Continuity is further established by a short introduction by sister Communist Elizabeth Gurley Flynn.

280   MOTHER BLOOR CELEBRATION COMMITTEE. Mother Bloor's 75th Anni-
      versary Souvenir Book. Staten Island, N.Y.: The Committee,
      1937, 36 pp.
          Published to honor Ella Reeve Bloor, this pamphlet records
      her radical activities over the decades and collects tributes
      from friends and comrades.

Braden, Anne (1924-)

281   BRADEN, ANNE. The Wall Between. New York: Monthly Review,
      1958, 306 pp.
          Anne Braden has been one of the outstanding white Southern
      radicals of the century. Along with Joyce Williams, she is one
      of the few women to emerge as a national figure. As she relates
      here, she descended from early Kentucky settlers and grew up in
      Alabama and in Mississippi. Appalled by racism at an early age,
      brought to political consciousness by the war against fascism,
      Anne Gambrell embarked on a career in journalism so that she
      might speak publicly against racial segregation. She married
      Carl Braden, a radical journalist and son of an ardent Socialist,
      and with him campaigned for the Progressive party in the late
      1940s and for its successor organizations in Louisville. While
      working for a Left-oriented union, the Farm Equipment Workers,
      she came to believe that human relations rather than ideology
      would remove the onus of racism from American society. This
      principle has guided her political activities since the 1950s.
          The Wall Between depicts the Bradens's involvement in an
      especially tense case for racial desegregation. The Bradens
      bought a house in an all-white district and resold it to a black
      family. After rounds of terrorism directed at both parties, the
      Bradens were charged with sedition, for allegedly plotting to in-
      cite violence by placing a black family in the midst of a settled
      white neighborhood. The Bradens stepped into the national spot-
      light for their role in this early fight against racial desegre-
      gation in the South.
          Anne Braden later became a leader in the Southern Confer-
      ence Educational Fund, which published Southern Patriot. Since
      her husband's death in the 1970s, she has been especially active
      defending civil liberties.

Budenz, Margaret Rodgers (1908-)

282   BUDENZ, MARGARET R. Streets. Huntington, Ind.: Our Sunday

Visitor, 1979, 494 pp.

In writing her memoirs, Margaret Budenz chose to focus on her marriage to mercurial Louis Budenz, who rose from Catholic activism in the 1920s to Communist leadership in the 1940s, and after reconverting to Catholicism, became a favorite friendly witness before HUAC hearings on "Communist subversion." She also traces her own political development.

Margaret Deaumer Rodgers grew up in working-class Pittsburgh and attended the local university on a scholarship. She became an idealistic young YWCA reformer and, after graduation, took up social work and joined A.J. Muste's Committee for Progressive Labor Action. There, in the 1930s, she met a fellow-Socialist, Louis Budenz.

Once settled with Louis, Margaret shared his political dedication. By the late 1930s she had followed her mate into the Communist party, but she preferred to serve as his clerical aide-de-camp while overseeing their growing family. When he recanted his marxist calling, she followed.

Budenz shows little understanding of her odyssey from social worker and Communist to Catholic and Republican. But this shortcoming is also a virtue, for she recaptures her Left years in anecdotal fashion and without bitterness. What stands out in her narrative is her isolation from the party mainstream. Lacking ethnic or cultural ties to the centers of the Communist movement, Budenz seemed always on the periphery. Thus her story provides insight into the experiences of an essentially moral reformer in an era when marxist ideology held unquestioned formal sway.

Damon, Anna (?-1944)

283 INTERNATIONAL LABOR DEFENSE. Equal Justice and Democracy in the Service of Victory; Continuing the Work of Anna Damon. New York: International Labor Defense, 1944, 31 pp.

A veteran trade unionist, editor of Working Woman during the 1930s, and Communist for twenty-five years, Anna Damon served also as secretary of the International Labor Defense. She worked energetically for the two major campaigns of the 1930s, the struggle to free the Scottsboro boys and Angelo Herndon.

Her death in 1944 was marked by the publication of this pamphlet, a collection of short essays on civil rights and tributes from her many friends and colleagues.

Day, Dorothy (1877-1980)

284 DAY, DOROTHY. The Long Loneliness. New York: Harper, 1952, 288 pp. Reprint. New York: Curtis Books, 1972, 320 pp.

Dorothy Day presided over the Catholic Worker movement from 1933 until her death. In her autobiography she traces her political evolution, assigning to Roman Catholicism, which she adoped in 1932, the role of guiding spirit.

Born in Brooklyn, one of five children, Day found little

in her childhood to prepare for either social activisim or religious dedication; she describes herself during these years as agnostic at best. Yet during her teens she read Kropotkin and enjoyed her first taste of anarchist ideas. When she attended the University of Illinois, she soon became involved in a small circle of radicals and took out membership in the Urbana, Illinois, chapter of the Socialist party.

In 1916 Day moved to New York City and bloomed. She found a job as a reporter for the Socialist daily, the Call, and served for six months on the staff of the Masses. She lived in Greenwich Village, became an outspoken anarchist and free-lover, and consorted with the avant-garde. Among her acquaintances were Leon Trotsky, Hippolyte Havel, John Reed, Floyd Dell, and Max Eastman. A friendship with Mike Gold lasted until his death in 1967. She also became a seasoned activist: a militant woman suffrage protest in Washington, D.C. resulted in her first imprisonment for civil disobedience.

As the radical climate shifted in the 1920s, Day felt increasingly at odds with the times. She netted a small profit from the screen rights to The Eleventh Virgin to buy a cottage on Staten Island, where she settled with her common-law husband, Forster Betterman and their child, Tamar, born in 1927. She began to consider Catholicism as an answer to her spiritual needs. A decision to baptize her daughter in the Catholic church precipitated a break in her relationship with Betterman, and by 1932, after five years of self-searching, she was a prime candidate for conversion.

Day does not look back with bitterness at her past radical involvements, but interprets them as steps on a path toward her final destination in the Catholic fold and under the tutelage of her beloved Peter Maurin, an itinerant philosopher. Maurin provided her with religious inspiration and channeled her social activism into a vocation. Together in 1933 they founded the Catholic Worker movement.

At this point her autobiography recounts the lives of both Day and Maurin, their programs to assist the unemployed and to promote the burgeoning labor movement of the 1930s and 1940s, and to adher to Maurin's dictum, "personalism and communitarianism." Her story ends with Maurin's death in 1949. In a postscript she adds: "We have all known the long loneliness and we have learned that the only solution is love and that love comes with community."

Dennis, Peggy (1909-   )

285   DENNIS, PEGGY.   The Autobiography of an American Communist: A Personal View of a Political Life 1925-1975.   Westport, Conn.: Lawrence Hill & Co., 1977, 302 pp.

Peggy Dennis, née Regina Karasick, joined the Communist party in 1925 when she was sixteen. In her autobiography, Dennis chronicles her years as a prime activist and wife of a party leader, until 1976 when she issued a formal resignation.

Dennis provides a fascinating account of her remarkable political life. She lovingly describes her childhood among the Jewish revolutionary emigrés resettled in Los Angeles. But the most engrossing sections of her book concern her exploits as a courier for the Comintern: life in Moscow during the 1930s; subrosa and dangerous journeys across Europe and to Shanghai and other Asian ports. Reassigned to the United States in 1935, Dennis and her husband helped build the CIO unions and Communist party in Wisconsin. In 1937 Dennis hoped to join the antifascist war in Spain but instead found herself once more in Moscow. In 1938 she relocated in New York City, where she lived with her husband, now a top party leader, until his death in 1960.

There is much sorrow and bitterness in this story, for the glory of political adventure is constantly undercut by the authoritarian control of the Comintern and by the insensitivity of Dennis's husband. For example, obedience to the dictates of the party leadership prevented her from rearing her first-born child. Dennis poignantly describes her feelings when the Comintern ordered her to leave her son, born in Moscow during the 1930s, in the Soviet Union. She was told a Russian-speaking child in a Wisconsin community might raise unwanted questions about his parents' political identities and recent histories. Although Dennis describes the joy of living with her son in Moscow briefly in the late 1930s and meeting openly with him in the United States in the 1950s, the fact of his Russian upbringing looms heavily over the narrative of her personal life. Similarly, when in the late 1930s Dennis hoped to find comfort in another child, her husband insisted upon an abortion. Dennis suggests throughout the book that her husband honored the party line over his wife's feelings, and failed, moreover, to recognize her sizable political achievements.

The focal point of Dennis's autobiography is a stoicism of personal survival. Writing from the perspective of the mid-1970s, she helps another generation of radical women understand the situation of women in the Old Left, particularly the overwhelming personal isolation caused by the absence of a women's movement. As Dennis admits, the Communist party made few provisions for a woman who hoped to be both a wife and an activist.

286   ____. "Memories from the 'Twenties." Cultural Correspondence 6, 7 (Spring 1978):84-86.

Dennis recalls her childhood in the Los Angeles Left. Before the age of six she engaged in Yiddish recitations and daily readings of the Freiheit, the major Socialist newspaper in Yiddish. Slowly she "assimilated" into the English-language sector. She grew up in the radical movement, attending cultural events and joining its youth organizations, the Young Pioneers and, at age sixteen, the Young Communist League. Her first assignment was to lead the children's organizations; she taught music from the Little Red Songbook and arranged original theatrical productions.

"Not until I was specifically asked the question a few weeks ago did I realize that yes, radical culture in its broadest sense had been a major influence in my first exposures as a child to the revolutionary movement," Dennis admits. Unsure what conclusions to draw, she leaves that task for future scholars, reminding them that the influences were indeed strong on her and her fellow youthful comrades.

287 _____. "A Response to Ellen Kay Trimberger's Essay, 'Women in the Old and New Left'." Feminist Studies 5 (Fall 1979):451-60.
        Dennis strongly disagrees with the conceptual approach in Ellen Kay Trimberger's essay, which appeared in the same issue of Feminist Studies (see entry 288). Dennis lambastes Trimberger for failing to offer a "solid analysis of the objective realities" in which culture and personal life are rooted.

288 TRIMBERGER, ELLEN KAY. "Women in the Old and New Left: The Evolution of a Politics of Personal Life." Feminist Studies 5 (Fall 1979):432-50.
        Trimberger compares Peggy Dennis's The Autobiography of an American Communist (1977) to Elinor Langer's autobiographical essay, "Notes for the Next Time, A Memoir of the 1960s." She notes a "distinct sensibility of women active in the Old Left," which she characterizes as a lack of political perspective on the dynamics of personal life and intimate relationships. Trimberger briefly contrasts the ideology and organizational structure of the Communist party and the New Left, and concludes that the latter fostered a psychological and cultural vision of revolution and thus paved the way for women's liberation. She also discusses the generational experiences of both Dennis and Langer. She traces Langer's unique sense of political subjectivity to the development of women's networks among middle-class families in the 1950s and an eventual critique of these institutions.

Dodd, Bella Visono (1904-1969)

289 DODD, BELLA. School of Darkness. New York: P.J. Kenedy & Sons, 1954, 264 pp. Reprint. New York: Devin-Adair, 1963, 264 pp.
        Expelled from the Communist party in 1949, Dodd became a practicing Catholic under the guidance of Monsignor Fulton J. Sheen. Although she has few kind words for Communists, she faithfully recounts her years when party membership directed her life. Despite the bitterness of disillusionment, Dodd's memoirs are full of rare insights into rank-and-file activity in New York City during the 1930s and 1940s.
        Born in southern Italy in 1904, Bella Visono came into the Communist party from pure idealism; neither her parents nor future husband, John Dodd, had shared her commitment. Rather, the radical milieu of Hunter College, where she attended undergraduate school and later served as a faculty member, pushed her

to the Left. In the early 1930s Dodd joined the party and became a leading functionary in the Teachers' Union. In the 1940s she was "the moving spirit in establishing the School for Democracy." She could not, however, survive the internal reorganization of the Communist party in the late 1940s; she could not accept the leadership of Foster or Dennis, and openly criticized the party's involvement in third-party ventures in 1948.

Duncan, Isadora (1878-1927)

290 DUNCAN, ISADORA. My Life. New York: Boni & Liveright, 1927, 359 pp. Reprint. New York: Liveright, 1972, 359 pp.

Isadora Duncan, one of the originators of modern dance, symbolized revolution in the early twentieth century. In both her personal life and art, she expressed the democratic impulse for freedom and broke scores of conventions. In 1921 she accepted an invitation to open a school for dance in Moscow and, inspired by the Russian Revolution, created the "International" and "March Slav," two dances that offended the sensibilities of many Americans when performed in this country.

Published shortly after her tragic death in 1927, her memoirs detail her successful European tours and her brief stints in the United States. Her freedom of expression and her desire to show the beauty of nature through the unrestrained movement of a disrobed body proved unsettling to many audiences, particularly those in the United States, and overwhelmingly exciting to others. She writes: "So here I was, a perfect pagan to all, fighting the Philistines." Only in New York, among the avant-garde, did she find the receptive audience she wanted in her native country.

Duncan concludes her autobiography by describing her final hope for acceptance. Summoned to the Soviet Union, she expresses her faith in its revolutionary fervor: "Now for the beautiful New World that had been created! Now for the World of the Comrades!"

One reviewer claimed that Duncan's memoirs constituted "a great document, revealing the truth of her life as she understood it, without reticence or apology or compromise." Indeed, Duncan wrote as candidly and poetically about her ambitions to transform dance as about her adventuresome love life, but the symbolic interpretations she gives to events are truly her own.

291 MACDOUGALL, ALLAN ROSS. Isadora: A Revolutionary in Art and Love. New York: Thomas Nelson, 1960, 296 pp.

A competent biographer, Macdougall served as Duncan's secretary in 1916-1917 and accompanied her on several important dance tours. He focuses primarily on Duncan's contributions to modern dance and her remarkable career, rather than her personal life or political leanings.

292 SEROFF, VICTOR. The Real Isadora. New York: Avon Books, 1971, 480 pp.

Seroff, a musician, was a close companion of Duncan during her later life. He writes this biography to correct the errors in earlier studies and to modify some of the sensational claims Duncan made in My Life. Most of all, he aims to show his appreciation for "the greatest performing artist that the United States ever produced."

Especially valuable for its firsthand description of Duncan's later career, Seroff's biography portrays her radical sympathies as an imaginative quirk. Although he treats in detail her famous post-Russian Revolution tour of the United States, when, accompanied by her Bolshevik lover, she proclaimed herself a "red" and advocated friendship between the two countries, Seroff cannot interpret Duncan's behavior. Instead, he delves into her personal relationships and expresses his own, sometimes petty opinions of her friends and co-workers.

Flanagan, Hallie (1890-1969)

293 FLANAGAN, HALLIE. Arena: The History of the Federal Theatre. New York: Benjamin Blom, 1940, 1965, 470 pp.

In 1935 Harry Hopkins of the Works Progress Administration asked Flanagan, who was then director of the Vassar Experimental Theatre, to develop a plan to help unemployed actors during the Great Depression. Under her tutelage, the Federal Theatre Project became perhaps the most innovative program in the history of performing arts in the United States. Between 1935 and 1939, the Federal Theatre arranged over 1,200 productions across the United States and used a wide variety of forms to reach large audiences unfamiliar with live theater. Its principal purpose was, in Flanagan's words, to create a theater "conscious of the implications of the changing social order." The House Committee on Un-American Activities also recognized its aim, and in the late 1930s criticized its work. Despite Flanagan's strong defense, Congress cut its funds and brought the successful venture to an end in 1939.

Flanagan returned to her teaching post at Vassar where she and a small staff produced this history. Because she was the major figure in the conception and organization of the Federal Theatre, this record of its life also serves as her memoirs of the Depression decade. A detailed production record of all performances constitutes a useful appendix.

Fisher, Minnie (1899-)

294 FISHER, MINNIE. Born One Year Before the 20th Century: Minnie Fisher/An Oral History. New York: Community Documentation Workshop of the Preservation Youth Project at St. Mark's Church-in-the-Bowery, 1976, 30 pp.

Minnie Fisher was a dedicated functionary in the Yiddishe Arbeter Universitet (Jewish Workers University), which was organized by Communists in the 1920s to offer workers a broad

136

education in the liberal arts and politics. This pamphlet records
her major activities in this institution as well as Fisher's rich
reminiscences of Jewish life, from the peasant village of her
childhood in White Russia to the exciting radical enclaves of
New York's Lower East Side, where she settled in 1914. Fisher
describes her first job in a garment factory and original contact
with Socialists in the trade. The most poignant sections of her
memoirs detail her extensive involvement in the Yiddish culture
movement of the 1910s and 1920s, an experience rarely told from
a woman's point of view.

Flynn, Elizabeth Gurley (1890-1964)

295 FLYNN, ELIZABETH GURLEY. The Alderson Story. New York:
International Publishers, 1963, 223 pp. Reprint. New York:
International Publishers, 1972.
Elizabeth Gurley Flynn was arrested in June 1957 by FBI
agents, charged with violating the Smith Act "for teaching and
advocating the violent overthrow of the government when and if
circumstances permit." Later convicted, Flynn was sentenced to
three years of hard labor.
The Alderson Story, first published in 1963, recounts
Flynn's incarceration in the Federal Penitentiary for Women in
West Virginia. Flynn describes her daily routine and provides
intimate details of her friendships and acquaintances. She also
includes her analysis of the situation, such as her impression
that many former Army women became prison officials after World
War II and were responsible for the newly instituted military
ways. Much like Kate Richards O'Hare's earlier prison memoirs,
this volume was produced to bring public attention to the in-
humane aspects of prison life and especially to initiate an
official investigation into conditions at the Alderson Penitentiary.

296 LAMONT, CORLISS, ed. The Trial of Elizabeth Gurley Flynn by
the American Civil Liberties Union. New York: Horizon Press,
1968, 222 pp.
This book reproduces the stenographic transcript of the
ACLU meeting that resulted in the expulsion of Elizabeth Gurley
Flynn from the board of directors on the grounds that she was a
member of the Communist party and on two minor charges. Lamont
charges that "feminist--new style" Dorothy Dunbar Bromley initi-
ated proceedings at the behest of Roger Baldwin, who believed a
woman would have a better chance in pressing charges against the
heroic crusader whose fight for civil liberties dated to her
arrest in 1910 in the IWW Spokane, Washington, free-speech campaign.

Gartz, Kate Crane (1865-1949)

297 GARTZ, KATE CRANE. The Parlor Provocateur; or from Salon to

Soap-box: The Letters of Kate Crane Gartz. Pasadena, Calif.:
Mary Craig Sinclair, 1923, 138 pp.
    Gartz delighted in describing herself as the first "parlor
Bolshevik." The daughter of Chicago industrialist and philan-
thropist Richard T. Crane, sister of Chicago Socialist and strike
activist Frances Crane Lillie, Gartz moved from reform to revolution with the currents of the Russian Revolution and World War I.
Her unique form of protest was letter-writing.
    This volume, which includes a laudatory introduction by
Mary Craig Sinclair, contains newspaper clippings of her noteworthy deeds, a documentary of her evolution to radical politics.
There are samples of her many letters to famous personages such
as President Warren G. Harding and Eugene Debs, and to various
newspaper editors. It also includes a few letters to her. Crane
expresses her sympathy with communism, her hatred of war, and her
general commitment to civil liberties.

298 _____. Letters of Protest. Pasadena, Calif.: Mary Craig
    Sinclair, [1925?], 151 pp.
        This second volume, edited by Mary Craig Sinclair, contains
    Gartz's letters from 1923 to 1925. She continues her discussions
    of bolshevism and speaks strongly in defense of civil liberties.

299 _____. More Letters. Pasadena, Calif.: Mary Craig Sinclair,
    [1926?], 151 pp.
        Aptly titled, this entry gathers Gartz's letters from 1925
    to 1926. Several concern Anna Louise Strong and offer a strong
    endorsement of her activities; others summarize the author's
    arguments in favor of pacificism.

300 _____. A Woman and War. Long Beach, Calif.: Mary Craig
    Sinclair, [1928?], 184 pp.
        In addition to Gartz's letters 1927-1928, this volume con-
    tains letters written by her son, Captain Crane Gartz, during
    World War I.

Graham, Martha (1893-   )

301 McDONAGH, DON. Martha Graham: A Biography. New York:
    Praeger Publishers, 1973, 341 pp.
        Martha Graham, one of the creators of American modern
    dance, intermittently supported radical causes in the 1930s and
·   early 1940s. She appeared at meetings against fascism and at
    benefits for the survivors of the Spanish Civil War. McDonagh
    minimizes her sympathies along this line and, oblivious to the
    impact of the Popular and United Fronts, insists that Graham was
    inspired only by "American" themes. "Graham's pre-eminence and
    moral fiber," he writes, "proved an immoderate attraction for
    causists in the 1930s. But where they wanted political commentary,
    she provided moral parables."

Hansberry, Lorraine (1930-1965)

302 HANSBERRY, LORRAINE. To Be Young, Gifted and Black: Lorraine
Hansberry in Her Own Words. Adapted by Robert Nemiroff. New
York: New American Library, 1969, 271 pp.
Hansberry, most notable of the younger generation of black
women artists to emerge before the 1970s, is also a study in the
troubled black radical esthetic. Hansberry grew up in Chicago in
a middle-class family. Niece of a world-famous scholar of African
antiquity, she nevertheless early confronted crowds hostile to
her family's move into a nonblack neighborhood. She studied
under W.E.B. DuBois in New York, working on Paul Robeson's
monthly, Freedom, close to the Communist party and adamantly committed to cultural pluralism.
Hansberry did not leave an autobiography. Her literary
executor, Robert Nemiroff, has selected portions of her writings
and correspondence for this volume. Notable for James Baldwin's
tribute to "Sweet Lorraine" as a dedicated and politically conscious artist in the pioneering years of a new black cultural
revolution, the book also offers insight into Hansberry's world
view. Her childhood in Chicago, her attacks on segregation and
the Vietnam War during the rise of the civil-rights movement, her
support of the Student Nonviolent Coordinating Committee and
their demand that white liberals become radical all illustrate
what she called her "revolutionary" commitment. Theatrical
pieces, like "New York: Baby, You Could Be Jesus in Drag," suggest how much she remained a product of the integrated, semi-
boheimian environment before the rise of Black Power.

Hawes, Elizabeth (1903-1971)

303 HAWES, ELIZABETH. Hurry Up Please, It's Time. New York:
Reynal & Hitchcock, 1946, 245 pp.
In the 1940s, shortly after she suspended a successful
career as leading fashion designer, Elizabeth Hawes took a job in
the educational department of the United Auto Workers' Union.
Hurry Up Please, It's Time serves as both her memoirs of the exciting union drives of World War II and a call for socialism.
Contemporary reviewers were baffled by this book, especially its harsh portrait of union leader Walter Reuther and its
passionate hatred for red-baiters. Nor could they understand why
Hawes, a Vassar graduate who was not a Communist, should share
the party's advocacy of political action and its disgust with
American capitalism.
Readers today will be intrigued by Hawes's unique stand on
the Woman Question. Although she exhibits few traces of sisterly
feeling--at one point she even criticizes a "fanatical feminist"--
Hawes delineates carefully the problems women faced in the UAW
and its auxiliaries and attacks the industry's discrimination
against working women. She offers ample evidence of rampant
sexual exploitation of female union organizers. Highly personal-

ized, Hawes's account provides a rare and fascinating insight into the sexual politics of the UAW and its Left political campaigns during World War II.

After the war Hawes returned to the fashion industry and reissued several functional designs from the 1930s. In 1967 the Fashion Institue of Technology staged a retrospective of her work.

Hellman, Lillian (1905-)

304   HELLMAN, LILLIAN. <u>An Unfinished Woman: A Memoir</u>. Boston:
      Little, Brown & Co., 1969, 280 pp. Reprint. New York:
      Bantam Books, 1970, 244 pp.
         Lillian Hellman, one of America's leading playwrights, achieved a reputation on the Left for her anti-Fascist activities in the 1930s and 1940s. Several of her most successful plays and stories concern the threat of fascism, at both home and abroad.

      Less than an autobiography, Hellman's memoirs are highly selective. One reviewer called them "an unfinished book." There is a chronological structure to the major sections, but an episodic character, which is compounded by the elusive quality of Hellman's revelations about herself, makes the story less than straightforward.

      Hellman begins conventionally. Born in New Orleans, she describes her childhood divided equally between the Southern city and New York. It is a psychological portrait, focused on Hellman's feelings toward her parents and her black surrogate mother, Sophronia. She accounts briefly for her two-year stint at New York University, where between 1922 and 1924 she learned "nothing." Her first job at Horace Liveright's publishing house, which she took at age nineteen, elicits righly humorous anecdotes about her adventures with the literary sophisticates of the era.

      The most compelling chapters deal with the 1930s and 1940s, when Hellman's political perspectives became clearer. She discusses life in Hollywood and life with Dashiell Hammett, the famous mystery writer and her companion of thirty years. Her European trips, especially her stay in Spain during the Civil War in 1937, become focal points. These episodes remained vivid in Hellman's memory as genuine adventures and political acts. So, too, a trip to the Soviet Union in 1944. The last three chapters are portraits of Dorothy Parker, a close friend, Helen Jackson, both friend and cook, and Hammett.

305   _____. <u>Pentimento: A Book of Portraits</u>. Boston: Little,
      Brown & Co., 1973, 297 pp. Reprint. New York: New American
      Library, 1974, 245 pp.
         Like the final chapters of <u>An Unfinished Woman</u>, this second volume of memoirs is constructed as sketches of several friends and moves equally casually between narrative and commentary.

      The best-known portrait is of Hellman's "beloved friend" from childhood, Julia, who was killed in the 1930s for her anti-

Fascist activities in Vienna. In 1976 this story was produced as
a motion picture starring Jane Fonda as Hellman and Vanessa
Redgrave in the leading role.

306 _____ . Scoundrel Time. Introduction by Gary Wills. Boston:
       Little, Brown & Co., 1976, 155 pp. Reprint. Boston: G.K.
       Hall & Co., 1977, 211 pp.
       Hellman recounts with little bitterness and uncommon de-
tachment her experiences with the House Un-American Activities
Committee in 1952. Counseled by her attorney and by Dashiell
Hammett, Hellman chose not to play the heroine, but nevertheless
stood before the committee as an unfriendly witness. She tells
her story with a touch of humor and deep understanding of the
crisis among intellectuals during the McCarthy era.
       This small book created a stir when it appeared in 1976,
for the "scoundrels" Hellman lambastes included not only Senator
McCarthy but the intellectual "bystanders" who stood passively
and allowed the "witch-hunt" to take place. Initial reviewers
were enthusiastic, and the book achieved a twenty-three-week run
on the best-seller list. Within a few months, however, intellectuals like Sidney Hook and Diana Trilling led a counterattack,
challenging both Hellman's accuracy and underlying assumptions.

307 FALK, DORIS V. Lillian Hellman. New York: Frederick Ungar
       Publishing Co., 1978, 180 pp.
       Falk calls Hellman "a grande dame of the literary estab-
lishment in America," someone as likely to inspire rancor as
respect but an important personage above all. Her study focuses
on two areas of Hellman's achievement: her contributions to the
theater and innovations in the genre of autobiography.

308 MOODY, RICHARD. Lillian Hellman, Playwright. New York:
       Pegasus, 1972, 372 pp.
       Moody, an unrestrained admirer, constructs a personal and
literary biography, pairing episodes in Hellman's life with her
artistic development. Although he acknowledges her political
idealism and its inspirational role, he tends to cast Hellman in
a more narrow role of playwright. Thus he concludes: "Her moral
and political convictions were deeply rooted in her thinking, in
her naked view of the world's malaise, in her own torture by the
witch-hunters, yet, just as she refused to run wild with the
radical political packs, in her plays she avoided bare-faced
propaganda."

Konikow, Antoinette Bucholz (1869-1949)

309 FEELEY, DIANNE. "Antoinette Konikow: Marxist and Feminist."
       International Socialist Review 33 (January 1972):42-46.
       Antoinette Bucholz Konikow, Russian-born revolutionary,
dedicated her life to the Socialist movement. After immigrating
to the United States in 1893, she helped organize the Boston

Jewish Workmen's Circle and joined the Socialist Labor party and later, the Socialist Party of America. She participated in the founding of both the Communist party in 1919 and the Socialist Workers party in 1938. At all times Konikow was firmly committed to women's rights, particularly their right to control their bodies. She was an early pioneer of the birth-control movement. A physician and lecturer, she continued to advocate reforms in medical law through the 1930s and 1940s.

Feeley's essay provides rare biographical information and details Konikow's activity in the post-1920 Left movements in the United States. A short bibliography lists her major works, most on family planning and hygiene.

Lee, Sirkka Tuomi

310 LEE, SIRKKA TUOMI. "The Finns." Cultural Correspondence 6, 7 (Spring 1978):41-49.

Sirkka Tuomi Lee recalls her childhood in a Finnish-American radical community, with its rich cultural life of music, theatre, and athletics. Her account of women's activities is especially interesting: women taught Sunday schools in Finnish, offering as their counterpart to biblical tales the story of Spartacus and the legacy of Finnish peasant uprisings; they directed the children's chorus in songs of proletarian trial and revolution; and they led the children's theatre, with a combination of skits, recitations, music, and Isadora Duncan-style dancing. Lee also recalls children's activities of the 1920s and 1930s and emphasizes their participation in virtually all phases of adult cultural life. Her strongest message underscores the strength of Finnish-American radical womanhood.

Le Sueur, Marian

311 LE SUEUR, MERIDEL. Crusaders. New York: Blue Heron Press, 1955, 94 pp.

In this brief biography, Le Sueur describes the Midwestern radical activities of her parents, Arthur and Marian Le Sueur. She comments extensively on her father's life, his role in the Socialist movement, and Non-Partisan League, and other aspects of his remarkable career. Marian Le Sueur, a Socialist, Wobbly, and civil libertarian, receives only a thumbnail sketch. Le Sueur draws constrained lessons from their lives of dedication: "Their compass points toward the inevitable weapon of Marxism. . . ."

Lumpkin, Katharine Du Pre (1897-?)

312 LUMPKIN, KATHARINE Du PRE. The Making of a Southerner. New York: Alfred A. Knopf, 1947, 247 pp. Reprint. Athens: University of Georgia Press, 1981, 261 pp.

The more consistently radical sister of proletarian novelist Grace Lumpkin, Katharine Du Pre Lumpkin wrote extensively on

labor and race relations. The South in Progress (1940) stands as
a major statement.

Born to an old slave-holding family of Georgia, Katharine
Du Pre Lumpkin describes her triumph over the racism of her childhood and youth. She tells how her grandfather and father, who
fought for the Confederacy during the Civil War, perpetuated the
romantic myths of the Old South and upheld the principle of white
superiority for their children. Lumpkin recalls her unquestioning
acceptance of her ancestors' views and her own part in a children's
section of the Ku Klux Klan. But, she writes, "the dynamics of
the South itself in its glaring incongruities began to arouse in
me a chronic state of doubt. . . ." Observing the hardships endured by black field hands, she began to question the wisdom of
her family's beliefs.

The real impetus, however, was an outward path from her
family and friends. In 1912 Lumpkin left home for college and
came into contact with the liberal leaders, black and white, of
the campus Young Women's Christian Association who were cautiously
challenging the caste structure of the South. After World War I
Lumpkin attended Columbia University and received a broader education from Northern blacks. When she returned to the South in the
1920s, she joined the field staff of the YWCA, worked for a time
in a shoe factory, and most important, recognized that a turning
point in race relations had been reached.

The Making of a Southerner received mixed reviews when it
appeared in 1947. Several critics commented unfavorably on its
uneasy combination of autobiography, history, and political
treatise. Most applauded Lumpkin's sensitive handling of her
racism and the way she overcame it. Readers today might yearn
for a more direct discussion of her political affiliations during
these critical decades. They will, however, find that the afterword by the author in this new edition provides significant insights.

McKenney, Ruth (1911-1972)

313 McKENNEY, RUTH. Love Story. New York: Harcourt Brace, 1950,
303 pp.

Ruth McKenney was a highly successful commercial writer,
best known for humorous sketches of her family. She was an active member of the Communist party, and conducted a weekly column
called "Strictly Personal" in the Left literary magazine, the
New Masses.

This fictionalized autobiography focuses on the first
dozen years of McKenney's marriage to New Masses editor and
writer Richard Branstein, here called "Mike Lyman." McKenney and
Branstein met in 1937, when both were working on books on the
labor movement. They married after a whirlwind courtship of
twelve days and settled in Greenwich Village. There McKenney
completed Industrial Valley and collected her rent-paying New
Yorker pieces into the best-selling My Sister Eileen (1938),

which soon served as the basis for a successful movie and Broadway play.

McKenney tells some anecdotes about her left-wing experiences, but the many vignettes that fill this book reveal mostly
her domestic situation: her partnership marriage with "Mike,"
daily work routine, and adventures in motherhood. Publishing
four years after she and her husband were expelled from the Communist party, McKenney looks back upon her period of class-con-
sciousness as a youthful escapade. She displays little affection
for her former comrades and considerable irritation at their
rough handling of her major proletarian novel, Jake Home.
McKenney's penchant for humor, however, spares the reader from
bitter tirades or unpleasant political memories. The trials of
domesticity have filled the void. A reviewer in the New York
Times (February 12, 1950) described her story accurately as "the
transition of a militant left-winger into a petty bourgeoise."

Millay, Edna St. Vincent (1892-1950)

314   MILLAY, EDNA ST. VINCENT. Letters of Edna St. Vincent Millay.
       Edited by Allan Ross Macdougall. New York: Harper & Brothers,
       1952, 384 pp. Reprint. Westport, Conn.: Greenwood Press,
       1973, 384 pp.
            In the 1920s Edna St. Vincent Millay was the most popular
       poet in America. Many of her early poems celebrated the "new
       woman" and embodied the energy she garnered from the cultural
       experimentalism of the previous decade. Youthful and romantic,
       these poems lack sophistication and tend toward melodrama, but
       they remain her best-known works.
            In the late 1920s Millay developed a more politically in-
       formed style. She had for years associated with the radical
       artists and writers of Greenwich Village, where she lived since
       graduating from Vassar in 1917. The crusade to stay the execu-
       tion of Sacco and Vanzetti crystalized her sentiments into a
       political commitment. She participated in the protest marches
       before the State House in Boston, and was deeply moved by their
       failure. From this point, her poetry became less personal and
       more explicitly social and economic in content.
            Millay did not publish an autobiography. This collection
       of her correspondence, 1900-1950, affords a few insights into her
       complex and often troubled personality. The bulk of letters date
       to her youth; after her marriage in 1923 her husband, Eugen Jan
       Boissevain, managed her correspondence. The letters from the
       1920s document her friendship with leading literary and cultural
       figures of the era: Edmund Wilson, Max Eastman, Ida Rauh, Djuna
       Barnes, and Eugene O'Neill. Beginning in 1927 several selections
       indicate the impact of the trial and execution of Sacco and
       Vanzetti on Millay's sensibility. For the most part, however,
       the collection reveals only slight glimpses of her growing radi-
       cal feelings during the late 1920s.

315 ATKINS, ELIZABETH. Edna St. Vincent Millay and Her Times.
     Chicago: University of Chicago Press, 1937, 265 pp. Reprint.
     New York: Russell & Russell, 1964, 266 pp.
          Atkins's critical study of Millay traces the development
     of her work as a function of changing esthetic values in the
     United States since the early 1920s. Thus Millay's growing social
     consciousness, sparked in particular by the Sacco and Vanzetti
     trial and execution, becomes understandable and, according to
     Atkins, even commendable. Unlike recent critics and many of
     Millay's contemporaries who favored her personal verse, Atkins
     defends her subject's right to comment on political systems and
     events: "A poet who is not deeply moved by political questions
     in a day like ours is deformed and insensitive." Millay, Atkins
     added, succeeds where others too often fail; she allows her
     poetic sensibility to hold her back "from merely journalistic
     expression" and its consequence, "limpid poetry." "The Buck in
     the Snow," the critic concludes, marks a significant advance in
     Millay's examination of good and evil.

316 BRITTIN, NORMAN A. Edna St. Vincent Millay. New York:
     Twayne Publishers, 1967, 192 pp.
          An entry in the Twayne series on American authors,
     Brittin's study fits the prescribed format. It contains a brief
     biography of Millay and concentrates on a literary analysis of
     her major works, including plays.

317 CHENEY, ANNE. Millay in Greenwich Village. University:
     University of Alabama Press, 1975, 160 pp.
          Cheney discusses the influence of four men--Floyd Dell,
     Edmund Wilson, Arthur Davidson Fiche, and Eugen Boissevain--on
     the psyche of Edna St. Vincent Millay. To Dell she attributes
     Millay's transition from lesbian to heterosexual identity.
     Boissevain, whose first wife was the militant suffragist and
     martyr to the cause, Inez Milholland, played a different role.
     He encouraged Millay to become more politically involved, a
     process that led to a decline in the quality of her poetry as she
     tried to work with social rather than personal themes. Although
     the Sacco and Vanzetti execution and fascism in Europe became her
     special interests in midlife, Greenwich Village, Cheney states
     unequivocally, was the formative influence on Millay and her
     poetry.

318 GOULD, JEAN. The Poet and Her Book: A Biography of Edna St.
     Vincent Millay. New York: Dodd, Mead & Co., 1969, 308 pp.
          Gould hoped that the counterculture of the 1960s might
     recognize Millay as a kindred spirit and foster a revival of her
     poetry. The biography therefore emphasizes the poet's sensitive,
     rebellious nature. Unfortunately, it provides few insights into
     Millay's personality or poetry. A factual chronology of her life
     written without apparent help from friends or family, Gould's
     story is remarkably flat. Moreover, the author has only scant

knowledge of Millay's cultural or political milieu.

319 GURKO, MIRIAM. <u>Restless Spirit; The Life of Edna St. Vincent Millay</u>. New York: Thomas Y. Crowell, 1962, 271 pp.
In lieu of a definitive, scholarship biography, Gurko's study serves a specific function in that it follows Millay's life through the 1930s and 1940s, when the major political concerns of the era affected her poetry and personality. The biography is straightforward, suitable for young adult readers.

Mitford, Jessica (1917-   )

320 MITFORD, JESSICA. <u>A Fine Old Conflict</u>. New York: Alfred A. Knopf, 1977, 333 pp. Reprint. New York: Vintage Books, 1978, 333 pp.
Better known for her best-seller, <u>The American Way of Death</u>, Jessica Mitford was foremost an activist in the Communist party during the 1940s and 1950s. She was born to a noble British family, and came to the United States in 1939 with her first husband, Esmond Romilly, who later died in the war. Mitford joined the party as soon as she obtained citizenship in 1944, and served prominently in California. She worked chiefly for its front organization, the Civil Rights Congress, which defended blacks and victims of the Cold War. When the Civil Rights Congress was dissolved during the upheaval following the Khrushchev report of 1956, Mitford lost her central role. Finally, in 1958, she and her husband, Bob Treuhaft, resigned.
Mitford's memoirs provide excellent insights into the life of a rank-and-file activist. She tells her story without bitterness or recrimination, and a fine sense of humor overlays the narrative. Anecdotes about her unusual family, which was inundated with famous Fascists, add color as well as intimacy to her descriptions of daily life.
Mitford retained her idealism long after she left the party. She remained active throughout the 1960s, supporting various antiwar and civil rights organizations. In a concluding passage she credits her sustaining activism to her early training in the Communist party, to its role in educating her to take part "in what she perceived as the crucial battles of the day."

Molek, Mary (1909-1982)

321 MOLEK, MARY. <u>Immigrant Woman</u>. Dover, Del.: M. Molek, 1976, 167 pp.
Mary Molek, an archivist and museum curator, was a member of the Yugoslav Socialist Federation in the 1930s and 1940s and leading contributor to its newspaper, <u>Prosveta</u> (Chicago), edited by her husband, Ivan Molek. She offers this story of Slovenian-American working-class life in the first decades of the twentieth century. Ostensibly a fictionalized biography of her mother, and illustrated with family photographs, <u>Immigrant Woman</u> is a heart-

146

rending memoir of Molek's own childhood in a Kansas coal-mining town. The oldest child, she describes in free-form, episodic fashion her mother's struggle to keep her family together and to rear her three daughters to adulthood.

Parker, Dorothy Rothschild (1893-1967)

322 KEATS, JOHN. You Might as Well Live; The Life and Times of Dorothy Parker. New York: Simon & Schuster, 1970, 319 pp.
        Known primarily for her light verse and satire, Dorothy Parker contributed steadily to Left causes throughout her productive years. The execution of Sacco and Vanzetti in 1927 firmed her dedication to activism; in 1934 she issued her notorious and purposefully wry proclamation: "I am a Communist." In the 1930s Parker used her wealth and prestige to support strikes, raise money for the Scottsboro defense, and serve as a leading organizer for the Screen Writers' Guild. She took greatest pride in her anti-Fascist activities: her role in forming the Hollywood Anti-Nazi League in 1936; her contribution to a pro-Loyalist film documentary about Spain in 1937; and her trip with Lillian Hellman to the site of the Spanish Civil War in 1937. In 1949 Parker was oficially blacklisted.
        Keats's biography attempts to explain the complexity of Dorothy Parker. Although he neither shares nor fully understands her Left sympathy, he relates it honestly and respectfully. He also draws heavily on reminiscences of Parker's closest friends and associates and thereby balances his own interpretation with several perspectives on her elusive personality.

323 KINNEY, ARTHUR F. Dorothy Parker. Boston: Twayne Publishers, 1978, 204 pp.
        In contributing to Twayne's United States Author Series, Kinney provides a biographical sketch of Parker as a preface to a survey of her major published works. He considers it a tragedy that she produced relatively little in her lifetime, but honors Parker as "the best epigrammatic poet in our country, in this century."

Plotkin, Sara (?-1982)

324 PLOTKIN, SARA. Full-Time Active: Sara Plotkin, An Oral History. Edited by Arthur Tobier. New York: Community Documentation Workshop, 1980, 49 pp.
        Sara Plotkin has rendered a beautiful, inspirational oral history of her lifelong dedication to political activism. She speaks with the charming lilt and directness characteristic of the best Yiddish storytellers. A sense of humor and integrity pervades her narrative.
        It is significant that Plotkin recounts her life story only insofar as it illuminates her political involvements. There is room for little else. Born just before the turn of the century

in White Russia, she remembers her youth in the shtetl--the
poverty, the grind of daily life, the oppressive religious atmos-
phere--and her awakening socialist consciousness, finally, in
1917. At age nineteen, Plotkin decided to meet a Bolshevik. She
took off for the nearest city, walked the forty-mile distance
from her home, and eventually achieved her goal: at the local
Bund office she encountered a young man who she immediately recognized as a Bolshevik and asked to join his ranks.

After immigrating to the United States in 1922, Plotkin
became an organizer for the Communist party. During the Depression she helped unionize cafeteria workers in New York City and
steel workers and coal miners in Pittsburgh and in Wheeling, West
Virginia; she also rallied the unemployed and helped people ob-
tain welfare.

Despite her memories of police brutality and frequent
arrests, Plotkin describes the 1930s and 1940s as decades of
important activity. She recounts her first serious disillusionment in the late 1940s, when the Communist party failed to rally
behind the Rosenbergs. The retrenchment during the 1950s, the
inability of the party to fight back against McCarthyism, and the
increasingly sectarian drift within the organization further
alienated her. Still "full-time active," Plotkin longed for the
earlier decades when the party could sustain the fervor of devoted political organizers.

Sara Plotkin closes her narrative in 1964. Once more
brought in for questioning by the FBI, she asks the young agent,
who she perceives as a man interested in his country, why he
isn't doing something useful, such as helping register the black
voters of Mississippi.

Rosenberg, Ethel Greenglass (1915-1953)

325 ROSENBERG, ETHEL, and JULIUS ROSENBERG. Death House Letters.
New York: Jero Publishing Co., 1953, 168 pp.

Ethel and Julius Rosenberg were brought to trial and convicted of conspiring to commit espionage in 1951. Victims of the
Cold War, they were executed in 1953.

Born on New York's Lower East Side, Ethel Greenglass as-
pired to be a singer and actress, but the hard times of the
Depression directed her into clerical work. In 1935 she helped
organize a union in her firm and established herself as a local
labor activist. The next year, at a labor rally, she met Julius
Rosenberg, a member of the Communist party. They married in 1939.

In the early 1940s Ethel Rosenberg supported the United
States involvement in World War II as a further step in the continuing fight against fascism. By the end of the decade, her
two small sons, born in 1943 and 1947, absorbed her energies.

In 1950 her period of domesticity came to an end. Her
husband was accused of giving secrets on the atom bomb to the
Soviets. Shortly after his arrest and imprisonment, she was
called to appear before a grand jury. Shortly thereafter she,

too, was arrested. Although the case against her was weak, the chance that she might "confess" to spare the life of her husband kept her a potential witness in the government's eyes. For two years she was held at Sing-Sing prison. Allowed to meet only once a week, husband and wife communicated chiefly though letters.

Published just as Chief Justice Vinson refused a stay of execution, these letters stand as testament of innocence, undying love for each other and their two sons, and refusal to renege on their principles. The letters are poignant. Especially moving are Ethel Rosenberg's expressions of concern for the welfare of her sons and frustration with her mother.

326 GARDNER, VIRGINIA. The Rosenberg Story. New York: Masses & Mainstream, 1954, 126 pp.

Gardner, a longtime Left journalist, expanded a series of essays she wrote originally for the Daily World as appeals for a new trial. She interviewed forty people who were acquainted with the Rosenbergs, and recorded their memories and reactions to the arrest and imprisonment. What emerges is a collective portrait of the couple, their love for one another and for their two sons, and their steadfast idealism in the shadow of imminent death. Particularly interesting are friends' reminiscences of Ethel during her youth and before her marriage.

327 MEEROPOL, ROBERT, and MICHAEL MEEROPOL. We Are Your Sons: The Legacy of Ethel and Julius Rosenberg. Boston: Houghton Mifflin & Co., 1975, 419 pp. Reprint. New York: Ballantine Books, 1976, 471 pp.

The Rosenberg sons present a personal history of the trial and execution of their parents as well as reminiscences of the dissolution of their family. Michael writes, "I can still hear her on the telephone telling me she was under arrest. I have been told that my reaction was a heart-rending scream, which continued to give her nightmares the rest of her life. I have completely blocked it out."

Adopted in 1957 by Anne and Abel Meeropol, after several years of legal battles over custody, Robert and Michael continue the story into the 1960s and discuss their own political development during the Cold War and through the period of the New Left. The first half of the book, written by Michael Meeropol, covers the years 1950 through 1954 and includes many excerpts from his parents' prison correspondence. The second section, written by Robert, traces the sons' history over the next two decades.

Shavelson, Clara Lemlich (1886-1982)

328 SCHAPPES, MORRIS U. "Three Women." Jewish Currents 29 (September 1975):5-7.

As a backdrop for International Women's Year proclaimed by the United Nations for 1975, Schappes contributed very brief biographical sketches of Ernestine L. Rose, Emma Lazarus, and Clara Lemlich.

329   SCHEIER, PAULA. "Clara Lemlich Shavelson: 50 Years in Labor's
      Front Line." Jewish Life 8 (November 1954):7-11.
         Scheier documents Clara Lemlich's famous part in the 1909
      shirtwaist makers' strike in New York as well as other union
      drives during the first years of the century. She also describes
      Lemlich's Socialist activities during the suffrage campaigns be-
      ginning in 1910, and later community work among housewives for
      the United Council of Working Class Women, which was renamed in
      1935 the Progressive Women's Council. Based on interviews,
      Scheier's brief biography underscores the lifelong dedication of
      a woman too often remembered only for her youthful bravado.

Sinclair, Mary Craig Kimbrough (1883-1961)

330   SINCLAIR, MARY CRAIG (KIMBROUGH). Southern Belle. Foreword
      by Upton Sinclair. New York: Crown Publishers, 1957, 407 pp.
         Mary Craig Sinclair, a daughter of luxury provided by the
      Southern cotton economy, shocked her proper family by marrying
      the newsworthy radical, Upton Sinclair. Her autobiography juxta-
      poses the glorious social life of her youth with the stark ordeal
      of her marriage.
         Upton Sinclair, a famous muckraking novelist, supported
      many radical causes and believed in living simply, without many
      material comforts. His wife describes her adaptation to this
      style and dedication to his work, including practical assistance
      on his many political treatises. "I understand the radical move-
      ment and my heart belongs to it," she writes, but also admits
      that despite great love and admiration, she found it hard to
      carry on the crusade in private as well as public life.

Smedley, Agnes (1890-1950)

331   SMEDLEY, AGNES. Battle Hymn of China. New York: Alfred A.
      Knopf, 1943, 528 pp.
         Whereas Daughter of Earth traces the outline of Smedley's
      life through World War I, these memoirs of her later years in
      China serve as a sequel. Smedley begins by recounting briefly
      her childhood in Colorado and early adulthood in the radical New
      York environs, but focuses on her remarkable experiences in China.
         When the revolution began, Smedley went to China as a
      correspondent for European Left newspapers and moved close to the
      Red army. Battle Hymn of China, one of several books on the
      revolution, is her partisan diary covering the exciting years
      1929 to 1941. It is rich in both anecdotes of people she has met
      and sympathy for a country struggling against its feudal past.
      Although not a skillful writer, Smedley was an honest and out-
      spoken reporter.

Strong, Anna Louise (1885-1970)

332   STRONG, ANNA LOUISE. I Change Worlds: The Remaking of an

American. New York: Henry Holt & Co., 1935, 422 pp. Reprint, with introduction by Barbara Wilson. Seattle: Seal Press, 1979, 422 pp.

When Anna Louise Strong died in Peking, the New York Times ran a front-page obituary: "For almost half a century . . . Strong dedicated herself passionately to glorifying China." And before China, the Soviet Union.

Born in Friend, Nebraska, to Congregational missionaries, educated in Oberlin, Bryn Mawr, and the University of Chicago, where she received a doctorate in 1908, Stong became a Socialist during World War I. In 1919 she took part in the Seattle general strike, and her newspaper reports catapulted her to fame as a radical reporter. Disappointed by the strike's failure, she joined the American Friends Service Committee relief mission to eastern Europe, where she imbibed the excitement of the Russian Revolution. Strong spent the next fourteen years in the Soviet Union, studying Communist doctrine, establishing the John Reed Children's Colony for victims of the Volga famine, and writing reports for the American press.

I Change Worlds recounts this odyssey from America to the Soviet Union. Strong tells of her early life in this country, her experiences in the Mexican and Chinese revolutions of the 1920s, and her adventures in the USSR. She relates her story with enthusiasm. As one reviewer commented in 1935 when the book first appeared: "this story of a born Puritan who has renounced capitalism for communism belongs with the major autobiographies of the twentieth century."

333 _____. My Native Land. New York: Viking Press, 1940, 299 pp.
In 1935 Strong took a cross-country motor trip to study the impact of the Great Depression on the spirit of the American people. Her memoirs, written at the suggestion of Eleanor Roosevelt, record new "forces ready to carry us onward to new ventures through and beyond the New Deal."

Roger Baldwin criticized My Native Land for its stereo-typed Left interpretation of American capitalism. But Strong does provide insight into the militant resistance of sectors of the populace, particularly in labor-torn areas like Minneapolis and Flint, Michigan. She also underscores the problems of the South, centered in the ownership of the land and the ensuing racial tensions.

334 DUKE, DAVID C. "Anna Louise Strong and the Search for a Good Cause." Pacific Northwest Quarterly 66 (July 1975):123-37.
This essay provides a useful factual summary of Strong's life and a judicious interpretation of her political inclinations. Duke describes Strong as driven by two principles: a desire to obliterate social injustice and "a deep personal need to be part of a great cause or movement." Although she tried to satisfy her longings in the United States, she became extremely pessimistic about the possibilities for social reconstruction after World

War I, a feeling prompted by the failure of the Seattle general
strike of 1919. In the Soviet Union Strong found a more promising
situation, especially, as she wrote, "the faith that we human
beings by the twin tools of human co-operation and science, are
able to conquer all problems presented by nature, even the problem
of our very backward souls." Twenty years later, China represented a similar, if not grander, opportunity for sacrifice and
heroism.

Weisbord, Vera Buch (1895-)

335 WEISBORD, VERA BUCH. A Radical Life. Introduction by Paul
     Buhle and Mari Jo Buhle. Bloomington: Indiana University
     Press, 1977, 330 pp.
          Growing up in New York, Vera Buch followed the path of
     many precocious women of her time and secured a solid education
     at Hunter College. Drawn toward the radical movement, she rapidly
     abandoned the usual career aspirations for the revolutionary
     promise of bolshevism. The foundling Communist movement in the
     United States, driven underground by the Palmer raids and divided
     into competing sects, proved difficult to locate, let alone join.
     Buch nevertheless kept to her dedication, and by the mid-1920s
     emerged as one of the handful of prominent Communist women activ-
     ists.
          Buch's renown had two principal sources. She threw her
     energies into the series of strikes where Communists aided the
     hard-pressed textile workers. Passaic in 1926 and Gastonia in
     1929 were Buch's baptism of fire, with arrests and persecution,
     glorious moments and great disappointments. Buch also became
     linked with Albert Weisbord, mercurial strike leader at Passaic.
     When the two broke with the Communist party in 1930 over differ-
     ences of leadership and strategy, they resolved themselves to
     relative isolation and sectarian involvement. Buch recalls their
     life together with vividness and candor, offering a rare insight
     into one woman's place within the private sectors of the Com-
     munist movement.

Whitney, Anita (1867-?)

336 RICHMOND, AL. Native Daughter; The Story of Anita Whitney.
     San Francisco: Anita Whitney 75th Anniversary Committee,
     1942, 199 pp.
          In 1940, when she had reached seventy-three years of age,
     Anita Whitney was elected to the highest governing committee of
     the Communist party. Her biographer describes this distinction
     as a mark of her leadership; more likely, the election acknowl-
     edged her twenty years of active service.
          Whitney was born in San Francisco in 1867 to a middle-
     class family of old Yankee stock. She graduated from Wellesley
     College in 1889 and, like so many women of her generation, worked
     for a time in a settlement house on the Lower East Side of

Manhattan. Called back to California by her father's death, she
established herself in Alameda County's charity organization.

The dramatic California woman suffrage campaign of 1911
pulled Whitney into politics. In 1914 she took up membership in
the Socialist party; five years later, she joined the Communist
Labor party.

Whitney became a cause celebre in the 1920s. In 1919 she
was charged with criminal syndicalism, and for the next seven
years became the center of a campaign to end political harassment
and imprisonment. Once freed from these charges, she worked in
the International Labor Defense. At age sixty, Whitney had become a standard bearer for the California Communist party, a
regular candidate in local elections.

Published to celebrate Whitney's seventy-fifth birthday,
this laudatory biography celebrates her long devotion to social
justice. Richmond, in tune with the party line during wartime,
describes her as a "daughter of America in whose veins flows the
blood of the nation's revolutionary creators." The source of her
Communist devotion, Richmond explains, was Whitney's "attachment
to the American tradition."

337 WHITTEN, WOODROW C. "The Trial of Charlotte Anita Whitney."
     Pacific Historical Review 15 (September 1946):286-94.
         Whitten details Whitney's famous trial for criminal syn-
     dicalism and its impact on her later political development.

Williams, Joyce (?-1977)

338 NAISON, MARK. "Claude and Joyce Williams: Pilgrims of Jus-
     tice." Southern Exposure 1 (Winter 1974):38-50.
         Claude and Joyce Williams were major figures in the strug-
     gles of miners and sharecroppers in Arkansas during the early
     1930s, and later participated in the CIO Southern organizing
     drive. During World War II they worked in Detroit on the United
     Auto Workers' interracial committees.
         Although focused on Claude's role in the Southern Farmers'
     Tenant Union and directorship of Commonwealth College, Mena,
     Arkansas, this essay provides essential information on Joyce's
     activities in their joint venture, the Progressive Institute of
     Applied Religion. Under its auspices, the Williamses helped
     counter Fascist and racist elements in the South and promoted
     trade union campaigns.

Winter, Ella (1898-1980)

339 WINTER, ELLA. And Not to Yield: An Autobiography. New York:
     Harcourt, Brace & World, 1963, 308 pp.
         Ella Winter was a distinguished radical journalist and
     authority on life in the Soviet Union. She reported on strikes
     of California farm workers and longshoremen in the 1930s, and
     produced two highly acclaimed studies, Red Virtue (1933) and I

Saw the Russian People (1945). In addition to writing and lecturing, Winter managed to meet virtually every Left intellectual
and artist of the early twentieth century in the United States
and abroad. Her first marriage to Lincoln Steffens, the famous
muckraker who was thirty years her elder, opened the avant-garde
circles of the first decades; her second marriage to Donald Ogden
Stewart, the leading film writer of the 1930s and 1940s who later
became a victim of the blacklist, brought contact with Hollywood
stars and "progressive" entertainers of all types.

In her autobiography, Winter tells about her personal life,
especially her happy marriages, but concentrates on compiling a
litany of the famous personages she met over decades of radical
involvements. The list is impressive, but as reviewers have
pointed out, the subjects themselves remain shadowy figures.
Winter does little better with her own character. Although she
records her three visits to the Soviet Union, the last in 1957,
she writes surprisingly little about problem issues such as the
impact of the Nazi-Soviet pact or the rise and fall of stalinism.
A pervasive lack of political reflection thus limits her memoirs
and reduces her life to a series of uninterpreted events and un-
analyzed friendships.

Despite its shortcoming, the autobiography does attest to
Winter's unyielding idealism. She ends her story with yet another
visit to a country in the throes of a revolutionary experiment.
In 1958, at the invitation of the Chinese National Women's Federation, Winter made a cross-country tour of the mainland. Once
more she affirmed her faith in the process of revolution. She
concluded: "If my life has taught me anything, it is that one
must fight."

BOOKS AND PAMPHLETS ON
THE WOMAN QUESTION

The publications covered in this section document the changing
place of the Woman Question in the Old Left. Between 1929 and 1935,
the so-called Third Period of American communism, the party upheld
the class struggle as its principal strategy for revolution, and concurrently downplayed women's issues as secondary to the needs of the
working class. The pamphlets published during the Third Period de-
rided feminism and expressed antipathy toward the Equal Rights Amendment as potentially damaging to working women. Writers tended to
address women singularly as members of the working class. Hostile to
mainstream women's organizations, they upheld the example of the
Soviet Union and demanded absolute loyalty to the Communist party and
its representatives in the trade unions. During the Popular Front
between 1935 and 1939, the Communist party broadened its appeal and
allowed more room for discussion of the Woman Question.

The advent of World War II, however, fostered a series of dramatic
shifts in party line. During the Popular Front the party organized
both working- and middle-class women around the issue of peace, and

154

continued to call upon women to resist conscription and preparedness
campaigns following the historic signing of the Nazi-Soviet pact. In
1941, with the German invasion of the Soviet Union, the party reversed
its position suddenly and dramatically. Writers who just a few months
before took a solid noninterventionist stand now supported the entry
of the United States into the war, and rallied women to take jobs in
defense industries. They asked women to help maintain the home front
in the heroic war against fascism. Only in the late 1940s and 1950s,
in the midst of the Cold War, did the party return to its advocacy of
peace.

Over the entire period, writers addressed several key issues.
The place of women in industry and their role in the trade union movement were primary considerations. Special attention was given to the
"triple oppression" of black women workers, especially after World
War II as the Communist party backed the growing campaigns for racial
integration. Women's work in the home, however, was more problematical
and inspired a rare exchange of differing opinions in the late 1930s;
Mary Inman and Avrom Landy emerged as the chief antagonists in a
heated debate that returned in the 1970s over the value of housework.

340 BARTON, ANN. Mother Bloor. New York: Workers Library, 1935,
    24 pp.
        Communist writers often presented leading party women as
role models. This pamphlet, written during the Third Period,
depicts Mother Bloor as a heroine of the class struggle.
        Barton traces Bloor's propensity for rebellion from her
childhood through various political movements--the Socialist
Labor party and Socialist party in some detail--to the Communist
party, when at age fifty-seven she became one of its first members. She offers a factual summary of Bloor's activities since
1919, underscoring her role in the struggle of miners and their
wives, farmers, machinists, steel workers, and men and women in
the needle trades. The conclusion reads: "At nearly seventy-
three, she [Bloor] is a stirring and inspiring example of one who
has been woman, mother, and class fighter. Her attitude towards
the workers and their struggle could have led her nowhere else
but into the ranks of the Communist Party."

341 _____. Mother Bloor: The Spirit of '76. New York: Workers
    Library, 1937, 31 pp.
        Barton updates her earlier publication on Mother Bloor to
bring the interpretation in line with the party's new emphasis on
"mass organizing" among women. Instead of describing the revered
Communist as "class fighter," Barton now presents Mother Bloor as
loyal citizen, a native-born activist in the tradition of the
American Revolution.

342 BEECHER, KATHERINE. Wives or Widows? New York: Women's
    Division, New York Council, American Peace Mobilization,

[1941?], 31 pp.

The Communist party, especially during the Popular Front, organized many women around the issue of peace. Until the Soviet entry into World War II in the summer of 1941, writers addressed women primarily in their traditional roles of wife and mother and emphasized their special interests in preventing war.

This pamphlet, published in the last days of the Hitler-Stalin pact, opposes United States entry into the war. Addressed to women, it discusses such issues as the potential conscription of women into wartime service, the loss of husbands and sons in battle, and the effect of wartime economics on the cost of living, especially housing and household commodities.

343 BLOOR, ELLA REEVE. Women in the Soviet Union. New York: Workers Library, 1938, 15 pp.

For most American Communists before the Khrushchev report of 1956 when the human toll of Stalin's program became widely known, the Soviet Union served as the supreme model. Writers on the Woman Question similarly looked abroad for leadership. Journalists Jessica Smith, who wrote Women in Soviet Russia (1928) and Ella Winter, who wrote Red Virtue (1933) had witnessed firsthand the strides of women since the Revolution and described favorably their impressions of women's achievements. As the Great Depression deepened in the United States, writers compared the situation of women in this country to the alleged full employment and welfare of women in the Soviet Union.

Ella Reeve Bloor offers a typical, uncritical account of the Soviet Union as a model of women's emancipation. She describes the "phenomenal growth of child care and the protection of motherhood in a land where human life comes first. . . ." She also discusses the prominence of women in public life, especially in the professions.

344 BRANT, MARIE, and ELLEN SANTORI. A Woman's Place. Los Angeles: New Writers, 1953, 23 pp.

Rare in a decade of quietude on the Woman Question, this pamphlet speaks for an independent group of former trotskyists inspired by Pan-African theorist C.L.R. James. The authors surveyed the plethora of contemporary literature about women's restlessness and judged them insufficient because women's own initiatives or efforts at self-emancipation are ignored. The authors seek for clues in what the New Left would call "everyday life" and find signs of rebellion: "Women are finding more and more that there is no way out but a complete change. But one thing is already clear. Things can't go on the way they are. Every woman knows that."

345 CALLER, FAY. Shall It Be Girls in Uniform? New York: Workers Library, 1941, 16 pp.

Addressed to young women, this tract warns against alleged government plans to draft women into wartime service. The author outlines the program of the Young Communist League and takes a strong stand against American entry into the "imperialist war."

346 COWL, MARGARET. Women and Equality. New York: Workers Library, 1935, 14 pp.
    "It is an undisputed fact that all women are in an unequal position with men in all countries with the exception of the Union of Soviet Socialist Republics," writes Cowl. She quotes Frederick Engels on the origins of women's oppression in the system of private property, and explains how the issue is not the antagonism between men and women but between workers and capitalists. She calls upon men and women to struggle together for social legislation, and to educate the masses about the position of women in the Soviet Union. Such struggles, she contends, are "links in the chain of struggle that will eventually break the shackles that bind woman and lead her forth into that world of freedom and happiness that only a Socialist Society can give."

347 _____. The High Cost of Living: How to Bring It Down. New York: Workers Library, 1937, 16 pp.
    This chatty talk with housewives addresses timely questions of the Depression economy: how wages have been lowered relative to production via the speedup; why inflation serves the rich. One section, "Women Can Win," recommends the formation of trade union auxiliaries and housewives' organizations wherein women might fight increases in taxes and prices. Cowl outlines tactics such as "baby parades" of strollers to city halls, and calls upon women to join the Communist party.

348 EPSTEIN, IRENE, and DOXEY A. WILKERSON, eds. Questions and Answers on the Woman Question. New York: Jefferson School of Social Science, 1953, 20 pp.
    Mimeographed for use by the Jefferson School and drawn from its experiences, this pamphlet was inspired by the wisdom of Stalin and the light of the Soviet Union. Issued on International Women's Day, 1953, its marshals factual materials on conditions in the USSR and United States, especially the place of black women, in catechetical form.
    "What is Feminism? Why must it be fought against?"--answered by the argument that bourgeois ideology provokes struggle against men rather than against the social system.
    "Will male supremacist ideology be completely eliminated under Socialism?"--answered, "Yes, but not immediately," as the experience of the USSR shows.
    Perhaps the most interesting aspect of this pamphlet is neither its predictable attack upon feminist programs, like the Equal Rights Amendment, nor the usual praise of the USSR, but rather the brief descriptions of international revolutionary women leaders, past and present, and most especially the American women who have led Communist-influenced mass movements but who have been largely forgotten.

349 FILLEY, JANE, and THERESE MITCHELL. <u>Consider the Laundry</u>
     <u>Workers</u>. New York: League of Women Shoppers, 1937, 64 pp.
     The League of Women Shoppers, organized in New York in
1935 and nationally in 1938, described itself as "an organization
of consumers whose purpose is to provide its members with impartial
and authentic information about labor conditions in factories and
stores so the public can use their buying power for justice."
The League advocated consistently three main strategies: higher
wages, lower living costs, and trade unions for workers. Although
the League claimed at its peak in the late 1930s over 4,500 women
of varied political and religious leanings, its leading members
and organizers were Communists; some historians describe the
League as a Popular Front organization.
     This pamphlet constitutes the results of an investigation
of the laundry industry. Committees of League members interviewed
employees in their homes and employers in their places of business,
and compiled lengthy questionnaires on working conditions, wage
standards, and attitudes. The pamphlet includes a brief history
of the industry, very intimate and informative sections culled
from the personal interviews, a survey of labor conditions, and
finally, a statement of recommendation. Unlike the National Consumers' Union, which stressed legislative measures, the League
of Women Shoppers advocated consumer boycotts and trade unions as
the most "complete solution" to the problems facing workers.

350 FLYNN, ELIZABETH GURLEY. <u>I Didn't Raise My Boy To Be a</u>
     <u>Soldier--for Wall Street</u>. New York: Workers Library, 1940,
     15 pp.
     Prepared for International Women's Day, this pamphlet
appeals to women to resist American preparations for another war.
Flynn explains how wars are caused primarily by groups of imperialist bankers and industrialists, and warns that capitalists,
seeking to control world markets, are already aligning for another
major conflict. She notes, however, that although Communists do
not support imperialist wars like World War I, they are not non-
resistant pacifists and would have participated in the American
Revolution and Civil War.

351 _____. <u>Daughters of America: Ella Reeve Bloor and Anita</u>
     <u>Whitney</u>. New York: Workers Library, 1942, 14 pp.
     Reflecting the change in party line, Flynn wrote this
pamphlet to promote the Communist-sponsored campaign to support
the war effort.
     To honor Whitney on her seventy-fifth birthday and Bloor
on her eightieth, the national committee of the Communist party
staged a huge birthday celebration on July 4, 1942, which was
followed by local festivities across the country. Flynn uses the
occasion to underline the United Front evocation of patriotism.
She describes Bloor and Whitney as daughters of the American
Revolution, documents "their lifelong struggle for human freedom
everywhere," and praises them for turning their birthday parties

into war rallies. She presents the political biographies of the
two women as sterling examples of active service, a model for
American women during wartime.

352 _____. Women in the War. New York: Workers Library, 1942,
31 pp.
In a brief introduction William Z. Foster described Flynn's
pamphlet as "the Communist position toward women in the war."
Flynn calls upon women to fight on the home front by taking production jobs. She insists that women can perform well in war
industries if certain programs are instituted, such as the establishment of day-care centers and the guarantee of equal wages for
equal work. Unions, too, must recognize their obligations toward
this new sector and advance women to positions of leadership.
Flynn pays special attention to the wartime needs of black women.
This pamphlet also includes several resolutions of trade
unions on child-care centers, job training for women, union
leadership programs, and women's auxiliaries.

353 _____. Women Have a Date With Destiny. New York: Workers
Library, 1944, 31 pp.
A United Front appeal, this pamphlet praises the accom-
plishments of the Roosevelt administration and commends Eleanor
Roosevelt for setting a new standard for presidents' wives.
Flynn implores American women to meet their date with destiny--
election day, 1944--by casting their ballots for FDR. She warns
against a vote for the Republican nominee, Thomas E. Dewey, and
discusses other "enemies of the people," like Martin Dies and
Clare Booth Luce.

354 _____. Woman's Place--in the Fight for a Better World. New
York: New Century Publishers, 1947, 16 pp.
Flynn wrote this pamphlet to commemorate International
Women's Day. She provides a brief history and correctly credits
American Socialists with organizing the first celebration. She
also discusses the international significance of this holiday and
urges contemporary women to join the March 8 celebrations. Most
of all, she asks women to claim the holiday in the name of world
peace.

355 GORDON, EVELYN B. Weaving the Future. New York: Workers
Library, 1937, 23 pp.
Addressed to workers in the textile industry, including
the many women employed, this pamphlet aims to quell fears aroused
by red-baiting of the union movement. The author narrates a long
history of "Red" participation in textile organizing, from the
efforts of the 1830s through the famous Lawrence, Massachusetts,
strike of 1912. Workers are asked to join both the National Textile Workers' Union and the Communist party.

356 GORDON, EUGENE, and CYRIL BRIGGS. The Position of Negro

Women. New York: Workers Library, 1935, 15 pp.
     The double oppression of Negro women is the subject of this pamphlet. Gordon and Briggs discuss the temporary effect of World War I on black women workers, their movement into well-paying factory jobs just before and during the war, and their "discharge" during the 1920s. They discuss the current situation of the majority of workers in domestic and personal service, the discrimination against blacks in white-collar and teaching professions, the impact of unemployment, and inequities in the NRA codes. To achieve the racial harmony and sex equality guaranteed in "the shining example," the Soviet Union, the authors call for unity of white and Negro workers in the Communist party.

357 HUTCHINS, GRACE. Women and War. New York: CPUSA, 1932, 31 pp.
     Grace Hutchins (1885-1969), a graduate of Bryn Mawr College and former Christian social reformer, was the Communist party's leading writer on wage-earning women. Along with her lifelong companion and leading marxist scholar, Anna Rochester, Hutchins sponsored the Labor Research Association, which produced scores of books on working conditions in the United States. An active party member from 1927 until her death, Hutchins was concerned primarily with the welfare of the American working class and wrote with special focus on women and children.
     This pamphlet begins as a short story about a group of women factory workers who are discussing their fear of another war. One of their rank quotes the Daily Worker to explain the imperialist nature of World War I and the current plans to smash the Soviet Union. She tells about war preparations in the United States, referring to the fact that women are already replacing men in industries and thus easing the way for wartime production schedules. She predicts that women will be drafted for combat duty during the next war.
     To prevent the drift toward war, Hutchins asks women to organize under the leadership of the Trade Union Unity League and under the banner of the Communist party. She advises women to be wary of the propaganda issued by the American Federation of Labor and Women's Trade Union League, and subscribe instead to the party's Woman Worker.

358   _____. Women Who Work. New York: International Publishers, 1932, 31 pp.
     Hutchins outlines the major points that would be more fully developed in her 1934 publication under the same title. She discusses the plight of working-class women during the Great Depression and compares their unfavorable situation to the security and status women enjoy in the Soviet Union. She accuses mainstream women's organizations of trying to bring working women under their "bourgeois" influence, and holds up the programs of the Communist party and the Trade Union Unity League.

359 _____. Women Who Work. New York: International Publishers, 1934, 285 pp.

Women Who Work is a classic document of the Third Period. It has a dual purpose: to attack the "bourgeois" feminist concepts of freedom and equality; and to present an alternative vision as illustrated by the emancipated position of women in the Soviet Union.

Hutchins opens with an examination of the elitist basis of freedom as espoused by middle- and upper-class feminists, and continues with an abbreviated history of the oppression of working-class women under capitalism interspersed with quotations from Marx and Lenin. She thereby hopes to persuade her readers that contrary to the promises of bourgeois feminists, full liberation requires the abolition of private property, a Communist economy. She details women's hardships in contemporary American society, their "double burden" of household and wage-labor, their situations on the farms and in the factories, various conditions of labor, hours, wages, and health, and especially the failure of the National Recovery Administration to ease unemployment and discrimination.

To demonstrate the inadequacy of capitalist policies in regard to women, Hutchins includes a lengthy chapter, "How It Is in the USSR." Soviet women, she claims, have achieved equality both in theory and in practice. She describes the freedom women enjoy in maintaining a career, the ample public services that eliminate household drudgery and manage child care, and women's role in policy making at all levels of government. The section on "Women Heroes of Socialist Construction" makes the essential argument for political equality as a function of a Communist state.

Hutchins offers a strategy for American women. She relates a long history of their participation in strikes and labor movements in the United States, beginning early in the nineteenth century and continuing to the 1930s. She documents the role of bourgeois women's organizations in opposing class struggle: "They are made up largely of middle-class women who run true to form as petty capitalists [and] teach individual achievement." Hutchins attacks not only the Young Women's Christian Association and the National Woman's party, but the Socialist party and American Federation of Labor; none offers women any hope, but stands against their liberation, she claims. Once more, the Trade Union Unity League is the answer. Only through this means, as organized workers or as members of women's auxiliaries, will women be able to carry "forward the struggle to real emancipation and equality. . . ."

360 _____. What Every Working Woman Wants. New York: Workers Library, 1935, 16 pp.

American Communists in the mid-1930s frequently detailed the programs for maternal protection established in the Soviet Union, such as day-care facilities for infants, special counseling

for mothers, maternity leaves and reduced hours, and additional
food allowances. Such programs, they averred, allowed women to
participate fully in industry without jeopardizing their family's
welfare or risking their own health.

Drawing on the Soviet model, Hutchins encourages American
women to support the New Deal's proposed social legislation and
to call for the inclusion of a "Mother's Bill of Rights." She
advocates the establishment of free birth-control clinics and day
nurseries, and maternity insurance that would cover both medical
costs and leaves of absence before and after confinement.

361   _____. Women Who Work. New York: International Publishers,
        1952, 96 pp.

Writing for the Labor Research Association, Hutchins up-
dates her 1932 study of working women to account for the impact
of World War II and the current situation of women in the labor
force. The first half of the pamphlet discusses problems con-
fronting working women "On the Job and at Home," such as the
double burden of housework, discriminatory wage-and-benefit
structures, and the party's position on the proposed Equal Rights
Amendment. The second half contains several sections on black
women, reflecting the party's strong commitment to civil rights.
A series of short chapters on women's organizations discusses
women's involvement in several progressive movements where the
party played an important role: Emma Lazarus Federation, National
Council for American-Soviet Friendship, the Progressive Party,
and American Women for Peace.

362 INMAN, MARY. In Woman's Defense. Los Angeles: Committee to
     Organize the Advancement of Women, 1940, 174 pp.

Although the majority of women members of the Communist
party were housewives, leaders and theoreticians paid little
attention to their situation. At best they described women's
domestic role as the root of their subjugation and insisted that
only women's participation in wage-labor would advance sex equality. During the Popular Front in the 1930s, several important
strategists began to reassess the party's complacency toward its
female majority. In inner-party councils and in the pages of
the press, a heated discussion took place about the wisdom of
prevailing attitudes toward housework. Mary Inman, a party journalist, presented the major challenge.

In Woman's Defense is a collection of Inman's articles
first published in the Daily People's World (San Francisco) in
1939. The bulk of short essays addresses contemporary issues of
sex stereotyping and oppression: the overemphasis on beauty and
femininity in American culture, the sexual double standard, and the
class basis of women's subjugation. The most controversial pieces
concern the housewife's role in social production.

Against the many Communist writers who viewed housework as
unproductive and the housewife a parasite living on her husband's
wages, Inman argues for a strikingly different position. She

insists that housewives are "the Pivot of the System" because their contributions to the maintenance of the family are essential services and therefore an "indispensible part of production." The work women do in the home, Inman claims, is just as important as the labor men perform in factories or offices. She calls upon her comrades to revise their notions, grant the respect due women in their domestic roles, and address the strategic significance of their labor in party policy.

363   _____. Woman Power. Los Angeles: Committee to Organize for the Advancement of Women, 1942, 88 pp.
        Inman updated her analysis for the wartime situation. She issues a strong critique of Bukharin and other discredited Communist authorities, arguing that the need to organize for victory over fascism demands the full utilization of women's energies and, on a theoretical level, the recognition of their contribution to labor power, be it in the factory or in the home. Inman continues to challenge the orthodox Communist position that the housewife does not create value or indirectly earn wages.

364   _____. Thirteen Years of C.P.U.S.A. Misleadership on the Woman Question. Los Angeles: The Author, 1948, 39 pp.
        Continuing her argument with those Communists who, in her opinion, belittle the role of housewife, Inman documents the party's position and presents her own case for the social value of housework.

365   _____. The Two Forms of Production Under Capitalism. Long Beach, Calif.: The Author, 1964, 43 pp.
        This pamphlet updates Inman's argument outlined in Woman Power (1942). She continues to chastize Left theoreticians for focusing almost exclusively on the form of production that produces surplus value and disregarding the other form that produces commodity labor power, namely women's household work and care of family. "This onesideness," she writes, "helped create a climate favorable to the growth of fantastic ideas about women in society."

366   JONES, CLAUDIA. An End to the Neglect of the Problems of the Negro Woman! New York: National Women's Commission, Communist Party USA, 1949, 19 pp.
        During the 1940s the Communist party played a significant role in fostering racial equality within the union movement. After the war, in advance of the great civil-rights campaigns of the next decade, it devoted special attention to the Negro Question, which Jones argues is "prior to, and not equal to, the woman question."
        Jones begins by stating: "An outstanding feature of the present stage of the Negro liberation movement is the growth in the militant participation of Negro women in all aspects of the struggle for peace, civil rights, and economic security." She considers various economic hardships of black women and discusses

their important role, dating to slavery, within the family. She
claims that black women are the chief forces "in all institutions
and organizations of the Negro people." Consequently, the Communist party should, in her opinion, take advantage of their
unique capabilities and advance black women to positions of
leadership.

This essay is reprinted from Political Affairs, June 1949.

367 _____. Women in the Struggle for Peace and Security. New
York: National Women's Commission, Communist Party USA, 1950,
16 pp.

During the Cold War, American Communists reconvened their
peace campaigns and addressed the traditional vanguard of such
agitations, women. Written for International Women's Day, this
pamphlet calls upon women to oppose the "Truman-bipartisan war
policy," especially H-bomb production.

Although Jones catalogs the peace activities of various
women's groups and local peace committees, she reaffirms the
party's stand against bourgeois feminism and warns of the dangers
posed by the Equal Rights Amendment in "its original reactionary
form." She compares the status of American and Soviet women,
highlights the situation of Negro women, and commends William Z.
Foster for his contributions to women's equality.

368 JOHNSTONE, JENNY ELIZABETH. Women in Steel. New York:
Workers Library, 1937, 30 pp.

During the late-1930s organizing drives of the CIO Communists actively supported the formation of women's auxiliaries,
especially in mining, auto, and steel industries. This pamphlet,
addressed to wives of steelworkers, explains the history and purpose of the Steel Workers' Organizing Committee (SWOC) and its
women's auxiliaries, which bring women "into the beautiful life
of group work."

The National Negro Congress, which had allied with the
CIO, encouraged black women to join auxiliaries. Thus Johnstone
offers detailed advice on organizing a committee and emphasizes
the role of Negro women in the leadership of many chapters. She
concludes: "We will work in our towns in cooperation with other
organizations for a life free from tyranny and misery--a life with
cultural opportunities for our children, with plenty for all."

369 LANDY, AVROM. Marxism and the Woman Question. New York:
Workers Library, 1943, 64 pp.

This text represents the major theoretical response from
Communist orthodoxy to Mary Inman's challenge. "The key to the
ultimate emancipation of women is to be found in the arena of
modern industry and the historical struggles attached with it,"
Landy answers. He strengthens his argument by assessing the
impact of wartime production on a woman's life: "It transforms
her from a relatively dormant into an active force in social
progress, providing the labor movement, the most decisive factor

of all, with a new source of vitality and strength."
Landy primarily attacks Inman through an exegesis of the classics, citing Marx, Engels, and Lenin against Inman's heterodox theories of a family wage. Housework, Landy argues, is not paid; rather, as part of the employed husband's total output, the domestic element in the reproduction of labor power is unpaid. It follows from this curious conclusion that only by entering into wage-labor can a woman become part of modern society in the determinate productive sense. Landy disagrees with Inman's proposal to call for greater self-respect for the housewife. He wrote, "The difficulties and misery connected with the home under capitalism, and not the usefulness or dignity of the work performed in it, are the ground out of which the immediate issues of struggle grow." Landy thus closes the official Communist debate about the value of housework.

370 LAPIN, EVA. Mothers in Overalls. New York: Workers Library, 1943, 30 pp.
Lapin surveys the gains made by women as they moved into factory jobs during World War II and discusses the remaining problems. She calls attention to the poor wages still paid to women in the service sector, the lack of recreational facilities, health and safety issues, and especially the pressing need for child-care facilities. She even chastises progressive unions like the United Auto Workers and United Electrical Workers for failing to respond sufficiently to women and to educate them to the tradition of trade unionism. Lapin advises women to join community-wide committees on Women in Industry, to join the CIO and assume leadership positions, and to support "political action" campaigns to get women to vote.

371 Love--Family Life--Career: Behind the Soviet Law Limiting Abortions and Increasing Aid to Mothers. New York: Woman Today Publishing Co., [n.d.], 14 pp.
Abortion had been legalized in the Soviet Union under the Family Laws established after the revolution. In 1936, a change in legislation proposed to limit abortion, and American Communists engaged in a heated discussion about the political implications. Eventually they came to defend the new Soviet policy.
This pamphlet includes the text of the Soviet bill on abortions and aid to mothers, and emphasizes its continuing sanction of healthy family relations based upon women's economic independence and marriage shaped by "real love" and comradeship. Unlike the United States where economic insecurity drives women to abortionists, the Soviet Union, according to this pamphlet, takes pride in its rising birth rate as an important sign of female equality.

372 McCONNELL, DOROTHY. Women, War and Fascism. New York: Workers Library, 1935, 18 pp.
McConnell, a freelance journalist and social reformer, was

active in the American League Against War and Fascism, a coalition
of left groups dominated by Communists that was formed in 1933.
In this pamphlet she illustrates the use of women as cheap labor
under fascism, as well as the simultaneous propaganda for large
families and discrimination against employed mothers. A Third-
Period document, the essay also suggests parallels between Fascist policies and aspects of the New Deal, specifically provisions
in the National Recovery Administration codes barring the employment of married women from civil service if their husbands were
employed by the government. Refusing to accede to feminist principles, however, McConnell insists that such discrimination was
not a matter of "sex antagonism," but solely the result of a competitive society. She advocates a campaign to defeat all discriminatory legislation as part of a struggle against fascism in
the United States.

373 MILLARD, BETTY. Women Against the Myth. New York: International Publishers, 1948, 24 pp.
        This pamphlet attempts to explain the myth of women's in-
feriority, and describes the historic struggles to achieve equality. It opens with a brief overview of the economic, legal, and
political barriers against women and shows how their secondary
status was maintained in the nineteenth century by religion.
Millard then assesses women's position since World War II, especially the emergence of freudian psychology as the new authority
of women's subordination; Marynia Farnham and Ferdinand Lundberg's
Modern Woman: The Lost Sex (1947) serves as the chief example of
popular arguments in this line. To counter such propaganda,
Millard summarizes Frederick Engels's theory of women's oppression and asserts that only as women enter industry and struggle
for their rights will they gain emancipation. The positive example is the Soviet Union, where women have achieved equality because they play an important role in the productive processes.
Millard concludes by outlining the American strategy: "Women
must continue to be a major force in their own advance, but they
can move ahead only in common action with labor." She calls upon
women to join the Congress of American Women and to support a
progressive third party, to fight for price and rent controls,
child-care facilities, protective legislation, and to support the
rights of "triply oppressed Negro women."

374 _____. Women on Guard: How Women of the World Fight for
Peace. New York: New Century Publishers, 1952, 31 pp.
        This pamphlet is the best example of the party's postwar
efforts to mobilize women in the campaigns for world peace.
Millard spent two years abroad as a member of the secretariat of
the Women's International Democratic Federation and toured Europe
and Asia, talking with other women pledged to end the "madness
for war." She discusses the work that went into a massive international petition, which by April 1952 collected signatures of
over 600 million advocates of disarmament. She also describes
the role of American women in Women for Peace clubs, which by the

early 1950s were organized in about 100 cities to protest United States intervention in Korea.

375 MITCHELL, LOUISE PEARSON. Food Prices and Rationing. New York: Workers Library, 1943, 15 pp.

During World War II the federal government instituted a partial rationing and price-control system to prevent severe food shortages and to help ease the high rate of inflation. This pamphlet, addressed to women who care for their family's well-being, calls for strict enforcement of measures and a truly universal and democratic rationing program. Mitchell, the Communist party's expert on consumer affairs and staff writer for the Daily Worker, asks women in their mothers' groups, clubs, and defense councils to rally Congress to address this crucial issue.

376 _____. Hold That Rent Ceiling. New York: New Century Publishers, 1947, 15 pp.

At the close of World War II, the acute housing shortage and inflation in rents became major political issues in many communities. Mitchell focuses on the situation in New York City and advocates the formation of a broad coalition of labor, community, and women's groups to fight for rent control, a moratorium on evictions, and an end to racial discrimination in housing. "Decent housing for all people," she writes, "cannot be achieved so long as home building remains a private business for profit only."

377 MITCHELL, THERESE. Consider the Woolworth Workers. New York: League of Women Shoppers, 1940, 64 pp.

This pamphlet is similar in design and purpose to Consider the Laundry Workers. It surveys the history of women's employment in dime-stores and details contemporary conditions of labor. It endorses a major union drive among Woolworth employees.

378 RIVINGTON, ANN. No Gold Stars for Us. New York: Workers Library, 1940, 19 pp.

Rivington, the editor of the Sunday Worker (New York) women's page during the 1930s, wrote this pamphlet during the Nazi-Soviet pact. She appeals to mothers, asking them to refuse to accept the government's offer of gold stars in recognition of sons killed in battle. She discusses the imperialist aspects of war and describes the preparedness campaigns under way, especially propaganda promising more jobs during wartime. She asks women to inform themselves of the political machinations behind the war drive, to write letters of protest to newspaper editors and public officials, and most of all, to organize neighborhood groups into a party-led Women's Council for Peace.

379 _____. Women--Vote for Life! New York: Workers Library, 1940, 15 pp.

This pamphlet asks women, "How are you going to vote in

1940?" Rivington states the major issue of the election, peace-
time mobilization, and describes a plot of big business and the
Republican and Democratic parties to force America into war and
overthrow democracy. She emphasizes the threat of fascism at
home and abroad, and lists the Communist party's promises to
women, such as equal pay, social welfare legislation, free education, and the abolition of child labor.

380 SMALL, SASHA. Women in Action. New York: Workers Library,
     1935, 16 pp.
        A Third-Period document, this pamphlet emphasizes the role
women have played in working-class struggles. The author lists
scores of strikes that garnered women's energies, in part to dis-
pell the prevailing myth that women's place is in the home. A
litany of contemporary labor heroines emerges, including Edith
Berkman, Stella and Ann Resefske, Ella May Wiggins, Clara Holden,
and Ann Berlak. Small describes briefly their role in strikes
from Rhode Island to California, as well as the contributions of
women to labor defense and campaigns against war and fascism and
various civil-rights activities. She relates the principal message: "We gather strength from those who came before us, because
their actions laid the foundation for the huge powerful wall of
solidarity, a human wall of men and women together against their
common enemy--the ruling class--which oppresses us all." A concluding statement calls upon women to join the Communist party
and "march shoulder to shoulder with all toiling masses toward a
Soviet America."

381 _____. Heroines. New York: Workers Library, [c. 1937], 48
     pp.
        This collection of very short biographies relates the
heroism and valor of fourteen women from history, ranging from
Mollie Pitcher, Lucretia Mott, and Harriet Tubman to Clara Zetkin
and Nadyezda Krupskaya to Mother Jones, Ella Reeve Bloor, and
Elizabeth Gurley Flynn. The purpose is to affirm the important
role women have played in public life and thereby counter the
threat posed by the Fascist examples of Germany and Italy, where
women's sphere is limited to the home and service to men. Small
also raises the example of women's freedom in the Soviet Union
and concludes: "But with the glorious heritage of the past and
the splendid promise of the future we are taking our places in
defense of peace, freedom and democracy to stay until the battle
is won."

382 The Woman Question: Selections from the Writings of Karl
     Marx, Frederick Engels, V.I. Lenin and Joseph Stalin. New
     York: International Publishers, 1951, 96 pp.
        This collection comprises short excerpts from the writings
of the leading marxist theoreticians. Selections are arranged
by topic: the enslavement of women; the emancipation of women;
the bourgeois family; women in the struggle for socialism; social-

ism and the emancipation of women; and women in socialist reconstruction. Clara Zetkin's "Lenin on the Woman Question" constitutes an appendix.

The brief preface states the purpose of this volume: "As
a whole, the book is a guide to understanding the role and position of women today. Taken with current writings on the subject,
it provides both historical perspective and theoretical insight
into the tremendous force for peace and progress which women can
become."

383 The Women's Fight for Equality: Maternity and Childhood Pro-
    tection. New York: Communist Party USA, New York District,
    1935, 23 pp.
        To prepare women for the 1936 elections in New York, this
    pamphlet dramatizes the hard times since the 1929 crash, exposes
    the false promises of the LaGuardia-Lehman machine, and describes
    the favorable position of women in the Soviet Union. It summar-
    izes the Communist party's planks on women: equal pay for equal
    work, equal rights; broad social welfare legislation; reduction
    of prices on foods and utilities; free birth-control clinics,
    maternity hospitals, and municipal child-care facilities. It
    advises women to "Vote Every Hammer and Sickle!"

PERIODICALS

The precipitous decline in a feminist radical press reflected the
gloomy facts of the emerging era. The suffrage amendment passed, and
the mainstream women's movement now had no essential rallying point
and no militant Left wing. The Communists, for their part (leaving
aside the special case of the Finns), had no room for feminist journalism except that which met specific tactical purposes. Women
writers and editors found their way to the literary New Masses or,
more generally, to the mainstream press.

384 Working Woman. New York, 1929-1935.
        Produced during the Third Period of American communism,
    1928-1935, Working Woman maintained the ultra-Left position of
    incipient class warfare. The editor, Anna Damon, therefore fea-
    tured the militant strike activities of women and blacks, and
    provided coverage of party-sponsored organizations such as the
    National Textile Workers' Union, Trade Union Unity League, Unem-
    ployed Councils, and the United Councils of Working Class Women.
    The party's best journalists contributed regularly, including
    Myra Page, Grace Hutchins, Charlotte Todes, Rose Wortis, Sasha
    Small, and Margaret Cowl.

        In March 1933 the publisher, the Central Committee of the
    Communist party, changed the format from a newspaper to a maga-
    zine. Working Woman continued to report strike and organizational
    activities, especially anti-Fascist campaigns and defense of the

Scottsboro boys, and it also included household tips and health
and birth-control information. Each issue contained some fiction
by leading writers such as Meridel Le Sueur, Ella Winter, Grace
Hutchins, and Grace Lumpkin.

385 Woman Today. New York, 1936-1938.
        The successor to Working Woman, Woman Today reflects the
change in political emphasis as the Communist party moved into
the Popular Front and made antifascism rather than class struggle
its principal strategy. The format resembles mainstream women's
magazines and is designed to reach a wide audience.

FICTION AND POETRY

Even before the stock market crash of 1929, a number of events
foreshadowed a turn from experimental, avant-garde forms that had
dominated American literature since the early 1920s. The trial and
execution of Sacco and Vanzetti in 1927 rallied scores of intellectuals to attack injustice and line themselves up with the victims of
capitalism. The Gastonia strike of 1929 dramatized the plight of unskilled workers, especially in the South. In response, young artists
and some veterans writing in the New Masses, founded in 1926, investi-
gated the possibilities of social realism and regional literature,
and soon found ample material. By the 1930s a major revival had
taken place in the literature of protest.

During the Great Depression, when American capitalism seemed on
its last legs, artists and writers, most from the lower middle class
that historically produces discontented intellectuals, promoted a new
genre--proletarian literature. Sympathetic to the Communist party,
most writers nevertheless kept their political distance. Too many
proved overnight wonders, capturing the preferred vision of oppressed
workers "converted" to commuism through heroic strikes at the close
of the narrative. Clara Weatherwax Strong gained short-lived recognition for exemplifying this purpose in her only novel.

For many writers, the form proved discordant with, and ultimately
destructive to, their developed styles. Genevieve Taggard, for
example, practically lost the poetic voice she had created in the
bohemian years of World War I. Others flourished for a time because
they needed no special political impetus to make the social thematic
their own. Olive Tilford Dargan, Catherine Brody, and Josephine
Winslow Johnson, among others, relied little on formula. Others such
as Meridel Le Sueur, Grace Lumpkin, Adriana Spadoni, and Josephine
Herbst used the form in their own ways and sometimes with considerable
skill, attracting a relatively large readership that might not other-
wise have appreciated their work.

The maturation of the proletarian novel toward the end of the
1930s ironically took place just as the genre lost its political

value for Communists. The proclamation of the Popular Front, the attack on European fascism, and a defense of American democratic traditions prompted the Left to heroize the famous and sympathetic writers, the progressive-but-not-revolutionary theme. Lillian Hellman and Dorothy Parker stepped into the spotlight for a moment.

Ultimately, the Cold War all but killed both tendencies. The stress and strain of political life drove complex writers such as Ruth McKenney away from the Left. Oldtimers like Le Sueur held fast, while newcomers on the scene remained at a political distance for decades. The civil rights movement brought a single outstanding talent, Lorraine Hansberry, toward the Old Left.

386 BISNO, BEATRICE. Tomorrow's Bread. Philadelphia: Jewish
     Publication Society of America, 1938, 328 pp.
        A thinly disguised fictional version of Abraham Bisno's autobiography, Tomorrow's Bread is one of the best treatments of immigrant radicalism. Written by his daughter, the novel captures the "tragedy of a man whose vision intellectually is so far ahead of his time that he is doomed never to complete himself." The novel also describes in detail the labor and political movements in Chicago and New York at the turn of the century.
        Sam Karenski rises in the Chicago Jewish ghetto of the 1880s, leading fellow-tailors into union activities, the Knights of Labor, and the fringes of the radical movement. In the midst of the turbulent events following the Haymarket tragedy, he learns a crucial lesson: workers are more interested in immediate improvements than in vistas of utopia. Although a Socialist, Karenski is hereafter a practical man. He plays an important role in the campaigns for government regulation of sweatshops while maintaining his distance from doctrinaire Socialists. In private life, however, he finds it impossible to reconcile his conflicting beliefs, torn between loyalty to his family and his strong attraction to free love. The candid treatment of the protagonist's complicated sexual adventures, drawn from the author's childhood memories, adds a perspective rare in histories of this period.
        Karenski's is foremost a story of immigrant life. "The struggles of these aliens to get a foothold in America constitutes a sort of folklore of an ancient race in modern setting," Bisno wrote. Her protagonist drifts from union work to real estate, and back to manage the Protocol of Peace in the New York garment unions. Along the way he romances Florence Kelley. In the midst of all the confusions, an industry comes of age--bosses and workers, management and union, and with it Jewish-Americans.

387 BRODY, CATHARINE. Nobody Starves. New York: Longmans Green,
     1932, 281 pp.
        Brody tells a dismal story of a young couple, Molly and Bill, who face the hardships of the Great Depression. The story

171

opens with Molly working as a mill hand in a factory; it is an
interesting portrayal of work relations drawn from the author's
own experiences. Molly's one dream is to marry and thereby escape
the drudgery of the job. She succeeds, but pays a heavy price
for dependence.

Bill Redding, convinced that Detroit offers economic security, uproots his young wife from the town of her childhood.
Things do look promising for a while--until the layoffs begin.
Chagrined, Molly goes back to work, but soon she too gets a pink
slip. As the couple nears destitution they discover Molly is
pregnant. Bill responds first by walking out. He returns, they
try to live together again, but their resources continue to
dwindle. The story ends on a grim note: Bill shoots Molly, and
failing to kill himself, is taken away by the police.

Except for the final scene, the story is told from Molly's
perspective. She is not a strong character, however, but rather
a weak symbol of class victimization. A boring job and financial
insecurity have made her aimless and extravagant, ill-equipped to
deal emotionally with the deprivation of Depression life. She
appears petty and selfish, a bad match for her thoughtless, sulky
husband. Despite Brody's effort to tell the story as an epic of
the Depression, too often the plight of Bill and Molly seems a
result of their individual temperaments rather than of social injustice and hard times.

388   _____. Cash Item. New York: Longmans Green, 1933, 303 pp.
       Brody again uses the Great Depression to frame a dismal
story. The protagonist, Deena Plodget, is an aspiring actress
who is bound to her witless family in a dreary, small Ohio town.
In the first chapter, a disheartened Deena returns home to witness
the death of her father, a drunk who is killed in a train accident. It is she who must carry the burden of his burial expenses
and remain to share a sordid home with her thankless mother,
feckless sister, and brother.

Deena's prospective lover, Lawrence Yomans, symbolizes the
depravity of upper-class life in Micmac. The son of a wealthy
businessman, he has refused the responsibilities of his station to
work instead as a bank teller. Worse, he consorts with lower-
class women like Deena. Although his stuffy mother and prissy
sister tolerate his amusements, they pay a heavy price when Larry
is exposed as an embezzler. He serves only a short prison term,
but his family must cover his debt to the bank, and in the process they lose both status and fortune.

After scores of grim details about class and family relations during the Depression, the novel has an ironically happy
ending. Larry and Deena decide to escape their families by
marrying and moving to California. In the last scene, Deena's
family hosts a surprise bridal shower!

389 CABRAL, OLGA. Cities and Deserts. New York: Roving Eye
     Press, 1959, 69 pp.

172

Born in the West Indies, raised from age ten in New York
City, and married for many years to noted Yiddish poet Aaron
Kurtz, Olga Cabral first began publishing poetry in the little
magazines of the 1930s and then abandoned her work only to return
to it in the 1950s. She subsequently won three Poetry Society of
America awards, published several books for children, and steadily
pursued her craft. Famed Left poet Walter Lowenfels described
Cabral:

> Between the office kitchen and husband-lover
>   this voyager goes through her
>   18 hour shift
>   in a Dead Man's Float
>   and gives nobody a tumble
>   that a poem goes on.
>
> When her brain reaches the level
> Where she can't breathe anymore
>   her electronic tongue triggers
>   the language and a poem
> saves us from the Sargasso Sea
>   of drowning in our daily prose.

In most of her poems Cabral reflects upon the conditions of
civilized life, especially for minorities, in what had once been
Walt Whitman's native land.

390 DARGAN, OLIVE TILFORD. Call Home the Heart. New York:
     Longmans Green, 1932, 432 pp.
     Dargan (1869-1968), who wrote social novels under the
pseudonym Fielding Burke, specialized in local color narratives
of Southern mountain folk and dealt sensitively with woman's
place in class society. She spent most of her life in her native
state, Kentucky, and received several awards for her contributions
to Southern literature. She was a close friend of Rose Pastor
Stokes.
     Call Home the Heart is Dargan's first and most successful
novel; it is also considered the best of the six leading novels
on the Gastonia strike of 1929. The story features Ishma
Waycaster, a young mountain woman who yearns for a better, richer
life. Like other women of her background, Ishma's aspirations
are kept in bounds by marriage, family, and poverty. Eventually
desire overcomes commitment, and she runs away with a lover to a
burgeoning mill town. Searching for excitement, Ishma experiences
instead a stark awakening: she discovers the overwhelming hardship of urban working-class life. She asks herself, "Ambition,
the burning intellect, the vain reachings out, what meaning could
they have if they did not in some way add to human happiness?"
Ishma tries and readies herself to assist the workers in the
great strike. Despite her intellectual growth, however, she had
not yet satisfied her personal needs. Unable to counter her

prejudice against blacks, eager to regain her husband's love,
Ishma deserts the strikers for the peaceful splendor of her
mountain home. Her return home symbolizes the victory of personal
desire over principle.

391   _____. A Stone Came Rolling. New York: Longmans Green, 1935,
      412 pp.
      This sequel to Call Home the Heart continues the saga of
Ishma into the Piedmont's Great Depression. Ishma again confronts
herself: "To watch things grow, to eat good food, to sleep be-
side the man she loved; there were moments when these seemed
enough." In this round, set against intensified class and racial
violence, Ishma does not give in to the contentment of personal
life. She witnesses the murder of her beloved husband and suffers
personally at the hands of antilabor vigilantes, but stays in the
fight.
      Reviewers noted that Dargan grappled more skillfully in
her sequel with the complexities of Southern society, especially
the religiosity and racism equally indigenous to the white working
class. They also commended her deep feeling for the oppressed
and portrayal of the abuses of capitalism.

392 DAY, DOROTHY. The Eleventh Virgin. New York: A. & C. Boni,
      1924, 312 pp.
      Similar in plot to the early portions of Day's autobiog-
raphy, this novel traces the maturation of a young woman destined
to lose her virginity, sexually and, metaphorically, politically.
The protagonist June leads an exciting political life in pre-
World War I in New York. She works as a reporter for a Socialist
newspaper, the Clarion, and covers the exciting birth-control
campaigns of the era. Lured by a couple of declassé intellectuals,
she takes a position on the Flame, a Left cultural magazine, and
eventually joins three men in a cooperative living arrangement
replete with salon.
      Left adverturism ends abruptly with the Red scare, which
kills the Flame and sends to jail many of June's radical friends.
The climax of the woman suffrage campaigns, and an especially
harrowing incident involving militant demonstrations in Washington, D.C., bring to a simultaneous conclusion the political phase
of June's life and the radical movement.
      June achieves her second goal in the 1920s. She falls in
love and finally loses her virginity. Her lover, who has pro-
fessed only temporary affection, leaves on the birth of their
baby. The story ends with a deflowered, depoliticized but mature
June.

393 GILES, BARBARA. The Gentle Bush. New York: Harcourt Brace,
      1947, 552 pp.
      Written during the period of Communist party advocacy of
black and white unity, Giles's first novel is a study in both
class loyalty and racial prejudice. In epic proportion, it

follows the decline of a Louisiana planter family of the new
South, focusing on three characters who break tradition and thereby shake the fragile foundation of white rule. Their course is
determined by fate, for they are the inheritors of a legacy rooted
in slavery, a "tyranny which functioned like a machine, powerful
and smooth, destroying the tiniest non-conformity." Adrift, the
younger generations can find no alternative to the stability and
superiority that had once been their family's right as overseers
of that barbaric system.

Set against the declining aristocracy is the hope of the
future, the white and black proletariat of the new South. Racial
prejudice, however, undercuts their potential strength, as white
workers lynch a local black and ruin one of the few of their
ranks who was not tainted by racism.

Ultimately, Giles's saga is not a lesson in despair. It
is a symbolic treatment of Carl Sandburg's "Let the gentle bush
dig its roots deep and spread upward to split one boulder." The
indigenous struggle against the heritage and remnants of slavery
waged by the Southern working class--the gentle bush--will triumph
in the end.

394   HANSBERRY, LORRAINE. A Raisin in the Sun, The Sign in Sidney
      Brustein's Window [and] the 101 Final Performances of Sidney
      Brustein: Portrait of a Play and its Author, by Robert
      Nemiroff. New York: New American Library, 1966, 318 pp.
      This volume collects Hansberry's two best-known plays.
Raisin in the Sun, which swept Broadway and went on to some 530
performances, made her the youngest American and only black playwright to earn the Best Play of the Year award. In time, it
would be perfomed in thirty countries and be adapted for film, a
musical, and a television series based on its themes and characters.

The play recalls Chicago's South Side in the decades since
the late 1940s, and studies the various plans concocted by members
of the Younger family to escape ghetto miseries. The dilemma of
the first step, through potential business success, rise to professional status, or geographical relocation, confronts and ultimately vitiates the common aspiration. Most important, perhaps,
Hansberry, who viewed herself as a playwright who happened to be
black, showed good and bad characters of both races.

By the 1960s the play had also become a football for political discussion of esthetics. Writers ranging from Nelson Algren
to Harold Cruse accused Hansberry of reformist-integrationist
illusions, for depicting black aspirations as only upwardly mobile
within the existing system. James Baldwin, Julius Lester, and
others came to her defense, responding that she had given honest
treatment to personal dilemmas. Freedomways, successor to
Freedom, devoted an entire issue in 1979 to her vindication.
Clearly, Hansberry had captured a certain perspective with rather
precise historical contours; that perspective could be rejected,
seen by many as archaic or accomodationist, but it would remain a

real part of the black radical world view.

The Sign in Sidney Brustein's Window, Hansberry's second
commercially produced play, had no luck on Broadway and was widely
misunderstood by critics, yet it expressed another essential as-
pect of the author's experience.

This play features a white couple, an artist who had been
burned (although only by implication) in the McCarthy era for his
Left-wing commitments and is struggling back from alienation and
rage. Largely a domestic drama, the play seemed to many observers
a mere personification of opinions. To its supporters who raised
money and elicited support from prominent theatrical personalities, it was an evocation of the moral commitment not seen on the
stage since the dawn of the Cold War. Hansberry died during the
play's run and did not see its later production in a dozen countries, including a French rendition by translator-producer Simone
Signoret.

395   _____. Les Blancs and The Last Plays of Lorraine Hansberry.
        Edited by Robert Nemiroff. New York: Random House, 1972,
        370 pp.
        A prescient depiction of the African revolutionary impulse
in the 1960s and 1970s, the drama from which this book takes its
title was also Hansberry's own favorite among her works. A
Westerner becomes involved willy-nilly in an African situation,
producing an interracial dialogue that Hansberry believed utterly
essential. When produced in 1970, the play characteristically
evoked cries of antiwhite racism, although Hansberry had sought
to make clear that she intended to move the discussion beyond
race as such, beyond guilt feelings, to the worldwide political
imperative. As Julius Lester writes in a sensitive introduction,
her refusal to take a racist posture toward whites proved
Hansberry's cross to bear and her vindication.

396 HELLMAN, LILLIAN. The Collected Plays. Boston: Little,
        Brown & Co., 1972, 815 pp.
        This volume contains Hellman's eight original plays and
additional adaptations. The best were written during the peak
of political drama, between 1929 and 1950, when a call for social
action was at the heart of much creative endeavor. For example,
during the 1935-1936 Broadway season, over one-fifth of productions addressed social or political issues. Hellman's unsuccessful attempt to base a play on labor unionism, Days to Come, appeared in 1936. In her subsequent works, Hellman found her
metier. The Little Foxes (1939) and Another Part of the Forest
(1947) revealed capitalist decadence in the South; Watch on the
Rhine (1941) and The Searching Wind (1944) dealt with the danger
of fascism. All are realistic in form, or what Hellman termed
melodrama in its true sense, the purposeful portrayal of violence.

In 1960 Hellman announced that she disliked "theme" plays,
a reflection on her later work. Her plays written during the
McCarthy period and later indicate a disjuncture between her

steadfast political commitment and playwrighting; they are usually described as chekhovian because rather than shaped around clear issues they excel in character development and mood. Yet one quality remains throughout—a hard-driving sense of morality.

397 HERBST, JOSEPHINE. Pity Is Not Enough. New York: Harcourt Brace, 1933, 358 pp.
     The story of an American family from the Civil War to the 1930s, Herbst's "proletarian" trilogy is her major literary contribution. Herbst (1892-1969) had been prepared for the task by a strong Midwestern background and first-rate esthetic training. Raised in Sioux City, Iowa, the daughter of a farm-implement salesman, she attended various universities when financially able, and entered New York's radical literary circles in 1919, making friends with the likes of Genevieve Taggard and Max Eastman. She left for Europe in 1922 after personal tragedy, but at the end of the decade she returned to rural Pennsylvania where she spent the rest of her life.
     Herbst had acquired some of the skill and styles of the "Hemingway school," and published two well-received novels in the 1920s. During the 1930s she devoted much energy to political causes and reportage, from Iowa farm strikes and the Scottsboro case, to Cuban revolutionary activities and the Spanish Civil War. Meanwhile she wrote her monumental trilogy. The political bent did not diminish her careful portrayal of the background shaping the lives of her main characters; indeed, many readers and critics were unable to find enough action or even development amid the richness of details.
     While Herbst's early novels dealt with the disillusionment of expatriate bohemians, Pity Is Not Enough returned to the American saga as a microcosm of the development of modern society. Tracing the Trexler family from 1868 to 1896, the novel links three characters to the respective economic institutions of the day. Joe goes to the Reconstruction South from Philadelphia as a carpetbagger and becomes involved in the rampant political corruption, loses his early fortune, and lives out his days a pathetic searcher of an elusive American dream. Anne marries and travels to Iowa to a life of farm poverty. David moves toward riches through profiteering in government flour, symbol of the staff of life bent through manipulation and deceit. Toward the end of the book, daughters of the Iowa couple grow up to support the famed 1919 Seattle general strike. The family has taken the bad and the good.

398 _____. The Executioner Waits. New York: Harcourt Brace, 1934, 371 pp. Reprint. New York: AMS Press, 1977, 371 pp.
     In the second installment of her trilogy, first published in 1934, Herbst followed the Trexler descendants from the turn of the century to the stock-market crash of 1929, using the Industrial Workers of the World, World War I, and the economic boom of the 1920s as social backdrop. For David, the era brought financial

good times and an illusion of well-being that ends abruptly in
the book's final scene when he observes the burial of a striker
in the 1930s. Meanwhile, his niece Rosamund dies in an automobile
crash, sending her husband to despair and eventual recovery in
strike support work. Victoria, David's other niece, becomes a
bohemian in New York circles before settling down to an apparently
peaceful marriage. The decay of the middle class, materially and
morally, underlines the entire epic; the spiritual growth of the
proletariat, although obviously intended, is less evident.

    The economic analysis and fructifying character and plot
development seemed to many reviewers a substitute for subjectiv-
ity; Herbst's merciless examination of the middle class is almost
too much for the average reader. Courageous, even remorselessly
patient in her descriptions, Herbst created a literary monument
that is almost forbidding.

399   _____. Rope of Gold. New York: Harcourt Brace, 1939, 429 pp.
    Published in 1939, this novel completes Herbst's trilogy.
From the early 1930s to the sitdown strikes of 1937, the lives of
Victoria and her intellectual husband, Jonathan, pass through the
turbulence of political commitment, sexual misalliance, and re-
cuperation amid heightening struggles. The disintegration of the
middle class and the American social structure in general now
quicken, and Herbst herself seems more comfortable with her subject matter. She, and the revolutionary potential of the times,
apparently rush toward a conclusion.

    But even here, Herbst remains at her best in handling the
patient literary chores of describing speech-patterns and physical
and psychological scenery. Still, she paints an overly dense
canvas. She tries to squeeze in the whole pattern of American
life at the middle of the Great Depression, when the Left passed
from hysterical overconfidence to a strategic confrontation with
the situation but not yet to the cooptation and suppression to
come later. Although ever brilliant in short flashes, Herbst
never managed to sustain a whole, gripping narrative.

400 JOHNSON, JOSEPHINE WINSLOW. Now in November. New York:
    Simon & Schuster, 1935, 1970, 231 pp.
    An outstanding, little-appreciated author of regional
literature since the 1930s, Johnson (1910-) won a Pulitzer
Prize for Now in November when it first appeared in 1935. She
subsequently produced a series of novels, short stories, poetry,
and nature essays without returning to any notable renown. One
of the most effective but also subtle literary radicals, she
skillfully weaves narrative and description with the love of
nature and semirural life. "I hate standardization, ugliness,
narrowness of life," she has said, and wished that "everyone
could see the significance and beauty of ordinary things." She
has remained obscure, one might suggest because she has remained
loyal to these values and to a form that places poetic voice
above action.

Now in November could be called a prerevolutionary novel.
The reminiscences of daughter Marget West about ten years of farm
existence record her family's ceaseless and ultimately unsuccessful struggle against agricultural conditions and economic arrangements. The protagonist characteristically compares the smallness
and folly to the beauty and power of the countryside. "We--I--
seemed like a disease on earth compared with the other things.
Our lives, buildings, our thoughts even, a sort of sickness that
earth endured," she reflects. For herself (and the author), the
glory of the seasons is unsatisfying only because it cannot
economically sustain human existence. A strike of tenant farmers
passes, not unnoticed but unsuccessful. As the crops die from
drought and her mother wastes away, the sense of imminent disaster
pervades. "Love and the old faith are gone," she ends, "But there
is the need and the desire left, and out of these hills they may
come again. I cannot believe this is the end."

401   . Winter Orchard and other Stories. New York: Simon &
     Schuster, 1935, 308 pp.
     Regional literature with a radical touch, Winter Orchard
is a collection of twenty-two remarkable short stories. Johnson
offers a critique of racism as powerful as any contemporary white
author, and describes the fear internalized by blacks, the callousness of most whites, and the guilt of others, especially
women. Reviewers have compared Johnson with Emily Dickinson, for
she too expresses the inner brooding, suppressed feelings, and
problems of social life. She seems to know best woman's loneliness and, by extension, the isolation experienced by beaten men.
Nature is her counterpoint, representing life without doubt or
guilt.

402   . Jordanstown. New York: Simon & Schuster, 1937, 259
     pp. Reprint. New York: AMS Press, 1976, 259 pp.
     One of the best yet most obscure proletarian novels,
Jordanstown captures the conflict in a small border town between
North and South. Originally published in 1937, Johnson's later
work continues some of the principal characters from Winter
Orchard and brings in small farmers and sharecroppers, black and
white, and a smattering of sympathetic small businessmen. Together
they constitute a group struggling to reappropriate money from a
project to fund a city monument and turn it over instead to relief. Their grievances are articulated by protagonist Allen
Craig, a grocery clerk who publishes a militant daily paper in
his evening hours. Craig's friend Dave, who "seems to have belief instead of blood in his veins," stars as the activist leader.
With their following they build a hall of their own and march
toward it gloriously on Labor Day, only to be clubbed and shot by
police. Mobs of "respectable" citizens smash their newspaper
operations and lock their leaders away in prison.
     Johnson avoids stereotypes in describing heroes and vil-
lains. The ordinary folk are despairing but not oblivious to the

source and meaning of their pain; they do not have to be awakened
by a Red Evangel, merely shown the means to fight. The enemy is
not only capital but the "rust-covered god of precedent and tradition," the fear of impropriety that restrains even sympathetic
middle-class observers, the injustice of a society somehow artificial and false. Still, as the newspaper publisher testifies:
"I believe still in the decency of men and in their courage. I
believe this suffering is a perversion, and not a necessity. . . .
We shall go on planning and protesting and building until we see
the earth again a great altar where the fruit and grain wait as
communion for all men."

403 Le SUEUR, MERIDEL. Salute to Spring. New York: International
     Publishers, 1940, 1977, 171 pp.
          Born in Iowa in 1900, Meridel Le Sueur writes most poig-
     nantly about the Midwest. Her parents were active Socialists
     there, and Le Sueur herself emerged as an organizer and writer in
     the late 1920s, during the farmer-labor upsurgency in Minnesota.
     During the Depression she made her literary mark in the field of
     journalism. She also served on the editorial staff of the New
     Masses.
          Salute to Spring, first published in 1940, is Le Sueur's
     best-known collection. Within the canon of proletarian litera-
     ture, her stories stand out for their Midwestern focus, their
     delicate style, and their female perspective. Like Thornton
     Wilder, Le Sueur cuts through the sentimentality often associated
     with small-town life and paints instead the rigidity and shallow-
     ness of character spawned by the ingrown society. "Like many
     Americans," she writes, "I will never recover from my sparse
     childhood in Kansas." Against this emotional depravity she juxta-
     poses woman's signal link with humanity--her life-giving capacity.
     Her stories are thus rich in maternal imagery and symbolism; many
     involve pregnancy or mother-daughter relationships. Although the
     hard economic reality of the Depression underpins her narrative,
     Le Sueur salvages an affirmation of life in motherhood.

404 _____. Harvest: Collected Stories. Cambridge, Mass.: West
     End Press, 1977, 93 pp.
          This anthology of Le Sueur's stories from the 1930s and
     1940s describes the tribulations of mostly Midwestern and Plains
     states women beset by poverty, misunderstanding or brutal men,
     and vicious state institutions. Including some labor reportage
     of the Minneapolis general strike of 1934 and some straightforward
     regional fiction, Harvest shows Le Sueur at her most versatile
     and poignant. She demonstrates her strongest writing in escape
     from outright political stylization and in a protofeminist con-
     sciousness that is vivid when the social context gives full sway
     to her skills of observation. At such times, she says all she
     needs to say through implication.

405 _____. The Girl. Cambridge, Mass.: West End Press, 1978,

148 pp.

Written in the 1930s, rejected by publishers, and rewritten slightly in 1978-1979 for publication funded in part by the National Endowment for the Arts, The Girl is a rare novel by Le Sueur. It relates a proletarian journey of a Minnesota girl unable to understand the poverty-stricken society around her, the sexual ruses that her friends use to get by, the brutality and selfishness of the men whom she loves and fears. She does understand, in characteristic Le Sueur fashion, the deep significance of her own biological womanhood; and when she has given birth, even the death of her father and the attempt of the state to take away her infant cannot dim her firm dedication to the continuity of life across generations. Politics play a peripheral role in this work, an occasional glimpse at the alternatives that only a few of the protagonists can perceive against a hellish social order.

406 LUMPKIN, GRACE. To Make My Bread. New York: Macauley Co., 1932, 384 pp.

To Make My Bread follows a Southern mountain family to its destiny in a new mill town. The story takes place during the first three decades of the century and focuses upon Emma McClure, the female protagonist. Through Emma's keen but tired eyes, the reader observes the transformation of her father, herself, and her children. Each generation reacts differently to mill life. "Granpap" McClure is too old to work and suffers the greatest dislocation. Emma tries to ignore the hardships because she wants desperately to see her children educated. Her children do indeed attend school briefly, but inevitably they take their places alongside their mother in the mill. Uprooted from the rural homestead, this last generation seems the most resigned to the breaking pace of labor in the mill and the overwhelming poverty of the village. In the 1920s, however, the situation changes dramatically as the millowners introduce new labor-saving machinery and dismiss a large number of hands whom they had previously lured away from their mountain homes. A dramatic and bloody strike closes the story and ushers in a new era of unionism.

Grace Lumpkin's first novel, To Make My Bread won deserved praise when it appeared in 1932. It won the Maxim Gorky award as the best labor novel of the year, and in 1935-1936 was adapted for the New York stage as Let Freedom Ring. Critic Robert Cantwell wrote that he could not imagine "how anyone could read it and not be moved by it."

Lumpkin (ca. 1903-), who grew up in the South, had once organized a night school for farmers and their wives and worked for a time in the rural counties of South Carolina. She was exceptionally deft in capturing the vernacular and customs of the region. To Make My Bread is thus a close portrait of Southern mountain folk, especially the distinct traditions of men and women. Effective propaganda, the novel is also good social history.

407 _____. A Sign for Cain. New York: Lee Furman, 1935, 376 pp.
      Described as "entertaining radical propaganda," Lumpkin's
second novel examines race relations in the South. The story is
set in a small reactionary town ruled by an old white family, the
Gaults, that has been declining materially and spiritually since
its glory during the Confederacy. The aged Colonel Gault, the
family patriarch, embodies the paternalism and condescension
towards blacks typical of his caste and generation. His off-
spring, in comparison, typify decadence and in the case of his
eldest, alcoholic son, blatant racism. On his land live a family
of black sharecroppers whose son, Denis, has returned from the
north ostensibly to care for his infirm mother. Denis, however,
is a Communist; he aims to help organize black and white sharecroppers to fight against their masters.
      The story culminates in the brutal slaying of Denis and a
black friend. The two men had been arrested and jailed for a
murder they did not commit. They barely survive a lynching attempt by an angry crowd only to die at the hands of the drunken
Gault son, who is the actual guilty party. Lumpkin uses this
dramatic incident to underscore the racism of a Southern community
that would turn the despicable murderer, Jim Gault, into a local
hero.

408 McDONALD, GRACE LOIS [Margaret Graham]. Swing Shift. New
      York: Citadel Press, 1951, 494 pp.
      The story of a "typical coal miner's family," Swing Shift
is based on "authentic historical data," according to its author.
It follows the protagonist, J.E. McCaffrey (Mac) through many
union struggles near and far, including the Soviet Union in the
1920s. The novel is actually a compendium of miscellaneous facts
and anecdotes about the history of the American labor movement
since 1900, and lacks true character development. A contemporary
reviewer aptly summarized its chief flaw: "The bulky narrative
is jam-packed with a wealth of detail and an almost stupefying
plethora of scenes."

409 McKENNEY, RUTH. Industrial Valley. New York: Harcourt Brace,
      1939, 379 pp. Reprint. Westport, Conn.: Greenwood Press,
      1968, 379 pp.
      McKenney recounts in artful detail events in Akron, Ohio,
during the Great Depression that culminated in the rubber workers'
strike of 1936. Considered by critics and author alike her best
book, Industrial Valley won the Writers' Congress prize for non-
fiction in 1938 and again in 1939. McKenney used newspaper
clippings to produce what one reviewer called "the most original
and readable piece of American labor history ever written." She
used fictitious names for two characters, and wrote the social
and political history of the strike as a rich narrative. Malcolm
Cowley called Industrial Valley a "collective novel" of the times.

410 _____. Jake Home. New York: Harcourt Brace, 1943, 503 pp.

McKenney's protagonist is the archetypal proletarian hero.
Jake Home is born to poverty in 1901; his mother labors three
days before delivering by cesarean section a twelve-pound "natural
accident." From that moment, Jake's life is one of pure bravado
and adventure. At age eleven he enters the coal mines of Luyskill,
Pennsylvania; within a decade he emerges a union leader. Jake
Home is a giant among the working class.

The story traces Jake's struggle to find a niche for himself in the labor movement of the 1920s and 1930s. For a brief
period he is derailed from his main course by his first wife,
Margaret Agar, a Greek-American beauty set on middle-class respect-
ability. But a violent strike brings Jake to his senses, and he
takes off, leaving behind a wife pregnant with his child. In New
York City he goes to work on the waterfront for the Trade Union
Unity League and becomes a Communist. Reacting to the Sacco and
Vanzetti case, organizing in the South where he barely escapes
death, and touring the Midwest, he continually asks, "Am I on the
right road?" In 1932, at the novel's close Jake Home has become
"Big Red." He is leading a parade of unemployed workers against
New York's City Hall--and he is happy.

Reviewers criticized <u>Jake Home</u> for its larger-than-life
hero, but as one critic noted, it is McKenney's "feeling for detail that puts her book head and shoulders over most fiction."
The character of Jake Home, moreover, is more complex than stereo-
types allow.

One of the most compelling features of Jake's personality
concerns his problematical relationships with women. McKenney
paints an unsympathetic portrait of his first wife, a woman who
desires foremost a story-book marriage, including a new home,
plump babies, and a white-collar husband. But Jake had been completely oblivious to Margaret's aspirations before their marriage,
for he was, and remained, attracted solely by her physical charms,
his major measure of womanhood. Without any insight into
Margaret's passion to rise above her immigrant background, Jake
watches passively as she tries to construct her dream life until
the situation becomes intolerable.

His second wife, Kate McDonough, a political opposite of
Margaret, fares no better. Kate is an independently wealthy
"liberated" woman working on the Sacco and Vanzetti case when
Jake meets her. Again, it is Kate's flair for fine clothes and
vivacious personality that attracts the rough proletarian. Soon,
however, Jake insists upon marriage and domesticity as the only
"proper" relationship. Kate resists for a long time but, at a
crucial moment, relents. After they marry, Jake pushes Kate to
give her money to the party, makes her feel inept as an organizer
and party member, and as a housekeeper. Eventually, Kate crumbles
under Jake's pressure and turns to alcohol for relief. Although
she eventually recovers from her breakdown, their marriage does
not. Jake walks out.

Jake Home, who is fatally drawn to attractive women, understands them not at all. His inability to relate honestly to

women, to exhibit any sensitivity whatsoever, emerges as one of
the central themes of the novel. Thus McKenney's story of Left
activism in the 1920s and early 1930s offers interesting insights
into the interpersonal rather than merely political dimension of
movement life.

411 MILLAY, EDNA ST. VINCENT. Collected Poems. Edited by Norma
       Millay. New York: Harper & Brothers, 1956, 1975, 738 pp.
          This volume is considered the definitive collection of
Millay's works, excluding plays. Norma Millay, the poet's sister,
has gathered poems and sonnets representing the celebration of
individual freedom in the 1920s and reflection on social issues
in the 1930s and 1940s.

412 OLSEN, TILLIE. Tell Me a Riddle. Philadelphia: J.B.
       Lippincott Co., 1961, 156 pp. Reprint. New York: Dell Pub-
       lishing Co., 1976, 125 pp.
          Tillie Olsen has published relatively little but neverthe-
less stands as one of America's most highly revered authors. She
writes about people who have been frustrated by the circumstances
of their lives, especially poverty or the limitations imposed by
race or gender. She relates, often in painful detail, "the un-
natural thwarting of what struggles to come into being but cannot."
          In her first book, published originally in 1961 when Olsen
was forty-eight, she collected four stories about personal relationships and family life. "Here I Stand Ironing" studies a
mother's reflections upon her almost grown daughter's childhood,
which was marked by illness and intense insecurity, and the
mother's inability to rise above the situation. The title story,
considered Olsen's finest work and winner of the O'Henry Award
for best American short story of 1961, examines the unhappy marriage of an aging Jewish couple, the mutual antagonism yet dependence that centers a relationship now devoid of the constraints
of child-rearing and full-time labor. The critic R.M. Elman
described some of the stories in this volume as "perfectly real-
ized works of art."

413 PAGE, [DOROTHY] MYRA. Gathering Storm: A Story of the Black
       Belt. New York: International Publishers, 1932, 374 pp.
          A story about the Gastonia strike and its roots in poverty
and exploitation, Page's first novel follows mill worker Marge
Crenshaw from her childhood at the turn of the century to her
political awakening in the late 1920s. Page draws an interesting
character who reflects on the special hardships women endure,
such as their frequent pregnancies and endless domestic responsibilities.
          Unlike other novels on Gastonia, Gathering Storm deals at
length with black-white relations in the community and during
the strike. Page also makes explicit her allegiance to the Communist organizers who speak, as one reviewer put it, in "half-

digested sociological slogans." As the story closes, the mill
community sees the promise of a Soviet America: "Marge could
feel the lash of the wet wind, the tremor of rushing bodies. . . .
She was riding a gale! Now swept along, but deliberately, joyously
a fore-runner, a marshaller of the gathering storm."

Both a student and native of the South, Page (ca. 1899-)
was well prepared to write Gathering Storm. With advanced degrees
from Columbia and the University of Minnesota, she published her
doctoral dissertation, Southern Cotton Mills and Labor, in 1929.
She also had firsthand experience in labor organizing. In the
1920s she worked for a time in the industrial department of the
Virginia Young Women's Christian Association, and finding its
local leadership too conservative, gained broader experience with
the Amalgamated Clothing Workers. In the 1930s Page was a leading
labor journalist and member of the Revolutionary Writers' Federation.

414   . Moscow Yankee. New York: G.P. Putnam's Sons, 1935,
     292 pp.

In the early 1930s Page visited the Soviet Union, where
she worked as a journalist and lived among other intellectuals
and artists. Moscow Yankee is drawn from her impressions of
Soviet life and serves as a vehicle for the author to lavish
praise on the great experiment.

Moscow Yankee features an ordinary American worker, Andy,
who escapes the woes of the Great Depression by joining the production line of the Red Star truck factory in Moscow. The story
opens with an account of Andy's relationship with his avaricious,
snooty Detroit girlfriend, Elsie, and closes with his marriage to
his fellow-worker and self-sacrificing Communist, Natasha.

The book was well-received by critics during the liberal
years of the mid-1930s. One reviewer called it a "gripping, profound, thrilling story." Its depiction of sexual relations is
still very interesting.

415   . Daughter of the Hills: A Woman's Part in the Coal
     Miners' Struggle. New York: Citadel Press, 1950, 245 pp.
     Reprint. New York: Persea Books, 1977, 245 pp.

Published as With Sun in Our Blood in 1950, Daughter of
the Hills is a fictionalized biography of Page's friend Dolly
Hawkins Cooper, a woman who struggled for survival in the harsh
coal-mining territory in the Cumberland Mountains of Tennessee.
The daughter of a widowed miner, Dolly Hawkins represents the
love of her people for Appalachia. Her story is linked to John
Cooper's, an equally gripping tale of a young man who wanders
into Dolly's household one rainy night, woos her, and eventually
shares her life in the coal-mining industry. Together John and
Dolly find love and happiness amid tragedy. They struggle against
the indignities of poverty and against the injustices levied by
the coal operators. Their hopes for a better life are passed on
to their children.

Page tells their story in the lyrical style of local-color realism. Richard Wright called her protagonist "one of the most impressive proletarian characters in our literature."

416 PALEY, GRACE. The Little Disturbances of Man. Garden City, N.Y.: Doubleday & Co., 1959, 189 pp. Reprint. New York: Viking Press, 1968, 189 pp.

Grace Paley (1922-) emerged during the 1960s as an anti-war activist and visited Hanoi and Moscow as a member of peace delegations during the Vietnam War. The Little Disturbances of Man, a collection of short stories first published in 1959, continues to enjoy the favor of critics. Paley's stories focus not on plots but on characters, on their struggles to overcome the complexities of life and determine their own fate. Set in New York, they describe Jewish lower- or middle-class relationships between parents and children, husbands and wives.

417 PARKER, DOROTHY (ROTHSCHILD). The Portable Dorothy Parker. New York: Viking Press, 1973, 1980, 610 pp.

In 1939 Dorothy Parker addressed the League of American Writers: "It is no longer the time for personal matters—thank God!" This volume reflects her determination to shift from light verse to social themes. The first part constitutes the original 1944 edition, which Parker herself compiled from her two collections Here Lies (1936) and Not so Deep as Well (1939). Her stories and poetry of the 1930s depict the banality of New York upper-class existence, especially as lived by women, as well as a growing sensitivity to the horrors of war and racism. Her later stories, reviews, and articles are also included in this edition, along with a brief introduction by Brendan Gill.

418 REPLANSKY, NAOMI. Ring Song. New York: Charles Scribner's Sons, 1952, 57 pp.

Ring Song is the only volume by a promising poet of the postwar and McCarthy years. Published in high-culture journals like Twice a Year and in the Left press alike, Replansky is clever, deft with words, and equally capable of writing political or ostensibly personal poems. Protest against social conditions stands alongside protest against the difficulties that modern life presents the individual, especially the American woman. As she writes in "Housing Shortage":

> Excuse me for living,
> But, since I'm living,
> Given inches, I take yards,
> Taking yards, dream of miles,
> And a landscape, unbounded
> And vast in abandon.

419 RIDGE, LOLA. Sun-Up, and Other Poems. New York: B.W. Huebsch, 1920, 93 pp.

This volume contains a section, "Reveille," that calls upon workers to rise up and pays tribute to Ridge's friends, Alexander Berkman and Emma Goldman.

420 _____. Red Flag. New York: Viking Press, 1927, 103 pp.
This volume contains the most social of Ridge's poetry. The title section celebrates the Russian Revolution and includes "Moscow Bells, 1917" and "Russian Women," both passionate tributes to revolutionary ardor.

421 _____. Firehead. New York: Payson & Clarke, 1929, 218 pp.
In the 1920s Ridge became active in the campaign to save Sacco and Vanzetti from execution. This poem, inspired by their death, is essentially a religious metaphor, the Crucifixion standing for the martyrdom of many others.

422 _____. Dance of Fire. New York: Harrison Smith & Robert Haas, 1935, 104 pp.
Described as a poem of earth's ending, Dance of Fire is Ridge's last tribute to Sacco and Vanzetti. It is considered her most successful poem; in 1935 she won the Shelly Memorial Award and soon thereafter was honored with a Guggenheim fellowship.

423 SARTON, MAY. Faithful Are the Wounds. New York: Rinehart & Co., 1955, 281 pp.
Popular novelist May Sarton (1912-) writes about the birth pangs of the McCarthy era and the feeble response of the liberal community. Presaging Lillian Hellman's Scoundrel Time, Faithful Are the Wounds is a bitter indictment of those Left-leaning liberals who refused to read the danger signals of the oncoming political repression. The novel is also a thinly disguised depiction of the actual suicide of the noted literary critic, F.O. Mathiesson.
The story is set in Cambridge, Massachusetts, in 1949, shortly after the defeat of Henry Wallace's campaign for the presidency. It concerns the suicide of Edward Cavan, a distinguished Harvard professor, and his sister, colleagues, students, and friends who try to determine the meaning of his sudden death.
Cavan, a Socialist since the late 1920s, had tried to wage a defense against a growing anticommunism on campus and in the American Civil Liberties Union. When his Boston chapter received a directive from the national organization to remove known Communists from its executive offices, Cavan had fought the measure only to witness the capitulation of his long-time liberal friends. He tried similarly to rally his Harvard colleagues to prepare to fight infringements on their academic freedom. Again he failed. The complacency of his associates at this critical moment, the realization that the political tide had turned fatally for the worse, pushed this reclusive and sensitive individual to suicide.
At first his circle of intimates express only shock and

disbelief, but Sarton reveals the ultimate meaning of Cavan's
death in a chapter entitled "Epilogue: November, 1954." The
scene is the Massachusetts State House, where Cavan's associates
are gathered before a committee investigating "Communist sub-
versives" in the state. Only at this moment do they heed Cavan's
warnings, too late to stop the political repression coming down
but in time to regain their own integrity by refusing to play the
part of friendly witness.

424 SEGAL, EDITH. <u>I Call to You Across a Continent</u>. New York:
    People's Press, 1955, 23 pp.
       Dedicated to Morton Sobell in Alcatraz and to the memory
of Julius and Ethel Rosenberg, this is the first adult volume by
a noted dance teacher and children's guide in the Left summer
camps and schools since the 1940s. Segal, growing up on New
York's Lower East Side, won a prize for her music and lyrics at
the Henry Street Settlement, worked in the old Neighborhood Play-
house on Grand Street, and came into the Left as a "people's
artist." Her poems often express anger at the miscarriage of
justice, as in the title poem:

           What does the Hudson mean to you?
           To me it once meant Palisades--
           an all day ride on the River Line
           Now it means the Rosenbergs
           Death House on the Hudson

425 SLESINGER, TESS. <u>The Unpossessed</u>. New York: Simon &
    Schuster, 1934, 357 pp. Reprint with afterword by Lionel
    Trilling. New York: Avon Books, 1966, 333 pp.
       Tess Slesinger (1905-1945) grew up in a middle-class
Jewish family in New York and attended the Ethical Culture Society
School, Swarthmore College, and Columbia University. In 1928,
while working as a book reviewer for the <u>New York Post</u>, she married Herbert Solow, assistant editor of the <u>Menorah Journal</u>, a
magazine of secular Jewish thought, and joined its left-wing
circle of intellectuals. Here she found the cast of characters
for her only novel, <u>The Unpossessed</u>, published originally in 1934.
       The novel studies the Left intellectual of the 1930s as a
social phenomenon. With equal measures of vindictiveness and
compassion, Slesinger exposes the self-destruction in his quest.
At the center is the troubled relationship of Miles and Margaret
Flinders, which was modeled on the author's own first marriage.
The husband's self-centered yet ineffectual intellectualism is
set against Margaret's desire for life, especially her need for
loving companionship. Written shortly after her divorce from
Solow, the book stands as an incisive commentary on the sterility
of the male intellectual.
       That the intellectual seeking to be "possessed" by revo-
lutionary fervor is male is no minor point. Slesinger portrays
women as equally adrift but as forced upon an unfamiliar course

by their menfolk. Dragged into the intellectual mire, women
suffer confusion and humiliation; or, pushed toward ultra-
sophistication, they find men too weak to satisfy their longings.
As Lionel Trilling noted in the afterword, it is Slesinger's
awareness of the sexual dynamics of the intellectual circle that
makes The Unpossessed most clearly the product of a woman's insight. "It is scarcely surprising," he wrote, "since the dialectic is between 'spirit' and 'nature,' that a woman should have
been the first to take note of the state of things." The novel
thus not only reveals the impotence of the Left intellectual of
the 1930s, but studies in revealing detail the undercurrent of
sexual politics.

426   . On Being Told that Her Second Husband Has Taken his
     First Lover and Other Stories. Chicago: Quadrangle, 1971,
     396 pp.
        While married to Herbert Solow, Slesinger kept a diary and
reflected often on her husband's intellectual circle around the
Menorah Journal. She began publishing short stories based on her
observations, many concerning the bitter feelings between husbands and wives. In 1932 Slesinger divorced Solow and wrote
"Missis Flinders," her most admired story and pivotal piece for
The Unpossessed. In the wake of critical acclaim, she wrote a
dozen more short stories about New York intellectuals and parlor
Socialists.
        These stories, including "Missis Flinders," are collected
in this volume, which appeared originally in 1935 as Time: The
Present. In a review in the New York Times, Edith Wharton compared Slesinger to Dorothy Parker, and the label stuck. Like
Parker's, Slesinger's stories are ironic, witty, sometimes
acerbic, but more often sympathetic portrayals of middle-class
sophistication and ennui. Slesinger's sensitivity to the hard
times of the Depression, however, make her work less flippant
than Parker's.
        Although Slesinger resented the comparison, her later
career resembled Parker's. In 1935 she went to Hollywood and
with her second husband, Frank Davis, became a successful screen
writer and leading organizer in the Screen Writers' Guild. She
died of cancer in 1945.

427 SMEDLEY, AGNES. Daughter of Earth. New York: Coward-McCann,
     1929, 344 pp. Reprint. Old Westbury, N.Y.: Feminist Press,
     1976, 413 pp.
        Writing in the Nation (March 20, 1929), Freda Kirchwey
described Daughter of Earth, published originally in 1929, as the
"first feminist-proletarian novel to be written in America."
This description is apt, for Smedley created a protagonist, Marie
Rogers, whose destiny is clearly shaped by the gender and class
systems of the small Missouri town of her childhood. Social discrimination, poverty, and domestic violence engulf Marie's youth.
She longs to escape but dreads the choice available to woman: to

become a household drudge, like her physically and spiritually
broken mother; or to become a prostitute, like her Aunt Helen.
Marie determines to cast her own lot by securing an education and
by vowing never to love or to marry. The story traces Marie's
struggle for emotional and economic independence through her
brief college years at Berkeley and her World War I adventures in
New York City, where she heroically aids the Indian freedom movement. At the novel's conclusion, Marie is a dedicated Socialist,
more hopeful about the prospects for revolution than for women's
emancipation. The protagonist's failure to achieve an unfettered
sexual relationship--even to enjoy sex without guilt--gives this
novel a poignant and contemporary flavor.
          Reviewers described Daughter of Earth as "too passionately
authentic" to be a work of fiction. The main story is the autobiography of the young Agnes Smedley (1890-1950). The Feminist
Press edition contains an afterword by Paul Lauter focused on
Smedley's later years in China, where she worked as a revolutionary
journalist.

428 SMITH, LUCY ELLIOT. No Middle Ground: A Collection of Poems.
     Philadelphia: Writers Division, Philadelphia Council of the
     Arts, Sciences and Professions, 1952, 30 pp.
          Born in 1916, Lucy Elliot Smith wrote "progressive" free
verse about social and political issues during the Cold War.
Many of her poems concern the victims of society, especially
blacks and the poor, and express hope for a better world dedicated
to peace and brotherhood.

429 SPADONI, ADRIANA. Not All Rivers. Garden City, N.Y.: Double-
     day, Doran & Co., 1937, 336 pp. Reprint. New York: AMS
     Press, 1976, 336 pp.
          This novel is a study of a woman's search for identity and
her eventual realization of self in the class struggle. Although
its plot development is weak, the handling of this potentially
didactic theme is not. If anything, the formal political conclusion is too subtle.
          Set in the Bay Area in the first decades of the twentieth
century, the opening chapters describe the childhood of strong-
willed, curious Rhoda Townsend. Her character remains fixed
through the story of her enrapturing first marriage to a Berkeley
professor, who had seduced Rhoda when she was his student and who
drifts back to this habit soon after their marriage. Rhoda
secures a divorce, and begins to reconstruct her life.
          The second half of the novel, which carries the story into
the turbulent 1930s, continues the theme of Rhoda's search for
self. An answer appears in the form of a gentle, sincere liberal
lawyer, David Evans. They marry, and Rhoda tries to live as devoted wife and, when that role proves too limiting, as devoted
mother. Restlessness will not let go, however. Her husband encourages her to join the staff of the New People, a Communist
party newspaper. Rhoda works hard and fills her days, but not the

troublesome emotional void. Finally, at the novel's unexpected gripping conclusion, after her husband had been badly beaten by some antilabor thugs, Rhoda grasps the true meaning of the class struggle and its meaning to her life. Along with David, she pledges herself to the fight for a better world.

The major tension in the story is Rhoda's battle with her emotions, her conflicting desire for excitement and need to be useful. Although Not All Rivers fails to meet the criteria of the "proletarian novel," for it focuses on left-wing intellectuals rather than workers, it presents an interesting perspective on the political climate of the 1930s. The protagonist's dilemma, framed by woman's point of view, makes Spadoni's novel a unique contribution to the genre.

430 STRONG, ANNA LOUISE. Wild River. Boston: Little, Brown & Co., 1943, 327 pp.

Strong raised funds for the John Reed Children's Colony, a refuge for orphans of the Volga famine following the Russian Revolution, and had a special knowledge of Soviet youth. In this, her first novel, she moves beyond journalism to fiction to relate their nobility and heroism to an American audience. Set against a German invasion, the story involves two Russian orphans, a peasant girl and petty thief, as they struggle to fulfill the promise of the great experiment. In building the Dneiper dam and in establishing a collective farm, the two protagonists mature and become leaders of their community.

431 STRONG, CLARA (WEATHERWAX). Marching! Marching! New York: International Publishers, 1935, 256 pp.

Marching! Marching! won the prize for a proletarian novel awarded in 1936 by the New Masses. The story follows the mobilization of lumber workers, aided by their Communist allies, against the Bayliss Lumber Company, a murderous West Coast firm. Weatherwax describes in graphic detail the inhumanity and violence of this local class war. Her characters suffer poverty, humiliation, and fear; they are maimed emotionally and often physically, yet they are also capable of heroic deeds. The story ends with the staging of a massive strike against the lumber baron, the workers singing in unison "Hold the fort for we are coming . . ."

Weatherwax, described on the inside flyleaf as a descendant of pre-Mayflower New England stock, provides interesting local color. She presents female characters who manage to star amid this male-dominated labor setting: women emerge as the key organizers in the community. Weatherwax also describes the ethnic character of the lumber community. The most perceptive section of the novel highlights the Finnish Communist sector and its cooperative institutions.

432 TAGGARD, GENEVIEVE. Collected Poems, 1918-1938. New York: Harper & Brothers, 1938, 164 pp.

Genevieve Taggard (1894-1948) became a Socialist during

her college years at Berkeley shortly before 1920. Although she later joined the Teachers' Union, she never became an activist. She was foremost a poet, although she also taught at Bennington College and Sarah Lawrence.

This collection documents the evolution of her poetry from its early lyricism, mostly a celebration of love and nature, to its later social and revolutionary themes. "At Last the Women Are Moving," written in 1935, celebrates the participation of women in a militant march. Thus she introduces the volume: "Many poems in this collection are about the experiences of women. I hope these express all types of candid and sturdy women. . . . All those who try to live richly and intelligently." A biographer of Emily Dickinson, Taggard shares a lot in form and theme with her mentor.

433 _____. Long View. New York: Harper & Brothers, 1942, 113 pp.
This volume contains Taggard's most political poetry. The bulk of poems celebrates themes common to the 1930s Left: the Soviet Union, the Spanish Civil War, and the "Negro people."

434 TOBENKIN, ELIAS. The Road. New York: Harcourt Brace, 1922, 316 pp.
The story follows the development of a young woman from a small Wisconsin town as she becomes a class-conscious Socialist and free woman. The main message concerns the double standard of morality and the artificiality of the marriage contract.

Hilda Thorsen has been deserted by her childhood lover, Raymond Evert. She pulls up stakes and moves to New York City, where she becomes a self-supporting factory worker and has Evert's child. There she also meets Ada, a recent widow who had self-consciously dispensed with the marriage ceremony altogether. Ada, in converting Hilda to socialism, delivers a major speech on marriage as a barbaric custom. She describes the hypocrisy of most Socialists, who in theory believe in free love, but in practice regard women like Hilda and herself as degraded species.

The remainder of the story is insignificant although dramatic. Hilda escapes a fire in the shirtwaist factory where she works (presumably the triangle fire of 1911), whereas her beloved friend dies. Hilda then takes a position as secretary for the United Mine Workers' Union and moves to Colorado during the great strike. Unexpectedly she meets her former lover who, after graduating from the University of Chicago, is serving on the government commission investigating the strike. Although he now offers his hand in marriage, Hilda considers him a class enemy and, equally important, herself a free woman fully competent of raising their son alone. She turns down his offer. At the novel's conclusion, Hilda has joined the American relief party to the Soviet Union at the close of World War I.

435 VORSE, MARY HEATON. Strike! New York: Horace Liveright, 1930, 376 pp.

This novel is a fictionalized account of the 1929 textile
strike in Gastonia, North Carolina, where Vorse served as an
organizer for the Amalgamated Clothing Workers of America. It is
an action drama of violence, including murder, directed against
the downtrodden mill workers and narrated by Northerner Roger
Hewlett, a labor journalist covering the strike.

"These women are militant workers," Vorse concludes a
chapter. Women and children stand prominently in her rendition
of the strike, especially Mamie Lewes, mother of four children
and chief ballad-singer, who is killed in a climatic scene. A
woman organizer, Irma Rankin, also emerges as a dedicated warrior
against injustice. Vorse describes vividly the role of women
within the union struggle and also their impoverished family life.

Mike Gold called Strike! a "burning and imperishable epic,"
although most contemporary reviewers expressed more reserved
opinions, advising readers to judge the book as something other
than a work of fiction; Sinclair Lewis aptly describes Strike! as
"more a statement of facts than a novel." However melodramatic,
the story does ring true.

436 ZUGSMITH, LEANE. A Time to Remember. New York: Random House,
1936, 352 pp.

Like many social novels set in the Great Depression, A
Time to Remember exposes the profound sense of personal dislocation suffered by many during this long period of financial insecurity. Zugsmith gracefully weaves the stories of several such
individuals, each of whom is trapped psychologically by family or
friends who themselves are the spiritual victims of poverty.
Fatefully, a dramatic strike in a leading New York department
store reverses the course of their lives. Through the heroic and
collective struggle for the union, the protagonists rise above
their personal tragedies and gain an essential inner strength and
peace.

Critics rightfully praised A Time to Remember when it appeared. Skillful at characterization, Zugsmith created two
strong female protagonists, and through their eyes the reader discovers the finely drawn world of their differing social milieus.
A member of the League of Women Shoppers, a Left variant of the
Consumers' League, Zugsmith (1903-1969) also offers unique insights into working conditions in department stores. She artfully
captures the vernaculars of clerks and sustains, as Alfred Kazin
noted, a "sharp portrayal that never stoops to exclamation."

437 _____. The Summer Soldier. New York: Random House, 1938,
290 pp.

Zugsmith once described herself as an anti-Fascist and advocate of American democracy, economic as well as political.
This novel takes that theme as its focus and studies a group of
assorted Northern liberals who travel South to investigate the
massive violence directed against union organizers in Chew County.
Three are exposed as "summer soldiers" when they choose to return
to their complacent lives.

1965-1981

Civil rights, campus unrest, and the Vietnam War gave birth to a
new era of radicalism in the 1960s. Different from its predecessors
in both structure and strategy, the New Left owed allegiance to no
political party or leadership and spoke at first only hesitantly in
the name of socialism or communism. At its peak in 1969-1970, the
movement staged massive protests against the war and sponsored scores
of campus and community organizations working for social change. Although sectarian politics and the altered political climate of the
1970s fractured the movement, the intense experience of the preceding
decade left its mark on the lives of many young men and women, now
avowedly Socialist.

Although several historians have examined the events of this
turbulent era, few have studied women's part in detail. Only Sara
Evans has contributed a scholarly work tracing the roots of women's
liberation to the civil-rights and student movements of the 1960s.
Others have written from personal experience, often to dissociate
themselves from their former involvements. The few sources in this
section all bear the imprint of participants' reflections upon an
important stage in history and in their own lives.

438 CANTAROW, ELLEN; SUSAN O'MALLEY; and SHARON STROM. Moving the
     Mountain: Women Working for Social Change. New York: Femi-
     nist Press, 1980, 166 pp.
        This volume contains three essays, based primarily on oral
     histories, on important twentieth-century activists. Sharon
     Hartman Strom relates the remarkable continuity in the political
     life of Florence Luscumb, a Boston radical born in 1887, beginning
     in 1910 in the woman suffrage campaigns and progressing through
     various civil rights, third-party movements, and peace activities
     to the present-day women's liberation movement. Ellen Cantarow
     and Susan Guskee O'Malley describe the civil-rights activities of
     Southerner Ella Baker, who was born in 1903. Cantarow also
     sketches the political biography of Mexican-American Jessie Lopez,

born in 1919, an organizer for the United Farm Workers in recent decades. Each essay includes lengthy transcriptions of portions of the original interviews.

439 CLUSTER, DICK, ed. <u>They Should Have Served that Cup of Coffee: Seven Radicals Remember the Sixties</u>. Boston: South End Press, 1979, 268 pp.

Cluster has collected a sample of reminiscences of the 1960s movements, including two contributions by Socialist feminists. Ann Popkin, in "The Personal Is Political: The Women's Liberation Movement," recounts her experiences in the Bread and Roses collective, which gathered approximately 150 core activists in 1969-1971. Although Popkin had been active since her high school days in various phases of the civil-rights and antiwar movements, the women's movement marked a turning point in her political development. She discusses its impact on her own life and describes its origins in the 1960s movement and political structure.

Leslie Cagan, also a Boston activist, was a "red diaper baby." Like her friend Popkin, she began political work when she was growing up in New York City. During the mid-1960s she took part in the student movement at New York University, visited Cuba, came out as gay, and joined the antiwar struggles. She describes her evolution in "Something New Emerges: The Growth of a Socialist Feminist."

440 EVANS, SARA MARGARET. <u>Personal Politics: The Roots of Women's Liberation in the Civil Rights Movement and the New Left</u>. New York: Alfred A. Knopf, 1979, 274 pp. Reprint. New York: Vintage Books, 1980, 274 pp.

A former activist in the civil-rights movement and the New Left, Sara Evans chronicles an important chapter in the political history of the 1960s. She shows how women gained spaces for themselves within male-dominated organizations, developed various skills and accumulated resources, and eventually came to chart their own independent course in women's liberation.

The strongest chapters of <u>Personal Politics</u> concern the formation of the Southern civil-rights movement in the late 1950s and early 1960s. Born and educated in the South, Evans carefully traces the regional roots of social activism to indigenous institutions, especially the Protestant churches and Christian organizations like the Young Women's Christian Association. She discusses the campaigns against lynching and racism conducted by black and white women since the early decades of the century as important precedents for the generation of women who came to civil rights via their own church and campus organizations of the 1950s. Religious and moral idealism thus encouraged a sense of political responsibility and served as the philosophical backdrop for the "Freedom Summer" of 1964, when large numbers of Northern students volunteered to help register Southern black voters. Evans examines the racial and sexual dynamics within the Student

Nonviolent Coordinating Committee (SNCC) between 1963 and 1965, especially the rebellion of black women who "struck the first blow for female equality" within the organization.

The second half of the book follows women's actions within the Northern student movement, particularly Students for a Democratic Society (SDS). As she examines the moral ethos of the Southern civil-rights movement, Evans analyzes the intellectual modes of SDS and its abstract commitment to participatory democracy. Evans assigns the SDS desire to change the quality of human relations as primary to the emergence of feminist consciousness among activist women. The various community organization projects sponsored by SDS between 1963 and 1965 encouraged the personal growth of a core group of women. By 1967 the Woman Question became a major issue of Left politics; by the following year women's groups formed at a rapid pace across the country.

An institutional history, Personal Politics is based on an extensive series of oral interviews with leading activists. Evans conducted her research from 1973 to 1978.

441 FREEMAN, JO. The Politics of Women's Liberation: A Case Study of an Emerging Social Movement and Its Relation to the Policy Process. New York: David McKay Co., 1975, 253 pp.
Freeman describes the emergence of an independent women's liberation movement from its dual origins in the New Left and the mainstream women's movement associated primarily with the National Organization of Women. More in tune with NOW politics, Freeman traces her own roots to the student movement at Berkeley and civil-rights activism in the South during the 1960s. She is decidedly critical of the New Left phase and underscores the blatant sexism and discrimination characteristic of the movement. Unlike Sara Evans, who recognizes the personal and political gains women achieved in the New Left, Freeman describes those same experiences as negative and women's break as a logical consequence of their mistreatment by male activists.

442 FRITZ, LEAH. Dreamers & Dealers: An Intimate Appraisal of the Women's Movement. Boston: Beacon Press, 1979, 293 pp.
By her own description, Fritz was a middle-class housewife and mother during the halcyon days of the late 1960s, too far "uptown" to participate fully in the radical movements. She did find time to take her children down to the "liberated zones" of Lower Manhattan, for happy afternoons of sightseeing. Despite her distance from the movement, Fritz offers her intimate memoirs as an authoritative statement on women's position in the New Left.

Fritz's history of the rise of radical feminism is both shoddy and irrelevant to her purpose. She is part of a small circle of antimarxist feminists, Andrea Dworkin the most prominent, who hope to discredit the New Left--and men in general--as a patriarchal conspiracy to prevent the consolidation of the women's movement. Fritz's prime examples are tragic case histories of Weatherwomen. Jane Alpert, Susan Saxe, and Bernadine

Dohrn, who were forced underground for their terrorist activities, are described as victims of male manipulation and later, betrayal. As other reviewers have pointed out, Fritz's narrative and chronology are ridden with errors. Her book is best read as a polemic of the late 1970s, a sad commentary on the disintegration of a movement.

443 RED APPLE COLLECTIVE. "Socialist-Feminist Women's Unions: Past and Present." Socialist Review 8 (March-April 1978):37-58.

This essay addresses the decline in Socialist feminist organizations since 1975. It begins by tracing the rise of the Socialist feminist movement in the early 1970s to its peak in 1975, when more than 1,800 women representing groups and unions from across the country assembled at the Yellow Springs Socialist-Feminist Conference to share their experiences. Three years later, most of these organizations had dissolved. The authors analyze the situation within the Socialist feminist movement, focusing on four categories: theory, practice, organizational form, and internal process. They conclude by offering a list of suggestions, including the formation of single-focus groups and national networks for communication, establishing firmer links with the mass women's movement, and maintaining the social and cultural traditions of the Socialist feminist movement.

This essay was written collectively by a workgroup of the Valley Women's Union, Northampton, Massachusetts, which was facing a serious decrease in membership from over one hundred in 1974-1975 to forty by 1977, shortly before it disbanded.

AUTOBIOGRAPHIES AND BIOGRAPHIES

The events of the 1960s fell hardest on women born in the 1940s. As their memoirs attest, their generational experience was as much personal as political in the formal sense. Very few had grown up with much understanding of their role as women in American society or with a well-defined interest in politics. Consequently, the civil-rights and antiwar movements, and the women's liberation movement that sprang from them, transformed their lives and fostered a host of unbounded expectations for the future.

Writing from the vantage point of less than a decade later, these women, now in their thirties, reflect a quieter mood. Their reminiscences nevertheless capture aspects of the 1960s experience. Many reveal an intense concern for self-realization, especially in the sphere of sexual relations. Only the pre-World War I radicals approached this generation's flair for introspection and, in some cases, sensationalism. In perhaps twenty or thirty years, as the disappointments of the 1970s fade and the larger meaning of the previous decade becomes clearer, the story might be worth retelling.

For those veterans who met the 1960s less as a revolution in private life than as a release from the politically repressive atmosphere of the Cold War, the era poured new energy into aging bodies. Dorothy Day, for example, found new causes to sustain her dedication. Literary artists Barbara Deming, Denise Levertov, Tillie Olsen, and Muriel Rukeyser gained new audiences for their works of protest and sometimes, new insights into themselves as radical women.

Alpert, Jane (1947-)

444 ALPERT, JANE. Growing Up Underground. New York: William Morrow, 1981, 372 pp.
    In 1974 Jane Alpert, who had gone underground to avoid conviction for several bombings in New York City, surrendered to government agents. She renounced her previous Left affiliations, declared herself a militant feminist, and soon began a two-year term in prison, where she worked on her memoirs.
    Alpert's roots in the Left were never very deep. Although she pays tribute to her grandparents' Socialist leanings, she herself grew up in a comfortable Jewish family set on upward mobility. At Swarthmore in the mid-1960s, she preferred the campus newspaper over nascent New Left activism. After her graduation in 1967, Alpert took a handsome position at Cambridge University Press in New York and pursued graduate studies in classics at Columbia University.
    Alpert moved only gradually to the Left. Her first antiwar act was participation in April 1967 in the National Mobilization to End the War in Vietnam. At Columbia she met a recruiter for Students for a Democratic Society and became involved in its Community Action Committee. Real change began only when she moved into a collective on East Eleventh Street and fell among a group drawn to terrorism.
    Although Alpert cannot explain her political development during this period, she manages to describe in ample detail her sexual adventures. Her affair with Sam Melville, who later died in Attica prison, becomes a focal point.
    The turbulent era of the late 1960s serves only as background to Alpert's self-realization. Her memoirs are, in a way, too personal. Yet she writes with honesty about her lack of political sense: "Certainly personal rage and pain, more than politics, had led me to break violently with my parents in adolescence, to bomb buildings, and later to reject the left with all the hostility I could muster."

Baez, Joan (1941-)

445 BAEZ, JOAN. Daybreak. New York: Dial Press, 1968, 159 pp.
    Throughout the 1960s Joan Baez was the leading female folksinger in the United States. By the decade's end she was equally renowned for her antiwar sentiments and activities, so

much so that her best-selling record albums were banned by Army
PXs. To many she appeared the symbol of the antiestablishment
generation: she wore simple black dresses, long, straight hair,
no make-up; and when she felt comfortable with her audience, she
performed sans shoes.

Daybreak is in part her autobiography and statement on
nonviolence, which she describes simply as "organized love." She
reflects on her brief term in the Santa Rosa Prison, which she
served for civil disobedience at the draft induction center in
Oakland, California; Quaker meetings, Harvard Square coffee
houses, the blind children she tried to teach; her sisters, and
in great pseudopsychoanalytic detail, her parents. Labeled a
"unique self-portrait," dedicated to "the flower children," Daybreak is a rambling sketch of Baez's youth and youthful philosophy.

Davidson, Sara (1943-)

446 DAVIDSON, SARA. Loose Change: Three Women of the Sixties.
     Garden City, N.Y.: Doubleday & Co., 1977, 367 pp.
     Davidson follows the lives of her two former sorority
sisters and herself from 1960, when they entered the University
of California at Berkeley, until 1972. Susie Berman, who married
a self-centered, sexist political activist, painfully travels
from commune to commune and sleeps with over one hundred men before entering medical school at the story's conclusion. Tasha
Taylor, a sketchy figure throughout, escapes the youth rebellion
for an equally tumultuous life within the New York art circle.
Sara herself has divided loyalties: a well-paying career in
journalism and a flirtation with the counterculture. In recalling
their journeys, Davidson hoped to "piece together a social history of the Sixties." She hoped, too, to frame answers to the
important questions, "What went wrong? All these bright, idealistic committed people--how could they have miscalculated so
badly?"

     Davidson admits her failure to find answers, or even to
keep the questions in focus. But there is a graver shortcoming--
her inability to interpret, however partially, the significance
of the social upheaval of the previous decade. A skilled journalist, she paints scenes very well: the revolution in women's
fashion; street demonstrations at Berkeley; violence at the
Rolling Stones concert in Altamont; dope-smoking orgies at hippie
communes. But her descriptions, engaging as they are, serve
merely as colorful backdrops, never as historical context, for
personal interaction.

     Somewhere along the way, Davidson confused the era's keen
perception, the personal is political, and reduced political activism to a very individualistic, insipid search for self-realization. For this reason she delights in describing in graphic detail the many sexual encounters of her protagonists. What
Davidson presents as their gradual feminist awakening thus comes
across primarily as success in achieving the perfect orgasm.

Then, too, as one reviewer noted, she seems to have writeen with
movie rights in mind; here, she proved prescient, for NBC-TV
adapted Loose Change for a miniseries in 1978.

Davis, Angela (1944-)

447 DAVIS, ANGELA YVONNE. Angela Davis--an Autobiography. New
     York: Random House, 1974, 400 pp.
         Davis, a prominent member of the Communist party since
     1968, framed her autobiography by her arrest and trial of 1972.
     The internal narrative traces her political development since
     childhood, beginning at age four when her parents moved to a
     white neighborhood in Birmingham, Alabama, and Davis first grap-
     pled with the issue of racism. Her later experiences in New York
     in the late 1950s, her college years at Brandeis, her sojourns in
     Europe and Cuba are all related to explain Davis's eventual deci-
     sion to join a marxist-leninist organization. A large, tightly
     constructed section concerns her work in California in SNCC and
     with the Black Panthers, and provides the most insight into the
     nature of Davis's political commitments.

448 APTHEKER, BETTINA. The Morning Breaks: The Trial of Angela
     Davis. New York: International Publishers, 1975, 284 pp.
         Unlike other descriptions of the trial, this version is
     told through the eyes of a longtime acquaintance. Aptheker de-
     scribes the proceedings in detail and also includes a brief but
     interesting prologue relating her first meeting with Angela Davis.
     They were both fifteen and attending a session of Advance, a
     Socialist club that convened in Aptheker's home. They met again
     nine years later in 1969 when Aptheker was an assistant editor on
     the People's World and Davis had just been fired from the Univer-
     sity of California because of her membership in the Communist
     party. Aptheker's narrative of the trial includes her own ex-
     periences as a member of Davis's defense committee.

449 NADELSON, REGINA. Who Is Angela Davis? The Biography of a
     Revolutionary. New York: Peter H. Wyden, 1972, 208 pp.
         Nadelson, a high school friend, offers a sympathetic ac-
     count of Angela Davis's political development. She interviewed
     various family members, acquaintances, and influential intellec-
     tuals such as Herbert Marcuse to explain why Davis cast her lot
     with the Communist party. She covers Davis's childhood and col-
     lege years especially well.
         Although most reviewers acknowledged the value of
     Nadelson's somewhat propagandistic biography, Toni Morrison (New
     York Times Book Review, October 29, 1972) expressed outrage at
     what she perceived as Nadelson's condescending attitude toward
     blacks, exemplified by her selection of mostly white interviewees.

450 PARKER, J.A. Angela Davis: The Making of a Revolutionary.
     New Rochelle, N.Y.: Arlington House, 1973, 272 pp.

A black conservative, Parker uses the biography of Angela
Davis to attack black militancy. He skims over Davis's childhood
and college years to create a forum for his own opinions in detailing her involvement in the Communist party and the affairs of
the Soledad brothers and George Jackson.

Although Parker's biography received an expectedly warm
review in the right-wing National Review, it was dismissed by
other commentators as a diatribe against socialism.

Day, Dorothy (1897-1980)

451　DAY, DOROTHY. On Pilgrimage: The Sixties. New York: Curtis
　　Book, 1972, 383 pp.

　　　Written as monthly journal entries, Day's account of the
1960s attests to her continuing involvement in causes of social
justice. Although she describes communal life in Catholic Worker
settlements, as she did in previous publications, and the inspiration she found in the life of Peter Maurin, she finds new material
in her role as titular head of the movement since Maurin's death.

　　　On Pilgrimage traces Day's journeys to cities across the
United States and to Cuba and Rome; it also documents her responses to the major political developments of the decade. She
begins defending Cuba and Fidel Castro, moves into civil-rights
activity in the South by the mid-1960s, and concludes by relating
her support to Cesar Chavez's farm workers' strike and antiwar
demonstrations at the decade's end. Since the 1930s Day had led
her life by one principle: "Love is the measure by which we will
be judged."

Deming, Barbara (1917-　)

452　DEMING, BARBARA. Prison Notes. New York: Grossman Publishers,
　　1966, 183 pp.

　　　Deming and thirty-five friends were jailed in Albana,
Georgia, in 1964 for their participation in a freedom walk for
civil rights. The book constitutes her reminiscences of their
treatment in prison, their relations with and feelings for one
another during the ordeal, and their steadfast dedication to
their ideals over the two months of their confinement.

453　FRITZ, LEAH. "Barbara Deming--The Rage of a Pacifist." Ms. 7
　　(November 1978):97-101.

　　　Drawn from an interview with Deming, this essay describes
her radical activities since 1960, with special emphasis on her
pacifist involvements.

Fonda, Jane (1937-　)

454　KIERNAN, THOMAS. Jane: An Intimate Biography of Jane Fonda.
　　New York: G.P. Putnam's Sons, 1974, 358 pp.

　　　Oscar-winning Jane Fonda was the most famous Hollywood

personality to take an unpopular stand against the war in Vietnam.
Her political activism of the early 1970s prompted this unofficial
and unwelcomed biography. Kiernan traces Fonda's life from childhood and tries especially to understand her political evolution.
He dates her shift in consciousness to the Tate murders and a
subsequent sojourn to India. When Fonda returned, he writes, she
drifted toward radical movements, first toward the civil-rights
struggles of Native Americans and the Black Panthers, and finally
to the antiwar movement.

　　　　Kiernan presents Fonda as a simple and impressionistic
young woman. He attributes her political development to romantic
involvements with men: Fred Gardner, a leading activist among
soldiers opposed to the war; Donald Sutherland, an actor; and Tom
Hayden, who allegedly confirmed "her radical legitimacy." Kiernan
concludes: "Jane's life has been a mirror of our times--neurotic,
extreme, violent, confused, naive, guilt-ridden, compressed,
contradictory, transformed. . . ."

Langer, Elinor (1939-)

455　LANGER, ELINOR. "Notes for the Next Time: A Memoir of the
　　　1960s." Working Papers for a New Society 1 (Fall 1973):48-83.
　　　　Langer, born in 1939, writes a eulogy for the New Left of
her generation. Her essays divides into two major parts, the
first assessing the political dynamics of the movement, the second
discussing personal life within.

　　　　Langer terms this piece a political autobiography. She
discusses her own childhood as a Jew growing up in the suburbs of
Boston in the 1950s, her intensely intellectual but apolitical
years at Swarthmore, and her transformation from a professional
journalist and middle-class wife to a full-time activist beginning
in 1965 with the free-speech movement in Berkeley. The bulk of
her reminiscences center on the political dynamics of the New
Left, especially what she pinpoints as the search for an "agent
of change"--the working class, students, GIs, blacks, the third-
world, women, gays, and so on--which symptomized a dearth of
theory. As to the personal side of movement life, she writes:
"Life in the movement was difficult. . . . I think personal un-
happiness is the real reason most people left the movement."

　　　　The last section of the essay denies the seeming bitterness
of Langer's exposition and looks forward to a better period.
"Let us bury the New Left with the praise and dignity it deserves,"
she admonishes. She concludes: "This is a strange and confusing
period. But there is at least as much chance that the sun is
rising as that it has set."

Levertov, Denise (1923-)

456　LEVERTOV, DENISE. The Poet in the World. New York: New
　　　Directions, 1973, 275 pp.
　　　　The poet and antiwar activist Levertov collected her prose

writings to demonstrate "the essential interrelatedness and
mutual reinforcement of the meditative and the active" in her
life. The essays mostly present her views on poetry and teaching,
but a substantial portion document her stand against the Vietnam
War, her early peace activities, and impressions formed during a
visit to North Vietnam in the early 1970s.

Morgan, Robin (1941-   )

457 MORGAN, ROBIN. <u>Going Too Far: The Personal Chronicle of a
     Feminist</u>. New York: Random House, 1977, 333 pp. Reprint.
     New York: Vintage Books, 1978, 333 pp.
        Robin Morgan, a self-defined radical feminist, has compiled
     her various letters and political essays from the mid-1960s and
     1970s. She has arranged the selections to document her feminist
     evolution, including her highly publicized break with the "male"
     New Left. Her notorious "Goodbye to All That," reprinted from
     the women's issue of the underground newspaper the <u>Rat</u>, stands as
     an important statement of disenchantment with the politics of an
     era.

Olsen, Tillie (1913-   )

458 OLSEN, TILLIE. <u>Silences</u>. New York: Delacorte Press, 1978,
     306 pp.
        A collection of essays, <u>Silences</u> constitutes Olsen's re-
     flections upon her experiences as a writer in light of the twenty
     years when she did not write. Born in 1913, she married Jack
     Olsen, a printer in 1936, and spent the next two decades working
     in low-paying, tedious jobs, maintaining a household, and raising
     four daughters. Olsen claims that she followed the course of
     most women, placing the needs of others before her own and keeping
     inside the ideas which "seethed, bubbled, clamored, peopled me."
     She discusses various obstacles in the path of creativity that
     affect women most of all. A polemic rather than scholarly work,
     <u>Silences</u> is a personal statement of frustration.

Oughton, Diana (1942-1970)

459 POWERS, THOMAS. <u>Diana: The Making of a Terrorist</u>. Boston:
     Houghton Mifflin Co., 1971, 225 pp.
        In March 1970 Diana Oughton, a twenty-eight year old stu-
     dent activist, died with two others in a bomb explosion that
     leveled a townhouse in Greenwich Village. Her story, the author
     claims, was "also the story of the Weathermen."
        A reporter for the United Press, Powers gathered informa-
     tion from Oughton's family and from extensive research into the
     New Left and created a chronicle of the Weather underground. He
     traced Oughton's life from her upper-class childhood in Dwight,
     Illinois, her stint in VISTA in the mid-1960s, to her experimental
     teaching positions in Philadelphia and Ann Arbor. By the winter

of 1968-1969 Oughton had become a regional organizer for the Students for a Democratic Society in Michigan.

Although Oughton's life is factually represented, Powers delves less into her particular psychology than into the fatal shifts within SDS that brought a small but important minority to advocate violence. The alienation and rage of this sector becomes the political context for Oughton's own transformation from "the prize girl" of her family into a revolutionary terrorist.

Rukeyser, Muriel (1913-1981)

460 KERTESZ, LOUISE. <u>The Poetic Vision of Muriel Rukeyser</u>. Baton Rouge: Louisiana State University Press, 1980, 412 pp.

Not a biography, this detailed study focuses on the forms and themes of Rukeyser's poetry. Kertesz describes Rukeyser as a traditionalist, closer in form to Emerson than to other proletarian writers of her generation, as "not a poet of Marxism, but a poet who has written directly about the tragedy of the working class."

Stern, Susan (1943-1976)

461 STERN, SUSAN. <u>With the Weathermen; The Personal Journal of a Revolutionary Woman</u>. Garden City, N.Y.: Doubleday & Co., 1975, 374 pp.

Susan Stern traces her personal history from August 1966 when she arrived in Seattle to attend the School of Social Work, to June 1972 when she was released from Purdy State Prison for Women. She provides a detailed narrative of her moves through SDS into Weathermen, her participation in key events like the October 1969 "days of rage," and her arrest and trial on conspiracy charges as a member of the Seattle Seven. Intimate details abound. Proudly attuned to the whims of the leadership, Stern describes most thoroughly her reactions to various men in the movement, which ones she likes, fears, distrusts, or lusts for. She also records her many acts of heroism amid the exciting and violent street scenes of the late 1960s, as well as her sacrifices for the movement. So determined to illustrate this dedication, Stern alleges at least three times in her narrative to have stripped herself of all worldly belongings collected since her middle-class childhood. Her hatred for "the pigs," her love for the revolution--such emotive claims substitute for either analysis or sensitivity.

Above all this story is highly personalized. Stern cavalierly assesses the characters of her friends and enemies, including her estranged husband, as if they were mere players in a fictional drama and thereby devoid of feelings. As Susan Brownmiller pointed out, Stern's voice is unquestionably authentic. "What is missing," Brownmiller noted, "is a sense of honor and integrity, the slightest hint of introspection, a concept of morality" (<u>New York Times Book Review</u>, June 15, 1975). Unwittingly, Susan Stern provides a convincing portrait of the arche-

typal Weatherman. From a self-proclaimed revolutionary terrorist
to the author of a sensational and exploitative book begun while
she was still in prison, Stern remains basically unchanged.

BOOKS AND PAMPHLETS ON
THE WOMAN QUESTION

Even in the television age, when young women moved with greater
ease into organizations and institutions of higher learning, radical
tracts retained a significant value. As in previous eras, local
branches of political movements ordered them by the hundreds and sold
them at meetings, liberal bookstores, and literature tables in student cafeterias. College teachers also ordered them for classroom
use. Timely in content and style, they generally aged fast and became relics in a few years, soon, like Shulamith Firestone's Dialectic
of Sex, mementos of times past.

The women's liberation movement fostered the rebirth of a Socialist women's continent, much smaller than in previous eras but more
independent and consciously feminist. The first sizable group of
radical women to have benefitted from college education, Socialist
feminists of the 1970s proved highly theoretical and prolific scholars,
agitators, and journalists. They collected the important tracts of
the 1960s and went on to produce pamphlets and books detailing the
theoretical underpinnings of their aspirations. They also produced a
set of didactic tracts, many of which were first printed (or reprinted
from periodicals) by the New England Free Press and later collected
into commercially published, highly successful anthologies.

In the same years, Old Left groups came to rely on the short
pamphlets as their staple. Stymied for the most part by the rapid
ascendance of the women's liberation movement, they sought to make up
in quantity what they lacked in innovation. Communists (New Outlook)
and the Socialist Workers party (Pathfinder) produced scores of pamphlets, while proliferating factions and grouplets of the Old Left
offered their positions ad infinitum, often beyond the range of this
cataloging. Communists and other hard-line "proletarian" groups
clung to the traditional attack on "bourgeois feminism" in the name
of workers' unity; the Socialist Workers party and most other entities
took up the cause of women's liberation as a factor in the victory of
socialism. In the flurry of publishing, vintage materialist tracts
enjoyed a revival, most notably Frederick Engels's Origins of the
Family.

462 ALTBACH, EDITH HOSHINO, ed. From Feminism to Liberation.
     Rev. ed. Cambridge, Mass.: Schenkman Publishing Co., 1980,
     322 pp.
        This collection of essays focuses on the origins of the
     women's liberation movement in civil rights and the New Left.

The four parts of the book are divided into the emerging women's liberation movement, cultural and material origins, the family question, and movement strategy. Among the contributors are Sara Evans, Marlene Dixon, Naomi Weisstein, and Selma James. The anthology includes "classic" documents of the early years of women's liberation, such as Kathy McAfee and Myrna Wood's "Bread and Roses," Margaret Benston's "The Political Economy of Women's Liberation," and Peggy Morton's "A Woman's Work Is Never Done."

Many of the essays in From Feminism to Liberation first appeared in Radical America, February 1970. In this revised and expanded version, Altbach reflects on the women's liberation movement ten years later and offers these essays as historical documents. She hopes they will serve former activists who need to understand their past involvements and who must now record the history of their movement for future generations.

463 BALLAN, DOROTHY. Feminism and Marxism. New York: World View Publishers, 1971, 69 pp.

Ballan, a trade-union organizer, offers four essays on the relationship between women's liberation and the class struggle. The first essay, "The Woman in History," begins with the premise that it is impossible to understand the present status of women without first studying the origins of their oppression from a historical materialist standpoint; it offers a brief summary of Frederick Engels's The Origin of the Family, Private Property, and the State. Other essays consider the sexual revolution aided by "the pill" and the role of the Russian Revolution in fostering sexual freedom. The most original essay in this volume, "The Lines on Women's Liberation," discusses the limitations of Kate Millet's Sexual Politics (1970). Ballan criticizes Millet for employing a "theory of sexual politics" rather than a class analysis, and for failing to establish the origins of women's oppression in class society. Ballan characterizes Millet's approach as "bourgeois" and "bankrupt."

464 BOGGS, GRACE LEE. Women and the Movement to Build a New America. Detroit: National Organization for an American Revolution, n.d. [1980?], 29 pp.

Boggs, along with her husband, black author James Boggs, is the leading ideological force in the National Organization for an American Revolution, a group indirectly born out of divisions within the trotskyist movement of the 1940s. An Asian-American schooled in philosophy, Grace Lee Boggs notably contributed in the 1940s and 1950s to a political break with notions of a "vanguard party" then prevailing within the Left. This document suggests a curious outcome. Originally delivered at a celebration of International Women's Week at the University of Massachusetts, it calls for a change in ethics, with a cultural revolution led by women to make human relationships more democratic and significant as a preface to the political-economic revolution.

465 Break the Chains! Unleash the Fury of Women as a Mighty Force
     for Revolution. Chicago: RCP Publications, 1979, 32 pp.
          Taken from the 1979 International Women's Day addresses by
     leaders of the Maoist Revolutionary Communist party, this largely
     rhetorical tract reveals an effort to restore the uncompromising
     vigor of Third-Period American communism for the modern era. The
     RCP, most prominent among the descendents and undertakers of the
     1960s New Left, is noted for its condemnation of homosexuality
     and its reduction of social contradictions to class terms.

466 COLÓN, CLARA. Enter Fighting: Today's Woman, a Marxist-
     Leninist View. New York: New Outlook Publishers, 1970, 95 pp.
          This pamphlet outlines the Communist party's position on
     the Woman Question in 1970. Colón provides a brief assessment of
     current conditions, particularly black and white women's place in
     the labor market. She also delineates the party's interpretation
     of major issues, such as day care, the Equal Rights Amendment,
     the family, and the women's liberation movement. Criticizing the
     separatist tendencies of young radical women, Colón affirms sex
     solidarity as long as "it helps build the unity of the working
     class and the alliance of labor with Black people." The final
     chapter, "The Communist Party and the Struggle for Women's Free-
     dom," reprints its twelve-point program, which includes the liber-
     ation of black women, defense of home and family, a fight against
     male supremacy, and a critique of mass media.
          Clara Colón, who had been active in the Communist movement
     since the mid-1930s, is the author of several pamphlets on legal
     defense.

467 COWLEY, JOYCE. Pioneers of Women's Liberation. New York:
     Pathfinder Press, 1971, 15 pp.
          A brief and nonscholarly history of the nineteenth-century
     women's rights movement, Cowley's essay emphasizes feminists'
     activities in relation to struggles for black freedom. She ends
     her narrative with the passage of the Nineteenth Amendment in
     1920, and concludes that the campaign for legal and political
     rights was "meaningless" as long as women's "position in economic
     and family life remains basically unaltered." Only "the coopera-
     tive atmosphere of a socialist commonwealth," Cowley explains,
     will bring liberation.
          This essay appeared originally in International Socialist
     Review and was reprinted in Mary Lou Thompson, ed., Voices of the
     New Feminism (1970).

468 DAVIS, ANGELA Y., and others. If They Come in the Morning:
     Voices of Resistance. Foreword by Julian Bond. New York:
     Third Press, 1971, 281 pp.
          This volume collects various letters, essays, and poetry
     by the principles in the Soledad brothers' defense and by Davis
     herself. Included are a brief political biography of Davis and
     statements in her behalf by Coretta Scott King and Shirley Graham

DuBois. Of special interest is the document "A Call to Black
Women of Every Religious and Political Persuasion."

469   DEMING, BARBARA. Revolution & Equilibrium. New York:
      Grossman Publishers, 1971, 269 pp.
          Deming collects a sample of her political essays, mostly
      written in the 1960s for the Nation and Liberation. She offers
      this anthology to people in the "movement" who know little about
      the contribution of pacifists to the radicalism of the 1960s.
      The collection also traces Deming's own contribution, beginning
      in 1960, when a meeting with Fidel Castro shook her from her self-
      avowed liberalism, to the antiwar and women's movements at the
      decade's close.

470   _____. We Cannot Live Without Our Lives. New York: Grossman
      Publishers, 1974, 191 pp.
          Long-time civil-rights and peace activist, Deming collects
      some of her publications from the New Left era. Her essays and
      letters mostly address issues of women's liberation from a radical
      feminist perspective, discuss the relationship of black and women's
      liberation, and redress male Left leaders for their inability to
      appreciate the significance of the Woman Question. Deming also
      includes a large selection of her poetry and memorials to recently
      deceased activists like A.J. Muste and Paul Goodman.

471   DIXON, MARLENE. Women in Class Struggle. San Francisco:
      Synthesis Publishers, 1980, 83 pp.
          This volume collects Dixon's essays published originally
      in Synthesis, journal of the League for Proletarian Socialism
      centered in San Francisco. Dating to 1977, the essays address
      the "super-exploitation of women" in the family, the wages-for-
      housework argument, "bourgeois" morality, antifeminism in the
      Left, and feminist criticism of Labor and Monopoly Capital by
      Harry Braverman. Two essays constitute overviews of the women's
      liberation movement during the previous decades, especially in
      relation to the development of a Socialist feminist perspective.

472   DUNAYEVSKAYA, RAYA. Woman as Reason and as Force of Revolution:
      Writings of Raya Dunayevskaya on Women's Liberation. Detroit:
      Women's Liberation-News and Letters Committees, 1981, 29 pp.
          Dunayevskaya, the founder of the philosophy of marxist
      humanism, has been active in the Left for over four decades. She
      is the foremost figure in the News and Letters Committees, an
      erstwhile trotskyist faction.
          Published for International Women's Day, 1981, this pam-
      phlet collects four essays on women's liberation, the earliest
      dating to 1951. Dunayevskaya reflects on both history and litera-
      ture to relate aspects of female creativity to a philosophy of
      liberation. A short piece on "Women in the Iranian Revolution;
      In Fact and Theory," by Neda, an Iranian woman revolutionary,
      constitutes an appendix.

473 EDELMAN, JUDY. Women on the Job: The Communist View. New
     York: New Outlook Publishers, 1973, 53 pp.
          Former SNCC worker, National Labor Secretary of the Young
     Workers Liberation League, and member of the Trade Union and
     Women's Commission of the Communist Party USA, Edelman analyzes
     discrimination against wage-earning women and outlines the party's
     program on women's rights. Because discrimination is an employer
     strategy to divide the working class, Edelman attests, men and
     women must fight together; similarly, the struggle for women's
     rights is "part and parcel of the struggle of the working class
     as a whole." Edelman calls upon women to organize into unions
     and to demand a national program of federally funded day-care
     centers. She also puts forth the party's position on the Equal
     Rights Amendment.
          This pamphlet is an updated and expanded version of Women
     on the Job: A Marxist-Leninist View, published originally in
     1970.

474 EHRENREICH, BARBARA, and DEIDRE ENGLISH. For Her Own Good:
     150 Years of the Experts' Advice to Women. Garden City, N.Y.:
     Anchor Doubleday, 1978, 369 pp. Reprint. Anchor Books, 1979,
     369 pp.
          Socialists Ehrenreich and English have interpreted advice
     to women on various issues ranging from health and sexuality to
     child-rearing. Their approach is historical and sociological,
     focused on an analysis of experts' response to shifts in gender
     roles over the past century. How "establishment" men--physicians,
     philosophers, and scientists--presented themselves as authorities
     on women is the subject of this clearly written study. The
     authors ground their interpretation in an analysis of the material
     conditions of the patriarchal order of industrial capitalism, es-
     pecially with reference to the changing needs of the market econ-
     omy.

475 EISENSTEIN, ZILLAH, ed. Capitalist Patriarchy and the Case
     for Socialist Feminism. New York: Monthly Review, 1978, 394
     pp.
          Contributor Rosalind Petchevsky quotes a colleague: "We
     are Marxists to our feminist sisters and feminists to our Marxist
     brothers." The seventeen essays in this anthology address various
     aspects of this dual identity. Activists and scholars, the
     authors discuss the current strengths and weaknesses in the
     Socialist feminist synthesis. Editor Eisenstein explains their
     goal: "This volume is devoted to understanding the dynamic of
     power involved which derives from both the class relations of
     production and the sexual hierarchal relations of society."
          Eisenstein supplies two lead essays on theoretical prob-
     lems at hand, especially pinpointing the nature of patriarchy.
     In a companion piece, Nancy Hartsock continues this analysis but
     considers the tactical methods in organizing a mass movement for
     social change. The second section of the anthology, "Motherhood,

Reproduction and Male Supremacy," contains essays by Nancy Chodorow and Linda Gordon that substitute "sex-gender system" for the loosely defined concept of patriarchy. The third section, "Socialist-Feminist Historical Analyses," constitutes two essays on nineteenth-century American women; Ellen DuBois discusses the theoretical and strategic limitations of the midcentury woman's rights movement, and Mary Ryan examines the ideological origins of feminism in the industrial revolution. Section four, "Capitalist Patriarchy and Female Work," is considered by several reviewers to be the strongest, most representative set of essays in the collection. Jean Gardiner, Batya Weinbaum, Amy Bridges, Heidi Hartmann, and Margery Davies provide insights into the sex-segregated labor forces as well as the complementary nature of women's unpaid domestic work and their wage-labor. Section five, "Patriarchy in Revolutionary Societies," contains essays by Carollee Bengelsdorf and Alice Hageman, and by Judith Stacey on women in Cuba and China. The last section, "Socialist Feminism in America," comprises statements by three contemporary Socialist feminist groups.

Although reviewers noted with favor the range represented in the essays in this volume, several found the quality either inconsistent or disappointing. Writing in Feminist Studies (Fall 1980), Liz Kennedy and June Lapidus conclude:

> Taken as a whole, Capitalist Patriarchy and the Case for Socialist Feminism reflects the current strengths of socialist feminism, in particular its capacity to transform social- ist theory through analyses of motherhood, sexuality, women's work in the home and the labor force, and feminist political activity. Yet is also reflects the current weaknesses-- inability to interpret all women's reality, the difficulty in developing a coherent theory and in relating theory to building a movement for women's liberation that has a chance for victory.

476 EISENSTEIN, ZILLAH. The Radical Future of Liberal Feminism. New York and London: Longman, 1981, 260 pp.

Eisenstein opens with the statement: "It is important for feminists of different political persuasions to recognize that mainstream feminism has the potential for radicalism." She documents this potential in the contributions of Mary Wollstonecraft, John Stuart Mill, Harriet Taylor, and Elizabeth Cady Stanton, all of whom shaped a feminist theory from the tenets of classic liberalism. At the center of Eisenstein's analysis is a consideration of the "contradictory base of liberal feminism," a tension between the patriarchal and individualist structure of liberalism and the egalitarian and collectivist character of feminism, which promotes an understanding of women as a sexual class. After a lengthy examination of nineteenth-century thinkers, Eisenstein turns to a study of Betty Friedan and examines her writings in a similar fashion.

477 FEELEY, DIANE. Why Women Need the Equal Rights Amendment. New York: Pathfinder Press, 1973, 15 pp.
        Unlike the Communist party, the Socialist Workers party in the early 1970s supported the women's liberation movement and especially the campaign for the passage of the Equal Rights Amendment. In this pamphlet, Feeley argues that the struggle for democratic rights abets revolutionary change. She presents a brief historical overview of the Equal Rights Amendment and analyzes its opposition by both conservatives and Communists. She also summarizes instances of legal discrimination against women and discusses women's economic status in regard to existing protective legislation.

478 FIRESTONE, SHULAMITH. The Dialectic of Sex: The Case for a Feminist Revolution. New York: William Morrow, 1970, 274 pp. Reprint. New York: Morrow, Quill, 1980, 274 pp.
        Firestone's treatise represents the first major criticism of Socialist feminism and outline of a radical feminist alternative. Its publication marked the definitive break of one sector of women from the New Left. Firestone was a cofounder of Redstockings and New York Radical Feminists.
        Dialectic of Sex opens appropriately with a formal critique of the marxist class analysis of women's oppression. Firestone chastises Engels for his propensity to "see sexuality only through an economic filter." But if Engels was shortsighted, Firestone continues, Marx was worse.
        She then sets out to improve upon the original materialist framework of history as originally outlined by Marx and Engels. She aims to "take the class analysis one step further to its roots in the biological division of the sexes." In her new categories, the historical dialectic becomes sexual antagonism; women's oppression finds its roots not in class society but in male domination of female nature. The solution therefore lies not in the overthrow of class society as defined by capitalism, but in the destruction of the principal agent of male domination, the biological family.
        In presenting her perspective, Firestone does not deprecate the revolutionary heritage per se. Rather, she sees women's liberation as a necessary prerequisite for successful revolution, which she envisions as cybernetic socialism. Radical feminism thus becomes a means for women to free themselves and to change society. Radical feminism, Firestone writes, "refuses to accept any existing leftist analysis not because it is too radical, but because it is not radical enough."

479 HAMILTON, ROBERTA. The Liberation of Women: A Study of Patriarchy and Capitalism. Winchester, Mass.: Allen & Unwin,

1978, 117 pp.

Hamilton uses a particular historical study, women in seventeenth-century England, to examine the affinity of feminist and marxist analyses in understandin women's role. For the past decade, Hamilton contends, scholars and activists have been discussing the relative merits of both modes. This book is thus her attempt to pose and answer the basic question about their complementary or contradictory relationship.

After "testing" the two theories as sufficient means to explain the condition of women in seventeenth-century England, Hamilton concludes that the problems inherent in both when applied singly are eradicated when combined with each other. She claims that marxist and feminist analyses are equally necessary components of historical analysis, and predicts that "at some point a marriage between Marxism and feminism may be possible."

480 HILDEBRAND, GINNY; CINDY JAQUITH; CATHY SEDWICH; and REBA WILLIAMS. How to Win the ERA. New York: Pathfinder Press, 1977, 31 pp.

Reprinted from the Militant and the Black Scholar, these essays discuss various aspects of the ERA campaign, especially black women's role and major strategic issues.

481 JACOBS, HAROLD, ed. Weatherman. Palo Alto, Calif.: Ramparts Press, 1970, 519 pp.

A representative selection of documents by and about Weathermen, Jacobs's book contains several key essays on the relationship of Weatherwomen to the Women's Liberation movement. Cathy Wilkerson's essay, reprinted from New Left Notes (July 8, 1969), calls for the formation of a women's militia, a revolutionary action group inviting young women, especially high-schoolers, into the armed struggle against imperialism and racism. "Honky Tonk Women," a polemic issued by the National War Council, criticizes separatist women's movement and outlines the Weatherman strategy for women's liberation: "The only way we can win is to build a consciously Communist white movement, ready to ally and fight with the rest of the world's people." As a rejoinder, "Weatherman Politics and the Women's Movement," by the Bread and Roses collective, offers sisterly criticism yet asserts the primacy of the position "that women must make revolutions for themselves as well as for other people." Essays by Karen Ashley, Bernadine Dohrn, Lorraine Rosel, Kathy Boudin, and Linda Evans are also included.

482 JAGGAR, ALISON M., and PAULA ROTHENBERG STRUHL, eds. Feminist Frameworks: Alternative Theoretical Accounts of the Relations Between Women and Men. New York: McGraw-Hill, 1978, 333 pp.

Feminist Frameworks is a clearly organized anthology of five types of writings about the nature of sexism. After demonstrating how contemporary social arrangements have created a need for both women's and men's liberation, editors Jaggar and Struhl

213

present what they term "feminist frameworks" that have developed as distinct approaches within the past couple decades. The five ideologies—conservatism, liberalism, traditional marxism, radical feminism, and Socialist feminism—set up an excellent comparative study not only of descriptions of women's oppression but prescriptions for improving the situation.

In the final section of the book, these frameworks are applied to practical problems: work, family, and sexuality. The often vague distinctions between radical/marxist/Socialist feminists are made lucid here through the selections and their placement in the appropriate context. Among the Socialist feminist writers are Gayle Rubin, Juliet Mitchell, Guiliana Pompei, Carol Lopate, Barbara and Michael McKain, Eli Zaretsky, and Sheila Rowbotham. Suggestions for further reading follow each section of the book and add to its usefulness as a guide to feminist theory and practice today.

483 JAQUITH, CINDY, and WILLIE MAE REID. Which Way for the Women's Movement? New York: Pathfinder Press, 1977, 31 pp.
This pamphlet constitutes two essays that outline the Socialist Workers party's position on the women's liberation movement. Jaquith's "What Strategy for Women's Liberation?" reprinted from the International Socialist Review of 1977, addresses the organizational problems inherent in building a mass-based movement, with special reference to the National Organization of Women and Committee of Labor Union Women. Reid's "Why Black Women Belong in the Women's Liberation Movement" challenges NOW to address the needs of minority women.

484 JAYKO, MARGARET. Reagan's War on Women's Rights: A Strategy to Fight Back. New York: Pathfinder Press, 1981, 38 pp.
This pamphlet examines Reaganism in terms of policy implications for women, especially concerning abortion and reproductive rights, the Equal Rights Amendment, and economic status. Jayko does not, however, place the blame entirely upon the Reagan administration, but traces what she terms "antiwoman ideas" to a bipartisan drive to roll back gains. The offensive against women merely intensified, the author contends, with the 1980 election. Jayko also reviews the response of prominent activists and spokeswomen, presenting as her principal example Betty Friedan. She lambastes Friedan for allegedly retreating from feminism in her recent book, The Second Stage (1981), and thereby complementing "the reactionary economic plans of the ruling class as they drive to reduce social services and transfer the burden from society back onto each individual family." In similar although milder fashion, Jayko also chastises the National Organization of Women for caving in under the weight of new oppositional forces, particularly by failing to defend wholeheartedly abortion rights.

Margaret Jayko is a member of the National Executive Committee of the Young Socialist Alliance and coordinator of women's liberation activities within the Socialist Workers party. She is also on the staff of the Militant, which printed the text of this pamphlet in its September 25, October 2, and October 9, 1981, issues.

485 JENNESS, LINDA, ed. Feminism and Socialism. New York: Path-
     finder Press, 1972, 160 pp.
        One-time presidential candidate for the Socialist Workers
     party, Linda Jenness has collected a representative sample of
     essays on the Woman Question from house organs International
     Socialist Review and the Militant. Jenness claims as her orga-
     nizing concept the thesis that "women's struggle against our
     oppression strikes at the very heart of capitalist society" but
     only a social revolution will bring women's full liberation.
        The book divides into four parts. The first section con-
     tains essays on the theoretical relationship of socialism and
     feminism by Caroline Lund and Mary-Alice Water, who then edited
     the Militant. Part two takes up major issues of the women's move-
     ment: the special oppression of black women and chicanas, abor-
     tion, the ERA, and the family. A literary section follows, in-
     cluding a forum on Sexual Politics and a response to Norman
     Mailer's Prisoner of Sex. The last section presents the resolu-
     tion adopted at the SWP's 1971 convention, "Toward a Mass Feminist
     Movement."
        One of the more interesting essays is Carol Lipman's
     examination of red-baiting in the women's movement. It is her
     response to NOW president Lucy Komisar, who introduced a resolu-
     tion before her organization condemning the SWP and the Young
     Socialist Alliance for "dividing and exploiting" the women's move-
     ment for its "own goals and purposes."

486 JENNESS, LINDA. Socialism and the Fight for Women's Rights.
     New York: Pathfinder Press, 1976, 15 pp.
        Jenness considers why people today question the comple-
     mentary nature of socialism and feminism. She reviews the history
     of the Socialist movement, underscoring its commitment to women's
     rights until "the political counterrevolution under Joseph Stalin."
     The split between feminism and socialism originated, Jenness as-
     serts, in Stalin's betrayal of the Russian Revolution. She also
     reviews current political choices before women, such as the New
     Left and the Democratic party, and concludes by calling upon
     serious feminists to help build the Socialist society through the
     Socialist Workers party.

487 JORDAN, JUNE. Civil Wars. Boston: Beacon Press, 1981, 188
     pp.
        June Jordan, poet and radical activist, collected her
     essays, letters, and lectures from the past two decades. Writing
     as both a black and a woman, she deals perceptively and often
     personally with the violence of the era. A central theme is the
     issue of feminism within the black community.

488   KOEDT, ANNE; ELLEN LEVINE; and ANITA RAPONE, eds. Radical
      Feminism. New York: Quadrangle, 1973, 1976, 424 pp.
         Although this anthology collects materials from a dis-
      tinctly radical feminist perspective, its editors include a few
      essays written by women who came through the New Left. Naomi
      Weisstein's "Psychology Constructs the Female," which has been
      reprinted widely, is a prime example. Meredith Tax's "Woman and
      Her Mind," which first appeared in Notes from the Second Year
      (1970) and in the 1970 list of the New England Free Press, also
      bears the imprint of her political upbringing. Then a member of
      Bread and Roses, a Boston-area Socialist women's liberation group,
      Tax examined the process by which women inculcate notions of
      feminity primarily in relation to the consumerist orientation of
      American capitalist society.

489   LEACOCK, ELEANOR. Myths of Male Dominance. New York: Monthly
      Review, 1981, 344 pp.
         Eleanor Leacock is an anthropologist who works within the
      historical materialist framework of the traditional Socialist
      canon. This volume collects her essays on sex relations written
      over the past three decades.
         Leacock presents her researches on women of the Montagnais-
      Naskapi of Labrador, which she describes as a "primitive-commu-
      nistic" people. She also examines in detail the thesis popular-
      ized by Frederick Engels that women's subordinate position is a
      historical development of class society, and presents new evidence
      in its favor. The most engaging essays express Leacock's strong
      disagreement with the recent feminist assertion that male domi-
      nance is a universal feature across societies and across history.

490   LONG, PRISCILLA, ed. The New Left: A Collection of Essays.
      Boston: Porter Sargent Publishers, 1969, 475 pp.
         One of the first published anthologies of New Left writings,
      Long's book includes only a few entries by women. Barbara Deming
      and Amy Cass contributed essays on radical visions of social
      change. On women's role is Sue Munaker, Evelyn Goldfield, and
      Naomi Weisstein's "A Woman Is a Sometime Thing."

491   LUND, CAROLINE. The Family System: Progressive or Oppres-
      sive? New York: Pathfinder Press, 1973, 22 pp.
         Lund's essay is primarily an indictment of the Communist
      party for its alleged "fear of an independent and radical Women's
      Liberation Movement." Lund reviews the positions of the Commu-
      nist party and the Progressive Labor party, and concludes that
      both organizations deny the oppression of women in the family.
      In contrast to their desire to bolster the working-class family
      as a bulwark against capitalism, the Socialist Workers party,
      Lund claims, refuses to compromise women's rights and demands,
      instead, the socialization of family functions that weigh heavily
      upon women.

492 MILLER, RUTHANN; EVELYN REED; and MARY ALICE WATERS. In De-
     fense of the Woman's Movement. New York: Pathfinder Press,
     1971, 15 pp.
         This pamphlet reprints three essays from the Militant,
     December 1969–February 1970. Miller criticizes childcare expert
     Dr. Benjamin Spock for his insistence that women take primary
     responsibility for child rearing. Waters reprimands New York
     Post columnist Pete Hamill for sexist remarks. Reed issues a
     salvo against the Communist party for its unjustified reverence
     of marriage and family.

493 MITCHELL, JULIET. Woman's Estate. New York: Pantheon Books,
     1971, 182 pp. Reprint. New York: Vintage Books, 1973,
     182 pp.
         In this book, British feminist Juliet Mitchell expands her
     widely circulated and highly praised essay, "Women: The Longest
     Revolution," which appeared in 1966. Considered by many the
     chief spokesperson for the Socialist feminist position, Mitchell
     divides her treatise into two sections. The first part explores
     the factors behind the emergence of the women's liberation move-
     ment in the late 1960s: civil rights and Black Power; the stu-
     dent movement; the youth rebellion. Mitchell also discusses at
     length the role of higher education in creating a vital mass from
     the postwar baby boom. The combination of these factors, she
     writes, produced a large sector of the population ready to revolt
     against the cultural values of the middle class. Thus the prime
     feature of the women's liberation movement is what Mitchell calls
     the "politics of experience," that is, the promotion of "feelings"
     to the realm of politics best expressed by the innovative con-
     sciousness-raising groups. Mitchell then reviews the leading
     contributions to the Woman Question, running through the works of
     Marx, Engels, Beauvoir, and Firestone. She pits "Radical femi-
     nists" against "Abstract socialists" and finds both guilty of
     overdetermination.
         The second section contains Mitchell's own analysis of
     women's oppression and theory of liberation. An editor of the
     British New Left Review, she shares their philosophical orienta-
     tion and produces a structuralist framework to take up her major
     task--asking feminist questions but trying to evoke marxist an-
     swers. She focuses on four key aspects of women's situation:
     production, or wage-labor; reproduction; sexuality; and the
     socialization of children. "The lesson," Mitchell concludes, "is
     that the liberation of women can only be achieved if all four
     structures in which they are integrated are transformed." Al-
     though abstruse, the major point of Mitchell's argument is that
     the family and personal relations are just as central to any
     theory of women's liberation as an understanding of women's place
     in the paid labor force. To emphasize her break with traditional
     marxist categories of analysis, she concludes with a brief note
     on psychoanalysis, presenting it as a useful tool for beginning
     the new task of examining women's condition in the family.

494 MORAGA, CHERRIE, and GLORIA ANZALDÚA, eds. This Bridge Called my Back: Writings by Radical Women of Color. Foreword by Toni Cade Bambara. Watertown, Mass.: Persephone Press, 1981, 261 pp.

    Toni Cade Bambara concludes her foreword with a call for the literature "to make revolution irresistable," and thereby sets the tone for this militant yet highly experimental collection of prose. Afro-American, Asian-American, Latino, and Native American writers contributed mostly short, crisp reflections on their status as minority women. Their statements are angry but rarely shrill.

495 MORGAN, ROBIN, ed. Sisterhood Is Powerful: An Anthology of Writings from the Women's Liberation Movement. New York: Random House, 1970, 577 pp.

    One of the earliest and most substantial anthologies, Sisterhood Is Powerful has become a classic. Its editor favored contributions expressing her own political leanings, radical feminism, but included a dozen essays by former SDS members: Naomi Weisstein, Connie Brown, Carol Glassman, Jean Tepperman, and Marge Piercy. Pat Mainardi's "Politics of Housework" and Karen Sacks's "Social Basis for Sexual Equality" help balance documents of WITCH, Redstockings, and New York Radical Feminists. Notes on contributors help identify the authors.

496 NATIONAL ORGANIZATION FOR AN AMERICAN REVOLUTION. Women and the New World. N.p.: n.p., [1976?], 55 pp.

    This pamphlet discusses sex roles and the origins of women's oppression, with special consideration of black women. Influenced by the West Indian marxist C.L.R. James, the authors stress the importance of the "subjective" struggle of the masses over material conditions. Thus they implore women to take advantage of the technological revolution since World War II and to engage in a "philosophical and political struggle" to control their lives by resisting sex stereotyping.

497 NOVACK, GEORGE. The Revolutionary Dynamic of Women's Liberation. New York: Pathfinder Press, 1973, 22 pp.

    Welcoming the rebirth of the women's liberation movement in the late 1960s, Novack presents a chronology of women's fight for liberation. He begins with the British civil war and French Revolution and carries his story to the nineteenth century in the United States. He devotes considerable attention to the relationship between the antebellum woman's rights movement and the antislavery campaign. This essay is reprinted from the Militant (October 17, 1969).

498 REED, EVELYN. Problems of Women's Liberation. New York: Pathfinder Press, 1970, 96 pp.

    Originally published in 1969, this fifth edition is, in the author's words, "a small contribution to the tremendous task

that awaits the women of our revolutionary epoch." It contains
five essays on theoretical issues of women's liberation from the
marxist standpoint. The first, "Women and the Family; a Historical View," dates to May 1969; delivered at a forum sponsored by
Students for a Democratic Society, it traces the origins of
women's oppression to class society and follows the analysis
ascribed by the author to Frederick Engels. The other essays expand this theme, for Reed believes that a study of prehistory
provides women with an understanding of their present dilemma as
well as guidelines for future struggle. "Women: Caste, Class or
Oppressed Sex," which appeared originally in International Socialist Review (September 1970), is a further discussion of basic
categories of analysis. Reed rejects the notion that women constitute a separate caste or class.

499 _____. Woman's Evolution from Matriarchal Clan to Patriarchal
      Family. New York: Pathfinder Press, 1975, 491 pp.
      Twenty years in the making, Reed's treatise revives the
theory of the matriarchal origins of society. She acknowledges
the controversy among scholars but affirms her position. She
writes: "It is only through the evolutionary approach . . . that
the concealed history of women--and of men--can be uncovered."

500 _____. Sexism & Science. New York: Pathfinder Press, 1978,
      190 pp.
      Sexism & Science is a collection of eight essays, several
of which appeared first in the International Socialist Review. A
supplement to Reed's major work, Woman's Evolution, this book exposes the sexist biases of scientific analyses that distort or
obscure facts to bolster male superiority. Reed examines the
antiwoman bias that has flawed the sciences closest to human life:
biology, sociology, anthropology, sociobiology, and primatology.
She attacks E.O. Wilson's biological determinism, Robert Ardrey's
and Desmond Morris's theories of innate human aggressiveness,
Lionel Tiger's concept of male solidarity and superiority, and
Claude Levi-Strauss's theories of kinship. She shows how the
methodology, data, and assumptions are improperly manipulated to
conceal the matriarchal epoch, and thus serve to perpetuate a
false myth that women have always existed in a preordained,
"natural" state of patriarchy.

501 REED, EVELYN, and CLAIRE MORIARTY. Abortion and the Catholic
      Church. New York: Pathfinder Press, 1973, 14 pp.
      This pamphlet reprints Reed's essay, "Why the Catholic
Church Hierarchy Opposes Women's Right to Abortion" from the
Militant (February 16, 1973) and Moriarty's "The Meaning of the
Catholic Church's Position on Abortion," from the International
Socialist Review (March 1973).
      Reed argues that because "women are no longer creatures of
blind nature" but instead victims of patriarchal class society,
they must struggle to gain complete control of their bodies. She

interprets the position of the Roman Catholic hierarchy as an example of contempt for women.

Moriarty's essay is less polemic and more historical. She surveys the Catholic Church's position on birth control and abortion since the first century and examines it as part of a larger sexual code that delimits women's autonomy.

502   REID, WILLIE MAE, ed. Black Women's Struggle for Equality. New York: Pathfinder Press, 1976, 15 pp.

Civil-rights activist Reid edits a volume of short essays on black women and feminism reprinted from the Militant and the International Socialist Review. Her lead article covers the recent history of black women's involvement in the women's liberation movement. Essays by Linda Jenness, Cindy Jaquith, and Pat Wright consider the Joan Little case, abortion and forced sterilization, and the ERA.

503   REITER, RAYNA R., ed. Toward an Anthropology of Women. New York: Monthly Review, 1975, 416 pp.

Since the early publications by Bebel and Engels, Socialist scholars have traditionally related women's status to specific forms of social organization. They have assigned the relations between the sexes under capitalism, as well as women's subordinate position, to the peculiar logic of the system of private property.

Since the late 1960s feminist scholars have begun to test the limits of this theoretical framework. Some argue that male domination is universal, that it transcends particular forms of social or economic organization, historically and cross-culturally. In challenging fundamental tenets of the Socialist canon, most radical anthropologists nevertheless tend to develop their arguments within the general outline of historical materialism.

Rayna Reiter has collected seventeen essays that examine the validity of the hypothesis assuming a historical specificity to women's subordination. By looking at social arrangements in so-called primitive societies, those not yet circumscribed by the logic of capitalist production, they ask hard questions about the causal relationship between economic arrangements and gender roles and hierarchies. Several scholars discuss the nature of women's position in developing countries such as Nigeria, Colombia, and the Dominican Republic, where the increasing presence of capitalist influences alters existing class and gender relations in fundamental ways. Others explore the historical basis of women's subordinate status by testing the classic evolutionary theories against new insights about the role of kinship in the origin of the state. Together these essays express the prevailing tension between Socialist and feminist approaches to the study of sex roles.

504   ROE, CHARLOTTE. The Rise and Fall of American Women. New York: Young People's Socialist League, n.d., 14 pp.

Responding to the rise of the women's movement in the

mid-1960s, and especially to the influence of Betty Friedan, the
author rehearses the history of the first feminist movement as a
middle-class protest that "concerned itself primarily with democratic rights and opportunities" and failed to grapple with the
great class issues of its era. Women do not need a revival of
that kind of movement, she insists, but rather a "democratic
socialist movement" with clear class content.

505 ROSZAK, BETTY, and THEODORE ROSZAK, eds. Masculine/Feminine.
New York: Harper & Row, 1969, 316 pp.
The editors selected essays addressing the processes of
sex-role inculcation, or the ways men and women learn their
gender identities. They drew on a wide range of example, from
statements by Nietzsche, Freud, and Shaw to feminist writers like
Alice Rossi and Simone de Beauvoir. A section entitled "The New
Militancy" includes classic documents from the early women's
liberation movement. Essays by Juliet Mitchell, Marlene Dixon,
Patricia Robinson, Beverly Jones, Gayle Rubin, and Robin Morgan,
which have been reprinted in several places, reflect on the New
Left origins of their perspectives.

506 ROWBOTHAM, SHEILA. Women, Resistance and Revolution: A History of Women and Revolution in the Modern World. New York:
Pantheon Books, 1972, 287 pp. Reprint. New York: Vintage,
1974, 287 pp.
The bold intention of this book is to describe the genesis
of the notion "that the liberation of women necessitates the
liberation of all human beings." British Socialist feminist
Rowbotham thus begins her study in the seventeenth and eighteenth
centuries and finds the crystalization of the central idea in the
pioneering works of Marx, Engels, and Bebel. She details their
contribution, yet acknowledges its shortcomings.
Later chapters chronicle the radical struggles of European
and American women in the labor movement and women's role in the
Russian, Chinese, and Third-World revolutions. Each chapter
represents a study in the imperfect synthesis of feminist and
Socialist ideals, a case study in the limitations of male-dominated movements in regard to women's emancipation.
Rowbotham concludes that feminism and marxism "cohabit in
the same place somewhat uneasily." Today's feminists, she hopes,
will recognize the historic problem and will extend marxist
theory as they construct a revolutionary feminist praxis; they
understand that women's liberation "will not follow a socialist
revolution automatically but will have to be made explicit in a
distinct movement now, as a precondition of revolution, not as
its aftermath."

507 SARGENT, LYDIA, ed. Women & Revolution: A Discussion of the
Unhappy Marriage of Marxism and Feminism. Boston: South End
Press, 1979, 400 pp.
Women & Revolution, a volume in the South End Press's

221

Political Controversies Series, focuses on the interaction of marxist and feminist theories, especially as regards to the patriarchal origins of class society, women's role in political movements, and the nature of sexism inside and outside the New Left. Essays elaborate on Heidi Hartmann's statement that "the marriage of marxism and feminism has been like that between husband and wife depicted in English common law; marxism and feminism are one, and that one is marxism. . . ."

Sargent traces the origins to this discussion to women's experiences in the civil-rights and New Left movements of the past two decades. Framed by this historical context, the twelve essays in this volume shed light on the political and theoretical question facing activists. A wide variety of opinions is included; radical, marxist, Socialist, liberal, black, lesbian, and anarchist feminists discuss the complexities involved in trying to build upon current feminist theory and practice as well as the pressing necessity to overcome differences in the decade ahead. Contributors include Iris Young, Christine Riddiough, Gloria Joseph, Carol Ehrlich, Sandra Harding, Azizah alHibri, Lise Vogel, Emily Hichs, Carol Brown, Katie Steward, Ann Ferguson, Nany Folbre, and Zillah Eisenstein. Lead essays by Sargent and Hartmann determine the contours of the discussion.

508   STONE, BETTY.   Sisterhood Is Powerful.   New York: Pathfinder Press, 1970, 15 pp.
       This pamphlet is the text of Stone's report to the Socialist Activists and Educational Conference held at Oberlin College in August 1970. Stone outlines the Socialist Workers party's position on women's liberation. After reviewing some of the schisms within the Old and New Left, she states: "We believe that the independent women's liberation movement is a powerful revolutionary force in itself. It is an inspiring and exciting movement precisely because, in a unique way, it gets to the root of what is wrong with this society."

509   TANNER, LESLIE B., ed.   Voices from Women's Liberation.   New York: Signet Books, 1970, 443 pp.
       Tanner collected a range of documents to give a historical dimension to the women's liberation movement of the 1960s. She begins with a long section on "Voices from the Past," which includes short statements by activists in the women's rights movement before 1920. From the present wave, Tanner reprints a dozen important manifestoes. The essays dealing with current political and cultural issues constitute several eclectic sections, although many represent a New Left perspective. Linda Gordon's "Functions of the Family" and Margaret Benston's "The Political Economy of Women's Liberation" deal most directly with the relationship between capitalism and women's oppression. Essays by Naomi Weisstein, Ellen Willis, Roxanne Dunbar, Patricia Robinson, Kathy McAfee, and Myrna Wood illustrate the impact of New Left thought on the early writings of women's liberation.

510   TROTSKY, LEON. Women and the Family. New York: Pathfinder
      Press, 1973, 78 pp.
           Whereas Communists reprint the classic works of Marx,
      Engels, and Lenin on the Woman Question, the Socialist Workers
      party gathers the pertinent writings of Leon Trotsky. This volume
      contains selections dating to Trotsky's participation in the
      Soviet experiment in the early 1920s and to his period of exile
      in the 1930s. The final selection from The Revolution Betrayed,
      written in 1936, reviews the situation of Soviet women as part of
      the degeneration of the revolutionary process under Stalin.
           In a brief introduction, Caroline Lund surveys some of the
      changes in women's situation and the family in the USSR since
      1919. She summarizes Trotsky's position that the Socialist revo-
      lution was only one necessary precondition for women's emancipa-
      tion, the other being the level of material and technological
      development, the root of the problem in the Soviet Union.

511   WANG, DIANE, and CINDY JAQUITH. FBI vs. Women. New York:
      Pathfinder Press, 1977, 47 pp.
           This pamphlet reprints short essays from the Militant,
      1976-1977, on the Federal Bureau of Investigation surveillance of
      the women's movement and the Socialist Workers party.

512   WATERS, MARY-ALICE. Feminism and the Marxist Movement. New
      York: Pathfinder Press, 1972, 43 pp.
           Waters reviews the history of the Socialist movement with
      regard to the Woman Question. She begins by assessing Marx and
      Engels's contributions and discusses the role of women in the
      Second International in Germany and the United States. The Third
      International under Lenin, Waters judged, had "a more advanced,
      revolutionary analysis of women's oppression and the road to
      liberation than any previous organization in world history." But
      as Stalin took power and betrayed the revolution, the mantle of
      women's freedom passed, via Leon Trotsky, to the Fourth Interna-
      tional and the Socialist Workers party. "Everything we do and
      say today," Waters notes, "is in harmony with this tradition, and
      a continuation of it." Before concluding, she reviews the role
      of the woman suffrage movement within the Left.

513   _____. Women and the Socialist Revolution. New York: Path-
      finder Press, 1976, 30 pp.
           This pamphlet offers a short history of the women's rights
      movement as a function of capitalist development in the nineteenth
      century. A large portion concerns the family, its history and
      current state in light of marxist theory. Waters concludes her
      study by measuring the revolutionary potential of the 1970s
      women's liberation movement.

514   WEINBAUM, BATYA. The Curious Courtship of Women's Liberation
      and Socialism. Boston: South End Press, 1978, 168 pp.
           This essay takes the critique of marxism one step further

223

in the direction of radical feminism. Weinbaum does not wish
merely to expand the traditional materialist analysis to include
the family and sexuality, but challenges Marx's entire critique
of political economy as "sex blind." She argues for a fundamental
recasting of theory premised on a study of kinship, the patriarchal
kinship system that determines the organization of production.
Weinbaum also suggests that marxists failed to predict a correct
strategy for liberating women because they, as patriarchs, feared
loosing their own women's labor power. To reach this conclusion,
she elaborates freely on freudian paradigms, viewing marxists as
fathers and women as their daughters, and posits a universal sexual dialectic as the historical source of women's oppression. A
less systematic thinker than Shulamith Firestone, Weinbaum shares
the earlier radical feminist's antipathy toward marxism.

515 WILLIS, ELLEN. Beginning to See the Light: Pieces of a
     Decade. New York: Alfred A. Knopf, 1981, 320 pp.
         This book gathers Ellis's essays from the Village Voice,
     Rolling Stone, the New Yorker, and other magazines from the
     period 1967-1979. They cover many issues--abortion, pornography,
     the Middle East--but the best examine various strains of American
     popular culture. A feminist of strong convictions, Ellis writes
     personally and with insight on controversial issues. Described
     by a reviewer as "a woman formed by the utopian hopes of the
     1960s," Ellis emerges a major feminist critic of American life
     and Left complacency, especially on women's rights.

516 Women's Liberation and the Socialist Revolution. New York and
     Sydney: Pathfinder Press, 1979, 93 pp.
         This booklet contains the major statement on women's
     liberation discussed at the World Congress of the Fourth Inter-
     national in 1979. It contains two major sections. The first
     places the question of women's status within a historical mate-
     rialist framework and considers the origins of oppression and the
     economic and ideological ramifications within class society; it
     also describes various political tendencies within the contempo-
     rary women's liberation movement and relates this surge of activity
     to women's struggles in colonial and semicolonial countries.
         The second section outlines the program of the Fourth
     International in regard to this struggle. It includes a list of
     six basic demands: "full legal, political, and social equality
     for women; the right of women to control their reproductive func-
     tions; an end to the hypocrisy, debasement, and coercion of
     bourgeois and feudal family laws; full economic independence of
     women; equal educational opportunities; reorganization of society
     to eliminate domestic slavery of women." It also outlines methods
     of struggle, which includes supporting and aiding the women's
     liberation movement. It states boldly, "There is no contradiction
     between building the independent women's liberation movement and
     building a revolutionary Marxist party of women and men." The
     statement concludes, "The struggle to liberate women from the

bondage in which class society has placed them is a struggle to free all human relationships from the shackles of economic compulsion and to propel humanity along the road to a higher social order."

517 WOODROOFE, DEBBY. Sisters in Struggle, 1848-1920. New York: Pathfinder Press, 1971, 31 pp.
     "Our history is a weapon of liberation," Woodroofe prefaces her essay. She focuses narrowly on the woman suffrage movement and fills her narrative with factual errors, ahistorical judgments, and a confusing chronology.

518 Working Papers on Socialism and Feminism. Chicago: New American Movement, 1975, 30 pp.
     This collection includes Barbara Ehrenreich's major address to the national Socialist Feminist Conference held in July 1975, in which she studies the strategic relationship between the two philosophies of social change. Essays by Roberta Lynch, Sara Evans, Betty Willett, and Eli Zaretsky continue this analysis.

519 Working Papers on Socialist Feminism. Chicago: New American Movement, 1972, 28 pp.
     Formed in 1971 to build a movement for democratic socialism in the United States, the New American Movement endorsed independent women's or gay feminist organizations. This collection reprints essays from the NAM newspaper and internal bulletins by Roberta Lynch, Michelle Russell, Renate Jaeger, and Eli Zaretsky. It includes NAM's "Political Perspective on Feminism," which pledged support to autonomous women's groups and chapters within the organization and welcomed criticism by feminists of the Socialist movement itself "as it gives the movement vitality and direction."

520 ZARETSKY, ELI. Capitalism, the Family, and Personal Life. New York: Harper & Row, 1976, 156 pp.
     This essay, which first appeared serially in Socialist Revolution in 1973, addresses the question of women's liberation in relationship to the emergence of family life under modern capitalism. Zaretsky begins by examining the texts of leading feminist writers Shulamith Firestone and Juliet Mitchell, and acknowledges their role in bringing to attention the importance of the family in feminist theory. He then constructs a brief overview of the changes in personal life in Great Britain and the United States.
     Zaretsky's central chapter, "Politics and Personal Life," criticizes radical feminists for failing to deal with the economy, and traditional marxists for ignoring the family. Like Juliet Mitchell, he credits the emergence of new political insights into the "separate sphere of private life" to the "personal radicalism" of the late 1950s and 1960s. A Socialist program, Zaretsky concludes, must address the quality of life in both the factory and the home.

PERIODICALS

The revival of Left journalism proved somewhat less substantial than its counterpart in literature. Thus radical writers and editors found their way to the mainstream <u>Ms.</u>, <u>Ramparts</u> (later <u>Mother Jones</u>), and the <u>Village Voice</u>. A few tenacious journals held on after the decline of the New Left in the early 1970s and served a loyal reader-ship dedicated to both socialism and women's liberation.

521 <u>Notes from the First Year</u>. New York, 1968, 33 pp.
     Announcing a definitive break with the New Left, this journal heralds the formation of an independent radical feminist movement. It contains Anne Koedt's "Women in the Radical Move-ment," a speech given to a convention of New York women's groups in February 1968 wherein she describes the low status accorded women in the New Left. It also includes Rosalyn Baxandall's whimsical "page of protest" against Left male chauvinists from Karl Marx to Staughton Lynd.

522 <u>Notes from the Second Year: Radical Feminism</u>. New York, 1970, 126 pp.
     Edited by Shulamith Firestone and Anne Koedt, this issue contains an important section delineating the independent position of radical feminists vis a vis the New Left. Reprinted is Ellen Willis's "Women and the Left" from the <u>Guardian</u> (February 1968), in which she states: "The women's liberation movement was created by women activists fed up with their subordinate position in radical organizations" (p. 55). Willis catalogs grievances against radical men and explains the necessity for "a specifically feminist radical consciousness." Essays by Carol Hanisch on her experiences in the Southern Conference Educational Fund, a civil-rights organization, and by an anonymous woman frustrated by her status in the New Left express a similar viewpoint.

523 <u>Off Our Backs</u>. Washington, D.C., 1970–present.
     <u>Off Our Backs</u> is a Left feminist publication. Begun in the early days of women's liberation, it chronicles the develop-ment of the movement by providing regular coverage of key events and important issues. The early volumes document feminist anti-war activities and the emergence of radical feminism. The edi-torial statement in the first number reads: "We seek, through the liberation of women, the liberation of all people." The writers draw on radical traditions, such as International Woman's Day celebrations, and pay tribute to past activists like Emma Goldman and Anna Louise Strong.

524 <u>Radical America</u>. Madison, Wis., and Somerville, Mass.: 1967–present.
     Begun as an unofficial journal of the Students for a Demo-cratic Society, <u>Radical America</u> has emphasized the historical

background to the struggles of labor and women. It has also continued the New Left traditions of seeking the roots of current
conflicts "from below," in social life more than in political
leadership; and in documenting the alternative cultures expressed
through feminist literature, crafts, and graphic arts.

Its first women's liberation issue (vol. 4, no. 2, February
1970), edited by Edith Hoshino Altbach, has been reprinted as
From Feminism to Liberation. Its first women's history issue
(vol. 5, no. 4, July-August 1971) included the major historiog-
raphical contribution to that date, "Women in American Society:
An Historical Contribution," by Mari Jo Buhle, Ann D. Gordon, and
Nancy Schrom. Assessing the outmoded perspectives, the authors
outlined a new model specifying the relationship between public
status and private roles within the history of capitalist development. A revised version of this essay appeared in Berenice
Carroll, ed., Liberating Women's History (1976).

A special double issue on women's labor (vol. 7, no. 7-8,
July-October 1973) took a theoretical approach to the question
and examined the relationship between household labor and wage-
labor. Accompanying documents from the British women's movement
complemented the American essays.

Several selections in vol. 13, no. 5 (September-October
1979) on feminism and leninism conduct a polemic against the
utility of older political frameworks on the woman question.
British author Sheila Rowbotham, a frequent contributor, joined
by Linda Gordon and Allen Hunter of the editorial board, outlined
this incisive viewpoint.

The double issue analyzing the New Right and its implications (vol. 15, no. 1, January-April 1981) brought the history
of the women's liberation movement up to a crucial stage in its
political development. Hunter and Gordon probed the origins of
the New Right's attitudes toward women and family, and Barbara
Ehrenreich sought to place that activism within the context of
declining energies of former feminist activists. Ellen Willis
traced the conflict to basic principles of Women's Liberation.

Other issues have featured a broad discussion of women's
history and culture in the United States and abroad. The women's
movement in revolutionary Portugal, Italy, and Great Britain;
the women's movement in the United States and its counterpart in
the labor movement; popular culture of quilts, soap operas, and
beauty parlors; and the lesbian and gay movements have been
featured. Contributors include Marlene Dixon, Selma James, Lyn
Lifshin, Margaret Randall, Lillian Robinson, Rosalyn Baxandall,
Lisa Vogel, Ntzoke Shange, Sara Evans, and Barbara Koppel.

525 Socialist Review (formerly Socialist Revolution). San Fran-
cisco, 1970-present.
This political journal carries frequent reports on and
analysis of the state of the women's liberation movement in the
United States, Europe, Latin America, China, and the Soviet Union.
Several issues concentrate on the relationship of feminist

organizations and the American Left. Ann Farrar's "The Seattle Liberation Front, Women's Liberation, and a New Socialist Politics" (September-October 1970) discusses the tendency within the women's liberation movement to reject Socialist politics as a partial response to the problems women face in dealing with the male Left. A lengthy forum on socialism and feminism (January-March 1974) continues this discussion. An essay by Barbara Easton describes various political tendencies within contemporary feminism as the basis upon which the Socialist movement might determine its contribution to the struggle for women's liberation; a statement by the Berkeley-Oakland Women's Union includes a brief history since January 1973, when the Union formed, and its principles of unity putting forth its conception of Socialist feminism; Eli Zaretsky and members of the New American movement take part in an exchange of ideas on the nature of the family under capitalism and Socialist politics. The National Conference on Socialist Feminism, July 1975 is reported by Barbara Dudley (October-December 1975), and includes speeches by Barbara Ehrenreich, the Berkeley-Oakland Women's Union, and Michelle Russell. Further discussion of the role of Socialist feminism in the New American movement appears in a forum, "Prospects for the Left: II," (January-February 1979).

526   Women: A Journal of Liberation. Baltimore, 1969-present.
        The opening editorial read: "This journal is intended to be of use to women engaged in struggle; struggle for greater awareness and struggle to change conditions. The Journal will serve as a forum of opinion and expression vital to a growing Women's Liberation Movement."
        Especially during its first four years, the journal published a run of articles on the relationship between the New Left and the women's liberation movement and on Socialist feminist positions within the larger movement. Its first number contains, for example, Ellen DuBois and Suzanne Gordon's "A National Action: A Women's Perspective," which criticized the SDS-Weathermen call for mass mobilization. In other numbers the journal revived the radical feminist past by publishing short biographical essays on notable revolutionary women. Its format, divided into thematic essays and perspectives on the political movement, allowed for a mixture of opinions and news of Socialist feminist interest.
        After 1975 the journal became more literary in orientation, its pages filled with short essays on issues of concern to the women's liberation movement and original feminist poetry and graphics.

FICTION AND POETRY

The modern period witnessed a renaissance of the literature of social protest in volume, content, and above all diversity. The novel, staple of previous generations, receded because the genre had suffered from the popularity of new forms, such as television and movies. Yet good novels and even better short stories found a reader-ship, and a handful of prose writers attained a stature equal to a Josephine Herbst, if not an Edward Bellamy of former times. Studied in the classroom, authors like Grace Paley and Tillie Olsen, coming late to their fame, established a radical and feminist voice. Poets did far better than before. Although poetry became increasingly an academic art, women gathered political audiences at public readings and generated an excitement few others could claim. Some, like Diane DiPrima, Denise Levertov, and June Jordon, found their work widely reprinted in the radical press. Here and there a playwright, such as Barbara Garson, hit home with enormous success on the local theatre circuit.

The old debates about "proletarian realism" or "aesthetic truths," so central to Left writers of the 1930s, scarcely existed outside of an occasional sectarian outburst. Ursula Le Guin became, without political fanfare, one of the leading science-fiction writers of the times. Muriel Rukeyser and Jayne Cortez continued poetic experimenta-tion begun decades earlier; Alice Walker gave Afro-American fiction a distinctly New Left taste. Without prescriptions or proscriptions, the writers devised their own rules, found their own audience, and if they suffered the lack of collective support Old Left artists occa-sionally garnered, they more than compensated with their free-ranging search for an appropriate popular aesthetic. A handful steadily re-ceived rave reviews in the leading literary journals; many others gained critical notice. Although radical women remained marginal to the best-selling authors in the mainstream, their readership per-severed even when the white-hot days of the movement faded from memory.

527 CABRAL, OLGA. *The Evaporated Man*. New York: Olivant Press, 1968, 58 pp.
    "A New Book of Anti-War and Other Poems," this volume again quotes Walter Lowenfels on Cabral: "You are the first woman poet I know in this country who has expressed a national spirit," in this case a spirit of protest. Many poems are reprinted from *Mainstream*, *Jewish Currents*, and *American Dialog*.

528 _____. *The Darkness in My Pockets*. San Francisco: Galli-maufry, 1976, 48 pp.
    This volume represents the author's tribute to the poetic craft. It is the most "internal" of her works, with only a sug-gestion of the political themes apparent in previous volumes. At best, she weaves surrealistic images with vivid satire and un-dying commitment to the human spirit:

>   Listen! I have lived from Spain to Spain.
>   I was young in Guernica. I grew old in Santiago
>   I tried to stop the blind bombing capability with my

fists and cries.

* * *

Listen! There is a wind that slices iron
The dead keep their accounts. The living grows stronger
I want to die a little each day living the deaths of the
    people
Bleeding because I'm alive.

529 _____. In the Empire of Ice. Cambridge, Mass.: West End
    Press, 1980, 80 pp.
        Published by a noted New Left press, this volume takes its
place appropriately among the works of older and younger writers.
Cabral joins them in a remarkable way, however. She has little
of the Socialist realist bias and much of the imaginative romantic
traditions unpopular with the Old Left. She has evolved in her
poetry from the early, instinctive rage toward a synthesis of
metaphor and political tone. She writes:

        The Polyvinal woman the industrial Venus
        Who surfaces in the stained air of cities
        Floats overhead assembled from molecules
        of factory wastes.
        Don't be misled by
        her gamboge yellow her pink alizarins
        her look of Norma Jean
        for she is Kali or Coatlicua
        in white caucasian skin
        Who dances
        Naked in a gas mask
        While we sleep.

530 CORTEZ, JAYNE. Pisstained Stairs and the Monkey Man's Wares.
    New York: Phrase Text, 1970, 16 pp.
        One of the most explicitly political and radical poets of
black experience, Cortez is definitely outside the mainstream
"protest" tradition. She is rooted not in realistic symbolism
but rather in an instinctive (and self-conscious) nonrealism or
surrealism. Spiritually allied with "free jazz," the African
Revolution and black eros, she draws upon tribal wisdom and im-
probable connections, uses wild metaphors, uproarious humor, and
savage bitterness to make a complex point about existence and
spiritual essence. Cortez, teacher and activist, has been in
recent years recognized as a leading black woman poet.
        Her first volume, Pisstained Stairs, is probably her least
overtly political. Her apotheosis of John Coltrane, her unasham-
edly erotic lyrics, and her general anger at white civilization's
treatment of blacks occupy her main themes. Illustrated by her
husband Mel Edwards, this work formally launched her unique
oeuvre.

531 _____. <u>Festivals and Funerals</u>. New York: Phrase Text, 1971,
   21 pp.
          More explicitly political, Cortez remains resiliently erotic
   in her commemoration and celebration of life lost and regained.
   She is immensely angry, but more precise in her identifications.
   For the first time, she captures the consciousness of factory
   life in the voice of a factory worker:

             My legs swollen from pressing pedals
             My hands stiff from pushing cloth
             I have a craving for food
             That's why I have to piece work my ass off

532 _____. <u>Scarifications</u>. New York: Bola Press, 1973, 64 pp.
          Cortez here investigates city life, most especially in New
   York, with the goal of subjective consciousness and sideways
   vision of the unspoken dreadful truth. She also hails African
   martyrs Amilcar Cabral and Kwame Nkrumah. We do not know whether
   she is being satirical or determined to bring beauty out of death
   when she says:

             It's nothing
             This tragedy in our arms
             We can invent new bones
             New fleshes against madness

   Perhaps she will not allow any simple, unambiguous answer.

533 _____. <u>Mouth On Paper</u>. New York: Bola Press, 1977, 63 pp.
          Recipient of a New York State Council of the Arts award,
   increasingly important cultural leader and outstanding figure in
   a multiracial radicalism (evidenced by her editorial role in <u>Free
   Spirits</u>, journal of City Lights Books), Cortez here takes a place
   at the center of poetic accomplishment. "i say dreams are like
   riots," she proclaims, and whether the subject is sex or revolution, the dream has always a riotous potential. She is an outspoken surrealist. Cortez retains nevertheless a wide compass
   for events and personalities within black America, as in her poem
   to the memory of Paul Robeson "even though you don't sing in the
   style of my choice."

534 DEE, RUBY, ed. <u>Glowchild and Other Poems</u>. New York: Third
   Press, 1972, 111 pp.
          A major protest anthology by an ill-fated Pan-African
   press, this volume brings together "gifted young Blacks" and
   other writers, most notably Dee herself. Born in Cleveland,
   raised in New York, educated at Hunter High School and College,
   Dee married actor-director Ossie Davis and became the black woman
   most steadily identified with Left causes since the 1950s.
   Actress in theatre, film, and television, she also writes poetry
   under the name Ann Wallace. In this volume, she writes "most

stimulating for me are the poems dealing with abstractions. Time,
Unity, Soul, Love, Peace, Freedom . . . beg for a more precise
definition in the minds of these young people." Her own poems
tend toward the humorous and personal.

535   di PRIMA, DIANE. Revolutionary Letters Etc. San Francisco:
      City Lights Books, 1971, 88 pp.
            Diane di Prima (1934-), the most influential woman among
      the Beat poets of the 1950s, also surpassed her milieu in em-
      bracing the revolutionary aspirations of assorted movements in
      the late 1960s. An activist only in the sense of her poetry and
      public readings, she nevertheless stands as a unique figure within
      radicalism and esthetics.
            The literary evidence is most abundant in this volume.
      Originally sent out in mimeographed form to Left political and
      underground publications, the Letters reached an audience far out-
      side traditional literary interests and at a critical moment.
      She wrote

                  When you seize Columbia, when you
                  seize Paris, take
                  the media, tell the people what you're doing . . .
                  forget to negotiate, forget how
                  to negotiate, don't wait for De Gaulle or Kirk
                  to abdicate, they won't, you are not
                  'demonstrating' you are fighting
                  a war, fight to win . . .

      as strategic and tactical advice, although her love poems about
      the land and the people she knew are equally serious by intent.
      Di Prima herself supplies the link with the further political
      aspirations of the modern age. Her grandfather, as she reveals
      in the first entry, was a close associate of the Italian-American
      anarchist leader and romantic Carlo Tresca. Her memories of the
      old man, his love of nature, culture, and uncompromising revolu-
      tionary ideals, have been a thread running through her entire
      oeuvre.

536   GARSON, BARBARA. MacBird! New York: Grove Press, 1967, 109
      pp.
            A political satire, Garson's play is a provocative adapta-
      tion of Shakespeare's Macbeth, with President Lyndon Johnson the
      chief antagonist. Garson (1942-) wrote MacBird! as an antiwar
      play for street theatre, a form of political demonstration that
      was very popular in the late 1960s. Highly acclaimed by the New
      Left in the United States and abroad, MacBird! achieved more than
      300 productions and sold over a half-million copies.

537   GELLER, RUTH. Seed of a Woman. Buffalo, N.Y.: Imp Press,
      1979, 314 pp.
            Seed of a Woman, Geller's first novel, is a study of the

development of the women's movement within the New Left. Set in
a university town between September 1969, and April 1970, the
story follows its protagonist, Becky, a graduate student in history, as she becomes absorbed by antiwar and campus activism.
Sexual relations, particularly with the professor Becky assists,
are central to the narrative and graphically described. At the
close, Becky and her friends have organized women's groups and
have begun to come to consciousness of themselves as women.

538 GILDEN, K.B. Between the Hills and the Sea. Garden City,
     N.Y.: Doubleday & Co., 1971, 549 pp.
        A little-appreciated and rare novel of defeat during the
late 1940s and early 1950s, this is the work of a husband-and-
wife writing team but primarily the craft of Katya Gilden. Its
outstanding feature is a careful portrayal of the industrial and
social dynamics of a blue-collar city dominated by the electronics
industry; here the intellectual quarrels that occupied most notable
Left writers in the 1940s and 1950s have little significance, and
even the debates between orthodox Communists and their opponents
are mooted.
        The story follows the marriage and activities of an in-
digenous labor radical, Mish, and his wife Priscilla, descendent
of left-wing local gentry. The two are in many ways complementary
opposites: she lacks his hardheadedness but also his pessimism;
he has the skills for industrial mobilization while she generates
enthusiasm in the community, particularly in the grim housing
complex where they make their home. One other female character,
union militant Mariuch Ucchini, is drawn in smaller scale but
also true to life as the shop-floor agitator who sustained the
Communist influence in the union through persistence, combative-
ness, and class-conscious antiracism.
        Between the Hills and the Sea, as perhaps no other novel
of the era, carries forward the best of the proletarian novel to
the breakdown of the Left, and illuminates the contradictions
facing the rank-and-file of the movement.

539 JORDAN, JUNE. Things That I Do in the Dark; Selected Poetry.
     New York: Random House, 1977, 203 pp.
        Born in Harlem, New York in 1936, educated at Barnard
College and the University of Chicago, June Jordan is an award-
winning poet and essayist of the black experience in America.
She is also one of her generation's outstanding radical poets.
        Her verse is free of artificiality, either political or
esthetic, because she roots it in an unclouded, imaginative reconstruction of the reality before her eyes. Her skill is most
apparent in satire, as in this "Memo to Daniel Pretty Moynihan"
from 1969:

             Don't you liberate me
             from my female black pathology

> I been working off my knees
> I been drinking what I please
>
>   * * *
>
> But you been screwing me so long
> I got a idea something's wrong
> with you
>
> I got a simple proposition
> You takeover my position
>
> Clean your own house, babyface.

She writes no less decisively about love or ecology. Her subject matter is, somehow, always political, her treatment always poetic.

540   . Passion: New Poems, 1977-1980. Boston: Beacon Press, 1981, 100 pp.
    This volume collects fifty-one poems on various themes, from street violence and racial and sexual oppression, to the search for love and for identity. It opens with a preface, "For the Sake of a People's Poetry: Walt Whitman and the Rest of Us," which outlines Jordan's stand. The many free verse poems in the collection reinforce her admiration of Whitman as the "great American poet of democracy as cosmos . . . poet of the many peoples as one people."

541 LAMB, MYRA. The Mod Donna and Scyklon Z: The Plays of Women's Liberation. New York: Pathfinder Press, 1973, unpaginated.
    The Mod Donna, or A Space-age Musical Soap Opera with Breaks for Commercials, appeared Off-Broadway during the 1970-1971 season. Focused on personal frustration and mutual exploitation in marriage, the play is a moral treatise about women's damaging obsession with sexuality. It is a polemic against modern marriage, described by Lamb as a "piece of agit-prop." The Mod Donna received widespread recognition as one of the earliest feminist plays of the second wave. Although some critics found it a bit too puritanical in its analysis of sex relations, Vivian Gornick, writing in the Village Voice, judged Lamb to be the "first true artist of the feminist consciousness."
    Scyklon Z, subtitled A Group of Pieces with a Point, also deals with contemporary themes of women's liberation. One selection, "But What Have You Done for Me Lately?" a short play about sex role reversal, was presented by the New York Socialist Workers party as a fund raiser for their 1970 campaign.

542 Le GUIN, URSULA K. Left Hand of Darkness. New York: Walker & Co., 1969, 286 pp.
    Ursula Le Guin (1929-) became one of the most respected science-fiction writers of the 1970s and gained many readers

outside the devotees of the genre. She attracted a large audience
intrigued by her stridently antiwar, antiimperialist, and anarcho-
Socialist views. Although Le Guin demonstrates no apparent faith
in marxist theories of historical progress or working-class triumph, she exposes the dread maladies of technocratic civilization.
Her novels and stories explore alternative political-economic
systems and underscore the hard struggle of the individual against
dehumanization.

Outstanding within a relatively small circle of women
writers of science fiction, Le Guin is the most prominent feminist
in the field. Left Hand of Darkness, which many critics consider
her most satisfying novel, deals imaginatively with sex stereotyping and gender roles. She describes life on a planet without
a sex-gender system and studies the implications by casting an
ordinary man from Earth into this alien culture. Although Le Guin
names fidelity and betrayal rather than androgyny as the main
theme of her novel, many readers have claimed her study of human
sexuality to be a landmark in feminist literature. Left Hand of
Darkness also won the favor of science-fiction fans and critics
and received the coveted Hugo and Nebula awards in 1969.

543   _____. The Word for World is Forest. New York: Berkley Pub-
      lishing Corp., 1972, 189 pp.
First published as a novella in 1969, The Word for World
is Forest is Le Guin's foremost protest against the American invasion of Vietnam. It is also a study of the irreversible effects
of history, the destruction of a civilization that had previously
perpetuated itself around the cycles of the seasons, life, and
death. In this sense, The Word stands as an interpretation of
the clash between technology and nature, between the fire power
of the former and the imagination of the latter.

An inner compulsion guided Le Guin's work. "What I wanted
to write about was the forest and the dream. . . . But the boss
wanted to talk about the destruction of ecological balance and
the rejection of emotional balance." The forest-dwelling primi-
tives of planet Athse face the invasion of Terran colonists who
have already reduced Earth to a poisoned dump and now seek fresh
resources of timber. They treat the Athse as unintelligent
beasts of burden, fail utterly to comprehend the native culture
based on dreams and dream-knowledge, and threaten to eradicate
the entire society. Athseans learn to fight back, but in the
process they are damaged, driven beyond innocence. On one level,
the story focuses on their need to win against an increasingly
barbaric and berserk military invader. On another level, it asks
deep questions about the balance of civilization and nature,
about the balance of conscious and unconscious forces in human
history.

544   _____. The Dispossessed. New York: Harper & Row, 1974, 341
      pp.
Subtitled An Ambiguous Utopia, The Dispossessed is one of

the outstanding political contributions to the genre of science
fiction, perhaps the most important utopian novel since Edward
Bellamy's Looking Backward. Unlike Bellamy, Le Guin offers no
blueprint of the ideal state and downplays any direct exposition
of its philosophy. Rather, she allows only glimpses of a non-
authoritarian society in operation, one struggling against material
deprivation and moral restrictions rather than achieving perfection.

The daughter of anthropologists Theodora Kracaw and Alfred
Kroeber, Le Guin deals foremost with the interaction of culture
and the individual. In this story, a colony of people, sickened
by the tyranny and corruption of their society, have willingly
left the fertile planet Urras to settle one of its moons, Anarres.
The utopians set out to construct an ideal society but must grapple with the philosophical dimensions of individual versus collective well-being, a classic utopian problem.

545 LEVERTOV, DENISE. The Sorrow Dance. New York: New Directions,
     1967, 94 pp.
     Levertov, who was born in 1923 and raised in England,
ranks highly among post-World War II American poets; she is
usually compared to William Carlos Williams and Ezra Pound. In
the late 1960s she became both an activist against the Vietnam
War and a political poet. This volume contains her first set of
poems in response to the horror, "Life at War," which deals primarily with the loss of poetic vision.

546 _____. Relearning the Alphabet. New York: New Directions,
     1970, 121 pp.
     The Vietnam War continues to be a major theme of Levertov's
poetry. In this volume she addresses the significance of her
shift in manner, the revolutionary potential of the moment, and
her relation to the antiwar movement.

547 _____. To Stay Alive. New York: New Directions, 1971, 86
     pp.
     By the poet's own judgment, this volume represents her
most successful attempt to weave together political and esthetic
themes. She stresses "the sense my individual history gives me
of being straddled between places [extended] to the more universal sense any writer my age—rooted in a cultural past barely
shared by younger readers, yet committed to a solidarity of hope
and struggle with the revolutionary young—must have of being
almost unbearably, painfully, straddled across time." In places
her text seems remarkably close to the immediate struggles, as
the creation of the People's Park in Berkeley or in confrontations
with police at antiwar demonstrations; in other places far away
to her intellectual, European self. As she says about a friend:

> There's a pulse in Richard
> that day and night says

```
        revolution     revolution     revolution

        and another
        not always heard:

        poetry      poetry

        rippling through his sleep,
        a river pulse.
```

548 LOZORAITIS, JEAN. <u>LOUDcracks/softHEARTS</u>. Boston: South End
     Press, 1979, 84 pp.
       "Dead Food Does Not Build Strong Bodies 12 Ways"

```
        Cookies, amerika loves its
        cookies; in the middle of
        all this poison floats a
        dollar bill/sign that
        amerika's citizens are
        dying of chemicals
        made for food and
        bombs alike . . . the
        ones in food are slow
        to kill, and can make you
        cancer or crazy. . . .
```

This stanza illustrates the tenor of Lozoraitis's analysis
of the capitalist system. Her collection illustrates further the
development of her consciousness from 1967 through 1978. The
heroines that emerge in her poems are strong women, be they poor
factory workers, lesbians, blacks, or herself. But the decade
itself that transformed Lozoraitis and provided her the clear
imagery of women's liberation is central. "Fascism, American-
style," written in 1977, is typical:

```
        as for me, i'll get used
        to hell/nothing new
        no reason to leave;
        all my beliefs, strength
        washed up --i'm just sittin here
        waitin to see if
        they're really gonna make
        Washington D.C. white
        by 1980; we really gonna be
        using nuclear power for energy;
        do Tampax really have a chemical
        that extracts more blood/
```

Lozoraitis, a writer from Worcester, Massachusetts, is a
teacher and community activist.

549 OLSEN, TILLIE. <u>Yonnondio: From the Thirties</u>. New York:
     Delacorte Press, 1974, 196 pp. Reprint. New York: Dell Pub-
     lishing Co., 1979, 132 pp.
          As reviewers remarked when the book appeared in 1974, this
     early and essentially unfinished document of Olsen's literary
     development is notable for its fine description, rhythmic prose,
     and weak character studies. Written in the period 1932-1937, re-
     vised during 1972-1973, this short novel recounts the bitter life
     of a poor Western family, always on the edge of starvation and
     moving from mining town to farm to city. Mazie, a child, is
     usually the protagonist, although her mother, Anna Holbrook, oc-
     cupies an increasingly central role as the story progresses. It
     is to the mother that the worst events befall. She is portrayed
     cutting corners to feed the children, threatened by frustration
     and the occasional physical abuse of her husband, and driven to
     hold onto family despite physical exhaustion. But she seems
     mentally stolid, psychologically mute. Thus <u>Yonnondio</u>, a powerful
     work inspired by Rebecca Harding Davis's "Life in the Iron Mills,"
     does not fulfill its potential. Nevertheless, many reviewers
     judge Olsen's elegiac novel one of the best products of the pro-
     letarian literature of the 1930s.

550 PALEY, GRACE. <u>Enormous Changes at the Last Minute</u>. New York:
     Farrar, Straus, 1974, 198 pp.
          Paley's second volume of collected stories reflects on
     personal themes over the previous fifteen years, including the
     autobiographical "a Conversation with My Father." Critics found
     the quality of the seventeen selections uneven. Some objected to
     oblique references to political issues like the Vietnam War or
     the welfare system, but most appreciated Paley's skill at con-
     veying a female sensibility and identity in second-generation
     ethnic New York.

551 PETERS, NANCY JOYCE. <u>It's In the Wind</u>. Chicago: Black Swan
     Press, 1977, 16 pp.
          Peters, codirector and editor of City Lights Books and
     coauthor with Laurence Ferlinghetti of <u>Literary San Francisco</u>, is
     perhaps the best-known woman poet among surrealists in the United
     States. <u>It's In the Wind</u>, a production of the Surrealist Group,
     combines an invocation of nature, utopian-revolutionary politics,
     and the imagination. Thus she writes, "I run out of my door/
     like the true aim of terror/ like the desire of the general
     strike/ onto that transfigured desert/ where nothing is quite
     certain/ except the chemical thrust/ of imagination/ willing the
     metamorphic world."

552 PIERCY, MARGE. <u>Breaking Camp</u>. Middletown, Conn.: Wesleyan
     University Press, 1968, 74 pp.
          Marge Piercy, the most outstanding and prolific feminist
     writer to emerge in the late 1960s, has continued to turn out
     novels and books of poetry at a time when political discouragement

and writer's block has silenced numbers of other promising artists. Born in 1936 in Detroit, Piercy attended the University of Michigan and Northwestern University, married briefly, participated in neighborhood integration struggles and antiwar movements, and became identified with the women's liberation movement.

In discussing her poetry, critics often compare Piercy to Walt Whitman because she, too, expresses--albeit differently--the dual imperative to love and to be free. Piercy herself has disclaimed "distinctions between private and social poetry." This first major collection, less overtly political than her later work, expresses outrage at poverty and inhumanity in American urban life. Rooted in her experiences in Chicago's South Side, the poems present stark images.

> You go on and I follow, I choose and follow.
> The mills of injustice darken the sky with their smoke,
>   ash floats on the streams.
> Soon we will be setting up camp on a plain of nails.
> Soon we will be drinking blood out of shattered bone.
> The dead will be stacked like bricks.
> The suns of power will dance on the black sky
>   and scorch us to dust.

553 _____. Going Down Fast. New York: Trident Press, 1969, 349 pp.

Although critics have praised Piercy's poetry, they have judged her prose a shade on a didactic side. Nevertheless, she has demonstrated a talent for creating individual characters and for casting scenes. Always timely in her subject matter, she may be regarded as the reincarnation of the nineteenth-century woman writer, proud of her womanhood and clear in her purpose.

Going Down Fast, her first novel, builds upon her experiences in Chicago in the mid-1960s. It concerns the heightening of tension in the ghetto neighborhoods around the University of Chicago and the awakening of erstwhile liberals to the radical imperative. Her portrayal of the period before radicalism became chic, the process of politicization just awakening to its internal contradictions, is singular and remains too little appreciated.

554 _____. Hard Loving; Poems. Middletown, Conn.: Wesleyan University Press, 1969, 77 pp.

The dedication reads "from the Movement for the Movement," but Piercy means more than politics in the usual sense. There are protest marches and demonstrations but also communes, marriages, relationships made and unmade, lectures on American history, glimpses of exile, much sex, and more introspection. In forceful imagery, Piercy forges a successful dynamic between poetry and polemics:

> Marching, a dream of wind in our chests,
> a dream of thunder in our legs,

> we tied up midtown Manhattan for half an hour,
> the Revolutionary Contingent and Harlem,
> but it did not happen
> because it was not reported in any newspaper.

555 _____. Dance the Eagle to Sleep. Garden City, N.Y.: Doubleday & Co., 1970, 232 pp.
   Piercy's first major experiment with science fiction and
her first political novel that can be described as Weatheresque,
that is, close to the mood of the late-1960 students-turned-
terrorists. The power of the book lay in reference to immediate
events: police riots, classroom rebellions, drugs, and sexual
experimentation. The story takes place in the near future and
follows a small army of alienated youth that declares itself a
nation apart from a dehumanized and oppressive system.
   While her first novel showed warm respect for the ghetto
community, Dance the Eagle suggests Piercy regarded all white
America, except its youth, as essentially one unrevolutionary
bloc. Despite this limiting perspective, she creates several
strong characters and many strong scenes. A growing feminist
consciousness foretells the direction of her later works.

556 _____. Small Changes. Garden City, N.Y.: Doubleday & Co.,
1973, 562 pp. Reprint. New York: Fawcett World Library,
1978, 542 pp.
   Catharine Stimpson wrote that in Small Changes "Piercy is
recording radical feminism giving birth to itself." Set in
Cambridge at the end of the 1960s, the story mainly concerns two
women's confrontation, in a very intimate way, with archetypal
"movement" men. The more self-confident and politically attuned
Miriam serves as a foil for the feminist evolution of her working-
class counterpart, Beth. Whereas Miriam never manages to come to
terms with the male milieu of the New Left and succumbs to a degrading domesticity, Beth grows painfully but inevitably to womanhood and demonstrates her new consciousness by joining a women's
commune. Sexuality looms large in the gradual transformation of
protagonists.
   Reactions to Piercy's explorations of liberated lifestyles
were strong and diverse. The unremittingly negative depiction of
men stirred the ire of some critics; Beth's solution in lesbianism
disturbed others. And while some critics appreciated Piercy's
attempt to make politics "personal," naming her the American
Doris Lessing, others found her presentation either overly didactic or insufficiently sharp.

557 _____. To Be of Use. Garden City, N.Y.: Doubleday & Co.,
1973, 107 pp.
   A poetic continuation of the women's liberation movement,
dedicated to the proposition that women must learn to see themselves anew and love themselves, this volume includes the famous
"Secretary Chant":

My hips are a desk
From my ears hang
Chains of paper clips

***
File me under W
because I wonce
was
a woman

Piercy proceeds from this bitterly humorous critique of
office work toward her sense of magic (a cycle of poems styled on
the Tarot) and finally, an evocation of death and renewal.
Calling back the faith of the martyred heroes of liberation, she
ends with a glorious poem to the Sun, "androgynous child" and
herald of a new day.

558 _____. Living in the Open. New York: Alfred A. Knopf, 1976,
108 pp.
Withdrawal from the 1960s into a quieter decade sets
Piercy's most avowedly autobiographical collection. "I need a
good fighter to be murdered by the CIA so I may care," she writes,
for her poetry and politics have "come unstuck." The first part
concerns life outside the metropolis: reconnoitering with
friends on Cape Cod restores the feeling of life, evokes themes
of nature. The second section concentrates on personal relations
with men and with women. The last part is a statement of feminism:

There is no difference between being raped
and being run over by a truck
except that afterward men ask if you enjoyed it.

559 _____. Woman on the Edge of Time. New York: Alfred A.
Knopf, 1976, 369 pp. Reprint. New York: Fawcett World
Library, 1978, 381 pp.
Piercy's outstanding experiment with science fiction,
Woman on the Edge of Time features a Mexican-American woman in-
carcerated for mental illness, isolated and fearful of losing her
family, and in contact with a being from the future. Two stories,
two planes of consciousness and struggle thus persist side by
side throughout the novel, for the future is no less hazardous
than the present. In a postnuclear-war civilization, a degree of
egalitarianism has been attained, but at a cost. Within the
commune, relations between men and women are formal, structured,
each member with "per" space guaranteed, and a heavy work load
for all. Outside the commune danger lurks in the form of a
possible invasion by some militaristic order. Connie Ramos, the
protagonist, explores this world while remaining in the prisonlike
mental institution and subjected to the indignities of paternal-
istic, racist, and sexist treatment.
Like much of Piercy's work, Woman on the Edge of Time

inclines toward sloganistic dialogue, the plot overshadowing character and scene. The portrayal of state mental hospitals, however, and most especially the treatment of minority women in them, rings true. Piercy's vision of semi-utopia has the power of complexity: as in the work of Ursula Le Guin, the problems of gender remain, despite changes in form and in definition.

560 _____. The High Cost of Living. New York: Harper & Row, 1978, 268 pp. Reprint. New York: Fawcett World Library, 1979, 268 pp.

The least overtly Socialist of Piercy's novels seems written essentially to portray the character of Leslie, a bold and remarkable lesbian, and to explore the native ground of Piercy's own lower-middle-class Detroit and its environs. A graduate student exploited and insulted by the professor who employs her, Leslie is drawn into the life of a girl on the verge of independent womanhood. As she seeks to quicken the process, she also becomes drawn to a homosexual male, Bernard. Her brief sexual episode with him, on an island in Michigan's polluted rivers, seems a metaphor of frustrated heterosexual relations. On the contrary, Leslie's own being--intellectual, motorcyclist, committed politico, sensitive and vulnerable woman--is a vindication of the 1960s women's liberation movement still far from its goals.

561 _____. The Twelve-Spoked Wheel Flashing. New York: Alfred A. Knopf, 1978, 130 pp.

Piercy writes about this book: "As I can't separate the personal and political in my life, as I will not separate emotion and intellectual judgment and experiences but try to weld them, as I go back and forth from the vital dying city with its wars of plunder I have tried to shape this book as a growth ring, the record of a year." Here she is on Cape Cod home turf, meditating about the significance of her glimpses of life in the post-Vietnam era:

> Now our armies too are withdrawn
> the armies of flowers and placards,
> the armies of raised fists and rocks,
> the handful of real homemade
> bombs. The war
> that goes on is our war
> for our own land. To take it
> to hold it
> to form it again new
> out of the nightmare splitting
> open into dream. . . .

This volume is self-evidently a mark of tradition, destination unknown.

562 _____. Vida: A Novel. New York: Summit Books, 1979, 412 pp.
Reprint. New York: Fawcett World Library, 1981, 480 pp.
    In this novel Piercy continues to explore the psychological
intricacies of the Weather underground. Its protagonist, wanted
by the FBI for a 1970 bombing, lives as a fugitive but tries desperately to maintain relationships, however unsatisfying, with
her husband and sister. She tries, too, to form a new friendship
with a fellow fugitive. How Vida manages to contact her relatives
and comrades aiding the underground, and what happens when they
manage a secretive meeting, provide dramatic tension. The supporting characters and Vida herself are complex, far from one-
dimensionally heroic. Rather, they are beset by their own problems, including growing individualism and desire for survival as
the political movement dissipates. In flashbacks covering the
crucial years from 1967 to 1974, Piercy offers her analysis of a
political epoch.
    Many reviewers praised Vida when it first appeared, calling
it a moving story and commending its insight into political history. Elinor Langer, writing in the New York Times Book Review
(February 24, 1980), described Piercy's novel as a "political
brief" but nonetheless an important portrait of the New Left.

563 PIERCY, MARGE, and IRA WOOD. The Last White Class: A Play
About Neighborhood Terror. Trumansburg, N.Y.: Crossing Press,
1980, 145 pp.
    Written during Boston's busing crisis, this nine-scene
play is drawn in story-line from a community play delivered in
the midst of the trauma. The central theme, of a black family
facing the terror of a white neighborhood, is explicitly intended
to foster antiracist sentiments. But The Last White Class is
also meant to be a comedy of sex roles.
    The play's title is a reference to the ethnocentric bias
of the curriculum of schools. Integration of the schools and
neighborhood thus represents the injection of black culture and
humanist values into a decaying white society. There is not much
room for rollicking humor here, and the pathos lends itself to
stark, sometimes one-dimensional characterization. The foreword
notes that the authors "struggled with each other as fiercely as
with any enemy to make [the play] at last come to light." Caught
up in the tumultuous events, Piercy and Wood obviously found it
impossible to move beyond agitational purposes. The result is a
drama with a certain power for examining one moment in history.

564 ROSEMONT, PENELOPE. ATHANOR. Chicago: Black Swan Press,
n.d. [1970?], 16 pp.
    Penelope Rosemont, artist and graphic designer of Arsenal:
Surrealist Subversion and other publications, activist at various
times in Students for a Democratic Society, the Workers Defense
League, and the International Typographers Union, is an "alchem-
ical" poet. Her writings, similar in a number of ways to those
of Jayne Cortez and Nancy Joyce Peters, bring forward overpowering

images not to be assimilated into any didactic political vision.

565 RUKEYSER, MURIEL. The Collected Poems. New York: McGraw-
      Hill, 1978, 588 pp.
          Surprised to witness the collection of her poetry during
      her lifetime, Rukeyser wrote a brief introduction to this defini-
      tive volume. The poems date from 1935 to 1976. The early works
      produced in the 1930s, when Rukeyser achieved fame as a proletarian
      writer, celebrate the stamina and bravery of common people--
      farmers, workers, blacks, and women--in the face of economic hard-
      ship and oppression. Somewhat unique to the canon, Rukeyser's
      poems unite social themes and the poet's own existential awareness.
      Described as a modern poet of sensibility, Rukeyser made liberty
      her central concept.

566 SEGAL, EDITH. Take My Hand: Poems and Songs for Lovers and
      Rebels. New York: Dialog Press, 1969, 127 pp.
          Introduced by Ossie Davis and published by the major Old
      Left literary journal of the 1960s, this volume compiles Segal's
      work over a twenty-year period. The selections range from World
      War II love letters to bitter reflections during the McCarthy
      era, to civil rights and antiwar lyrics of the 1950s and 1960s.
      Davis says she is "a people's poet--adamant, like Walt
      Whitman. . . . But for all her loving kindness, Edith is also a
      street fighter." She is, however, a more specific type, the en-
      during Left poet whose tributes to fallen comrades and to notables
      who have reached some important birthday are received as if in a
      family gathering. Noted more for political relevance than for
      poetic craft, her work has been translated for the Left press in
      Latin America and eastern and western Europe, saluted by Diego
      Rivera, Dr. Spock, Langston Hughes, Sean O'Casey, and Harry
      Golden.

567 _____. Poems and Songs for Dreamers Who Dare. Westport,
      Conn.: Lawrence Hill & Co., 1975, 96 pp.
          Segal's first commercially produced publication, introduced
      by Ruby Dee and illustrated by her husband, radical artist Samuel
      Kamen, includes many poems on the Vietnam War as well as on Chile,
      Cuba, civil rights martyrs, and Old Left institutions like Camp
      Kinderland. Again, the clipped style is her forte.

568 WALKER, ALICE. Meridian. New York: Harcourt Brace Jovanovich,
      1976, 220 pp. Reprint. New York: Pocket Books, 1977, 220 pp.
          Meridian, first published in 1976, is a New Left novel
      insofar as its theme and style are rooted in the 1960s. Alice
      Walker's protagonist, for whom the novel is named, seeks her
      liberation through her womanhood as much as her blackness, through
      personal growth as much as revolutionary politics. Married too
      young, she is an unwilling mother who breaks away to go to college
      and seek her own destiny. She meets a black militant who is
      terrible with women; he ultimately marries, and almost destroys,

Meridian's white friend, a dedicated civil-rights volunteer from
the North. Meridian attempts to intervene. On a broader political
level, she also rejects violence. Asked if she is willing to
kill for the revolution, Meridian cannot answer unequivocally.
Both decisions are troubling, for they symbolize tests of her
commitment.

The most vivid scene takes place in a black church during
a service for a murdered civil-rights volunteer. Here Meridian
appreciates the forces in process of mobilization, in the emotional intensity and unspoken but firm collective dedication of
the congregation. "I will come forward and sing from memory
songs [the people] will need once more to hear," Walker (1944-)
writes. "For it is the song of the people, transformed by the
experiences of each generation, that holds them together, and if
any part of it is lost the people suffer and are without soul."
Walker's dramatic shifts in style, brief chapters, and sharp
glimpses serve to dramatize literature as a disconnected song
more than a classic novel.

569 YGLESIAS, HELEN. How She Died. Boston: Houghton Mifflin Co.,
   1972, 338 pp.
      The first and highly praised novel of Helen Yglesias
(1915-) is a tale of death of Mary Moody Schwartz, a young political activist, and a once-vibrant Left movement. Mary,
stricken by cancer, is the daughter of a famous Communist woman
who was convicted on espionage charges and jailed during the Cold
War. Throughout her childhood, Mary had been the ward of a com-
mitte formed to agitate for her mother's freedom. Now she lives
in a small New York apartment with her feckless, apolitical husband, Matt, their two small children, and her infirm mother who
has been released from prison because of poor health. Responsible
to the end, the committee rallies to care for Mary during her
last, tragic months.

Most of the story is narrated by Jean, who has been hired
by the committee to watch over Mary. Jean, Mary's best friend,
soon moves into a love affair with Matt; concurrently, Mary begins behaving erratically, exhibiting signs of seemingly justifi-
able paranoia. Within a short time neither Jean nor Matt can
cope with Mary, and the family and committee agree to have her
institutionalized. Meanwhile, the story follows Jean, studies
her own problematical domestic situation and sexual involvements.

Political death is told through Bob, a Communist physician,
principal figure in the committee, and Mary's faithful guardian.
He tries hard to organize Mary's routine, and when he dies suddenly everything falls apart. Without Bob's leadership, the committee cannot manage and thus accedes to Matt's wishes and approves
Mary's confinement. While Mary succumbs to cancer, the committee,
a pathetic remnant of the Old Left, experiences its own equally
disorienting and humiliating death.

Yglesias's novel is a hard-hitting commentary on the devas-
tating effect of the Cold War on the Left, the political and

personal barrenness of life among the few remaining comrades.
Bob, the only idealist in the story, reflects on his life during
the exciting times of the 1930s and 1940s and compares his movement with the New Left. He tries to explain to Jean, a generation
younger: "Those were wonderful times. . . . People were different
then. Maybe we made mistakes, but we didn't make the major mis-
take they're making now, of going along with no theory and no
guidelines. We believed in something. Something positive. We
had a goal. We were working for the happiness of all mankind.
The New Left blames us now for the ills of the whole world, but
we were a force then. We stood for something. And we had our
influence. We changed things."

570 _____. Family Feeling. New York: Dial Press, 1976, 309 pp.
       A novel of Jewish life, Family Feeling concerns assimila-
tion, upward mobility as well as political dedication. The protagonist, Anne Goddard, a second-generation New York Jew, reflects
upon her paradoxical relationships with her dying parents and
seven brothers and sisters, particularly the extraordinarily successful Barry, eldest son and multimillionaire. Anne herself
achieves a stable middle-class existence and some prominence in
left-wing intellectual circles, but she finds herself always a
member of the family.

Selected References

571 CONLIN, JOSEPH R., ed. The American Radical Press 1880-1960.
     2 vols. Westport, Conn.: Greenwood Press, 1974, 720 pp.
         These volumes contain scholarly essays on radical periodi-
     cals from such movements and organizations as the Knights of
     Labor, Nationalism, the Industrial Workers of the World, the anar-
     chist, Socialist, and Communist movements and various splinter
     groups, and independent journals and magazines of the arts. Many
     were written as introductions for Greenwood Press's radical re-
     print series of microform or facsimile editions. Several are
     central to the history of radical women, such as Richard Drinnon
     on Mother Earth Bulletin, Madeleine B. Stern on The Forerunner,
     Mari Jo Buhle on Socialist Woman/Progressive Woman/Coming Nation,
     Dwight MacDonald and Dorothy Day on the Catholic Worker, and
     Richard Fitzgerald on the Masses and Liberator.

572 DAVIS, LENWOOD G. The Black Woman in American Society: A
     Selected Annotated Bibliography. Boston: G.K. Hall & Co.,
     1975, 159 pp.
         This general reference includes a lengthy section of books
     and articles on black women.

573 DELANEY, ROBERT FINLEY. The Literature of Communism in Amer-
     ica: A Select Reference Guide. Washington, D.C.: Catholic
     University of America Press, 1962, 433 pp.
         This lengthy, annotated bibliography, arranged by subject
     and indexed by author, contains both Communist and anti-Communist
     references.

574 DILLING, ELIZABETH. The Red Network: A "Who's Who" and Hand-
     book of Radicalism for Patriots. Kenilworth, Ill.: The
     Author, 1934, 352 pp.
         Dedicated to "Professional Patriots" and supported by the
     Daughters of the American Revolution, Dilling's book contains
     miscellaneous short essays on various aspects of the "red menace,"
     descriptive data on more than 460 organizations, and a list of
     about 1,300 persons allegedly involved in radical activity, in-
     cluding many women. Writing during the early years of the New

Deal, she is generous in her criteria for selection, but less than consistently accurate in compiling biographical data.

575   EGBERT, DONALD DREW, and STOW PERSONS, eds. Socialism and American Life. 2 vols. Princeton, N.J.: Princeton University Press, 1952, 776 pp, 575 pp.
       Volume 1 contains fourteen essays by specialists in various areas of radical history, particularly the European and religious origins of American socialism. Daniel Bell, Sidney Hook, and Paul Sweezy contributed interpretive statements on the philosophical character of American socialism and its relation to classic marxism. Although no writer focuses on women's role or on theories of women's emancipation, together they provide a detailed study of background and context.
       Volume 2, described as a selective and critical bibliography, is an invaluable research tool. The categorical arrangement of sources is complex and works against a quick survey, but sections on utopian communities, Left organizations, and doctrine contain ample numbers of citations for the persevering researcher. A short section on socialism and women offers an eclectic enumeration of American and mainly European sources.

576   FOGARTY, ROBERT S. Dictionary of American Communal and Utopian History. Westport, Conn.: Greenwood Press, 1980, 271 pp.
       This volume divides into two major sections on biographies and communities. It also includes two appendices, an annotated list of communal and utopian societies 1787-1919 compiled by Otokiko Okugawa, and a biographical essay on communal history in America.
       Among the biographies are prominent women: Elizabeth Byrne Ferm (1857-1944), educator at the Ferrer Colony; Marie Stevens Howland (1835-1921), of Topolobampo and Fairhope; Georiana Bruce Kirby (1818-1887), of Brook Farm; Ann Lee (1736-1784), founder of the Shakers; Martha McWhirter (1827-1904), founder of the women's Commonwealth; Helena Modjeska (1840-1909), of the Modjeska Colony; Mary Gove Nichols (1810-1884), of Memnonia Institute; Melusina Fay Peirce (1836-1923), writer on cooperative housekeeping; Sophia Willard Dana Ripley (1803-1861), of Brook Farm; Elizabeth Rowell Thompson (1821-1899), philanthropist of cooperative endeavors; Katherine Tingley (1847-1929), founder of Point Loma; Sojourner Truth (1797-1883), of Mathias Colony; Angelina Grimké Weld (1805-1879), of the Raritan Bay Colony; Jemima Wilkinson (1752-1819), of the Jerusalem Colony; Frances Wright (1795-1852), of New Harmony and Nashoba; and Lucy Wright (1860-1821), a Shaker.

577   GANNON, FRANCIS X. Biographical Dictionary of the Left. 4 vols. Boston: Western Islands, 1969-1974, 624, 632, 639, 667 pp.
       Designed to provide useful "facts" about potential subversives, this guide comprises lengthy entries on individual radicals,

including many women, but does not consistently convey accurate information.

578 GOLDWATER, WALTER. Radical Periodicals in America, 1890-1950.
New Haven, Conn.: Yale University Press, 1964, 51 pp.
Goldwater lists the major serials of the Left.

579 HABER, BARBARA. Women in America: A Guide to Books, 1963-
1975. Boston: G.K. Hall & Co., 1978, 216 pp. Reprint.
Urbana: University of Illinois Press, 1981, 360 pp.
Haber, curator of printed books at the Schlesinger Library
on the History of Women in America, Radcliffe College, selected
over 500 titles to summarize and to evaluate. Arranged by subject, and with an appendix of books published 1976-1979, the list
includes many recent publications on radical women, particularly
autobiographies and biographies, works of fiction, and sources
related to women's liberation.

580 HARRISON, CYNTHIA, ed. Women in American History: A Bibliography. Introduction by Anne Firor Scott. Santa Barbara,
Calif.: ABC-Clio Press, 1979, 374 pp.
This volume abstracts 3,395 articles in 550 periodicals
and five collections published between 1963 and 1976. The subject
index is excellent. The publisher plans to issue periodic supple-
ments.

581 HINDING, ANDREA; CLARKE CHAMBERS; and AMES SHELDON BOWER, eds.
Women's History Sources: A Guide to Archives and Manuscript
Collections in the United States. 2 vols. New York: R.R.
Bowker Co., 1979, 1114 pp., 391 pp.
Volume I describes 18,026 collections in 1,586 repositories
arranged geographically by state and city. Volume II constitutes
a name and subject index. This source is an invaluable guide to
the collected papers of major and minor radical women.

582 JAMES, EDWARD T.; JANET WILSON JAMES; and PAUL S. BOYER, eds.
Notable American Women: A Biographical Dictionary. 3 vols.
Cambridge: Belknap Press of Harvard University, 1971, 687,
659, 729 pp.
Among the many entries are brief biographies of radical
women, including: Martha Gallison Moore Avery, Kate Richards
O'Hare Cunningham, Elizabeth Glendower Evans, Elisabeth Gilman,
Emma Goldman, Carrier Rand Herron, Florence Kelley, Maria Maud
Leonard McCreery, Helen Marot, Caroline Amanda Sherfey Rand, Lola
Ridge, Agnes Smedley, Ellen Gates Starr, Rose Harriet Pastor
Stokes, and Frances Wright.

583 KEHDE, NED, ed. and comp. The American Left, 1955-1970; A
National Union Catalogue of Pamphlets Published in the United
States and Canada. Westport, Conn.: Greenwood Press, 1976,
515 pp.

This compilation lists 4,018 pamphlets, most published during the prime of the New Left. Sources on women and women's liberation are indexed.

584 KLOTMAN, PHYLLIS RAUCH. The Black Family and the Black Woman: A Bibliography. With Wilmer H. Baatz. New York: Arno Press, 1978, 231 pp.
     Part II of this work lists sources on black women, histories, autobiographies and biographies, and works in several disciplinary areas including arts and literature.

585 KRICHMAR, ALBERT; VIRGINIA CARLSON SMITH; and ANN E. WIDERRECHT. The Women's Movement in the Seventies: An International English-Language Bibliography. Metuchen, N.J.: Scarecrow Press, 1977, 875 pp.
     This volume lists numerous books and articles on a variety of topics related to women's liberation.

586 KRICHMAR, ALBERT; BARBARA CASE; BARBARA SILVER; and ANN WIEDERRECHT. The Women's Rights Movement in the United States, 1848-1970. Metuchen, N.J.: Scarecrow Press, 1972, 436 pp.
     This partially annotated bibliography covers sources on the legal, political, educational, economic, religious, and professional status of women since the formal founding of the women's rights movement in 1848. It includes 5,170 entries for books, periodical articles, doctoral dissertations, and a few government publications. A selected list of manuscripts and serials is appended. Beginning researchers in American history might find especially helpful its coverage of basic reference books in the field.

587 LOADER, JAYNE. "Women in the Left, 1906-1941: A Bibliography of Primary Sources." Papers in Women's Studies 2 (September 1975):9-82.
     Loader divides her annotated bibliography into three main parts: anarchism; the literary Left; and the Communist party (1920-1941). The major section on communism contains many entries from Left magazines and newspapers.

588 NEGLEY, GLENN. Utopian Literature: A Bibliography with a Supplementary Listing of Works Influential in Utopian Thought. Lawrence: Regents Press of Kansas, 1977, 228 pp.
     This volume lists but does not annotate books on utopian thought written since the sixteenth century and notes their location in major libraries. It includes a short-title and chronological index.

589 O'SULLIVAN, JUDITH, and ROSEMARY GALLICK. Workers and Allies: Female Participation in the American Trade Union Movement, 1824-1976. Washington, D.C.: Smithsonian Institution Press, 1975, 96 pp.

The book served as the catalogue of an exhibit on women and trade union history sponsored by the Smithsonian Institution Traveling Exhibition Service in conjunction with the bicentennial celebration. One section contains brief biographies of women associated with wage-earning women; the selection is eclectic rather than systematic, but includes entries for many radical women.

590 SEIDMAN, JOEL, ed. and comp. Communism in the United States--A Bibliography. Ithaca, N.Y.: Cornell University Press, 1969, 526 pp.
     This annotated bibliography contains "all writings of any consequence by a member of the Party," according to its compiler. The 7,000 entries represent books, pamphlets, and magazine and newspaper articles arranged alphabetically by author.

591 SICHERMAN, BARBARA, and CAROL HURD GREEN, eds. Notable American Women, The Modern Period: A Biographical Dictionary. Cambridge: Belknap Press of Harvard University, 1980, 733 pp.
     Under the listing "Socialism and Radicalism" the editors provide biographies of Angela Bambace, Ella Reeve Bloor, Elizabeth Gurley Flynn, Josephine Herbst, Jessie Wallace Hughan, Helen Keller, Carol Weiss King, Eslanda Cardoza Goode Robeson, Ethel Greenglass Rosenberg, Vida Dutton Scudder, Anna Louise Strong, and Mary Abby Van Kleeck.

592 SILVIN, EDWARD. Index to Periodical Literature on Socialism. Santa Barbara, Calif.: Rogers & Morley, Printers, 1909, 45 pp.
     This source cites a dozen entries in mainstream magazines on women and socialism.

593 TAMIMENT LIBRARY, NEW YORK UNIVERSITY. Guide to the Microfilm Edition of Radical Pamphlet Literature: A Collection from the Tamiment Library. Glen Rock, N.J.: Microfilming Corporation of America, n.d., 721 pp.
     Successor to the Rand School of Social Science, the Tamiment Library houses the major collection of labor and Left materials in the United States. This bibliography, compiled by Dorothy Swanson, lists its large holding of pamphlets.

594 WILLARD, FRANCES E., and MARY A. LIVERMORE, eds. American Women: A Comprehensive Encyclopedia of the Lives and Achievements of American Women During the Nineteenth Century. 2 vols. New York: Mast, Crowell & Kirkpatrick, 1897, 824 pp. Reprint. Detroit: Gale Research Co., 1973, 824 pp.
     Originally published in 1893 as Woman of the Century, this reprint of the revised 1897 edition contains 1,500 biographies and over 1,400 portraits. The majority are literary contributors, but many reformers are represented, including radicals like Populists Eva McDonald Valesh, Marion M. Todd, Annie L. Diggs, and Ella L. Knowles; Socialists Alzina Parsons Stevens and Marion

Howard Dunham; and many temperance workers. As a supplement to
Notable American Women, American Women is a surprisingly useful
reference tool for tracking less prominent figures.

595 WILLIAMS, ORA. American Black Women in the Arts and Social
Sciences: A Bibliographic Survey. Rev. ed. Metuchen, N.J.:
Scarecrow Press, 1978, 197 pp.
    This volume contains a comprehensive listing of reference
materials, biographies, anthologies, and published works on black
women in the arts and social sciences as well as a review of
works by and about selected individuals.

Index

abortion, 371, 484, 485, 501, 502, 515

Abortion and the Catholic Church, 501

Addams, Jane, 7, 209

Afro-Americans, 39, 187, 188, 274, 281, 302, 312, 320, 324, 333, 352, 361, 366, 367, 368, 384, 393, 394, 395, 401, 402, 407, 428, 433, 440, 447, 448, 449, 450, 466, 467, 468, 480, 483, 485, 487, 494, 496, 502, 530, 531, 532, 533, 534, 539, 540, 568, 572, 584, 595

Akron Rubber Workers' Strike, (1936), 409

Alarm, 39

Alderson Penitentiary, 295

Alderson Story, The, 295

Algren, Nelson, 394

AlHibri, Azizah, 507

All for One, 194

Alpert, Jane, 442, 444

Altbach, Edith Hoshino, 462, 524

Amalgamated Clothing Workers of America, 163, 413, 435

American Anarchist, An, 138

American Black Women in the Arts and Social Sciences, 595

American Century, An, 164

American Civil Liberties Union, 142, 296, 423

American Club Woman, 40

American Dialog, 527

American Fabian, 147, 232

American Federation for the Blind, 221

American Federationist, 40

American Federation of Labor, 37, 82, 357, 359

American Immigrant Women, 9

American Institute for Marxist Studies (New York), 144

American Journal of Eugenics, 87

American League Against War and Fascism, 373

American Left, 1955-1970, The, 583

American Radical Press, 1880-1960, The, 571

American Spiritualist Association, 44

American Way of Death, The, 320

American Women: A Comprehensive Encyclopedia, 594

American Women for Peace, 361

anarchism, 2, 21, 22, 31, 51, 72, 74, 75, 87, 104, 111, 112, 115, 117, 136, 138, 139, 140, 141, 142, 146, 152, 153, 154, 155, 156, 157, 158, 159, 160, 161, 162, 164, 191, 200, 207, 211, 212, 213, 244, 247, 257, 258, 265, 271, 587

"Anarchism and Idealism: Voltairine de Cleyre," 140

Anarchism and Other Essays, 212

"Anarchist-Feminist Response to the 'Woman Question,'" 21

Anarchist Woman, An, 200, 257

Anarchist Women, 1870-1920, 22

Ancient Society, 237

Anderson, Kristine, 106

Anderson, Margaret, 136

Anderson, Sherwood, 136

And Not to Yield, 339

Index

Andres, Chaya Rochel, 275
Andrews, Stephen Pearl, 51, 88
Angela Davis--An Autobiography, 447
Angela Davis: The Making of a Revolutionary, 450
"Anna Louise Strong and the Search for a Good Cause," 334
Anne Sullivan Macy, 177
"Anne Whitney, Art and Social Justice," 41
Another Part of the Forest, 396
Anthanor, 564
anticommunism, 276, 282, 289, 296, 423, 450, 491, 492, 573, 574, 577
antifascism, 301, 304, 305, 317, 322, 325, 363, 372, 379, 380, 381, 384, 396, 437
antislavery, 10
antisocialism, 24
"Antoinette Konikow: Marxist and Feminist," 309
Anzaldua, Gloria, 494
Appeal to Reason, 245, 251
Appeal to the Young, 142, 143
Apprentices to Destiny, 107
Aptheker, Bettina, 448
Arbeter Ring (Workman's Circle), 275, 309
Ardrey, Robert, 500
Arena, 293
"Are the Interests of Men and Women Identical?," 125
Arizona, 234
Arkansas, 338
Arling, Emanie Sachs, 46, 48
Arnold, Birch. See Bartlett, Alice Elinor
As Equals and as Sisters, 124
Ashbaugh, Carolyn, 39
Ashley, Karen, 481
Asian-Americans, 464, 494
Association for the Advancement of Women, 65, 67
Atkins, Elizabeth, 315
Autobiography, An (Sanger), 189
Autobiography of an American Communist, The, 285, 287, 288
Autobiography of Mother Jones, The, 165
Avery, Martha Moore, 24, 25, 52, 582
Avery, Rachel Foster, 76
Avrich, Paul, 138

Baatz, Wilmer H., 584
Baez, Joan, 6, 445
Baker, Ella, 438
Baker, Estelle, 248
Bakken, Douglas A., 30
Baldwin, James, 302, 394
Baldwin, Roger, 296, 333
Ballan, Dorothy, 463
Bambace, Angela, 591
Bambara, Toni Cade, 494
"Banishment of Kate Richards O'Hare, The," 185
Barber, Harriet Boomer, 89
Barnes, Djuna, 314
Bartlett, Alice Elinor, 90
Barton, Ann, 340, 341
Basen, Neil K., 129, 186
Baskin, Alex, 247
Battle Hymn of China, 331
Baxandall, Rosalyn Fraad, 144, 521, 524
Beals, May, 205, 249
Bebel, August, 2, 53, 64, 92, 173, 216, 240, 503, 506
Beecher, Catharine, 7
Beecher, Katherine, 342
Beecher-Tilton Scandal, 46, 47, 48, 49, 84, 88
Beginning to See the Light, 515
Bell, Alexander Graham, 170
Bell, Daniel, 575
Bellamy, Charles J., 91
Bellamy, Edward, 7, 18, 54, 69, 78, 91, 92, 93, 100, 111, 114, 116, 142, 232, 544
Bellamy Nationalism. See Nationalism, Bellamy
Bellanca, Dorothy Jacobs, 9, 12
Bengelsdorf, Carollee, 475
Benston, Margaret, 11, 462, 509
Bentley, Elizabeth, 276
Berger, Meta, 277
Berkeley, Calif., 441, 445, 446, 525, 547
Berkeley-Oakland Women's Union,

525
Berkin, Carol Ruth, 148
Berkman, Alexander, 138, 146,
    152, 155, 158, 207, 244, 419
Berkman, Edith, 380
Berks County, Pa., 273
Berlak, Ann, 380
Berman, Susie, 446
Better Days, 98
Betterman, Forster, 284
Between the Hills and the Sea,
    538
Biographical Dictionary of the
    Left, 577
birth control, 5, 32, 120, 121,
    133, 156, 186, 189, 190, 191,
    192, 193, 200, 221, 243, 244,
    247, 309, 360, 383, 384, 392,
    463, 501
"Birth Control and Social Revo-
    lution," 1
Birth Control in America, 191
Bisno, Abraham, 386
Bisno, Beatrice, 386
Black Family and the Black
    Woman, The, 584
Black Panthers, 447, 454
Black Scholar, 480
Blackwell, Alice Stone, 278
Blackwell, Elizabeth, 55
Black Woman in American Society,
    The, 572
Black Women's Struggle for
    Equality, 502
Blatch, Harriot Stanton, 18, 278
Bliss, W.D.P., 196
Blocker, Jack S., Jr., 13
Bloor, Ella Reeve (Mother), 279,
    280, 340, 341, 343, 351, 381,
    591
Blumberg, Dorothy Rose, 27, 32
Bodin, Jean Baptiste, 101
Bogan, Louise, 268
Boggs, Grace Lee, 464
Boggs, James, 464
Boisevain, Eugen Jan, 314, 316
Bolshevism: Its Cure, 24
Bond, Julian 468
Bordin, Ruth, 14
Born One Year Before the Twen-
    tieth Century, 294

Boston, Mass., 20, 24, 25, 31,
    41, 57, 63, 103, 177, 195,
    196, 197, 198, 265, 309, 438,
    563
Boston Globe, 31
Boston Social Science Club, 202
Boudin, Kathy, 481
Bower, Ames Sheldon, 581
Boyce, Neith, 126, 133
Boyer, Paul S., 582
Braddy, Nella, 177
Braden, Anne Gambrell, 281
Braden, Carl, 281
Branstein, Richard, 313
Brant, Marie, 344
Braverman, Harry, 471
"Bread and Roses," 462
Bread and Roses, 439, 462, 481,
    488
Breaking Camp, 552
Breaking Up the Home, 230
Break the Chains!, 465
Bridges, Amy, 475
Brief Sketches of the Life of
    Victoria Woodhull, 45
Briggs, Cyril, 356
Bristol, Augusta Cooper, 56
Brittin, Norman A., 316
Brody, Catharine, 387, 388
Bromley, Dorothy Dunbar, 296
Brommel, Bernard J., 184
Brook Farm, 576
Brown, Carol, 507
Brown, Connie, 495
Brown, Corinne Stubbs, 137
Brown, John, 200
Brownmiller, Susan, 461
Buck in the Snow, The, 315
Budenz, Louis, 282
Budenz, Margaret Rodgers, 282
Buenker, John D., 129
Buffalo, N.Y., 174
Buhle, Mari Jo, 119, 120, 121,
    129, 335, 524, 571
Buhle, Paul, 335
Bullard, Arthur, 250
Burden of Christopher, The, 95
Burke, Fielding. See Dargan,
    Olive Tilford

Cabral, Amilcar, 532

Cabral, Olga, 389, 527, 528, 529
Caesar's Column, 26
Cagan, Leslie, 439
California, 8, 81, 285, 286, 304,
    320, 322, 339, 380, 426, 429,
    445, 446, 455, 525, 547
Caller, Fay, 345
Call Home the Heart, 390, 391
"Call to Black Women of Every
    Religious and Political Per-
    suasion, A," 468
Cambridge, Mass., 7, 423, 556
Campbell, Helen, 92, 94, 150
Campbell, Rachel, 57
Camp Kinderland, New York, 567
Cantarow, Ellen, 438
Cantor, Milton, 120
Cantwell, Robert, 406
Cape Cod, Mass., 561
Capitalism, the Family, and Per-
    sonal Life, 520
Capitalist Patriarchy and the
    Case for Socialist Feminism,
    475
Carnegie, Andrew, 170
Carney, Jack, 179
"Caroline Hollingsworth
    Pemberton," 188
Carrigan, D. Owen, 24, 25
Carroll, Berenice, 524
Case, Barbara, 586
Cash Item, 388
Cass, Amy, 490
Castro, Fidel, 451, 469
Catholics, 24, 282, 284, 289, 501
Catholic Worker, 571
Catholic Worker Movement, 284,
    451
Central Committee, Communist
    Party, USA, 272
Challenging Years, 278
Chambers, Clarke, 581
Champney, Adeline, 202
Chandler, Lucinda, 19
Channing, Grace Ellery, 150
"Charlotte Perkins Gilman--The
    Economics of Victorian
    Morality," 149
Charlotte Perkins Gilman: The
    Making of a Radical Femi-
    nist, 150

Charlotte Perkins Gilman Reader,
    The, 253
Cheney, Anne, 317
Chicago, Ill., 13, 27, 37, 38,
    39, 58, 77, 80, 119, 134, 138,
    152, 165, 179, 206, 207, 222,
    234, 245, 251, 257, 258, 302,
    386, 394, 434, 522, 553
Chicago Daily Socialist, 119, 222
Chicago garment workers' strike
    (1910), 199, 163
Chicago Trade and Labor Assembly,
    58
Chicanas, 485
Children of Fantasy, The, 126
Children of Light, The, 252
Children's Crusade, (1922), 182
China, 331, 332, 334, 339, 427,
    506
Chodorow, Nancy, 475
Christian socialism, 20, 42, 55,
    67, 90, 94, 95, 109, 116,
    117, 195, 196, 197
Christian Socialism: Thoughts
    Suggested by the Easter
    Season, 55
Chrysalis, 1
CIO. See Congress of Industrial
    Organizations
Cities and Deserts, 389
Civil rights, 187, 188, 244, 281,
    296, 297, 298, 302, 311, 312,
    320, 324, 361, 366, 380, 438,
    439, 440, 441, 447, 448, 449,
    450, 451, 452, 454, 462, 468,
    470, 487, 493, 502, 507, 522,
    566, 567, 568
Civil Rights Congress, 320
Civil Wars, 487
Claflin, Tennessee C. See Cook,
    Tennessee C. Claflin
Clanton, O. Gene, 33
"Clara Lemlich Shavelson," 329
Clark, W.E., 203
"Claude and Joyce Williams," 338
Clemens, Samuel, 170
Cluster, Dick, 439
Cohen, Jannette, 275
Cold war, 276, 320, 324, 325,
    367, 394, 428, 566, 569
Collected Plays, The (Hellman),

396

Collected Poems, The (Millay), 411

Collected Poems, The (Rukeyser), 565

Collected Poems, 1918-1938 (Taggard), 432

College Settlement Association, 195

Collins, May, 59

Colon, Clara, 466

Colorado, 331, 434

Colorado strike (1903), 165

Colorado strike (1913-1914), 165

Colton, James, 152

Coltrane, John, 530

Coming Nation, 251, 571

Coming Nation. See Socialist Woman

Committee for Improving the Industrial Condition of Negroes, 187

Committee for Progressive Labor Action, 282

Committee of Labor Union Women, 483

Common Cause Society, 24

Commonwealth, The, 227

Commonwealth College, 338

Communism in the United States-- A Bibliography, 590

Communist Cadre, 272

Communist Manifesto, The, 44, 88

Communist party, 2, 142, 164, 270, 271, 272, 274, 276, 279, 282, 283, 286, 287, 288, 289, 296, 302, 309, 313, 320, 324, 325, 329, 335, 336, 340, 341, 342, 343, 347, 348, 350, 351, 352, 353, 355, 356, 357, 358, 360, 361, 362, 363, 364, 365, 366, 367, 368, 369, 371, 375, 379, 380, 381, 383, 384, 385, 393, 407, 429, 431, 447, 448, 449, 450, 466, 473, 477, 491, 492, 538, 569, 571, 574, 577, 587, 590

"Communist Party and the Struggle for Women's Freedom, The," 466

communitarian socialism, 2, 7,

36, 101, 109, 200, 252, 253, 254, 575, 576

Communist Action Committee, SDS, 444

Comrade Yetta, 250

Conditions of the Working Class in England in 1844, The, 27

Condition of Women Workers Under the Present Industrial System, The, 82

Conference on Socialist Feminism, 525

Conger-Kaneko, Josephine, 121, 204, 205, 235, 251

Congressional Union, 277

Congress of American Women, 373

Congress of Industrial Organizations (CIO), 4, 279, 285, 368, 370

Conlin, Joseph, 571

Consecrate Every Day, 161

Consider the Laundry Workers, 349, 377

Consider the Woolworth Workers, 377

Consumers' League. See National Consumers' League

Constitutional Equality, 60

Converse, Florence, 95, 199, 252

Cook, Blanche Wiesen, 1, 122, 210

Cook, Francis, 61

Cook, George Cram, 126, 151, 255, 256

Cook, Tennessee C. Claflin, 60, 61, 88

"Cooperation, the Law of the New Civilization," 79

Cooperative Commonwealth, The, 70, 92

cooperative housekeeping, 7, 16, 54, 222, 576

Corcoran, Theresa, S.C., 198

Cortez, Jayne, 530, 531, 532, 533, 564

Coser, Lewis, 53

Cott, Nancy F., 1

counterculture, 446, 461, 493

Cowl, Margaret, 270, 346, 347, 384

Cowley, Joyce, 467

Cowley, Malcolm, 409
Crane, John Mayo, 62
Crane, Richard T., 297
Creel, Herr Glassner, 206
Critics and Crusaders, 157
"Crusade for Child Laborers,"
    168
Crusaders, 311
Cruse, Harold, 394
Crystal Eastman on Women and
    Revolution, 210
Cuba, 397, 439, 447, 451, 567
Cupid's Yokes, 73
Curious Courtship of Women's
    Liberation and Socialism,
    The, 514

Daily People's World, 362
Daily Worker, 279, 357, 375
Daily World, 326
Dallas, Texas, 275
Damon, Anna, 283, 384
Dance of Fire, 421
Dance the Eagle to Sleep, 555
Dancis, Bruce, 123
Dargan, Olive Tilford, 390, 391
Darkness in My Pockets, The, 528
Darrow, Clarence, 165
Dash, Joan, 193
Daughter of Earth, 331, 427
Daughter of the Hills, 415
Daughters of America, 351
Daughters of the American Revo-
    lution, 574
Davidson, Sara, 446
Davis, Angela Yvonne, 447, 448,
    449, 450, 468
Davis, Frank, 426
Davis, Lenwood G., 572
Davis, Ossie, 534, 566
Davis, Rebecca Harding, 549
Day, Dorothy, 10, 243, 284, 392,
    451, 571
Daybreak, 445
"Days of Rage," (1969), 461
Days to Come, 396
Dear Remembered World, 173
Death House Letters, 325
de Beauvoir, Simone, 493, 505
Debs, Eugene V., 137, 279, 297
de Cleyre, Voltairine, 21, 22,

    74, 138, 139, 140, 141, 207
Dee, Ruby, 534, 567
de Ford, Miriam Allen, 205, 268
Degler, Carl N., 69, 149
Delaney, Robert Finley, 573
DeLeon, Daniel, 2, 25, 53, 128,
    208
Dell, Floyd, 11, 126, 133, 136,
    201, 209, 243, 255, 268, 284,
    317
Deming, Barbara, 452, 453, 469,
    470, 490
Democratic party, 194, 486
Denison House, Boston, 195
Dennis, Eugene, 285, 289
Dennis, Peggy, 285, 286, 287, 288
Depression, The Great, 270, 293,
    324, 333, 343, 347, 358, 387,
    388, 391, 399, 403, 405, 409,
    412, 426, 436, 549
Detroit, Mich., 387
Deutsch, Babette, 268
Dewey, Thomas E., 353
Dialectic of Sex, The, 478
Diana: The Making of a Terrorist,
    459
Diary of a Shirtwaist Striker,
    261
Diaz, Abby Morton, 63
Dickinson, Emily, 401, 432
Dictionary of American Communal
    and Utopian History, 576
Dies, Martin, 353
Diggs, Annie, 31, 40, 594
Dilling, Elizabeth, 574
Dillon, Mary Earhart, 13, 43
di Prima, Diane, 535
Dispossessed, The, 544
Dixon, Marlene, 462, 471, 505,
    524
Ditzion, Sidney, 2
Dodd, Bella Visono, 289
Dodd, John, 289
Dodge, Edward, 174
Dodge, Mabel. See Luhan, Mabel
    Dodge
Doenninges, Helene Von, 173
Dohrn, Bernadine, 442, 481
Donnelly, Ignatius, 26, 96
Donnelly, Kate, 26
D'Onston, Roslyn, 45

Index

Dorothy Parker, 323
Douglas, Amanda M., 97
Douglass, Emily Taft, 190
Drafted In, 89
Dreamers and Dealers, 442
Dreiser, Theodore, 136
Drinnon, Anna Marie, 153, 155
Drinnon, Richard, 153, 155, 156, 212, 507
DuBois, Ellen, 475, 526
DuBois, Shirley Graham, 468
DuBois, W.E.B., 187, 302
Dudley, Barbara, 525
Duke, David C., 334
Dunayevskaya, Raya, 472
Dunbar, Roxanne, 11, 509
Duncan, Isadora, 6, 174, 209, 290, 291, 292, 310
Dunham, Marion Howard, 594
Dunning, Nelson A., 68
Dworkin, Andrea, 442
Dye, Nancy Schrom, 124, 524

Earhart, Mary. See Dillon, Mary Earhart
Eastman, Crystal, 1, 11, 122, 130, 133, 210
Eastman, Max, 11, 126, 136, 243, 268, 284, 314, 397
Easton, Barbara. See Epstein, Barbara Leslie
Easy Wheel, An, 259
Eau Claire, Wisconsin, 74
Edelman, Judy, 473
Edna St. Vincent Millay, 316
Edna St. Vincent Millay and Her Times, 315
Edwards, Albert. See Bullard, Arthur
Edwards, Mel, 530
Egbert, Donald Drew, 575
Ehrenreich, Barbara, 474, 518, 524, 525
Ehrlich, Carole, 507
Eisenstein, Zillah, 475, 476, 507
Ek, Richard, 47
Eleventh Virgin, The, 284, 392
"Elizabeth Gurley Flynn: The Early Years," 144
"Elizabeth Morgan, Crusader for Labor Reform," 38
"Elizabeth Morgan: Pioneer Female Labor Agitator," 37
Elliot, T.S., 136
Ellis, Havelock, 191
Elman, R.M., 412
Ely, Richard T., 116
"Emma Goldman--Feminist and Anarchist," 159
"Emma Goldman on Mary Wollstonecraft," 162
Emma Lazarus Federation, 361
Empire of Ice, The, 529
End to the Neglect of the Problems of the Negro Woman!, 366
Engels, Frederick, 2, 27, 64, 88, 216, 234, 235, 346, 369, 373, 382, 463, 478, 489, 493, 498, 503, 506, 510, 512
English, Deirdre, 474
Enormous Changes at the Last Minute, 550
Enter Fighting, 466
Epstein, Barbara Leslie, 1, 15, 525
Epstein, Irene, 348
Equality, 93
Equal Justice and Democracy in the Service of Victory, 283
Equal Rights Amendment, 4, 270, 348, 361, 367, 466, 473, 477, 480, 484, 485, 502
Equal Suffrage Association, Arizona, 234
Espionage Act, 180, 181, 182, 183, 184
Essays on Social Topics, 61
Ethical Culture Society, 425
"Eva McDonald Valesh, Minnesota Populist," 40
Evans, Elizabeth Glendower, 582
Evans, Linda, 481
Evans, Sara, 440, 462, 518, 524
Evanston, Ill., 43
Evaporated Man, The, 527
Everett, Washington, 227
Evolution of the Family, 62
Executioner Waits, The, 398
Experiment in Marriage, An, 91, 112

Fabian Society, 278
Fagar, Peter, 172
Fairhope, Ala., 101, 576
Fairmont Field Miners' strike
    (1901), 169
Faithful Are the Wounds, 423
Fales, Imogene C., 65, 66, 67, 79
Falk, Doris V., 307
Fall and the Restoration, The,
    66
Familistère, The, 101
familistères, 7, 56, 101
family, 15, 21, 22, 24, 62, 64,
    70, 233, 234, 235, 236, 238,
    241, 371, 382, 462, 463, 471,
    482, 484, 485, 491, 492, 493,
    498, 499, 503, 509, 510, 514,
    520, 570, 584
Family Feeling, 570
Family System, The, 491
Farm Equipment Workers Union, 281
Farmers' Alliance, 17, 30, 32,
    68, 76, 99, 108
Farmers' Alliance History and
    Agricultural Digest, 68
Farmer's Wife, 86
Farnham, Marynia, 373
Farrar, Ann, 525
FBI vs Women, The, 511
Federal Theatre Project, 293
Feeley, Diane, 309, 477
"Female Support Networks and
    Political Activism," 1, 122
Feminism and Marxism, 463
Feminism and Socialism, 485
"Feminism and the Contemporary
    Family," 1
Feminism and the Marxist Move-
    ment, 512
Feminist Alliance, 133
Feminist Frameworks, 482
Feminist Studies, 287, 475
Ferber, Nat J., 146
Fergusen, Ann, 507
Ferlinghetti, Laurence, 551
Ferm, Elizabeth Bryne, 576
Festivals and Funerals, 531
Fetherling, Dale, 166
Fiche, Arthur Davidson, 317
Filley, Jane, 349
Fine Old Conflict, A, 320

Finnish-Americans, 127, 246, 310,
    431
Finnish Socialist Federation of
    the United States, 127, 246
"Finns, The," 310
Firehead, 421
Firestone, Shulamith, 478, 483,
    514, 520, 522
First International. See Inter-
    national Workingmens' Associa-
    tion
Fisher, Minnie, 294
Fitch, Anna M., 98
Fitch, Thomas, 98
Fitzgerald, Richard, 571
Flanagan, Hallie, 293
Flawed Liberation, 129, 237
Flint, Mich., 333
Flint Auto Workers' Strike,
    (1937), 201
Florence Crittenton Mission, 180
Florence Kelley: The Making of a
    Social Pioneer, 27
"Florence Kelley in Illinois," 29
Flower, Benjamin O., 90, 196
Flowering Stream, 31
Flynn, Elizabeth Gurley, 142, 143,
    144, 145, 189, 201, 243, 279,
    295, 296, 350, 351, 352, 353,
    354, 381, 591
Fogarty, Robert S., 101, 576
Folbre, Nancy, 507
Fonda, Jane, 305, 454
Foner, Philip S., 3, 4, 188, 122
Food Prices and Rationing, 375
Foote, Edward Bliss, 23
Footnote to Folly, A, 201
Ford, Mary Hanford, 99
Forerunner, The, 147, 242, 253,
    254, 571
"Forgotten Yankee Marxist, A," 25
For Her Own Good, 474
Forster, Dora, 23, 211
For the Common Good, 127
Foster, William Z., 289, 352, 367
Foundation Principles, 83
Fourier, Charles, 7, 8, 101
Fourth International, 512, 516.
    See also Socialist Workers
    Party
Fragmentary Record of Public Work

Done in America, 1871-1877, A, 44
Frances: A Story for Men and Women, 103, 104
Frances Willard: From Prayers to Politics, 13, 43
Frederick, Peter J., 196, 197
Freedom. See *Freedomways*
Freedom Summer, (1964), 440
Freedomways, 302, 394
free love, 7, 21, 22, 23, 44, 46, 47, 48, 51, 57, 62, 71, 72, 73, 74, 75, 77, 80, 83, 84, 85, 87, 88, 91, 103, 104, 110, 123, 126, 130, 133, 138, 152, 160, 174, 175, 176, 179, 186, 191, 200, 202, 209, 211, 214, 215, 217, 232, 236, 238, 244, 257, 258, 262, 267, 274, 434
Free Love and Socialism, 236
Freeman, Jo, 11, 441
Free Society, 74
free speech, 47, 142, 143, 152, 184, 219, 244, 296, 455
Free Spirits, 533
free thought, 2, 72, 74, 80, 83, 87, 88, 101, 103, 138, 152, 173, 207, 239
Free Union, A, 262
Freiheit, 152, 286
Fremantle, Anne, 6
Freud, Sigmund, 191, 256, 373, 505, 514
Frick, Henry Clay, 152
Friedan, Betty, 476, 484, 504
Fritz, Leah, 442, 453
From Feminism to Liberation, 462, 524
From Fireside to Factory, 224
"From Sisterhood to Self," 120
"From Sweatshop Worker to Labor Leader," 178
Fuller, Gertrude Breslau. See Hunt, Gertrude Breslau Fuller
Full-Time Active, 324
"Functions of the Family," 509
Future Relation of the Sexes, 75

Gag, Wanda, 130
Gage, Mathilda Joslyn, 203

Gale, Zona, 147
Gallick, Rosemary, 589
Gannon, Francis Z., 577
Ganz, Marie, 146
Garbutt, Mary, 205
Gardiner, Jean, 475
Gardner, Fred, 454
Gardner, Virginia, 326
garment industry, 3, 4, 37, 39, 58, 82, 119, 134, 163, 178, 194, 250, 279, 329, 386
Garson, Barbara, 536
Gartz, Crane, 300
Gartz, Kate Crane, 297, 298, 299, 300.
Gastonia Textile Workers' Strike (1929), 201, 335, 390, 406, 413, 435
Gathering Storm, 413
Gay, Bettie, 68
gay rights, 439, 524, 560
Geller, Ruth, 537
Generation of Women, A, 128
Gentle Bush, The, 393
George, Henry, 115, 173
Georgia, 312, 452
German-Americans, 2, 13, 27, 44, 94, 107, 116, 121, 173, 260
Ghetto, The, 264
Gilden, K.B., 538
Gilden, Katya. See Gilden, K.B.
Giesler-Anneke, Mathide, 9
Giles, Barbara, 393
Gill, Brendan, 417
Gilman, Charlotte Perkins, 7, 10, 11, 18, 69, 100, 133, 147, 148, 149, 150, 209, 225, 240, 242, 253, 254
Gilman, Elisabeth, 582
Gilman, Rhoda R., 40
Girard, Kans., 245
Girl, The, 405
Glaspell, Susan, 126, 133, 151, 255, 256
Glassman, Carol, 495
Glimpses of Fifty Years, 42
Glowchild and Other Poems, 534
God of Civilization, The, 110
Godwin, William, 2
Going Down Fast, 553
Going Too Far, 457

Gold, Mike, 284, 435
Golden, Harry, 566
Golden Bottle, The, 96
Goldfield, Evelyn, 490
Goldman, Emma, 1, 2, 5, 6, 9, 22,
    39, 122, 136, 138, 139, 142,
    146, 152, 153, 154, 155, 156,
    157, 158, 159, 160, 161, 162,
    174, 200, 209, 212, 213, 214,
    215, 244, 247, 419, 523, 582
Goldmark, Josephine, 27, 28
Goldstein, David, 24
Goldthwaite, Lucy, 194
Goldwater, Walter, 578
"Goodbye to All That," 457
Goodman, Paul, 470
Gordon, Ann, 524
Gordon, Eugene, 356
Gordon, Evelyn B., 355
Gordon, Linda, 1, 5, 125, 475,
    509, 524
Gordon, Suzanne, 526
Gornick, Vivian, 271, 541
Gould, Jean, 318
Graham, Margaret. See McDonald,
    Grace Lois
Graham, Martha, 301
Grand Domestic Revolution, The, 7
Greeley, Horace, 51
Green, Carol Hurd, 591
Greenback party, 81
Greenpoint Settlement, Brooklyn,
    187
Greenwich House Settlement, New
    York, 187
Greenwich Village, New York, 126,
    133, 151, 174, 175, 201, 209,
    264, 284, 313, 314, 317, 459
Greenwood Press, 571
Greer, Dr. J.H., 216
Griffen, Frederick C., 6
Grange. See Patrons of Hus-
    bandry
Grimké, Sarah, 10
Gronlund, Laurence, 70, 92
Growing Up Underground, 444
Guardian, The, 522
Guide to Microfilm Edition of
    Radical Pamphlet Literature,
    593
Guise, France, 56

Gurko, Miriam, 319

Haber, Barbara, 579
Hageman, Alice, 475
Hahn, Emily, 175
Haile, Margaret, 205
Half A Man, 187
Hamill, Pete, 492
Hamilton, Roberta, 479
Hammett, Dashiell, 304, 306
Hamtramck, Mich., 135
Hanisch, Carol, 522
Hansberry, Lorraine, 302, 394,
    395
Hapgood, Hutchins, 126, 174, 200,
    257
Harding, Sandra, 507
Harding, Warren G., 297
Hard Loving, 554
Harman, Lillian, 71
Harman, Moses, 23, 71, 87, 217
Harmon, Sandra D., 29
Harriman, Job, 8
Harris, Frank, 154
Harrison, Cynthia, 580
Harrity, Richard, 171
Hartmann, Heidi, 507
Hartsock, Nancy, 475
Harvest, 404
Hastings, Elizabeth. See Sherwood,
    Margaret Pollock
Havel, Hippolyte, 207, 212, 284
Hawes, Elizabeth, 303
Hay, John, 89
Hayden, Dolores, 7, 8, 16
Hayden, Tom, 454
Haymarket Square, 39, 134, 137,
    138, 152, 207, 258, 386
Haywood, William D., 143, 189
Helen Keller, Her Socialist Years,
    221
Hellman, Lillian, 304, 305, 306,
    307, 308, 322, 396, 423
Henry Worthington, Idealist, 113
Herbst, Josephine, 397, 398, 399,
    591
"Here I Stand Ironing," 412
Here Lies, 417
Heritage of Her Own, A, 1
Herland, 254
Herndon, Angelo, 283

Heroines, 381
Herron, Carrie Rand, 582
Heterodoxy (New York), 133
Heywood, Angela Tilton, 73
Heywood, Ezra, 2, 23, 73
Hichs, Emily, 507
High Cost of Living, The (Cowl), 347
High Cost of Living, The (Piercy), 560
Hildebrand, Ginny, 480
Hill, Joe, 143
Hill, Mary A., 150
Hiller, Gertrude, 273
Hillman, Bessie Abramowitz, 9, 163
Hillman, Sidney, 163
Hinding, Andrea, 581
Hirsch, Charlotte Teller, 258
Hilter-Stalin Pact. See Nazi-Soviet Pact
Hoffpauir, May Beals. See Beals, May
Hohl, Marden Walker, 145
Hold That Rent Ceiling, 376
Holden, Clara, 380
Hollywood, Calif., 304, 322, 339, 426
Hollywood Anti-Nazi League, 322
Holmes, Lizzie Swank, 39
Holocaust, 275
Homecoming, 209
"Honky Tonk Women," 481
Hook, Sidney, 306, 575
Hoopes, Hazelette, 273
Hope Mills, 97
Hopkins, Harry, 293
Hopkins, Mary Alden, 130
House Committee on Un-American Activities, 293, 306
House of Bondage, 260
housework, 7, 69, 86, 100, 108, 123, 125, 127, 130, 133, 222, 225, 227, 230, 233, 253, 274, 359, 361, 362, 363, 364, 365, 369, 384, 471, 475, 495, 524
How To Win the ERA, 480
Howe, Bertha W., 164
Howe, Julia Ward, 20
Howe, Robert Harrison, 218
Howes, Ethel Puffer, 7

How She Died, 569
Howland, Edward, 101
Howland, Marie Stevens, 7, 16, 101, 576
HUAC. See House Committee on Un-American Activities
Hughan, Jessie Wallace, 591
Hughes, Langston, 566
Hull House, 27
Humphrey, Robert E., 126
Hunt, Gertrude Breslau Fuller, 205, 259
Hunter, Allen, 524
Hurry Up Please, It's Time, 303
Hutchins, Grace, 164, 274, 357, 358, 359, 360, 361, 384

Ibsen, Henrik, 152, 156, 214
I Call to You Across a Continent, 424
I Change Worlds, 332
I Didn't Raise My Boy to Be a Soldier--for Wall Street, 350
If They Come in the Morning, 468
Illinois, 27, 28, 29
Illinois Compulsory Education Act, 37
Illinois Factory Inspection Act, 58
Illinois Woman's Alliance, 3, 37, 58, 134, 137
Immigrant Woman, 321
Impatient Crusader, 28
Index to Periodical Literature on Socialism, 592
Industrial Valley, 313, 409
Industrial Workers of the World (IWW), 5, 39, 132, 133, 134, 142, 143, 144, 145, 152, 179, 191, 200, 226, 247, 296, 311, 398, 571
"Influence of Women in the Alliance," 68
Inman, Mary, 274, 362, 363, 364, 365, 369
In Prison, 181
Institute for Marxism-Leninism (Moscow), 27
Institutional Marriage, 217

International Labor Defense, 283, 336
International Ladies' Garment Workers' Union (ILGWU), 194
International Socialist and Labor Congress, London, 147
International Socialist Review, 179, 467, 483, 485, 498, 500, 501, 502
International Typographers' Union, 564
International Women's Day, 241, 274, 348, 350, 354, 367, 465, 472, 523
International Workingmen's Association (First International), 44, 46, 60, 88, 101
International Working People's Association, 39
In This Our World, 100
Intimate Memoirs, 174
"Intolerant Populist? The Disaffection of Mary Elizabeth Lease," 33
In Woman's Defense, 274, 362
Iowa, 397, 403
Irish-Americans, 13
Irish Nationalism, 32, 142
Isadora, 291
I Saw Russia, 277
I Saw The Russian People, 339
Is Mankind Advancing?, 232
Italian-Americans, 142, 289, 535
It's In the Wind, 551
IWW. See Industrial Workers of the World

Jackson, George, 450
Jackson, Helen, 304
Jacobs, Harold, 481
Jaeger, Renate, 519
Jaggar, Alison M., 482
Jake Home, 313, 409
James, C.L. (Charles Leigh), 74, 75
James, C.L.R., 344, 496
James, Edward T., 34, 582
James, Henry, Sr., 51
James, Janet Wilson, 582
James, Selma, 462, 524
Jane: An Intimate Biography of Jane Fonda, 454
Jaquith, Cindy, 480, 482, 502, 511
Jayko, Margaret, 484
Jefferson School, 348
Jeffrey, Julie Roy, 17
Jenness, Linda, 485, 486, 502
Jewish Currents, 527
Jewish Workers University. See Yiddishe Arbeter Universitet
Jews, 9, 21, 146, 161, 173, 194, 248, 250, 264, 275, 294, 309, 324, 328, 386, 416, 425, 444, 455, 570
John Reed Children's Colony, 332, 430
Johns, Dorothy, 219
Johnson, Josephine Winslow, 400, 401, 402
Johnson, Lyndon, 536
Johnson, Oakley C., 164
Johnson, Olive Malberg, 220
Johnston, Johanna, 48, 49
Johnstone, Jenny Elizabeth, 368
Jones, Alice Ilgenfritz, 102
Jones, Beverly, 505
Jones, Claudia, 366, 367
Jones, Jack, 144
Jones, (Mother) Mary Harris, 3, 9, 10, 131, 165, 166, 167, 168, 169, 381
Jordan, June, 487, 539, 540
Jordanstown, 402
Joseph, Gloria, 507
Joyce, James, 136
"Julia," 305
Julianelli, Jane, 163
Jungle, The, 142

Kamen, Samuel, 567
Kaneko, Josephine Conger. See Conger-Kaneko, Josephine
Kansas, 32, 76, 87, 96, 108, 180, 226, 321, 403
Kansas Farm, A, 108
Karasick, Regina. See Dennis, Peggy
Karvonen, Hilja J., 127
"Kate Donnelly versus the Cult of True Womanhood," 26
Kate O'Hare Booklets, The, 180

Kate O'Hare's Prison Letters, 181
"Kate Richards O'Hare: A Mid-
    western Pacifist's Fight for
    Free Speech," 184
"Kate Richards O'Hare: The
    'First Lady' of American
    Socialism, 1901-1917," 186
Kauffman, Reginald Wright, 260
Keep, Jane, 136
Kehde, Ned, 583
Keller, Helen, 6, 132, 170, 171,
    172, 177, 221, 247, 591
Kelley, Florence, 27, 28, 29,
    386, 582
Kellie, Luna E., 30
Kellog, Charles Flint, 187
Kelly, Florence Finch, 31, 103,
    104
Kelly, Joan, 210
Kennedy, David M., 191, 192
Kennedy, Liz, 475
Kerr, Charles H., 222
Kerr, Katherine, 222
Kerr, May Walden, 222, 223
Kertesz, Louise, 460
Key, Ellen, 209, 240, 247
Khrushchev Report (1956), 271,
    343
Kiernan, Thomas, 454
King, Coretta Scott, 468
King, Carol Weiss, 591
Kingsley, Charles, 55
Kinney, Arthur F., 323
Kirby, Georgiana Bruce, 576
Kirchwey, Freda, 427
Kisner, Arlene, 85
Klehr, Harvey, 272
Klotman, Phyllis Rauch, 584
Knapp, Adeline, 105, 150
Knights of Labor, 32, 34, 40, 42,
    78, 80, 81, 108, 118, 165,
    178, 386, 571
Knights of the Golden Rule, 196
Knowles, Ella L., 594
Koedt, Anne, 488, 521, 522
Komisar, Lucy, 485
Konikow, Antoinette Bucholz, 309
Koppel, Barbara, 524
Korean War, 374
Kracow, Theodora, 544
Kreuter, Gretchen, 26, 40, 129

Kreuter, Kent, 129
Krichmar, Albert, 585, 586
Kroeber, Alfred, 544
Kropotkin, Peter, 142, 143, 156
Krupskaya, Nadyezda, 381
Ku Klux Klan, 312
Kurtz, Aaron, 389

Labor and Monopoly Capital, 471
labor legislation, 27, 28, 29, 37,
    38, 58, 82, 132, 134, 210, 477
labor movement, 2, 3, 9, 12, 15,
    22, 37, 39, 78, 82, 97, 121,
    124, 217, 132, 134, 142, 143,
    144, 145, 163, 165, 166, 167,
    168, 169, 178, 194, 201, 267,
    279, 281, 303, 324, 335, 338,
    340, 352, 355, 366, 368, 370,
    377, 380, 390, 391, 408, 409,
    431, 435, 436, 589
Labor Research Association, 357,
    361
Ladies' Federal Labor Union No.
    2703, 37, 134, 137
Ladies' Liberal League, 138
Lagemann, Ellen Condliffe, 128
Lamb, Myrna, 541
Lamont, Corliss, 296
Landy, Avrom, 369
Lane, Ann J., 253, 254
Lane, Mary E. Bradley, 106
Langer, Elinor, 288, 455, 562
Lapidus, Liz, 475
Lapin, Eva, 370
Larger Aspects of Socialism, The,
    240
Lasch, Christopher, 176
Lash, Joseph P., 172
Lassalle, Ferdinand, 173
Last White Class, The, 563
Lauter, Paul, 427
Law of Marriage, The, 74
Lawrence Textile Workers' Strike
    (1912), 134, 142, 143, 144,
    145, 177, 195, 198, 201, 221
Lazarus, Emma, 328
Leach, William, 18, 19
Leacock, Elinor, 489
League for Proletarian Socialism,
    471
League of American Writers, 417

League of Women Shoppers, 436
Lease, Mary Elizabeth, 32, 33, 34, 35, 40, 76
Lee, Ann, 576
Lee, Sirkka Tuomi, 310
Left Hand of Darkness, 542
Le Guin, Ursula, 542, 543, 544
Lemlich, Clara. See Shavelson, Clara Lemlich
Lenin, V.I., 270, 359, 369, 382, 510, 512
"Lenin on the Woman Question," 382
Les Blancs, 395
Lessing, Doris, 556
Lesson Outlines in the Economic Interpretation of History, 234
Lester, Julius, 394, 395
Le Sueur, Arthur, 311
Le Sueur, Marian, 311
Le Sueur, Meridel, 311, 384, 403, 404, 405
Letters of Edna St. Vincent Millay, 314
Levertov, Denise, 456, 545, 546, 547
Levine, Ellen, 488
Levinson, Harry, 35
Levi-Strauss, Claude, 500
Lewis, Lena Morrow, 129
liberalism, 476, 482
Liberal League, 80
Liberating Women's History, 524
Liberation, 469
Liberation of Women, The, 479
Liberator, 268, 571
Liberty, 202
Liebknecht, Wilhelm, 173
"Life in the Iron Mills," 549
Life of One's Own, A, 193
Lifshin, Lyn, 524
Lilienthal, Augusta, 121, 173
Lilienthal, Frederick, 173
Lilienthal, Meta Stern, 121, 173, 205, 224, 225
Lillian Hellman, 307
Lillian Hellman, Playwright, 308
Lipman, Carol, 485
Listener in Babel, A, 265
Literary San Francisco, 551

Literature of Communism in America, The, 573
Little, Joan, 502
Little Disturbances of Man, The, 416
Little Falls, N.Y., 132
Little Foxes, The, 396
Little Red Songbook, 286
Little Review, 136
Little Rock, Ark., 200
Little Sister of the Poor, 251
Livermore, Mary Rice, 7, 10, 92, 594
Living in the Open, 558
Living My Life, 152
Living My Life (abridged), 153
Living of Charlotte Perkins Gilman, The, 147
Llano del Rio, Calif., 8, 16
Loader, Jayne, 587
Long, Lily A., 107
Long, Priscilla, 167, 490
Long Loneliness, The, 284
Long View, The, 433
Looking Backward, 7, 69, 91, 92, 93, 111, 116, 142, 544
Looking Forward, 235
"Looking Forward Together," 18
Loose Change, 446
Lopate, Carol, 482
Lopez, Jessie, 438
Los Angeles, Calif., 8, 219, 285, 286
LOUDcracks/softHEARTS, 548
Louisiana, 8, 304, 393
Love--Family Life--Career, 371
Love, Marriage and Divorce and the Sovereignty of the Individual, 51
Love Story, 313
Lovin, Hugh, 185
Love in Freedom, 72
Lowe, Caroline, 205, 226
Lowell, Amy, 136
Lowenfels, Walter, 389, 527
Lower East Side, N.Y., 264, 294, 336
Lozoraitis, Jean, 548
Luce, Clare Booth, 353
Lucifer, the Light-Bearer, 74, 87
Lucy Parsons, 39

Luhan, Mabel Dodge, 126, 174, 175, 176, 189, 243
Lumpkin, Grace, 312, 384, 406, 407
Lumpkin, Katharine Du Pre, 312
"Luna E. Kellie and the Farmers' Alliance," 30
Lund, Caroline, 485, 491, 510
Lundberg, Ferdinand, 373
Luscumb, Florence, 438
Luther, Martha, 150
Lutz, Alma, 278
Lynch, Roberta, 518, 519
Lynd, Staughton, 521
Lysistrata, 83

Mabel: A Biography of Mabel Dodge Luhan, 175
McAfee, Kathy, 462, 509
McAlmon, Victoria, 130
Macbird! 536
McCall's Magazine, 276
McCarthy, Joseph, 306
McCone, Selma Jokela, 127, 246
McConnell, Dorothy, 372
McCormick, Fannie, 108
McCreery, Maria Maud Leonard, 582
McDonagh, Don, 301
McDonald, Dwight, 571
McDonald, Grace Lois, 408
Macdougall, Allan Ross, 291
McFarland, C.K., 168
McKain, Barbara, 482
McKain, Michael, 482
McKenney, Ruth, 313, 409, 410
McWhirter, Martha, 576
Macy, Anne Sullivan, 171, 172, 177
Macy, John Albert, 170, 177
Madison, Charles A., 157
Maglin, Nan Bauer, 199
Mailer, Norman, 485
Mainardi, Pat, 495
Mainstream, 527
Making of a Southerner, The, 312
Maley, Anna A. See Ringsdorf, Anna A. Maley
Malkeil, Leon A., 178
Malkiel, Theresa Serber, 121, 178, 228, 229, 261
Mallach, Stanley, 182

Mann, Arthur, 20
Mann, Prestonia. See Martin, Prestonia Mann
manuscript collections, 581
Marberry, M. Marion, 49
Marching! Marching!, 431
"March of the Mill Children," 165, 168
Marcuse, Herbert, 449
Marcy, Mary, 179, 230, 231, 262
Margaret Sanger: Pioneer of the Future, 190
"Margaret Sanger and Voluntary Motherhood," 192
Marot, Helen, 124, 243, 582
marriage, 2, 8, 22, 62, 64, 71, 72, 73, 74, 80, 91, 110, 130, 138, 193, 202, 211, 215, 233, 235, 238, 258, 262, 271, 285, 313, 330, 335, 339, 371, 387, 425, 426, 492, 538, 544, 549
Marriage, 80
Marriage and Morality, 71
Marriage, Morals and Sex in America, 2
Marsden, Dora, 209
Marsh, Margaret S., 21, 22
Martha Graham, 301
"Martha Moore Avery," 24
Martin, John Biddulph, 44
Martin, Mrs. John Biddulph. See Martin, Victoria Claflin Woodhull
Martin, Prestonia Mann, 232
Martin, Ralph G., 171
Martin, Victoria Claflin Woodhull, 2, 44, 46, 47, 48, 49, 50, 51, 60, 84, 88
Marx, Karl, 2, 44, 63, 88, 225, 237, 359, 369, 382, 478, 493, 506, 510, 512, 514, 521
Marxism and the Woman Question, 369
"Mary Elizabeth Lease, Populist Orator," 32
"Mary Elizabeth Lease: Prairie Radical," 35
Mary Marcy, 178
Mary Wollstonecraft, 162
Masculine/Feminine, 505
Mason, Caroline A., 109

Massachusetts, 309, 438, 443, 556, 561, 563

Masses, 133, 209, 243, 244, 268, 284, 571

maternity, 223, 236, 238, 360, 371, 383, 475, 478

Mattila, Emma, 246

Mattson, Helmi, 127, 246

Maurin, Peter, 284, 451

May Days, 268

Mayer, Maria Goeppert, 193

"Meaning of the Catholic Church's Position on Abortion, The," 501

Meeropol, Michael, 327

Meeropol, Robert, 327

Melting Pot, 239

Melville, Sam, 444

Memnonia Institute, 576

Memorial--Corinne Stubbs Brown, 137

Memories and Impressions of Helena Modjeska, 36

"Memories from the 'Twenties,'" 286

Memories of the Industrial Workers of the World (IWW), 143

Mena, Ark., 338

Menorah Journal, 425

Men, Women, and Issues, 120

Merchant, Ella, 102

Meridian, 568

Metzerott, Shoemaker, 116

Mexican-Americans, 438, 559

Meyer, Annie Nathan, 78

Michel, Louise, 138

Michigan, 333, 387, 560

Midstream: My Later Life, 170

Milholland, Inez, 317

Militant, 480, 484, 485, 492, 497, 501, 502, 511

Militia of Christ for Social Service, 24

Mill, John Stuart, 476

Millard, Betty, 373, 374

Millay, Edna St. Vincent, 126, 193, 268, 314, 315, 316, 317, 138, 319, 411

Millay, Norma, 411

Millay in Greenwich Village, 317

Miller, Ruthann, 492

Miller, Sally M., 129, 178, 237

Millett, Kate, 463

Milwaukee, Wis., 277

Mine and Thine, 118

Minneapolis, Minn., 333, 404

Minneapolis General Strike, (1934), 404

Minnesota, 26, 40, 333, 403, 404, 405

Minor, Robert, 243

Mississippi, 324

Missouri, 239

Mitchell, Juliet, 482, 493, 505, 520

Mitchell, Louise, 375, 376

Mitchell, Therese, 349, 377

Mitford, Jessica, 320

Mizora, 106

Mod Donna and Scyklon Z, The, 541

Modern Dance, 290, 291, 292, 301, 310

Modern Woman: The Lost Sex, 373

Molek, Ivan, 321

Molek, Mary, 321

Modjeska, Helena, 36, 576

Monroe, Marilyn, 48

Moody, Richard, 308

Moraga, Cherrie, 494

"More Corn, Less Hell?" 34

Morgan, Elizabeth, 37, 38, 58

Morgan, Lewis Henry, 64, 235, 237

Morgan, Robin, 457, 495, 505

Moriarty, Claire, 501

Mormons, 8

Morning Breaks, The, 448

Morris, Desmond, 500

Morrison, Toni, 449

Morton, Peggy, 462

Moscow Yankee, 414

Most, Johann, 152

Mother Bloor, 340

Mother Bloor Celebration Committee, 280

Mother Bloor's 75th Anniversary Souvenir Book, 280

Mother Earth, 74, 138, 146, 158, 202, 244, 264

Mother Earth Bulletin, 571. See also Mother Earth

"Motherhood, Reproduction and
Male Supremacy," 475
Mother Jones, the Miners' Angel,
166
Mother Jones, Woman Organizer,
167
"Mother Jones in the Fairmont
Field, 1901," 169
"Mother's Bill of Rights," 360
Mothers in Overalls, 370
Mott, Lucretia, 381
Mouth on Paper, 533
Movers and Shakers, 174
Moving the Mountain, 438
Mrs. Herndon's Income, 94
Mrs. Satan, 48
Munaker, Sue, 490
Muste, A.J., 282, 470
My Disillusionment in Russia, 154
My Further Disillusionment in
Russia, 154
My Life, 290, 291
My Native Land, 333
My Sister Eileen, 313
My Thirty Years' War, 136
Myths of Male Dominance, 489

Nadelson, Regina, 449
Naison, Mark, 338
Naisten Viiri. See Toveritar
Nashoba, Tenn., 576
Nation, 130, 427, 469
"National Action: A Women's
Perspective, A," 526
National American Woman Suffrage
Association, 277
National Assoication for the
Advancement of Colored
People, 187
National Consumers' League, 27,
28, 82, 113, 349
National Council for American-
Soviet Friendship, 361
Nationalism (Bellamy), 14, 18,
20, 24, 41, 42, 54, 63, 65,
78, 92, 94, 111, 114, 116,
147, 150, 571
National League for the Protec-
tion of Colored Women, 187
National Mobilization to End the
War in Vietnam, 444

National Negro Congress, 368
National Organization for an
American Revolution, 496
National Organization for a New
America, 464
National Organization of Women,
441, 483, 484
National Recovery Administration
(NRA), 194, 356, 359, 372
National Review, 450
National Rip-Saw, 239
National Society for Birth Con-
trol, 32
National Textile Workers' Union,
355, 384
National Woman's Alliance, 86,
108
National Women's Commission, Com-
munist party, 270
National Woman's party, 359
Native Americans, 494
Native Daughter, 336
Nazi-Soviet Pact, 339, 342, 378
Nebraska, 30
Neda, 472
Negley, Glenn, 588
Negroes. See Afro-Americans
Neidle, Cecyle S., 9
Nemiroff, Robert, 302, 394
New American Movement, 519, 525
New Aristocracy, A, 90
New Civilization, The, 65
New Deal, 194, 360, 372
New England Free Love League, 57,
73
New England Free Press, 488
New Feminism in the 20th Century
America, The, 11
New Harmony, Ind., 576
New Left, 288, 344, 440, 441, 442,
455, 457, 459, 462, 465, 470,
478, 486, 488, 490, 505, 507,
508, 509, 521, 522, 524, 525,
526, 529, 535, 536, 537, 548,
555, 556, 562, 568, 569, 577,
583
New Left Notes, 481
New Left Review, 493
Newman, Pauline, 9, 12, 124
New Masses, 313, 403, 431
New Nation, 54

New Orleans, La., 304
New Radicalism in America, The, 176
New Republic, 264
New Review, 164, 269
New Right, 524
News and Letters Committees, 472
New Slavery, The, 58
New Social Structure, The, 226
New Woman, The, 133
New York, N.Y., 27, 35, 82, 104, 124, 126, 129, 133, 134, 135, 146, 151, 173, 174, 175, 187, 194, 201, 256, 260, 264, 284, 285, 289, 313, 314, 317, 324, 333, 335, 376, 427, 439, 442, 444, 459, 532
New York Call, 164, 173, 178, 189, 221, 250, 261, 284
New Yorker, 313, 315
New Yorker Volkszeitung, 173, 178
New York Radical Feminists, 478, 495
New York Shirtwaist Makers' Strike (1909-1910), 134, 194, 250, 261, 329
Nichols, Mary Gove, 576
Nies, Judith, 10
Nietzsche, Friedrich Wilhelm, 152, 269, 505
Nkrumah, Kwame, 532
No Gold Stars For Us, 378
No Middle Ground, 428
Non-Partisan League, 278, 311
Northampton, Mass., 443
North Carolina, 17, 413
Norton, Mary Beth, 148
Notable American Women, 528, 594
Notable American Women, the Modern Period, 591
Not All Rivers, 429
"Notes for the Next Time," 288, 455
Notes From the First Year, 521
Notes From the Second Year, 488, 522
Not So Deep as Well, 417
Novack, George, 497
Nowhere at Home, 155
Now in November, 400, 401, 402
NRA. See National Recovery Administration
Nurmi, Maija, 127, 246

Oakland, Calif., 226, 525
O'Casey, Sean, 566
Off Our Backs, 523
O'Hare, Frank, 180, 181, 263
O'Hare, Kate Richards, 2, 120, 121, 131, 180, 181, 182, 183, 184, 185, 186, 233, 236, 295, 582
Ohio, 388, 409, 443
Ohio Liberal Society, 59, 71
Oklahoma, 226
Okugawa, Otokiko, 576
Olsen, Jack, 458
Olsen, Tillie, 412, 458, 459
O'Malley, Susan, 438
On Being Told That Her Second Husband Has Taken His First Lover, 426
O'Neill, Eugene, 314
One of "Berrian's" Novels, 114
One Thousand Dollars a Day, 105
On Journey, 195
Only a Flock of Women, 63
On Pilgrimage, 451
On the Inside, 104
O'Reilly, Leonora, 12, 124, 128, 134
O'Reilly, Mary, 205
Orlando, Fla., 164
Origins of the Family, Private Property and the State, 64, 463
O'Sullivan, Judith, 569
Oughton, Diana, 459
Our National Kitchen, 227
Out of Bondage, 276
Out of the Dark, 221
Out of the Dump, 179
Ovington, Mary White, 187

pacifism, 157, 158, 184, 297, 298, 299, 469
Pack, Emma D., 86
Page, [Dorothy] Myra, 384, 413, 414, 415
Paley, Grace, 416, 550
Pankhurst, Emmeline, 209
pantarchy, 88

Papa's Own Girl. See Familistère, The
Parce, Lida, 205, 234
Parker, Dorothy, 304, 322, 323, 417, 426
Parker, J.A., 450
Parlor Provocateur, The, 297
Parsons, Albert, 39
Parsons, Elsie Clews, 243
Parsons, Lucy, 39
Partisans of Freedom, 158
Parton, Mary Field, 165
Passaic Textile Workers' Strike, 1926, 201, 335
Passion, 540
Paterson Textile Workers' Strike, (1913), 174
patriarchy, 475, 479, 499, 500, 501, 507, 514
Patrons of Husbandry, 56, 78, 101
Payne, Elizabeth Rogers, 41
peace movement, 42, 83, 133, 152, 180, 181, 182, 183, 186, 221, 225, 263, 266, 354, 357, 366, 367, 374, 378, 379, 444, 445, 451, 453, 456, 469, 470, 527, 534, 536, 542, 545, 546, 547, 566
Pease, Leonora, 205
Peirce, Melusina Fay, 7, 576
Pennsylvania, 267, 324
Pentimento, 305
People's party, 13, 86, 99
People's World, 448
Perkins Institution for the Blind, 177
Perlin, Terry M., 140
Personal Politics, 440
Persons, Stow, 70, 575
Petchevsky, Rosalind, 475
Peters, Nancy Joyce, 551, 564
Philadelphia, Pa., 138, 168
Philomatheia Club, 24
Pickering, Ruth, 130
Piercy, Marge, 495, 552, 553, 554, 555, 556, 557, 558, 559, 560, 561, 562, 563
Pioneers of Women's Liberation, 467
Pisan, Christine de, 6

Pisstained Stairs and the Monkey Man's Wares, 530
Pitcher, Mollie, 381
Pittock, Mrs. M.A. (Weeks), 110
Pittsburgh, Pa., 324
Pity Is Not Enough, 397
Plays (Glaspell), 256
Plea for the New Woman, A, 59
Pleck, Elizabeth, 1
Plotkin, Sara, 324
Poems and Songs for Dreamers Who Dare, 567
Poet and Her Book, The, 318
Poetic Vision of Muriel Rukeyser, The, 460
Poet in the World, The, 456
Point Loma, Calif., 576
"Political Economy of Women's Liberation, The," 462, 509
"Political Perspectives on Feminism," 519
Politics of Domesticity, The, 15
"Politics of Housework, The," 495
"Politics of Reform, The," 13
Politics of Women's Liberation, The, 441
Popkin, Ann, 439
Popular Front, 142, 274, 301, 342, 349, 385
populism, 13, 14, 17, 26, 30, 32, 33, 34, 35, 40, 68, 76, 86, 96, 99, 108, 121, 180, 233, 594
pornography, 515
Portable Dorothy Parker, The, 417
Porter, Linn Boyd, 111
Position of Negro Women, The, 356
Potter-Loomis, Hulda L., 77
Pound, Ezra, 136, 545
Powers, Thomas, 459
Pratt, William C., 129, 273
Present Phase of Women's Advancement, The, 56
Princeton, Mass., 73
Prisoner of Sex, The, 485
Prisoners of Poverty, 94
Prison Notes, 452
"Private Woman, Public Woman," 148
Problem of Civilization, The, 32
Problems of Women's Liberation,

498
Prodigal Daughter, The, 57
Prof. Goldwin Smith and His
    Satellites in Congress, 81
Progressive Institute of Applied
    Religion, 338
Progressive Labor party, 491
Progressive party (1940s), 281,
    361
Progressive Woman. See Socialist
    Woman
Progressive Women's Council, 329
Prohibiting Poverty, 232
prohibition, 13
prostitution, 180, 200, 206, 211,
    215, 216, 226, 233, 235, 236,
    239, 243, 248, 250, 251, 260
Prostitution for Profit, 206
Prosveta, 321
protective legislation. See
    labor legislation
Protective Tariff Delusions, 81
Provincetown Players, 133, 151
"Psychology Constructs the Fe-
    male," 488

Questions and Answers on the
    Woman Question, 348
Quint, Howard H., 120

race suicide, 233, 236
Radical America, 462, 524
radical feminism, 442, 457, 470,
    478, 482, 488, 495, 514, 520,
    522, 523, 526
Radical Future of Liberal Femi-
    nism, The, 476
Radical Life, A, 335
Radical Periodicals in America,
    1890-1950, 578
Railways of Europe and America,
    81
Raisin in the Sun, A, 394
Rand, Caroline Amada Sherfey,
    582
Randall, Margaret, 524
Rand School of Social Science,
    242, 593
Raplansky, Naomi, 418
Rapone, Anita, 488
Rappaport, Philip, 235

Raritan Bay Colony, 576
Rat, 457
Rauh, Ida, 126, 133, 134
Reading, Pa., 129, 273
Reagan's War on Women's Rights,
    484
Real Isadora, The, 292
Rebel at Large, The, 249
Rebel Girl, The, 142
"Rebel Girl--Elizabeth Gurley
    Flynn, The," 145
Rebel in Paradise, 156
Red Apple Collective, 443
Red Emma Speaks, 213
Red Flag, 249
Red Flag (Ridge), 420
Redgrave, Vanessa, 305
"Red Kate O'Hare Comes to Madi-
    son," 182
Red Network, The, 574
Red scare, 154, 278, 335
Redstockings, 478, 495
Red Virtue, 339, 343
Reed, Evelyn, 492, 498, 499, 500,
    501
Reed, John, 126, 174, 284
Reichert, William O., 158
Reid, Willie Mae, 483, 502
Reiter, Rayna, 503
Reitman, Ben L., 152, 200
Relearning the Alphabet, 546
Religion of the Future, The, 67
Report of the International
    Council of Women, 79
Resefske, Ann, 380
Resefske, Stella, 380
"Response to Ellen Kay
    Trimberger's Essay, A," 287
Restless Spirit, 319
Reuther, Walter, 303
Revera, Diego, 577
Revolution & Equilibrium, 469
Revolutionary Communist party,
    465
Revolutionary Dynamic of Women's
    Liberation, The, 497
Revolutionary Letters, 535
Revolutionary Writers' Federa-
    tion, 413
Rhine, Alice Hyneman, 78
Rhode Island, 380

Richards, Ellen Swallow, 7
Richmond, Al, 336
Ricker, Allen W., 236
Riddiough, Christine, 507
Ridge, Lola, 264, 419, 420, 421, 422, 582
Ringsdorf, Anna A. Maley, 227
Ring Song, 418
Ripley, Sophia Willard Dana, 576
Rise and Fall of the American Woman, The, 504
Rising of the Women, The, 134
Rivington, Ann, 478, 479
Robeson, Eslanda Cardoza Goode, 591
Robeson, Paul, 533
Robins, Margaret Dreier, 209
Robinson, Lillian, 524
Robinson, Patricia, 505, 509
Rochester, Anna, 357
Rodman, Henrietta, 11, 133
Ritter, Ellen M., 37
Road, The, 434
Roe, Charlotte, 504
Rolling Stone, 515
Romance of American Communism, The, 272
Romilly, Esmond, 320
Roosevelt, Eleanor, 194, 333, 353
Rope of Gold, 399
Rose, Ernestine L., 328
Rose Door, The, 248
Rosel, Lorraine, 481
Rosemont, Penelope, 564
Rosenberg, Ethel Greenglass, 324, 325, 326, 327, 424, 591
Rosenberg, Julius, 325, 326, 327, 424
Rosenberg Story, The, 326
Ross, Albert. See Porter, Linn Boyd
Rossi, Alice, 505
Roszak, Betty, 505
Roszak, Theodore, 505
Rowbotham, Sheila, 482, 506, 524
Rubin, Gayle, 482, 505
Rukeyser, Muriel, 460, 565
Ruskin, John, 197, 265
Russell, Michele, 519, 525
Russian Revolution, 147, 154, 155, 213, 221, 246, 279, 292, 297, 332, 335, 420, 463, 486, 506, 512
Ryan, Mary P., 475

Sabaroff, Nina, 192
Sacco and Vanzetti Trial, 142, 279, 314, 315, 317, 322, 409, 421, 422
Sachs, Emanie. See Arling, Emanie Sachs
Sacks, Karen, 495
Salute to Spring, 403
Sandburg, Carl, 393
Sanger, Margaret, 5, 6, 11, 120, 121, 142, 156, 174, 189, 190, 191, 192, 193, 244, 247
Santori, Ellen, 344
Sargent, Lydia, 507
Sarton, May, 422
Saxe, Susan, 442
Sayles, Lita Barney, 79
Scarifications, 532
Schappes, Morris U., 328
Scharnau, Ralph, 38
Scheier, Paula, 329
Schlesinger Library, 579
Schloss, Helen M., 132
Schneiderman, Rose, 9, 12, 120, 124, 128, 194
School for Democracy, 289
School of Darkness, 289
Schreiner, Olive, 209, 240, 247
Schrom, Nancy. See Dye, Nancy Schrom
Scottsboro Boys, 283, 384, 397
Scoundrel Time, 423
Screen Writers' Guild, 322, 426
Scudder, Vida Dutton, 20, 195, 196, 197, 198, 199, 201, 265, 591
Scyklon Z, 541
SDS. See Students for a Democratic Society
Searching Wind, The, 396
Sears, Hal D., 23
Seattle, Wash., 332, 334, 397, 525
Seattle General Strike (1919), 332, 334, 397
"Seattle Liberation Front," 525

Second International, 240, 243, 512
Second Stage, The, 484
Sedwich, Cathy, 480
Seed of a Woman, 537
Segal, Edith, 424, 566, 567
Seidman, Joel, 590
Selected Works of Voltairine de Cleyre, 207
Seretan, L. Glen, 129
Seroff, Victor, 292
settlements, 7, 195, 197, 252, 265, 336
Seven American Utopias, 8
Seven Women, 10
Severance, Juliet H., 80
Sexism & Science, 500
Sex Radicalism as Seen by an Emancipated Woman of the New Time, 211
Sex Radicals, The, 23
Sex Revolution, A, 83
sexual liberation, 2, 5, 19, 87, 91, 93, 114, 133, 160, 207, 209, 211, 215, 231, 240, 243, 244, 247, 250, 256, 478, 482, 541, 556. See also free love
Sexual Politics, 463, 485
Shaffer, Robert, 274
Shakers, 8, 576
Shall It Be Girls in Uniforms?, 345
Shange, Ntzoke, 524
Shavelson, Clara Lemlich, 12, 328, 329
Shaw, George Bernard, 147, 214, 278, 505
Sheen, Monsignor Fulton J., 289
Sherwood, Margaret Pollock, 112, 113
Shively, Charles, 51
Shop Talks on Economics, 179
Showalter, Elaine, 150
Shulman, Alix Kates, 141, 159, 160, 213, 215
Sicherman, Barbara, 591
Sickels, Eleanor M., 131
Sign for Cain, A, 407
Sign in Sidney Brustein's Window, The, 394
Signoret, Simone, 394

Silences, 458
Silver, Barbara, 586
Silvin, Edward, 592
Simons, May Wood, 121, 129, 237
Sinclair, Mary Craig, 266, 297, 330
Sinclair, Upton, 142, 266, 330
single-tax, 101, 115
Sisterhood Is Powerful (Morgan), 495
Sisterhood Is Powerful (Stone), 508
Sister of the Road, 200
Sisters in Struggle, 517
Slesinger, Tess, 425, 426
Slinker, Elmina, 23
Sloan, John, 243
Small, Sasha, 380, 381, 384
Small Changes, 556
Smedley, Agnes, 331, 427, 582
Smith, Jessica, 343
Smith, Lucy Elliot, 328
Smith, Virginia Carlson, 585
Smith, Walker C., 200
Smith Act, 142, 295
SNCC. See Student Non-violent Coordinating Committee
Snyder, Robert E., 132
Sobell, Morton, 424
Sochen, June, 10, 133, 161
"Social Basis for Sexual Equality," 495
Social Democracy of America, 65
social evil. See prostitution
Social Evil and the Remedy, The, 216
Social Freedom, the Most Important Factor, 77
Socialism: The Nation of Fatherless Children, 24
Socialism and Motherhood, 237
Socialism and the Fight for Women's Rights, 486
Socialism and the Home, 222
"Socialism and Women in the United States," 123
Socialist, 39
Socialist Feminist Conference, (1975), 443, 518
"Socialist-Feminist Women's Unions," 443

Socialist Labor party, 24, 25,
27, 38, 39, 70, 78, 82, 178,
208, 220, 237, 279, 309, 340
Socialist Literature Company, 242
Socialist Party of America, 2, 3,
5, 14, 24, 27, 39, 121, 123,
125, 127, 129, 132, 134, 137,
142, 143, 164, 165, 166, 170,
172, 173, 177, 178, 179, 180,
181, 182, 183, 184, 185, 186,
187, 188, 189, 191, 206, 219,
221, 222, 226, 227, 234, 245,
249, 259, 273, 277, 278, 279,
284, 309, 311, 329, 332, 336,
340, 359, 571, 592
Socialist Review, 1, 520, 525
Socialist Revolution. See
Socialist Review
Socialist Trades and Labor Alli-
ance, 25
Socialist Woman, 245, 571
"Socialist Women and the 'Girl
Strikers,'" 119
Socialist Women's Society of
Greater New York, 178, 208
Socialist Workers party, 309,
477, 483, 484, 485, 486, 491,
508, 511, 512, 541
social purity, 19, 42, 120, 180,
233, 236, 245
Social Reform Club, 187
Social Science League of Chicago,
77
Social Significance of Modern
Drama, 214
Sociologic Society of America,
65, 79
Soledad Brothers, 450, 468
Solow, Herbert, 425
Sonnets by Mary Craig Sinclair,
266
Sorrow Dance, The, 545
Sorrows of Cupid, 233, 236
South, 281, 304, 312, 330, 333,
338, 390, 391, 393, 396, 406,
407, 413, 415, 435, 437, 438,
440, 441, 451, 452, 522
South Carolina, 406
Southern Belle, 330
Southern Conference Educational
Fund, 522

Southern Cotton Mills and Labor,
413
Southern Farmers' Tenant Union,
338
Southern Patriot, 281
South in Progress, The, 312
Soviet Union, 154, 155, 158, 201,
277, 279, 285, 290, 304, 332,
334, 339, 343, 346, 348, 356,
357, 358, 359, 360, 367, 371,
373, 381, 408, 414, 420, 430,
433, 434, 510
Spadoni, Adriana, 429
Spanish Civil War, 152, 213, 285,
301, 304, 322, 397, 428, 433
Spargo, John, 237
Speaking of Ellen, 111
spiritualism, 19, 44, 45, 50, 80,
83, 88, 164, 211
Spock, Benjamin, 492, 566
Stacey, Judith, 475
Stalin, Joseph, 348, 382, 486
Stanton, Elizabeth Cady, 10, 18,
278, 476
Starr, Ellen Gates, 582
Steel, Edward, 169
Steel Workers' Organizing Com-
mittee (SWOC), 368
Steffens, Lincoln, 339
Stern, Madeline B., 84, 571
Stern, Susan, 461
Stetson, Charles Walter, 147, 148
Steuben, Maine, 24
Stevens, Alzina Parsons, 39, 594
Steward, Katie, 507
Stewart, David Ogden, 339
Stirner, Max, 158
Stokes, James G. Phelps, 267
Stokes, Rose Pastor, 9, 267, 268,
582
Stone, Betsey, 508
Stone, C.H. (Mrs.), 114
Stone, Lucy, 20, 92, 278
Stone Came Rolling, A, 391
Stories for Cave People, 179
Streets, 282
Strike!, 435
Strike of a Sex, 83
Strom, Sharon, 438
Strong, Anna Louise, 10, 298,
332, 333, 334, 430, 523, 591
Strong, Clara Weatherwax, 431

Struhl, Paula Rothernberg, 482
Stuhler, Barbara, 40
Student Non-violent Coordinating
    Committee (SNCC), 302, 417,
    440, 473
Students for a Democratic Society
    (SDS), 440, 444, 459, 461,
    495, 498, 524, 526, 564
Sullivan, Anne. See Macy, Anne
    Sullivan
Summer Soldier, The, 437
Sunday Worker, 378
Sun-Up, and Other Poems, 419
Suppressed Desires, 256
surrealism, 528, 530, 551, 564
Survey, 28
Susan Glaspell, 151
Sutherland, Donald, 454
Swank, Lizzie. See Holmes,
    Lizzie Swank
Swanson, Dorothy, 593
Sweezey, Paul, 471, 575
Swing Shift, 408
Synthesis, 471

Taggard, Genevieve, 130, 268,
    397, 432, 433
Take My Hand, 566
Talks on Nationalism, 54
Tamiment Library, New York Uni-
    versity, 393
Tanner, Leslie, 509
Tax, Meredith, 134, 488
Taylor, G.R., 162
Taylor, Harriet, 476
Taylor, Tasha, 446
Teachers' Union, 432, 489
Teitler, Stuart A., 106
Teller, Charlotte. See Hirsch,
    Charlotte Teller
Tell Me a Riddle, 412
temperance, 14, 15, 30, 32, 42,
    43, 56, 68, 76, 121, 127,
    180, 233, 245, 279, 594. See
    also Woman's Christian Tem-
    perance Union
Templeton, Faith. See Barber,
    Harriet Boomer
Tennessee, 249, 415
Tepperman, Jean, 495
Terrible Siren, The, 46

Texas, 68, 275
textile industry, 97, 107, 111,
    132, 198, 224, 335, 355, 384,
    390, 391, 406, 413, 435, 463
These Modern Women, 130
They Should Have Served That Cup
    of Coffee, 439
Things That I Do in the Dark, 539
Third International, 512
Third Period, CPUSA, 274, 340,
    359, 372, 378, 384
Thirteen Years of CPUSA Misleader-
    ship on the Woman Question,
    364
This Bridge Called My Back, 494
Thompson, Bertha, 200
Thompson, Elizabeth Rowell, 576
Thompson, Fred, 165
Thompson, Mary Lou, 467
Thompson, Moses, 200
Thoreau, Henry David, 158
Thorpe, Herbert A., 247
"Three Proponents of Women's
    Rights," 127
"Three Women," 328
Tichenor, Henry Mulford, 239
Tiger, Lionel, 500
Tilton, Theodore, 50, 85. See
    also Beecher-Tilton Scandal
Time: The Present. See On Being
    Told That Her Second Husband
    Has Taken His First Lover
Time to Remember, A, 436
Tingley, Katherine, 576
Tobenkin, Elias, 434
To Be of Use, 557
To Be Young, Gifted and Black,
    302
Tobias, Roscoe Burdette, 231
Tobier, Arthur, 324
Todd, Marion Marsh, 81, 594
Todes, Charlotte, 384
Tolstoy, Leo, 197, 214, 265
To Make My Bread, 406
Tomorrow's Bread, 386
Topolobampo, Mexico, 16, 101, 576
To the Barricades, 160
Toveritar, 127, 246
Toward an Anthropology of Women,
    503
Trade Union Unity League, 357,

358, 359, 384, 409
Traffic in Women, 215
Transactions of the National
    Council of Women, 76
Tresca, Carlo, 142, 144, 535
Treuhaft, Bob, 320
"Trial of Charlotte Anita
    Whitney, The," 336
Trial of Elizabeth Gurley Flynn,
    The, 296
Trifles, 256
Trilling, Diana, 306
Trilling, Lionel, 425
Trimberger, Ellen Kay, 287, 288
Trotsky, Leon, 284, 510, 512
True Love and Perfect Union, 19
Truth, Sojourner, 576
Tubman, Harriet, 10, 381
Tucker, Benjamin, 31, 51
Twelve Daughters of Democracy,
    131
Twelve-Spoked Wheel Flashing, 561
Twice a Year, 418
Twin Falls, Idaho, 185
Two Forms of Production under
    Capitalism, 365
"Two Lines on Women's Libera-
    tion," 463
"Two Utopian Feminists," 16
Tyolaisnainen. See Toveritar

Ukrainian-Americans, 135
"Ukrainian Radicals and Women,"
    135
Unemployed Councils, 384
Unfinished Woman, An, 304, 305
Union Labor party, 32, 81
United Auto Workers' Union, 303,
    338, 370
United Cloth Hat and Cap Makers'
    Union, 194
United Council of Working Class
    Women, 329, 384
United Electrical Workers, 370
United Farm Workers' Union, 438
United Front, 301, 351, 353
United Mine Workers of America,
    165, 169, 434
Unpossessed, The, 425
Unveiling a Parallel, 102
Utopian Literature, 588

utopian socialism, 2, 16, 66, 91
    92, 101, 102, 106, 109, 110,
    114, 223, 253, 254, 544, 575,
    576, 588

Valesh, Eva McDonald, 40, 594
Valley Forge, Kansas, 71, 200
Valley Women's Union, Northampton,
    Mass., 443
Van Etten, Ida, 82
Van Kleeck, Mary Abby, 591
Vicky, 49
Victims of the System, 219
Victoria C. Woodhull, 50
"Victoria Woodhull and the
    Pharisees," 47
Victoria Woodhull Reader, The,
    84
Vida, 562
"Vida Dutton Scudder," 197
"Vida Scudder and the Lawrence
    Textile Strike," 198
"Vida to Florence," 199
Vietnam War, 302, 416, 451, 456,
    469, 527, 536, 543, 545, 546,
    547, 550, 566, 567
"Viewing Voltairine de Cleyre,"
    141
Village Voice, 515, 541
Vindication of the Rights of
    Women, A, 162
Violette of Pere Lachaise, 269
Visioning, The, 255
Vogel, Lisa, 507, 524
Voices from Women's Liberation,
    509
Voices of the New Feminism, 467
Voltairine de Cleyre, 139
voluntary motherhood. See birth
    control
Vorse, Mary Heaton, 201, 243, 435

Waisbrooker, Lois, 23, 83, 115
Wald, Lillian, 1, 122
Walden, May. See Kerr, May
    Walden
Walker, Alice, 568
Walker, Edwin C., 71
Wallace, Ann. See Dee, Ruby
Wallace, Zerelda, 18, 92
Wall Between, The, 281

Walling, Anna Strunsky, 269
Walling, William English, 240
Walls Came Tumbling Down, The, 187
Wang, Diane, 511
Warren, Josiah, 23
Washington, Booker T., 187
Washington, 332, 525
Watch on the Rhine, 396
Waterman, Arthur, 151
Waters, Mary-Alice, 485, 492, 512, 513
We Are Many, 279
We Are Your Sons, 327
Weatherman, 481
Weatherman, 526, 555, 562
"Weatherman Politics and the Women's Movement," 481
Weatherwax, Clara. See Strong, Clara Weatherwax
Weatherwomen, 442, 461. See also Weatherman
Weaving the Future, 355
Webb, Beatrice, 209
Web of Gold, A, 117
We Cannot Live Without Our Lives, 470
Wedekind, Frank, 214
Weidner, Bertha Tyson, 273
Weinbaum, Batya, 475, 514
Weisbord, Albert, 335
Weisbord, Vera Buch, 335
Weisstein, Naomi, 11, 462, 488, 490, 495, 509
Weld, Angelina Grimke, 576
Wentworth, Franklin Harcourt, 241
Wertheimer, Barbara Mayer, 12
West, Rebecca, 154
West Virginia, 169, 295, 324
We Were There, 12
Wexler, Alice, 162
What Every Working Woman Wants, 360
What Happened to Dan? See Sorrows of Cupid
"What Strategy for Women's Liber-ation?" 483
Wheeling, W.V, 324
Wherefore Investigating Company, The, 115
Which Way for the Women's Move-ment?, 483
Which Wins?, 99
White, Lillie, 23
white slavery. See prostitution
Whiting, Lilian, 31
Whitman, Walt, 552, 566
Whitney, Anita, 336, 337, 351
Whitney, Anne, 41
Whitten, Woodrow C., 336
Who Is Angela Davis?, 449
"Why Black Women Belong in the Women's Liberation Movement," 483
"Why the Catholic Church Hierarchy Opposes Women's Right to Abortion," 501
Why Women Need the Equal Rights Amendment, 477
Wiederrecht, Ann E., 585, 586
Wiggins, Ella May, 380
Wilder, Thornton, 403
Wild River, 430
Wilkerson, Cathy, 481
Wilkerson, Doxey A., 348
Wilkinson, Jemima, 376
Willard, Frances E., 12, 14, 15, 18, 42, 43, 86, 92, 121, 594
Willett, Betty, 518
Williams, Claude, 338
Williams, Joyce, 281, 338
Williams, Ora, 595
Williams, Reba, 480
Williams, William Carlos, 545
Willis, Ellen, 509, 515, 522, 524
Wills, Gary, 306
Wilson, Barbara, 332
Wilson, E.O., 500
Wilson, Edmund, 314, 317
Wilson, Lilith Martin, 273
Winter, Ella, 339, 343
Winter Orchard, 401, 402
Wischnewetzky, Lazare, 27
Wisconsin, 129, 277, 285
WITCH, 495
With Sun in Our Blood, 415
With the Weathermen, 461
Wittenmyer, Annie, 43
Wives of Widows?, 342
Wobblies. See Industrial Workers of the World
Wollstonecraft, Mary, 2, 162,

207, 476
Woman, 52
Woman, Man and Poverty, 203
"Woman and Her Mind," 488
Woman and Socialism, 223
Woman and Temperance, 14
Woman and the Socialist Movement,
    220
"Woman and the Social Problem,"
    129, 237
Woman as Reason and as Force of
    Revolution, 472
Woman as Revolutionary, 6
"Woman in History, The," 463
"Woman Is a Sometime Thing, A,"
    490
Woman of the Century, 594
Woman of Yesterday, A, 109
Woman of Yesterday and Today, 288
Woman on the Edge of Time, 559
Woman Power, 363, 365
Woman Question (Champney), 202
Woman Question (Marx, Engels,
    Lenin, and Stalin), 382
Woman Rebel, 191, 247
Woman's Body, Woman's Right, 1, 5
Woman's Christian Temperance
    Union, 7, 14, 15, 32, 42, 43,
    56, 279
Woman's Emancipator, 200
Woman's Estate, 493
Woman's Evolution, 500
Woman's Evolution from Matriar-
    chal Clan to Patriarchal
    Family, 499
Woman's Movement in the Seventies,
    The, 585
Woman's National Committee,
    Socialist party, 121, 123,
    129, 226
Woman's Peace Party, 133
Woman's Place, A, 218, 344
Woman's Place--in the Fight for
    a Better World, 354
Woman's Portion, The, 241
Woman's Progressive Political
    League, 86
Woman's Rights Movement in the
    United States, 1848-1870, The,
    586
Woman's Slavery, 204

Woman's Suffrage, 208
woman suffrage, 3, 11, 13, 22, 25,
    32, 42, 43, 52, 54, 60, 68,
    70, 76, 81, 84, 88, 121, 123,
    124, 127, 129, 130, 133, 134,
    147, 165, 166, 173, 178, 180,
    186, 194, 204, 208, 215 223,
    227, 234, 243, 245, 277, 278,
    279, 284, 329, 392, 438, 467,
    475, 512, 517, 586
Woman's Voice, 205
Woman's Work in America, 78
"Woman's Work in Industry," 78
"Woman's Work Is Never Done, A,"
    462
Woman Today, 274, 385
Woman Under Capitalism, 239
Woman Under Socialism, 53, 64,
    92, 240
Woman Who Wouldn't, The, 267
Woman Worker, 357
Women: A Journal of Liberation,
    215, 526
"Women: Caste, Class or Oppressed
    Sex?" 498
Women, Resistance and Revolution,
    506
"Women: The Longest Revolution,"
    493
Women--Vote for Life!, 379
Women, War, and Fascism, 373
Women against the Myth, 373
Women and American Socialism,
    1870-1920, 121
"Women and American Socialism:
    The Reading Experience," 273
Women and Economics, 69, 147,
    150, 253
Women and Equality, 346
Women and Freedom, 228
Women & Revolution, 507
Women and the American Labor
    Movement from Colonial Times
    to the Eve of World War I, 3
Women and the American Labor
    Movement from World War I to
    the Present, 4
"Women and the Communist Party,
    USA," 274
Women and the Family, 510
"Women and the Family: A His-

torical View," 498
"Women and the Left," 522
Women and the Movement to Build a New America, 464
Women and the New World, 496
Women and the Socialist Revolution, 513
Women and War, 357
Women as Sex Vendors, 231
Women as World Builders, 209
Women for Peace Clubs, 374
Women Have a Date with Destiny, 353
Women in Action, 380
Women in America, 579
Women in American History, 580
"Women in American Society," 524
Women in Class Struggle, 471
Women in Soviet Russia, 343
Women in Steel, 368
"Women in the Farmers' Alliance," 76
"Women in the Iranian Revolution," 472
"Women in the Left, 1906-1941," 587
"Women in the Old and New Left," 287, 288
"Women in the Radical Movement," 521
"Women in the Southern Farmers' Alliance," 17
Women in the Soviet Union, 343
Women in the War, 352
Women of America, 148
Women of Minnesota, 40
Women of the Future, 225
Women on Guard, 374
Women on the Job, 473
women's auxiliaries, 368
Women's Educational and Industrial Union, 63
Women's Charter, 270
women's clubs, 7, 32, 137, 234
Women's Commonwealth, 576
Women's Council for Peace, 378
Women's Fight for Equality, 383
Women's History Sources, 581
Women's International Democratic Federation, 374
women's liberation, 11, 159, 160, 190, 270, 271, 439, 440, 441, 442, 443, 457, 462, 463, 464, 465, 466, 467, 468, 469, 470, 471, 472, 473, 474, 475, 476, 477, 478, 479, 480, 481, 482, 483, 484, 485, 486, 487, 488, 489, 490, 491, 492, 493, 494, 495, 496, 497, 498, 499, 500, 501, 502, 503, 504, 505, 506, 507, 508, 509, 510, 511, 512, 513, 514, 515, 516, 517, 518, 519, 520, 521, 522, 523, 524, 525, 526, 539, 541, 548, 552, 553, 554, 555, 556, 557, 558, 559, 560, 561, 562, 563, 579, 583, 585, 586
Women's Liberation and the Socialist Revolution, 518
women's rights movement, 2, 10, 19, 21, 32
"Women's Struggles for Equality," 170
Women's Trade Union League, 120, 133, 134, 167, 178, 194, 250, 357
Women's Trade Union League of New York, 124, 194, 261
Women Who Work (1932), 358
Women Who Work (1934), 274, 359
Women Who Work (1952), 361
Wood, Myrna, 462, 509
Woodhull, Victoria. See Martin, Victoria Claflin Woodhull,
Woodhull & Claflin's Weekly, 61, 85, 88
Woodhull & Claflin's Weekly: The Lives and Writings of Notorious Victoria Woodhull and Her Sister Tennessee Claflin, 85
Woodroofe, Debby, 517
Woods, Katharine Pearson, 116, 117, 118
Word for World Is Forest, The, 543
Workers and Allies, 589
Workers Defense League, 564
Workers' Defense Union, 142
Working Papers, 288
Working Papers on Socialism and Feminism, 518
Working Papers on Socialist

Feminism, 519
Working Woman, 274, 383, 384, 385
working women, 3, 4, 12, 58, 78,
    82, 113, 119, 121, 124, 134,
    167, 173, 178, 220, 223, 224,
    230, 237, 243, 250, 261, 274,
    303, 349, 355, 356, 357, 358,
    359, 360, 361, 370, 377, 436,
    466, 473, 524, 589
Working Women's Society, 82
Working Women's Union, 39
Workman's Circle. See Arbeter
    Ring
Works Progress Administration,
    293
World Peace, 263
World War I, 121, 123, 133, 143,
    146, 180, 181, 182, 184, 191,
    201, 240, 266, 279, 297, 300,
    356, 357, 398, 427
World War II, 142, 274, 303, 325,
    338, 342, 345, 350, 351, 352,
    361, 363, 370, 375, 376, 378,
    566
Woroby, Maria, 135
Wortis, Rose, 384
Wright, Frances, 2, 9, 576, 582
Wright, Lucy, 576
Wright, Pat, 502
Wright, Richard, 415

Yankee Reformers in the Urban
    Age, 20
Years Have Sped By, 275
Yeats, W.C., 136
Yellow Springs, Ohio, 443
Yglesias, Helen, 569, 570
Yiddish, 161, 275, 286, 294, 324
Yiddishe Arbeter Universitet,
    294
Yonkers, N.Y., 178
Yonnondio, 549
Young, Art, 243
Young, Iris, 507
Young Communist League, 286, 345
Young Pioneers, 286
Young Socialist Alliance, 484,
    485
Young Women's Christian Associa-
    tion, 312, 359, 413, 440
Young Workers' Liberation League,
    473
Yugoslav-Americans, 321
Yugoslav Socialist Federation,
    321

Zaretsky, Eli, 482, 518, 519, 520
Zaturensky, Marya, 268
Zechman, Annie Pike, 273
Zetkin, Clara, 381, 382
Zugsmith, Leane, 436, 437
Zurich, Switzerland, 27